HITLER IN HELL

Books by Martin van Creveld

Clio and Me

Pussycats: Why the Rest Keeps Beating the West—and What Can Be Done about It

A History of Strategy: From Sun Tzu to William S. Lind

Equality: The Impossible Quest

A Biography of Conscience

The Privileged Sex

Wargames: From Gladiators to Gigabytes

The Evolution of Operational Art (ed., with John Olsen)

The Age of Airpower

The Land of Blood and Honey: The Rise of Modern Israel

The Culture of War

The American Riddle

The Changing Face of War: Lessons of Combat from the Marne to Iraq

Countering Modern Terrorism (ed., with K. von Knop and H. Neisser)

Defending Israel

Moshe Dayan

Men, Women and War

The Rise and Decline of the State

The Sword and the Olive: A History of the Israel Defense Force

The Encyclopaedia of Revolutions and Revolutionaries from A to Z (ed.)

Airpower and Maneuver Warfare

Nuclear Proliferation and the Future of Conflict

The Transformation of War

The Training of Officers: From Professionalism to Irrelevance

Technology and War: 2000 B.C. to the Present

Command in War

Fighting Power: German and US Army Performance, 1939-1945

Hitler's Strategy 1940-1941; The Balkan Clue

Supplying War: Logistics from Wallenstein to Patton

MARTIN VAN CREVELD

HITLER IN HELL

CASTALIA HOUSE

Hitler in Hell

Martin van Creveld

Published by Castalia House
Kouvola, Finland
www.castaliahouse.com

Cover: Steve Beaulieu
Editor: Vox Day

Contents

Prologue

I, Adolf Hitler, am in Hell, the place to which the victors assign their dead opponents. Not just the dead ones either, but that is a separate topic. Hell, let me tell you, is neither "a dungeon horrible" nor "torture without end" as John Milton, whom I read in German translation after my death, imagined. Far from it! In some ways it reminds me of Landsberg Prison, where I spent almost all of 1924. The main difference is that here I have no visitors and can receive no presents. That apart, conditions are quite similar. Not luxurious, but for a person like me, one whose material demands are moderate and who has always lived in a fairly austere manner, adequate.

There are no windows, and my spirit, or whatever it is, is not free to leave the compound, if it is one. As a result, I have no idea where it is located or what it looks like from the outside. If, indeed, it *has* an "outside." The light, which is artificial and on all the time, never varies. It seems to come from all directions at once, so there are no shadows. And there are no sounds, except for the few we handful of inmates make as, ghost-like, we flutter about. Even those seem to be muffled in a strange, unearthly way. For eight hours out of every twenty-four I am locked in my cell by guardian devils. They never—never—answer any questions, but they never do me any harm either. That is more than one can say for many people on Earth. At other times I can do much as I please. Who cares? I have no needs, I have no worries, and I have no one to fight. I suppose that accounts for my relatively mellow mood.

The souls I miss the most are those of my shepherd bitch, Blondi, and Frau Eva Braun. As to the former, there seem to be no dogs in

Hell. That depresses me, for I have always liked them very much. The scene in a certain film I will not name, where I am shown thoughtlessly shooting a little dog just because it was bothering, is pure invention. My first dog was a white terrier. I found him in the trenches, where he was chasing a rat. Originally, he had belonged to an English officer and did not understand a word of German. I called him Fuchsl, and he was with me for about a year and a half until someone stole him, causing me much grief. Several others followed. I was proud of them and taught them all sorts of tricks; when asked what young girls do, Blondi, who was the last of the lot, would roll on her back and lift her legs in the air.

As to the latter, Eva's most ardent wish had long been for me to marry her. Unfortunately, my duty to my people did not permit us to spend as much time together as I—and even more so she—would have liked. But what if I had done as she wanted? Throughout the war, I lived mainly at my various military headquarters. There, she would have been badly out of place with nothing to do all day long. All around were hundreds of males, many of them starved for sex, who would have stared at her. And gossiped. And sniggered.

I kept in touch with her by a daily telephone call as well as letters. But I saw to it that our correspondence should not fall into the wrong hands. As, for example, Napoleon's letters to Josephine and the telephone conversations of Prince Charles with his lover Camilla did, thereby revealing their intimate secrets for everyone to slaver over. My chief adjutant Julius Schaub, whose loyalty to me dated back to the very first days of the Party, and Eva's sister Gretl, were a great help in this respect. Shortly before the end of the war Eva defied my wishes for the first and only time. She had her car covered with camouflage paint, left Berchtesgaden, and took us all by surprise by unexpectedly turning up in Berlin, specifically in order to die with me. Doing so was an act of courage and love. At the time, just thinking of her made me happy; it does so still. Poor woman, with my modest needs she never knew what to give me as a present! Where she is, if she is, I have not the faintest clue.

All of us here seem to be staying the same age. We are indestructible. No one ever gets sick; no one ever dies. Nothing ever happens. To understand what a horrible torment *that* is, one must either have experienced it or have been with Gulliver on his trip to the land of the immortals. I am alive, yet I am dead; I am dead, yet I am alive. The main problem is what to do with my time. That is one very important reason why I decided to write this book. Now as in 1924, the faithful and artless, if sometimes moody, Rudolf Hess is helping me with my work. But there are a couple of differences. When I wrote *Mein Kampf,* I was still a comparative newcomer to the political scene. Imprisoned, I possessed very few personal documents. That is why much of what I wrote in volume I, which, unlike volume II, is largely autobiographical, had to be based mainly on my memory. Which, let me say, is excellent indeed.

Here in Hell things are very different. To help me keep up with what is happening, I have with me a couple of the world's leading experts on the Internetz, the so-called "Black Internetz" included. Germans and faithful followers, of course. They are better than those two mavericks, Julian Assange and Edward Snowden, combined! They provide me with access to *everything.* Meaning absolutely everything that has ever been written, filmed, recorded, videotaped, or whatever, right down to the present time. With the result that they can help me document my life and times much more thoroughly and much more faithfully than I could then.

So vast is the inflow of material that mastering it all might actually fill the unlimited time I have stretching out in front of me. More, much more, keeps being added day by day. There are books about my youth, books about my women, books about my alleged mental and physical diseases, books about the movies I did and did not like, books about the medicines I took, books about my attitude to the

Jews, and books about my headquarters and my performance as a military commander. There is even a book about how hard it is to write anything new about me! Not to mention an avalanche of books (and TV programs) about my alleged escape to South America after the war. I am told that, when I started working on this project in the spring of 2015, on Google I had about a hundred million "hits." Stalin only had thirty-three million; Mao Zedong, a paltry million.

But there is also another more important reason why I write. History, Schopenhauer said, is as riddled with lies as the body of a prostitute with syphilis. In this volume I am determined to tell my side of the story, set the record straight, and get even with my enemies—both my contemporaries and those who fed on my legend later on. And, on the way, I will put that bunch of feckless liars, meaning the countless "historians" who have done their best to present me as the worst monster in the whole of human memory, to shame. I shall beat them into a pudding, as Goebbels used to say. Doing so is my duty and my right. After all, isn't that what people occupying positions similar to mine have always done? Think of Julius Caesar, whose memoirs schoolchildren are being made to study right down to the present day. Or of that lying drunk, Winston Churchill. He even got a Nobel Prize for his efforts.

Finally, all my life I have believed in the "unconquerable will" (Milton again). Though I may be in Hell, "to bow and sue for grace, with suppliant knee"—that glory my enemies will never extort from me. "For the mind and spirit remains invincible." Down to the last breath I took, I gave my all fighting on behalf of the German people. Since then, I am told, there has come into being something called Godwin's Law. Meaning that, the longer two people argue, the more inevitable it is that at least one of them should call the other "Hitler." Countless lesser folks apart, those to whom my name has been (mis)applied include Egypt's President Gamal Abdul Nasser, Soviet President Nikolai Bulganin, Iraq's dictator Saddam Hussein, Iran's President Mahmoud Ahmadinejad (known, in his own country, as "The Monkey"), Russia's President Vladimir Putin, America's President Donald Trump…*Reductio ad Hitlerum,* one might say. The Israelis, who always claim to have a corner on suffering, especially like to play this game. I am, however, gratified that their enemies have caught on and are using the same tactics against *them,* as, for example, when someone calls a chatterbox like Prime Minister Netanyahu "Hitler." They wish they had just one percent of my stature. Each and every one of them.

Unfortunately, there is no way we here in Hell can contact those we have left behind. Thus pushing the latter in the right direction appears out of the question for the time being. But I am not about to throw in the towel. Not me! Ever since the first humans started walking the earth, they have always tried the most varied methods to get in touch with the dead and to learn what they have to say. There now exists a whole branch of science, if that is the word, whose aim is to do just that. You may be certain that, if and when the time comes, my voice will be heard.

Loud and clear.

Part I

The Road to Power

Chapter 1

In the Home of My Parents

I was born in Braunau-on-the-Inn on 20 April 1889. During the 1930s my birthday used to be celebrated with flags, ceremonies, and parades as if I were some saint. No more, of course: but neither has it been forgotten. My father, Alois, did not clearly know who his father had been. The outcome has been endless speculation. Decades after my death, it is still going on. Some have even claimed that he was the son of a Jew by the name of Frankenberger, or Frankenreiter, or whatever! As the fact that no person bearing those names could ever be found indicates, all these are simply lies. Originally, they were spread by my political opponents, who would have liked nothing better than to tar me with this particular brush.

That fact, and not any worry I felt about the matter, was why, no sooner had I become Chancellor than I sent my former attorney, Hans Frank, to gather and secure all possible information about my *Ahnen* (ancestors.) After all, didn't someone say that knowledge is power? Frank was an able if sometimes petty-minded lawyer who had often represented the Party in the courts. After our *Machtergreifung*, seizure of power, in 1933 I made him Bavarian minister of justice as well as head of the National Socialist Jurists' Association and the Academy of German Law. He carried out his task well enough, as he also did in occupied Poland, where he served as governor-general. Later, sitting in his Nuremberg cell as one of the so-called major war criminals, he wrote a book called *Im Angesicht des Galgens* (facing the scaffold), in which he repeated some of the rumors. Perhaps he was trying to curry favor with his captors.

The alleged Jewish connection apart, it did not really matter. Some historians have claimed that my father was the son, not of Johann Georg Hiedler but of his brother Johann Nepomuk Hiedler. This reminds me of the story about a certain philologist. A German one, needless to say. He spent his life trying to find out who wrote the Homeric poems. After thirty years, he concluded that it had not been Homer but another bard whose name was also Homer. Who cares? We all know that not even the strictest measures and worst punishments have ever been able to prevent the females of the species from having occasional fun. Not least the ones married to those effete snobs, the blue bloods. Recently, I read that even the British royal family has some interesting breaks in its DNA. The same applies to the Jews. Throughout history, no other people has tried as hard to keep their people free of foreign blood. Seen from this point of view, not a few of them were more "racist" than I! But Jewish women appear to be no better than the rest. That is why, as recent scientific advances have shown, a single gene all Jews have in common does not exist.

Let the professors, who are always so full of themselves, chatter away to their hearts' contents. What mattered was the fact that, unlike so many other rulers, most German ones included, I was not born in a palace. I did not have a "von," "zu," or "und" to my surname. "Hitler," sometimes spelled Hietler or Hütler, means "cottager." My ancestors came from the Waldviertel, far from Vienna and well known for being Austria's poorest district. Nor was I a *Herr Doktor*. I was a man of the people. And so, to the end of my earthly life and to the extent that my official duties permitted, I remained. I was *"Unser Hitler,"* our Hitler, as Goebbels liked to put it. As to my first name, it is a composite made up of two ancient Germanic words: *Adal* and *Wulf*. Noble Wolf. I liked wolves and often doodled them. During the period of struggle I sometimes used the cover name Wolf; one of those who first got to know me under that name was Eva Braun. Later, I named several of my field headquarters after them.

My father met my mother, Klara Pölzl, in 1876 when she entered his household as a servant. Nine years later, after he had been widowed for the second time, they married. He was thirty-nine, she twenty-five. Of their six children only my sister Paula, who was seven years younger than me, and I survived to adulthood. All the rest died very young. The household also included two older offspring from my father's previous marriages, my half-brother and sister Alois Jr. and Angela. Finally, there was my mother's spinster sister, Johanna. In the family she was known as Hanitante.

Some psychiatrists—in my time they used to be called "mad-doctors"—have engaged in the most cock-eyed speculations about my mental makeup. One, an American Jew named David Luck, wrote that I was possessed by a "malignant orality"—whatever *that* may be—and a sexuality "either completely narcissistic or pre-genitally perverse." Another, Robert Waite, claimed that I had witnessed my parents having sexual intercourse, which turned me into a "psychopathic god." All that, and much more, is pure invention whose purpose is to present me as some sort of maniac. Much of the rubbish can be traced back to my opponent, Otto Strasser, as well as to that big idiot, my one-time foreign press secretary Ernst ("Putzi") Hanfstängl. Mr. Cannabis-Stalk came from a highly artistic family and had been educated in America at Harvard. A snob, Putzi strongly resented my attachment to some people in my entourage, the *chauffeureska,* as he called them, who were not as sophisticated as he considered himself to be. So pompous was he that, in 1937, I decided to play an elaborate practical joke on him. It proved him a coward as well as an ass. Shortly after, Putzi left Germany and published a book in which he spread all kinds of lurid stories about me in the hope of making money at my expense.

The theory behind the speculations originated in the sick brain of that typical Jew, Sigmund Freud, who came up with the equally Jewish invention psychoanalysis, which he had the effrontery to call a science. A claim incidentally, which was denied by his fellow

Jews at the Hebrew University in Jerusalem who refused to include psychoanalysis in the curriculum. Freud claimed that most, if not all, mental disturbances originated in sexual problems. It was he who came up with the idea that witnessing one's parents during their "primal act" led to all kinds of mental disturbances. Judging by his published works, it is quite possibly his own personal experience he was speaking about here! Next, he and his clique, almost all of whom were also Jewish, foisted it on his unfortunate patients, presumably making many of them even crazier than they already were.

What the self-styled "analysts" overlooked was the plain fact that not everyone was a good bourgeois as they were. Nor did most people spend their lives in a spacious Viennese flat. Throughout history, most children have always lived with their parents in a single room or hut. Quite a large number of them grew up in tents. Like it or not, they witnessed everything—everything—practically from the day they could walk. And let's not mention what they could see happening all around them both in nature and on the farm! Yet nearly all of them grew up perfectly normal, Indeed, it is often the doctors, not their patients, who are as crazy as bats.

Others too spent their time obsessively looking for all kinds of anomalies in my body, mind, family, and what not. Working for the OSS, the CIA's parent organization, the American psychologist Walter Langer criticized my strict hygienic habits and fastidious taste in dress. As if walking about unwashed, with a dirty coat and a soiled collar, were a virtue; and as if I, having been poor and homeless, did not know the meaning of being unable to wash and change one's clothes much better than he did. This is a topic on which I could go on and on. But let the psychologists, past, present, and no doubt future, wallow in their morbid fantasies.

In fact the family in which I grew up was not at all unusual for those days. Partly because of the difference in age and partly because of my father's position in society—about which more in a moment— it was inevitable that he should seek to protect, direct, and, yes, dominate and discipline his wife up to a certain point. So, at a time when it was taken for granted that women should "love, cherish, and obey" their husbands and the great feminist revolt was still decades away, did a great many others. My father was not without his faults. However, he ran an intact household. He and my mother did not divorce as forty percent of married people in "advanced" countries do today. Assuming responsibility, he looked after his family as best he could. Nor did I grow up with step parents, lesbian "parents," homosexual "parents," transgender "parents," surrogate "parents," or God knows what other kinds of "parents" modern society keeps inflicting on its unfortunate offspring.

Socially and economically, we were lower middle class. Overcoming his humble origins as well as his lack of a formal education, my father worked his way up. In the end he occupied the respectable position of a KuK, meaning *kaiserliche und königliche,* customs official. As many of my biographers have noted, my father, partly because his bosses kept transferring him and partly because he wanted to, moved his family about quite a bit. The clear implication is that there was something very wrong with his life and that this "fact" had important implications for mine. But that, too, is nonsense. Many families throughout the world have moved much more often than mine did. This includes military families, which continue to do so down to the present day. And let us not mention business executives being "relocated" from one end of the world to another with little notice and less power to choose. Yet such movements do little, if anything, to explain their offspring's subsequent lives.

Nor is it is true that he smoked "like a chimney," as the English historian Ian Kershaw, by a mere sleight of hand and without any evidence whatsoever, has claimed. In reality he was no more addicted to the habit than most men at that time and place. Men considered smoking a sign of maturity and manliness. They were proud of doing so and often had themselves portrayed or photographed with a cigarette in their mouth. Franz Joseph, the first Austrian emperor who smoked, provided the example. Many libraries and clubs, which until 1860 or so had prohibited visitors from smoking on the premises, now permitted them to do so as a matter of course. Smoking was allowed—even expected—by every sort of committee and council during business hours. If you did not smoke, you did not count. More and more, that even applied to women; imitating men, they took it up as a sign of "independence."

My father also spent time in the *Kneipe,* or pub, drinking his glass of wine or beer. Here and there he may have drunk a little too much. Like so many others he had a temper. Like so many others he did not take opposition lightly. I being his chief opponent at home, he beat me at times. But he never seriously hurt me. In any case there was nothing extraordinary about that either. Almost everyone did it as a matter of course. As the Old Testament, which I studied at school, says, "He that spareth the rod hateth his son." Looking down from Hell upon Western society as it has developed since my time, I am inclined to agree.

As I explained at some length in *Mein Kampf,* most of the conflict between my father and me had to do with his expectations. He himself spent his life working in the service of Kaiser Franz Joseph, to whom he was both loyal and very, very grateful. Given this background, the effort he invested in his career, and the success he ultimately enjoyed, it is hardly surprising that he wanted me to continue in his footsteps. I was to become a government official. I, however, refused. On one occasion, to change my mind, he took me to the place where he worked and showed me around. But the effect was the opposite of what he had hoped for. Spending my life like a monkey in a cage, filling in forms? No way.

Instead, at the age of twelve and based on my talent for drawing, which was already becoming obvious even then, I decided I would become an artist. A painter. *A painter?* My father thought I had gone out of my mind. This was the turn of the twentieth century. Artists were famous—or, depending on one's view of them, infamous—for their Bohemian lifestyle and also for their inability to work steadily and to keep regular hours. Supposedly, they needed leisure and a certain amount of disorder to develop their creativity. A point of view, incidentally, with which I fully agree. In this way they represented the exact opposite of everything he himself stood for: duty, conscientiousness, industry, regularity, and punctuality. That's to say nothing of the fact that, then as now, for a young unknown man to make a living as an artist was anything but easy.

He and I often clashed over this matter and went on doing so until his death. As we did so my mother did her best to protect me. But she did not always meet with success. She was deeply religious, humble, devout, caring, and as sweet as sweet can be. Grieving for the four children she had lost, she did what she could to spoil my sister and me. Once again, this fitted the *Zeitgeist*. My home was not by any means the only one in which wives and mothers, fully accepting their lot and no doubt suffering some things in silence, acted as the family saint. Future U.S. President Richard Nixon, for example, said the same of *his* mother (who also suffered the death of some of her children). Judging by his biography, her influence on him seems to have been not a whit smaller than mine was on me. My mother, however, was the best of all. I loved her much more than I loved my father; what I had for him is better called respect.

My family's frequent moves took me to a number of different elementary schools. But in none of them was I ever more than a mediocre student. As you may well imagine, that was not because I had any difficulty understanding or remembering what we were taught. On the contrary, most of the material we learned and the tasks we were assigned were ridiculously easy. In any case, as I often said later on, I consider schools a much overrated institution. It is true that society cannot do without them. After all, it needs people who can read, write, and figure. But a lot of what they teach was and is rubbish. For example, are classical languages really needed? Furthermore, schoolmasters are hardly society's most successful members. Mine, I remember, were distinguished chiefly by their dirty shirts and unkempt beards. It's no wonder that, with few exceptions, they did little to prepare students for the reality of life.

My behavior at school, which one of my teachers described as "variable," reflected two factors. First, as I have just explained, it was a protest against my father's ambitions for me. As a result, I simply neglected anything that did not interest me. Second, instead of doing my homework, I much preferred to play outside. There was a group of us young scamps who were always on the outlook for games we could play. And in many of those games I was the leader of the pack. Much of our inspiration came from Karl May, the author of countless books on the Wild West, of which I read and reread as many as I could lay my hands on. They were so easy to follow, so vivid, so colorful, and so full of adventure and imagination; I was overwhelmed! We divided into groups, distributed roles, and "fought" each other.

Another source of inspiration was an illustrated book about the Franco–German War of 1870–71 I found in my father's library. Yet another one, newspaper—there were no "media" yet—reports about the Boer War of 1899–1902. We youngsters followed them avidly. Whatever some of my biographers may have said, there was nothing extraordinary about all this. To the extent that they are not glued to their computers, iPhones, and what not, children throughout the world still go on playing similar games.

Easily my best teacher, and the only one who left a lasting impression on me, was Professor Leopold Pötsch. Indeed, I would say that he helped determine my whole future life. Pötsch was an excellent speaker, as only someone who is enthusiastic about a cause can be. He had the gift of transporting us young students into the past while making that past come alive for us. As he did so, he turned me into a nationalist. I became aware of the endless life-and-death struggles between Germans and others: Romans, Huns, Magyars,

Latins, Mongols, Mohammedans—who twice laid siege to Vienna—
and, last but not least, Slavs. Thanks partly to its geographical position at the southeastern corner of the Reich and partly to its own
multinational nature, Austria was destined to play a crucial role in
these struggles—much more so than most of the Reich-Germans of
the time appreciated.

Starting with Otto the Great in 961 A.D., there had always been
some sort of German Reich. Only in 1805 did that Reich, subdued
by a foreign conqueror (Napoleon), cease to exist in the same form.
Another blow to German unity was delivered in 1866 when Austria
went to war against Prussia and lost. Later, in 1918–19, it was
the victorious Allies who, acting very much against the Austrian
people's will, threatened to use force in case the two parts of our
nation decided to join together. Given their declared principles, how
hypocritical *that* decision was hardly requires pointing out.

However, around 1900 that was still in the future. We young
people were convinced that the German nation should be reunited
in a single state as it had been for almost nine centuries. Also, we
felt that the chief obstacle standing in the way was the Hapsburg
Dynasty, with its long supranational tradition and egoistic determination to stay on top. We did our childish best to promote the cause
of Germandom against the great mass of non-German people who
inhabited the empire and, multiplying like rabbits, threatened to
engulf it, by wearing the appropriate insignia, waving the appropriate
flags, gathering pennies, and the like.

The second thing Pötsch taught me, which was closely linked to
the first, was the supreme importance of studying history, understanding history, and using history as it ought to be used. As I later
wrote in *Mein Kampf,* "To study history means to search for and
discover the forces that are the causes of those results which appear
before our eyes as historical events." In other words, we should
not just learn by heart what happened long ago; doing so, however

entertaining it may be, is useless. The real objective is to illustrate the present by means of examples from the past and to use the latter to draw lessons for practical life.

Much later, I once said that a man who does not know history is like a man who does not have a face. Not knowing the past, how can he (or, for God's sake, she) arrive at a considered judgment of the present and the future? The more important the post he occupies, the more true that is. That is a view I still maintain. Indeed one of Hell's greatest shortcomings is precisely that its routine is uniform and unvarying. It has neither a future nor a past to study and draw lessons from, making it a totally uninteresting place where nothing ever happens. That in itself makes it worthy of the name Hell.

The turn of the century found us living in Linz, a lovely town on the Danube which from that time on I have always regarded as the home of my youth and of which I have many pleasant memories. The conflicts with my father still persisted, causing my grades to deteriorate further. I just did not want to follow the path he had laid down for me; it was one in which, as he himself once said, thought was not required. When I was in my thirteenth year, he was taken from us. He was still in robust health when a stroke painlessly ended his earthly wanderings and left us all deeply bereaved. His most ardent wish was to be able to help his son advance in a career, sparing me the harsh ordeal he himself had gone through. But it seemed to him then that all his longings were in vain. Yet though he himself was not conscious of it, he had sown the seeds of a future which neither of us foresaw at that time.

Once my father died, I had little difficulty persuading my mother that I should indeed become a painter. I continued to attend a lower Realschule, a kind of secondary school. Not offering Greek and Latin, it was considered inferior to the gymnasium. It did not ultimately lead to the *Abitur*, or high-school leaving, diploma, and was meant for those who did not expect to attend a university. I soldiered on, more or less. Occasionally, I had to re-sit for examinations or change schools. I did well enough to become eligible for admission to the higher Realschule. However, school did not interest me more at that time than previously.

In 1905 I fell seriously ill with some lung disease, worrying my dear mother almost to death. After my recovery, I finally left my school years behind me. Exceptionally talented people often do. Steve Jobs, Bill Gates, and, in my own time, Joseph Stalin; none finished college, let alone took a postgraduate degree, as almost anyone who aims at becoming someone is obliged to do today. At least one, Richard Branson of Virgin Airlines fame, did not even complete high school. The reason is easy to find. Success requires originality and innovation. Yet school can only teach what teachers learned twenty-five years earlier. Keeping children at school against their will until they are eighteen, which today has become almost standard practice, serves no purpose. In not a few cases doing so actually prevents them from growing up and developing their talents. I thank my stars that, in my time, things had not yet reached that point. Or else God knows what, acting out of sheer boredom, I might have done.

The next two years were among the happiest in my life. Since I was not attending school, had no classmates, and did not receive grades, they are also among the least documented ones. These facts have enabled historians to rack their imaginations and have field days inventing all kinds of disturbed stories about me. Reality, though, was prosaic enough. Yes, I did lead "a life of parasitic idleness"—to quote Kershaw—in the comfortable flat which my mother, being relatively well off, had rented. Yes, I had "still never earned a day's income." Yes, I led "a drone's life without career prospects." I was, after all, still growing up and not thirty-something, like many of the so-called "boomerang children," who, early in the twenty-first century, are leading lives not so different from the one I led during that period.

Yes, I did like to dress well and go about town. Yes, I did often go to the theater and the opera. I did fall in love—an adolescent love, to be sure—with a girl, Stephanie. And yes, I did not have the courage to approach her. In fact, she never knew I existed. What is so unusual about that? Didn't school teach my biographers that *Honni soit qui mal y pense*?

My companion on those occasions was my friend August ("Gustl") Kubizek. Kubizek, who was eight months older than I, was the son of an upholsterer. His dream was to become a musician. After the end of each musical performance we attended, I used to talk to him about what we had just seen and heard. Truth to say, I did most of the talking while he did most of the listening, making us a well-matched pair! His subsequent account of those years went through various versions. It also lifted some passages straight out of *Mein Kampf*. Still, on the whole it is correct. Not for one moment in all that time was I bored. Boredom being something experienced only by those too dull to think for themselves. Not being bored, I never got into any trouble to speak of.

In the spring of 1906 I visited Vienna for the first time. It was, after all, the capital of a great, if already rickety, empire. Like so many others who visited it then and visit it now, I wanted to see the streets, the public squares, the buildings, the museums and the palaces. Also, I wanted to attend the famous Hofoper (Court Opera), which had much more to offer than its poor relative in the provincial town of Linz did. But the main attraction always consisted of the splendid buildings along the Ringstrasse. It would hardly be an exaggeration to say that they had a magical effect on me.

One outcome of my encounter with Vienna was to revive my hope of becoming an artist. In September 1907 I returned to the city to take the entrance examination to the Academy of Fine Arts. There were a hundred and thirteen candidates, and after various tests, only twenty-eight were selected. I was not one of them. It was a terrible blow, the more so because it was totally unexpected. But again, was it in any way unusual? Just look at the math.

In 2014, in my residence in Hell, I was shown a letter allegedly addressed to me by the academy. Written (typed) on 2 October 1907, it was signed by Christian Griepenkerl, the professor who had also signed my rejection that year (and also in the next one, when I tried again). The text says that, given my work, "We [the committee in charge of admissions] do not have a moment's doubt that you are suited to widen your horizons at our academy." Supposedly, the letter had been lost at the post office and only recently discovered after it had been sent, by mistake, to a certain Herr Can Ölmez, who lived at my old address in Linz. It is a useless, crude forgery produced by some sensation-seeking hack; one of countless others that have been produced to discredit me. But it does show how much, seven decades after my death, I—and everything concerning me—still remain in the public eye.

Having failed, I went to speak to the rector. He was frank with me, saying that the work I had submitted showed I was more suited for a career in architecture than in painting. But that road was closed to me because I did not possess a school-leaver's certificate. That was a fact which, at that time, caused me great regret. Accordingly, my dream of following an artistic career was in ruins.

In December of the same year my mother died of breast cancer, an agonizing disease if there is one. Johanna, my little sister Paula, and I took care of her. She was attended by our family doctor, Eduard Bloch, one of the very few decent Jews I have ever met or heard of. He did what he could for her. Recently, there has been a spate of stories alleging that he mistreated her and overcharged the family, causing me to become an anti-Semite. I want to take this opportunity to declare, as solemnly as I can: all that is simply a pack of lies. Or else, unless you consider me very stupid indeed, why do you think I allowed him and his family to leave Germany for the U.S. in 1938? Once he had arrived, he said and wrote some kind words about me. Never, he asserted, had he seen a young man as touchingly attached to his mother as I was. I had, in fact, done my best for her. Later, I had her photograph stationed in each one of my primary residences: in Berlin, in Munich, and at Berchtesgaden as well.

Once she had died and been buried, at considerable expense I must add, there was nothing left to hold me back in Linz. Accordingly, I moved to Vienna. I shall have more to say about my life there in the next chapter. Before doing so, though, I want to emphasize the obvious: namely that, if the family from which I came and the education I received were in some ways unique, so are every family and every kind of education that have ever existed and will ever exist.

Taking into account the time and the place, millions of others had experiences not too different from mine. Fathers, who except among the very poor were the sole breadwinners, tended to dominate their wives. They were supposed to do so, especially, if they were much older than their spouses, as mine was. Father-son conflicts were frequent, as they have always been and still remain. The same applies to the love between a mother and her boy. Wasn't it the aforementioned Freud who, somewhere in his voluminous but often fanciful writings, declared that it represented the strongest bond of all? And no one had heard of the idea that disciplining one's offspring by hitting them, if necessary, was harmful. Let alone some kind of crime.

Nor was I the only boy who hated school. Many American schools these days are protected by metal detectors, armed guards who patrol the premises, and what not. One or two even allow teachers to go armed and provide them with weapons! Even so, hardly two months pass in which some disturbed kid does *not* take up a machine gun— in the U.S., these weapons are easy to obtain—and kills everyone in sight before shooting himself. The feelings I had for school were and are widely shared; yet out of millions and millions of contemporary youngsters, not one developed the way I did or could point to achievements nearly as great as mine. The ways of Providence have always been a mystery. They remain so still.

Chapter 2

Vienna

My biographers are a pedantic pack. Many seem to believe that, even when I was still an unknown teenager with little money and even fewer prospects, I regarded each and every minute of my life as if it were of earth-shaking importance. That is why, every time they find some trifling error in something I said or wrote, they call me a cheat and a liar. If that is scholarship, then let me have no part in it. In any case they claim that I arrived in Vienna at some time between 14 and 17 February 1908. Finding a place to stay was easy; the streets of the poorer districts bristled with little pieces of paper saying, "Room to rent." I took up lodging at Stumpergasse 31, not far from the Westbahnhof. My landlady, the biographers don't forget to add, was a certain Czech woman, Frau Zakreys. Big deal.

On the 18th my friend Kubizek joined me. He had taken the train from Linz and arrived in a state of exhaustion. But such was my enthusiasm for the city that I gave him no rest. Instead, I immediately dragged him about to see the most important sights, enabling the indefatigable Kershaw to take this as more "proof" of what an insufferable person I had already become. Originally, Kubizek and I had planned to live at separate addresses. However, I soon managed to make him to change his mind. He and I stayed together in Frau Zakreys' modest flat, where we exchanged my small room for a larger one, paying double as a result. For a few months I kept up a correspondence with the rest of my family. In August 1908 I visited Hanitante, who had moved back to the Waldviertel, where she had relatives. After that, I lost contact with her.

There has been much speculation concerning my finances at this time. So here are the facts. First, I received a miserable pension of 25 kronen a month due to me as the son of a retired KuK official (the remaining 25 kronen went to my sister, Paula). Second, my family provided me with some money. Everything considered, I was not badly off. I had enough to live on and could even visit the opera provided that I contented myself with the cheapest available standing places. But I was certainly far from being rich. Anyone who says or writes otherwise is a liar.

A few days after his arrival, Kubizek received notice that he had been accepted as a student at the Vienna Conservatory. Consequently, he rented a grand piano at Feigel's Music Store in the Liniengasse, just around the corner, as Kershaw pedantically notes. Another big deal. He began to study regularly, filling our room with his music. Here and there we quarreled a little, especially because he insisted on playing his piano at times which were inconvenient to me. But we never argued nearly to the point where we separated or even came close to doing so.

Arriving in Vienna, I had in my pocket a letter of introduction. It had been sent to Professor Alfred Roller, a well-known painter, graphic designer, and set designer. (Hess told me he got these facts from Wikipedia.) The author was Roller's brother. He, in turn, had been contacted by the mother of a female acquaintance of mine who happened to know him and wrote on my behalf. Needless to say, I thanked her profusely, as courtesy demanded. Whatever other bad qualities I may have, ungratefulness has never been one of them. In any event Roller, who was no doubt a busy man, agreed to see me. However, I never took the opportunity. Looking back, I suppose I was too shy.

By and large, Kubizek's description of the life he and I led in Vienna is correct. Why shouldn't it be? Yes, the room we had rented was cramped. It left me very little space in which to pace to and fro as, from ancient Greece on, many people have always done when sunk in thought and as I myself went on doing throughout my life. Yes, I was often carried away and took up many fanciful projects that quickly proved to be beyond my powers. But doesn't building "castles in the air," as the saying goes, form an essential part of youth? Looking back, I think that whoever did *not* do so at this point in his life so has never been young. Yes, I talked a lot. I was overwhelmed by the great city in which I now lived and which made such a tremendous impression on me. I needed somebody to listen to my thoughts, and Kubizek was the only one who did. Yes, my self-confidence suffered as a result of my apparent failure "to get ahead" in life. In the long run, though, it only made me more determined to succeed. Yes, I went to sleep late and got up late. I understand that Churchill, when he was prime minister, did the same; not that I would use him as an example for anything.

And yes, I did read a lot. How much became clear recently when the historians at Munich's Institute for Contemporary History ana- lyzed *Mein Kampf* and pointed out the numerous texts that I had paraphrased or that had clearly influenced me. Kubizek went so far as to say that he cannot remember me ever being without armloads of books. Earlier, I had read *Robinson Crusoe, Gulliver's Travels,* and *Uncle Tom's Cabin.* Now I followed up with Dante, Herder, Ibsen, and Nietzsche. Much later, my sister Paula claimed that, after moving to Vienna, I had recommended *Don Quixote* to her, but I can no longer remember doing so.

At that time, I also read the German classicists, Lessing, Goethe, and Schiller. However, I did not like them very much; they were too cosmopolitan. They were typical representatives of the so-called Enlightenment and its dreams concerning the brotherhood of men, but they did not sufficiently understand the destructive role the Jews have always played in history. In particular Lessing, in *Nathan the Wise,* came close to betraying the race to which he belonged. Why couldn't they be more like Shakespeare, who gave the world not only *Julius Caesar* and *Hamlet* but *The Merchant of Venice,* too? Under the Third Reich, Shakespeare was performed more often in Germany than in Britain. After the outbreak of war, I personally made sure that his plays could still be produced by us. But the author I liked best was Schopenhauer. Just look at the title, *The World as Will and Representation,* and you will understand why.

In recent years several historians, hoping to find the clue to my personality, have taken the trouble to research what one of them called "Hitler's Vienna" at considerable length. For this I thank them, but I consider that their efforts have been largely wasted. To be sure, my environment was not without effect on my development. Even my birthplace at Braunau, very near the border between Germany and Austria that we young people sought to erase, might have been chosen by Providence. On the other hand, what distinguishes great men is precisely the fact that, unlike millions of others, they do *not* allow themselves to be shaped by circumstances. Instead, rising above them, they deliberately set out to shape themselves *and* transform the circumstances in question. As, for example, Julius Caesar, who was an epileptic, and Frederick II, originally a weak and dreamy youth, did.

We Germans have great respect for *Bildung,* variously translated (I am told) as education, knowledge, or learning. We always ask what diplomas a man has, not what he can do. What we often overlook is that learning, however great, in itself is useless. As the lives of a great many professors prove, beyond a certain point it can even turn into an obstacle to action. To make it useful it must be properly organized and registered. Above all, the essential must be separated from the inessential. The latter must be discarded, the former stored and re-membered. Once understanding has been achieved, any subsequent reading can serve either as a correction or as a reinforcement. It was especially during my years in Vienna that I taught myself to read in this way. All other forms of reading may help one idle the hours away. They cannot, however, substitute for the method I have just described.

Whoever wants to know what I learned during my years in Vienna needs only open *Mein Kampf.* That's easy because by now it has been translated into dozens of languages and because demand for it is quite strong. Here I shall do no more than provide a brief summary. First, I learned how obsequious, how utterly spineless and cowardly and untruthful the so-called "great" Viennese press really was. Superficially, it was "tolerant," "liberal," and "progressive." It could always be counted upon to support noble causes—bread for all, equality, freedom, what have you. This applied both at home and around the world. In reality, all it did was kowtow to the Hapsburgs at every step. No amount of flattery was considered too low. If it was "open to the world," as some of its loudest proponents said it was, then mainly in the sense that it admired, indeed worshipped, everything French. Supposedly, it was from Paris that everything good in the world had come. Above all, it totally failed to defend the German character of the state. As, by advocating union with Germany and opposing the claims of the various nationalities that formed the Empire, it should have done.

Second, I learned what democracy looks like. Close up! There were times when, with or without little Kubizek in tow, I visited parliament almost daily. The very fact that the deputies belonged to many different nationalities sufficed to repel a German nationalist like me. Besides, what a bunch of miserable crooks they were! Always talking and talking, or rather shouting and shouting. Always at loggerheads over every possible issue, including many that were of no interest to anyone except themselves.

By one count there were no fewer than fifteen different parties, big and small. But even the largest of them barely held 20 percent of the seats. As a result, they were never able to accomplish anything. Nor, perhaps, did most of them want to. After all, deeds mean taking responsibility. And responsibility was absolutely the last thing they wanted. They never ceased quarreling and fighting each other. On more than one occasion they even beat each other up. No wonder poor old Franz Joseph at one point said he wanted nothing to do with them (as if he had a choice). No wonder governments and ministers kept rising and falling like ninepins in a game of bowling. If what I saw is democracy, then I do not want any part of it.

Third, I became an anti-Semite. In Linz at the time there were few Jews (700 out of a population of 60,000), and no one took much notice of them. It is simply not true, as someone has claimed, that I imbibed my anti-Semitism at home. My father, after all, spent his youth in the countryside, where Jews were even less thick on the ground than in Linz. Later, he was too busy exercising his hobby, which was bee-keeping, to care about the few representatives of "the Chosen People" he may have met. As for my mother, she was too good and, truth to be said, too simple a soul to worry about such things. The idea that my anti-Semitism had anything to do with a supposed encounter with that confused Jewish philosopher, Ludwig Wittgenstein, is also false. It seems that he did in fact attend the same Realschule I did. But I never met him or heard of him. As far as I was concerned, he never existed.

Vienna, by contrast, had no fewer than 147,000 Jews in a population of almost 1.8 million. A few, with the Rothschilds at their head, were filthy rich. They aped, or tried to ape, the manners of the town's aristocracy and *haute bourgeoisie.* Many—especially those who, taking advantage of Emperor Franz Joseph's liberal policies, had newly arrived from Eastern Europe—were very poor. Dressed in their caftans, often filthy and unwashed, they were very conspicuous. Their presence simply could not be ignored. The greatest concentration was in Leopoldstadt, the island between the Danube and the Danube Canal. The locals used to call it "Matzos Island." They had a very high birth rate, with the result that Jewish students flooded the universities. Though I did not know it at the time, they comprised two-fifths of the students of medicine, a third of the law students, and a third of the entire student body. In 1889, the year I was born, of 681 lawyers practicing in Vienna, over half were Jewish.

I have described my own first encounter with these creatures in *Mein Kampf*. Then and later, I found them revolting, but they did arouse my curiosity. So I decided to try to learn more about them. The more I learned, the less savory they appeared. Not just because of their appearance (and smell), which were bad enough. But because of what they were and what they represented. Until then, I had accepted the common idea that they were simply people who adhered to a religion different from that of the majority. Now I understood that they belonged to a different *Volk* altogether. The Jews themselves agreed with this view. Had they not developed, from the 1860s onward, a movement called Zionism which insisted on precisely that point?

If anything, the power of the Jews was growing. In 1934, one source says, 73 percent of all textile plants and shops, 75 percent of banks, 82 percent of credit bureaus, 96 percent of advertising bureaus, and 100 percent (!) of scrap metal and metal dealerships were in their hands. And these are just a few fields out of a great many. Besides dominating the press, where they spouted the anti-German views that had made me so angry, the Jews ruled the arts and the cinema. They used their influence to put on shows that were the filthiest, most depraved productions imaginable. Jews also ran the workers' movements, making tens, if not hundreds of thousands, of simple, hardworking souls adopt socialism and turn against their own people.

The Jews' idea of socialism went against nature itself. They themselves were the lowest of the low. Well aware of that fact, they repudiated the aristocratic principle, the eternal privilege of force and energy. In its place they and their toadies put numerical mass and dead weight. In this way they prepared the way for their own triumph over the rest of mankind and the latter's destruction. Worst of all, the Jews were working in unison. The numerous sharp divisions that appeared to exist among them were just a façade intended to mislead gullible *goyim* so as to exploit them all the better. In reality they were following a plan that was as well-considered as it was demonic. Some, Goebbels included, considered the *Protocols* a forgery. Perhaps it was. But of the fact that it broadly expressed the Jews' objectives and methods there can be no doubt.

Naturally, I did not grasp all of this at once. Only much later did all the various pieces finally fall into place and form a complete picture. That is why, in *Mein Kampf,* I recommended that people should not enter politics before they are thirty years old. Thirty, incidentally, was exactly the age at which Roman citizens were first allowed to stand for election as public officials. Even so I continued to educate myself. Just at present I am using my place in Hell to familiarize myself with everything I find interesting; during my time at Landsberg I did the same. Like so many others before and after me, I made prison my university. At the time I brought my earthly existence to an end my private library comprised 16,000 volumes. The books were distributed between Berlin, Munich, and Berchtesgaden. At one time or another I read, or at any rate skimmed, almost all of them. Doing so, I developed my own original method. I would start in the middle of each volume. Next I worked my way in both directions to see if there was anything valuable in it.

Coming on top of my observations of what was going on around me, my reading enabled me to form my *Weltanschauung*. By that I mean my—the emphasis is on my—particular way of understanding history. And, through it, the way the world works and will always go on working. My *Weltanschauung* was the rock-solid foundation which, as I first entered politics, I did my best to turn into reality. Later, its rough outline came to be shared by millions of my fellow-Germans and, I can say without false modesty, quite a number of non-Germans as well. Needless to say, though, at the time I first started shaping it I did not have the slightest idea that this would or could happen.

I do not want to say that all my impressions of Vienna were negative. Great as its shortcomings were, the city also taught me a lot. To be sure, already at a very early age I ceased to believe in the nonsense the priests were always dishing out. At school I used to make fun of our teachers of religion, often leaving them speechless. But I *was* impressed by the way the Church used pomp and pageantry in order to attract the masses. So much so that, at one point during my childhood in Linz, I sang in a choir! Vienna, with its numerous grand baroque churches, their elaborate decorations, and their splendid ceremonies, completed my education in this respect. Above all, I came to understand the amalgam of hypocrisy and business acumen on which the Church rests. Halleluiahs and indulgencies, what a team! An organization that has managed to survive for two thousand years must have many lessons to offer. The contrast with spineless, leaderless Protestantism could not be greater. That is why it has divided into tens of thousands of different sects.

As instructive as the Catholic Church was its rival, the workers' movement. I certainly was no socialist. The Talmudic teachings of Karl Marx, his numerous fellow Jews, and his deluded followers never made any impression on me. So did his idea that history is governed by material factors. A notion that, by eliminating the will, reduces men to the level of amoebae. But coming as I did from a relatively simple family with no property to speak of, I *did* feel sympathy for the great mass of working people whose lot in life, as I well knew, was often very hard. The more so because I was soon to become one of their number.

On one occasion I watched, fascinated, an enormous workers' parade that went on for hours and hours. The participants may have been rough and untutored. Many were also unwashed; how could they not be, given that running water, let alone hot water suitable for use in Vienna's ice-cold winter, was a luxury very few of them could afford? But the timber of which they were made was sound. If only one could win them back from the turgid mass of "international" ideas their leaders had foisted on them toward their own people, I thought to myself. In that case, any- and everything would be possible.

Finally, there was Vienna's great burgomaster, Karl Lueger. At first I thought he and his movement, the Christian Socialists, were merely reactionaries. Later, as I got to understand them better, honesty obliged me to alter my judgment. Such were his achievements in all aspects of municipal life, both economic and cultural, that he almost single-handedly succeeded in reinvigorating the empire. He had the rare gift of insight into human nature, and he was always very careful not to take men as better than they really were. In this he was quite unlike some others, such as the head of the Pan-German Party, Georg von Schönerer. Schönerer's ideas concerning the need to keep Austria German and to reunite it with Germany were excellent. But he did not have what it takes to lead really large numbers of people.

Lueger was professedly anti-Semitic. But he saw anti-Semitism as a tool of politics, not as a key issue around which to organize a nation and a state. Whatever he may have said, under his administration Jews did not suffer much. He even permitted himself to have some Jewish friends! His most important insight was very different: namely, that the aristocracy and upper bourgeoisie were politically useless. In their time they had contributed mightily to build the empire along with all the cultural achievements for which it will be forever remembered. By the early twentieth century, though, they were a spent force. Well aware of their decline, the people in question were intent, if on anything at all, only on postponing the inevitable for as long as possible.

A true mass party, one capable of seizing power and, eventually, shaking the world, could only be built by enlisting the lower middle classes. This includes people such as small shop owners, teachers, low-level civil servants and clerks, and salespeople. It was they, not their social superiors, who had the necessary stamina and were ready to make the sacrifices any great struggle requires. To rally these people behind him, Lueger had to hold the promise of a better life in front of them. Doing so, he was even able to win over the young clergy. So much so, in fact, that their seniors either retired from the field or swallowed their pride and joined him. To all these insights he added his qualities as a superb tactician. He had everything a really great political leader needs to succeed. However, the empire, torn apart by the various nationalities of its inhabitants and too weak to get them under control, was long past saving. That, at any rate, was one point on which Schönerer was right and Lueger wrong.

In September 1908 I made another attempt to be accepted at the Academy of Fine Arts. This time the idiots in charge did not even allow me to sit for the entrance examinations. Besides, my financial situation was changing for the worse. The appropriately named Stumpergasse—literally, Miserable Bunglers' Alley—where Kubizek and I shared a room was dingy enough. Now, the money I got from my family started running out, leaving me with less and less to live on. I did not want to share my worries with Kubizek. Kindhearted as he was, he might have embarrassed me by offering me to share some of his own slender resources. How could I, who had always tried to impress him with my various projects, humiliate myself in front of him in such a way? That is why, as he was staying with his parents in Linz during the summer break, I left our room, and the life I could no longer afford, without saying goodbye and without leaving a forwarding address. But I did not forget him. In 1938, at the time of the Anschluss, I asked my people to find him. They had no difficulty in doing so, and we had a brief meeting which brought much joy to both of us.

My biographers, stumbling over one another, have left no stone unturned in their efforts to find out just how I lived and what I did during this period in my life. Doing so, they dug up all kinds of obscure people who claimed to have known me in one way or another. Some probably did; after all, I did not live in a desert. Others I cannot remember. At times I feel those bloodhounds knew more about me than I did myself. That, of course, is another example of their tendency to make, or at least to try to make, much of nothing. All supposedly in the service of "objective" science! I moved to the

Felberstrasse, which was also located near the Westbahnhof and where I was lucky to find a reasonable place to stay. Nearby there was one of those kiosks that sell newspapers and tobacco. I took the opportunity to buy some of the countless little brochures published by all kinds of groups and parties and read them. In August 1909 I moved to even more modest accommodations in the nearby Sechsauserstrasse but stayed there for just one month.

The next few months were the hardest in my life. The autumn of that year was windy, wet, and cold. At first I tried sleeping in the open. However, I, soon found out that the only way to stay alive was to move from one cheap café to another and to stay there until they threw me out. By Christmas my situation had become really bad. My body was infested with lice, and my clothes, which I had always kept scrupulously clean, were in tatters. I did not actually starve. But hunger, persistent hunger, was definitely my companion.

Along with a great many others in my situation, I turned to a large house for the homeless in the district of Meidling. At the time every European city had such a place or, in many cases, several such places. It offered soup and bread, a shower, and a bed. So bad were the conditions that I was obliged to sleep with my shoes under my head so as to prevent them from being pinched! Even worse, come morning, the residents were driven into the streets. The doors were locked behind us, and we were left to fend as best we could. Here and there I tried to do manual labor—shoveling snow or carrying luggage for railway passengers—only to find out that, not having an overcoat and haggard as I was, I was not up to it. I also learned that being a simple worker in a harshly competitive capitalist world is no fun.

It was at this shelter that I met Reinhold Hanisch. Hanisch was a Sudeten German, a vagrant and petty criminal with a police record. He had, however, spent some time in Berlin and could tell me a lot about that city. It was Hanisch who, learning that I could paint, suggested that I start doing so and promised to sell the products. The resulting income was to be shared between us. Hanisch was not the most savory character on earth. Much later, after I had become famous, he started hawking his own paintings, pretending they were mine. For this and other trivial offenses he was jailed several times.

Before his death, which took place in 1937, he told some journalists that, contrary to what I had written in *Mein Kampf,* at the time he knew me I had not yet developed into the strong anti-Semite I later became. In fact, he claimed, I actually preferred dealing with Jewish customers because they were more reliable. Of two other people who also sold my paintings, he said, one, Josef Neumann, was himself Jewish. As if one could believe a word a man like Hanisch said; and as if, given my circumstances, I had a choice.

In February 1910, though, he was still my partner. Having bought the necessary equipment, I started producing a more or less steady stream of views of Vienna. Assisted by the pennies I earned in this way, as well as by a small gift from Hanitante, I moved to a men's house in the Meldemannstrasse. The institute, which had only just opened its doors, drew praise from the papers and was considered a model of its kind. For just fifty Heller residents were given their own cubicles to stay overnight. There were also some public facilities for day use: a canteen (where people could prepare their own food), bathrooms, lockers, a laundry, a small library, and the like. The one I liked best was a sort of common room in which some of us social outcasts used to gather, read newspapers, and discuss politics. Even at this low point in my life my main interest was study. That is why, ignoring Hanisch's protests, I only produced as many works as were needed to keep body and soul together.

At one point Hanisch tried to cheat me out of some of the money that was my due. I complained to the police, who arrested him. He spent a few days in jail, after which he disappeared. I continued living at the Meldemanstrasse, painting and hoping for better times to come. Life was no longer quite as desperate as it had been in late 1909. But it remained very hard. Much as I tried, naturally, that fact was not without effect on my appearance and behavior. Yet somehow, amidst all the problems, I always kept my head above water. Far from being a threat to the social order, as so many others in my situation became, I was always in danger of being crushed by that very order. That was how things remained until the spring of 1913.

Given the unsavory nature of Austrian politics, the repugnant mixture of races that infested Vienna, as well as my own unpleasant experiences in that city, I may be forgiven for not liking it very much. That, incidentally, did not prevent the Viennese from giving me a welcome when I returned there in 1938. The cries of "Heil" went on for hours on end until our ears were ringing with them! More to the point, looking back, as I do, from a safe distance, I cannot honestly say that I regret the life I led as a pauper on its streets. In particular, I got to know the common people. People whom most politicians, coming from, and spending their lives in, a much "better" social milieu than I did, never meet and therefore cannot understand. Seen in this light, the experience was invaluable both for Germany and for myself. But for it, I have no doubt that Germany would have turned communist.

Above all, my life as a down-and-out in Vienna made me hard. Much harder, as I later found out, than most of those who did not go through a similar period could even imagine anyone can be.

Chapter 3

Munich

On the eve of what was later to become known as the Great War, the Hapsburg Empire was clearly tottering. Honeycombed by the numerous different squabbling nationalities and guided, to the extent that it was guided, by a bunch of senile courtiers, it was paralyzed by the democratic system it had recently adopted. As a result, it was incapable of taking decisive action in any direction. For a German nationalist such as myself the atmosphere had become stifling, threatening even. Nor could I see any hope on the horizon. Schönerer's Pan German Movement was ideologically sound but did not have what it took to attract mass support. The Christian Socialists were better at doing so. But after the death of their great leader, Lueger, in 1910, they lost their way. Instead of taking a firm stance, especially over the all-important Jewish question, they zigged and zagged. As I later learned, in the entire empire there was only one person, Chief of Staff General Conrad von Hötzendorf, who knew what had to be done and was prepared to do it. They did not let him have his way though, and the rest is history.

The entire question also touched me in a more immediate manner. Like most other countries, Austria-Hungary at the time relied on general conscription to fill the ranks. When it was my time to be called up, I decided, hell no, I wouldn't go. I did not want to do military service, and perhaps risk my life, solely to promote the cause, which in all probability was a lost one, of the Hapsburgs, their

aristocratic flunkeys, and their Jewish supporters. Feeling trapped, I
decided to move to the Bavarian capital of Munich.

On a personal level the decision proved to be among the happiest
I ever made. To me, the city immediately felt as if I had known it
for ages. To be sure, the district of Schwabing where, for economic
reasons, I settled, had its share of "artistic" crackpots. Much of what
went on had more to do with filth and pornography—the word, having been recently coined, was everywhere—than with sound, healthy
German art. Some called themselves Expressionists, some Cubists.
Others formed associations which carried strange names such as such
as The Bridge, The Blue Horseman, or whatever. The more absurd,
the better. What was one to say of people who painted red trees and
green skies? Or tried to reduce everything to cubes? Or spent their
time looking for all kinds of degenerates and putting them on show?
Or sculpted human torsos without heads and without limbs? Later,
I, and the German people acting through me, took the opportunity
to say all too clearly what we thought of such "art." Still Munich,
located far from Berlin and competing with it, was a real *German*
city. After the teeming, racially heterogeneous and often bastardized,
masses of Vienna, what a relief.

The weather on the day I arrived in Munich, 25 May 1913, was
fine; a good omen for the future. I rented a room in the Schleis-
sheimerstrasse, a relatively poor district in the north. If you want to
know the exact house number and floor, ask one of my biographers.
Next, I set up as a painter. After all, I still dreamed of becoming an
architect. However, given my lack of a proper school certificate, I
still could not see a clear way to pursue my ambition. Meanwhile,
I painted public buildings just as I had previously done in Vienna.
Among them were the Altes Rathaus, the Residenz, the Alter Hof,
the Propyläum, and the Hofbräuhaus; briefly, the most important
sights of Munich. As I had done in Vienna, I preferred to draw
them from postcards rather than from life—a technique often used
by other artists too. My work sold well enough to keep soul and body

together in a fairly decent manner. No small achievement, as many young budding artists can tell from their own experience.

I painted about two pictures per week. To be sure, I could have done more if my material needs had been greater than they were and if I had really set my mind to the task. However, an artist—and that is how, throughout my life, I have considered myself—needs time to think, rest, and, yes, idle. The kind of life, in short, that is the opposite of the one my father led. After all, is not *schole*, leisure, the source of all wisdom? I could name any number of famous artists who had their greatest inspiration not when they were absorbed in their work but at the most unexpected moments. Some were engaged in some other activity, preferably one that does not require thought, such as taking a walk. One of them was Nietzsche, who got his best ideas when walking, on his own, in the mountains of the Engadin. Trust no thought unless it was born in the fresh air, he said! Others were doing nothing in particular when the Muse, coming from God knows where, suddenly lighted on them.

Besides, I saw my modest art as a means to an end, not as an end in itself. I wanted to continue my education in the fields that interested me most, i.e. history and public affairs. Education, if it is to be worthy of the name and not to result in mere *Bildung*, takes time and effort. Perhaps even more important, it requires opposition—people who act as a sounding board and who are not ashamed to take up your ideas and to tear them to pieces if they can. Whoever thinks that lectures delivered by a professor, however brilliant, in front of tens of thousands of people, each of whom is sitting in his own private room in front of his own private screen, can provide anything like a real education is deluding himself. And, which is much worse, he deludes his students as well.

I also went on studying architecture and producing sketches. I often worked so deep into the night that my roommate, one Rudolf Hausler, moved out and rented another room in the same building. I was on friendly terms with my landlord, a tailor by the name of Herr

Popp, and had many political discussions with his family and him. But I also frequented coffee houses and beer halls, of which Munich had as many as any other city on earth. There, usually in the kind of modestly priced places I could afford, I talked. I argued. And, yes, when the spirit took me, I harangued. Occasionally, I got very angry at people who did not know what they were talking about or who voiced opinions that betrayed the German national cause. And they got equally angry at me.

To be sure, being a "beer-hall philosopher," as Kershaw has disparagingly called me, is not considered exactly the most exalted calling on earth. How many times have such characters not been made fun of by their self-appointed intellectual superiors! But pay heed. Addressing such an audience in such a way as to attract and keep its attention is not exactly easy. The penalty for failure is being thrown out into the streets and hearing the door slammed shut behind you. Let the *Herren Professoren,* most of whom have never done anything more ambitious than speaking in front of a captive audience of sheepish students in class, try it, if only for five minutes! I am told that, until a few years ago, London's famous Speakers' Corner had no shortage of spellbinding speakers who regularly addressed every subject under the sun. Spellbinding they had to be, or else no one would have listened to them. Briefly, it was the much-despised coffee houses and beer halls that first launched me on the road to developing the oratorical skills that later made me world famous. At the time, however, I did not have the slightest idea as to where they would lead me.

Meanwhile, the Austrian imperial bureaucracy was looking for me. Many people thought of it in terms of *österreichische Schlamperei,* Austrian sloppiness. In fact, thanks no doubt to legions of self-sacrificing officials like my father, it was one of the most efficient in Europe. The bureaucrats' tenacity in looking for me, a single insignificant individual, was impressive. First, they went to my relatives in Linz and the Waldviertel and then to the Vienna police. (Like everyone

else, when I arrived in the city, I had to register with them.) Then
they went to the men's home at the Meldemannstrasse. Finally, they
turned to the Munich police, with whom I had also registered. On
18 January 1914 one of the latter's officers knocked on the door.
Failure to present yourself for military service carried quite a hefty
fine whereas leaving the country in order to avoid it might cause one
to be imprisoned. No wonder I was shocked.

I was summoned to present myself two days later at Linz, which
is 200 kilometers away. To make sure I would comply, the Munich
police arrested me. Later it turned out that they had been sitting on
the summons for some time but had failed to deliver it. This worked
in my favor because I could argue that the time I was given was too
short to put my affairs in order. I appealed to the Austrian Consulate,
which showed some sympathy for my situation. I asked the people
in Linz for a deferment, only to have my request rejected. However,
their answering telegram only arrived on the morning of 21 January,
the day after the one I was supposed to present myself. Thereupon I
asked for permission to present myself on 5 February. This time my
request was granted, and the place changed to Salzburg, which was
much closer to where I lived.

To explain what had happened, I sent the authorities a letter three
and a half pages long. Naturally I could not inform them of the real
reason for my decision to leave Austria and, with it, its armed forces,
since doing so would only have made my situation worse. Instead
I said that my failure to register for service in 1909 had been due
to my bitter circumstances at the time; also that I had written to
them retroactively in February 1910. Having received no response, I
assumed everything was in order and had almost forgotten about the
matter. I reminded them that, though an orphan and in a difficult
situation, I had never been accused of any crime and had always
kept my name clean. In the event, my humble efforts proved to
be superfluous. On 5 February I took the train—at the consulate's
expense—to Salzburg and presented myself as I had been ordered to

do. I was examined and found physically unfit to serve, whereupon I was happy to return to Munich and resume my life.

I cannot vouch that every line I later wrote in *Mein Kampf* was already germinating in my mind at that time. That is just not the way memory, mine included, works. I did, however, find my attention increasingly directed toward foreign policy. Nor was there any cause for surprise in this. The Austrian monarchy had its enemies. The most important one was Russia, with which it was deeply embroiled in the Balkans. Another enemy was Italy, which, despite being a formal ally, was always looking for an opportunity to snatch South Tyrol, Dalmatia, and God knows what other territorial morsels. As I wrote earlier, though, the most important problems from which Austria suffered were internal.

The situation of the Reich was, or at any rate appeared to be, quite different. To this day, there are those who consider the Wilhelmine period the happiest one in the whole of German history. The treasonous idea of *multi-kulti* (multiculturalism) was so far in the future as to be unimaginable. The Jews apart, there were, as yet, few foreigners around. The country was superbly looked after, prosperous, and bursting to the seams with growth. Its army was far and away the best in the world, and its science and technology were widely respected.

Here in Hell I happened to come across a Sears and Roebuck Catalog for the year 1903. Leafing through it, I quickly learned that, in the U.S. at that time, the best way to praise any kind of product was to put the word "German" in front of its name. As, for example, in the case of the so-called "Heidelberg belt," a device supposed to restore sexual vigor by sending electric shocks through the male organ! Or take a look at Erskine Childer's best-seller, *The Riddle of the Sands,* which was published in the same year. It will not take you long to learn how much he admired the Kaiser, whom he actually called "a splendid chap." Many other Englishmen agreed.

There were cracks in the structure, particularly the Reichstag, which never stopped cackling and obstructing Wilhelm in any way it could. But these only became really serious during the World War and after it had ended. At this point I want to put it on record that foreign policy, whether waged by diplomatic methods or by armed force, is a brutal struggle for existence that has neither beginning nor end. To think, as many who observed Germany's prosperity did, that it can be waged, let alone won, by purely commercial means is an illusion, and a very dangerous one at that. No better illustration of this fact may be found than the rise, first of England and then of the United States. It is true that, partly because they were favored by geography, both were and are great trading nations. But it is also true that neither showed the slightest hesitation in using armed force whenever it saw the need to do so. As the English themselves said of themselves, trade followed the flag. Any attempt to deny this truth can only be characterized by a single world: absurd.

While the need for struggle forms an integral part of my *Weltanschauung*, it is not I who invented it. It is a fundamental law of nature. It was discovered at least as long ago as Heraclitus in the fifth century B.C. Wasn't it he who first said that war was the father of everything? So pervasive is it that nations, every single nation that has ever existed or will ever exist, *must* engage in it willingly or unwillingly. It is, so to speak, the way in which nature exercises its justice. In the long run it always is the stronger party that survives and prospers. Whereas the weaker one is defeated if it is lucky and subjugated and perhaps exterminated if it is not. To be sure, strength is made up of several factors. Among them are racial makeup (what, a hundred years later, mealy-mouthed people like to call ethnicity), numbers, geography, economics, industrial and technical development, and so on. And yet, as Schopenhauer taught, at the center of everything there is the will. The one thing for which there is no substitute; and without which all the rest are more or less worthless.

The first pillar of German foreign policy I came to criticize after my move to Munich was the alliance with Austria. I need hardly repeat that I, as someone who had been a German nationalist practically from birth on, would have liked nothing better than to see the Germans in the land where I was born united with their brethren in the Reich. What I had not anticipated was the extent to which people in the latter misunderstood the Habsburg Dynasty. Uniting with the Reich was the last thing Austria's ruling classes wanted. To the contrary, their survival depended on their ability to keep the two countries apart for as long as possible. It was only their fear of Russia, which in itself was perfectly justified, which induced them to ally themselves with Germany. The Reich-Germans also failed to appreciate the weakness of the monarchy and, in particular, that of the German element in it. Owing to its much lower birthrate, that element was losing power year by year. A nation that commits suicide in this way is doomed, and any others who ally themselves with it will suffer.

Unlike the Germans in Austria, the Reich-Germans were bursting with vitality. The population, which in 1871 had stood at 41 million, had now reached 68 million and was still growing fast. How to feed the hundreds of thousands being added each year? By bringing down the birthrate? Doing so might indeed have been possible. But only at the cost of seeing the country drop from the list of great powers and turn into some kind of larger Switzerland. We quite likely would have lost control of our destiny and become a protégé of Russia, whose population, estimated at 166 million, was increasing even faster than ours. That, incidentally, was what Chancellor Bethmann-Hollweg, "the Philosopher of Howenfinow," as, after his estate in Brandenburg, he was known, believed and feared. Even at the time, the joys of such "protection" could be seen all too plainly in Poland, which had been experiencing it for over a hundred years. After 1945, the whole of Eastern Europe, including parts of Germany itself, learned to know and appreciate them.

Another oft-discussed possibility was internal colonization, such as by opening new land for cultivation, increasing our industry, and exporting and importing. Our neighbors, the Netherlands, provided a very good example of this method. Such colonization might indeed present a solution—for some time at any rate. The more so because it goes well with our people's innate pacifism and preference for a half-slumbering existence. Not for nothing do foreigners often poke fun at our *Schlafmütze* (nightcaps). But there clearly were, and are, limits. Not every soil can be made to yield the crops people need. And what soil can be made to do so will, sooner or later, be exhausted.

From 1914 to 1918, the fact that we were cut off from our sources of fertilizer in Chile produced dire results for the health of our people. Estimates put the number of those who died because of the English blockade at anything between 424,000 and 763,000. Many of them were children and old people. If this reminds anyone of the problems we are periodically having in obtaining natural gas from Russia, then that is as it should be. Furthermore, a state which adopts such methods is like a man on a treadmill. That is due not only to the number of people constantly increasing, but, what is just as important, the way in which their demands for higher standards of living also keep growing. The final outcomes must always be unemployment, poverty, and hunger—or, as people like to call it today, an "economic crisis." I shall discuss the crisis of 1929–32 later in this volume. At this point, all I want to say is that such a one is quite capable of shaking the country to its very foundations. Unless proper foresight is exercised and preventive measures are taken, it can very well lead to the outbreak of diseases and mass starvation. Not to mention civil war.

Given its position in the center of Europe, Germany had always embraced a continental—some would say provincial—outlook. That was as true of the old Reich as it later became of both the most important German states, Austria and Prussia. To be sure, Frederick II took an interest in the New World. But there was little he, or, for that matter, his Hapsburg enemy Maria Theresa, could do about it. Hamburg, long a great commercial and seafaring center, was an exception. It was not always a welcome one though, since its citizens tended toward cosmopolitanism. Later, they had some trouble understanding why anti-Semitism was as vital to our well-being as it was. At any rate Hamburg only represented a drop in the German bucket. Of the states in that bucket, none ever built a proper navy or set out to acquire oversea colonies as Spain, France, England, and even little Portugal, the Netherlands, and Belgium all did.

At the turn of the century things changed. Everyone started talking of *Weltpolitik*, AKA geopolitics in non-German speaking countries. The term, and the science for which it stands, surfaced for the first time in the 1890s. Their most important exponent was not a German but an Englishman, Halford Mackinder. It was from Mackinder, who in his own way was a genuine genius, that everyone else took their cue. Among them were our own worthy Karl Haushofer and his onetime student Rudolf Hess.

During the years leading up to the war, as well as the war itself, the term *Weltpolitik* was on everyone's lips. After 1918, it all but disappeared from the printed page. Later, during my time as Chancellor, it underwent a moderate revival. After World War II, it again disappeared, only to experience a second revival after 1960. By that time, though, its meaning had been thoroughly changed. It no longer referred to Germany. Defeated, humiliated, and dismembered, our poor country hardly any more had the power to engage in any kind of foreign policy at all. Reduced to *Kettenhunde*, dogs on a chain, all its two parts could do was bark at each other while hiding under the wing of their respective masters, the U.S. and the USSR. Thus the frequency with which authors used the term, and the way in which they did so, faithfully reflected Germany's foreign policy as well as the none-too honorable position it was holding in the world.

Weltpolitik both summed up the foreign policy of Wilhelm II and reflected it. Wilhelm was highly intelligent and highly energetic.

However, initially, at any rate he was also young. And headstrong, and flamboyant, and, some would say, unstable. He was always speaking of "Huns"—a term, incidentally, that did us immense damage during the World War—sharp swords and shining armor. But he did not really mean it. He liked maneuvers, in which he could cut a splendid figure, much better than he liked war. He also rejected the sagacious advice of Bismarck, of whom he rid himself soon after assuming the throne. Indiscriminately lashing out in all directions, he sought to increase Germany's power in every quarter of the globe, however remote and unimportant. As he kept telling anyone who would and would not listen, "Germany's future is on the water." Never mind that, according to Reichskanzler Bernard von Bulow, who often accompanied him on the imperial yacht, he tended to suffer from seasickness.

I thought then, and I continued thinking to the last day of my earthly existence, that this policy was wrong. First, geography itself dictated that our chief competitors and enemies should be the French, *la grande nation* as they liked to call themselves, on one hand and the Russians on the other. Starting in 1892, when they signed a formal alliance, they encircled Germany from both the west and the east and were always threatening to overwhelm it. True, we were not entirely without allies. Austria-Hungary apart, they included Italy as well as much weaker ones in the form of Romania, Bulgaria, and Turkey. Italy and Romania ended by treacherously switching to the other side. The rest were not worth a fig. They did not help us; instead, we had to help them. We ended up sending some of our troops to fight as far afield as Iraq.

Under such circumstances, to aim at overseas expansion and thereby to add England, and later the U.S., which came to the assistance of its former mistress, to our enemies was sheer lunacy. Throughout the days of the Second Reich, all this policy achieved was to acquire for us a few worthless pieces of land in Africa and East Asia. Instead of adding to our resources, all proved a drain

on them. Far away as they were, none could be defended by force
of arms if necessary. When the time came, the heroic resistance of
some of our people in them—first and foremost, General Paul von
Lettow-Vorbeck in East Africa—was of no avail. Even worse was the
megalomaniac attempt to engage in an arms race with both France
and Russia (on land) and England (at sea) at the same time. Such a
policy ran contrary to the most elementary principles of strategy. It
could only end in disaster, as it eventually did.

Briefly, the only solution to our problems, one which states and
nations have always used, was territorial expansion. Not overseas,
as Wilhelm and his advisers hoped, but right here in Europe. To
the east of us there were the immense spaces occupied by the Slavs,
principally Poles, Balts, and, of course, Russians and Ukrainians.
They might be numerous, but they were also racially inferior, weak,
underdeveloped, and ill governed. To be convinced of this, all one
had to do was to look at the difference between prosperous West
and East Prussia on one hand and the lands known as "Congress
Poland" on the other. Not for nothing did we Germans speak of
polnische Wirtschaft (Polish economy) and *polnische Versager* (Polish
blunderers). In today's Germany using these expressions is strictly
verboten. But here in Hell, thank Satan, using them and some others
like them is perfectly in order.

Our entire foreign policy, our choice of allies, and our armament
should have reflected this necessity. Instead, in many ways we did
just the opposite from what was required. A few people, such as then
Colonel Erich Ludendorff, questioned the policies we had adopted
and demanded that the army be expanded to cope with our two most
important enemies. However, amidst the constant cries of "hurrah"
so characteristic of Wilhelmine Germany, no one paid any attention
to him. Instead, he was dismissed from the General Staff, where
he had been in charge for the critically important Department of
Mobilization, and was sent to command an infantry regiment! Had
it been up to the Reichstag, in fact, the military career of one of the

greatest German commanders of all times would have ended then and there. Ludendorff himself was convinced it would.

Kershaw and others have spilled large amounts of ink trying to find out precisely when, where, and why the various elements of my *Weltanschauung* were formed. So let me repeat: I cannot vouch that every one of these ideas was ripe in my young mind before the World War broke out, let alone that all the pieces of the puzzle had fallen into place, creating the rock-like, seamless whole they later became. That had to wait until the time of my imprisonment at Landsberg and even later. However, as far as my limited knowledge allowed, I had already begun thinking seriously about them and arrived at certain conclusions. Looking back from the vantage point provided by the post-1918 years, it seemed to me as if Providence itself was beckoning us to march in this direction. I shall have more to say about this later in the present volume.

Chapter 4

The World War

Interestingly enough, few, if any, of my "serious" biographers have ever heard a shot fired in anger. That already applied to one of the first, a man who was not only a Jew, but a liar to boot. Yet his manifest unreliability did not prevent his book, bristling with falsehoods as it does, from being used against me by all the rest. To the contrary, they were attracted to it like flies to a sack full of rotting trash.

Out of the two best-known post-1945 German ones one, Sebastian Haffner, betrayed his Motherland by absconding to England in 1937 just as it was his turn to be called up. The other, Joachim Fest, was born too late to see action. So was a third, Peter Longrich. Accidentally or not, neither of my two major English biographers, Alan Bullock and the aforementioned Kershaw, served. Nor did another well-known English historian, Richard Evans, who wrote no fewer than three volumes about the Third Reich. John Tolland, the American author of a supposedly "classic, definitive" biography, did spend seven years wearing a captain's uniform. However, at no time during the critical years from 1942 to 1945 did he set foot outside the Continental U.S. One author, the Australian John Williams, devoted an entire book to my service in the World War. But even he never came close to a real-life trench. Scant wonder that what they and many others who followed in their footsteps had to say about me is often misleading. Specifically, not one of them really understood the impact the war had on me as well as so many other front-soldiers of my generation.

The feeling that war, if not a world war (the term *Weltkrieg* itself only appeared for the first time in 1911) then a smaller one, was about to break out had been widespread in Europe for quite some years before 1914. The Continent, as the saying goes, was a powder keg waiting for a spark to explode it. Luckily, the spark, when it came, hit Austria first of all. Had it not been for that fact, Germany would have entered the war, which was inevitable, without any allies at all. That is not to say that I blame Austria. As everyone knows, and as a recent volume (Christopher Clark, *The Sleepwalkers*, 2014) has confirmed once again, the Serbs, assisted by the Russians, had long been giving the government in Vienna as much trouble as they could. All the assassination of Franz Ferdinand did was to push it, much against its will, to the point where it *had* to act. Surely any other government worth its salt would have done the same.

Scholars, driven to publish or perish, are always trying to prove their predecessors wrong. That is why some of them have tried to show that the war of 1914 was unwelcome. But that is nonsense. Not only was the war not forced on the people, but most of them desired it and even enthusiastically welcomed it. They hoped it would put an end to the general feeling of uncertainty once and for all. When it did in fact break out, it opened the eyes of the nation, enabling them to look clearly into the future. That alone explains why over two million German men and youths voluntarily joined the colors, ready to shed the last drop of their blood for the cause. The same, incidentally, happened in other countries, nowhere more so than in England, whose small professional army was flooded by so many volunteers that it soon changed its character altogether. So I repeat: whoever says the war was forced on the masses simply does not know what he is talking about.

As for me, during the boisterous years of my youth, nothing used to damp my spirit as much as to think that I had been born in an age when the only people worth honoring were businessmen. At times it looked as if the entire world was about to transform itself into a single gigantic department store owned, as was so often the case, by the Jews. As I already said, to the extent that my young mind allowed I took a lively interest first in the Boer War and then in the Russo–Japanese War, both of which I keenly followed in the papers. But I had all but given up hope that I myself might participate in such great events. That is why, when the moment came, I sank to my knees and thanked Heaven out of the fullness of my heart for the favor of having been permitted to live in such a time. As the famous photograph of the demonstration in Munich's Odeonsplatz shows, I was not the only one.

On 3 August I petitioned His Majesty, King Ludwig III of Bavaria, asking to be allowed to join his army. A positive answer arrived on the very next day; a speed that few modern postal services, for all the much-improved technical devices at their disposal, are able to match. So well did the *pneumatique,* as it was called, function in Munich and other cities which had it that one could even send a letter and get an answer on the same day. Very soon, I found myself wearing a German uniform and undergoing basic training. Like countless others in similar situations before and since, we recruits only feared one thing: that we would arrive too late to see any fighting. That is why, when crossing the Rhine by rail on our way from Munich to the front, we spontaneously broke into *Die Wacht am Rhein.*

And then, as the morning sun rose out of the mist after a damp, cold night spent marching in Flanders' Fields—

An iron greeting suddenly burst above our heads. Shrapnel exploded in our midst and spluttered in the damp ground. But before the smoke of the explosion disappeared, a wild "Hurrah" was shouted from two hundred throats, in response to this first greeting of death. Then began the whistling of bullets and the booming of cannons, the shouting and singing of the combatants. With eyes straining feverishly we pressed forward, faster and faster, until we finally came to close-quarter fighting, there beyond the beet-fields and the meadows. Soon the strains of a song reached us from afar. Nearer and nearer, from company to company it came. And while death began to make havoc in our ranks we passed the song on to those beside us:

> *Deutschland, Deutschland über alles,*
> *über Alles in der Welt…*

After four days in the trenches we came back. Even our gait had changed. Boys of seventeen looked more like men. The rank and file of the List Regiment [after its commander, Colonel Julius List] had not been properly trained in the art of war. But they knew how to die like old soldiers.

That was just the beginning. With death passing among us and cutting us down with its scythe, it did not take long for our enthusiasm to change into horror and fear. Only later—for some of us, much later—did fear in turn give way to an iron determination to stick it out. *Coute que coute.* For me this inner struggle ended in the winter of 1915–16. From then on my will triumphed, making me calm and resolute. And, yes, it also did much to immunize me to the sufferings of my fellow soldiers as well as those of the enemy troops we killed or injured as best we could. To see and hear men caught in barbed wire, their guts spilling out and begging for help, is not exactly a pleasant experience. First, they scream. Then they sob, then they moan, and then they fall silent. All this while the birds hover above, sometimes even attacking them when they are still alive. And all this amidst the inescapable stench of the battlefield, which even now I can smell in my sleep. A horrible mixture of cordite, rotting flesh, and shit. Day after day, month after month, year after year. Hell, at any rate in my experience, is kind by comparison. I had to become immune, or else I would have gone mad.

Ever since 1945, there probably has not been a single book about me that did not set out to calumniate me as much as it could. Accordingly, I am proud to say that all of them, without a single exception, agree that I was a brave soldier. And how could they do otherwise? As the German saying goes, *Selbstlob stinkt* (self-praise stinks). But quite a few of my comrades in arms have testified to my qualities and performance. Chief among them was Max Amman, my former company sergeant-major, who later became a publishing mogul. Another was Fritz Wiedemann, the regimental adjutant who was my direct superior; he later served as my own adjutant until I packed him off to represent Germany in San Francisco.

Then there were Hans Mend, a fellow dispatch runner and subsequent petty criminal and jailbird, Balthaser Brandmayer, a fellow soldier who was a newcomer to our group and of whom we initially made fun, and Ernst Schmidt, who was closest to me and who later occupied an important position in the NSDAP organization in Munich. Whatever took place later, throughout the war we were as close as only war can make men be. I did what I could for them. And they did the same for me. Without hesitation, we risked our lives for each other. Had things been otherwise, surely even fewer of us would have survived than was actually the case.

To reward my efforts I was decorated with the Iron Cross II and I. Though I did not mention the fact in *Mein Kampf*, the former was handed out to me by the Kaiser, who happened to be visiting the front, in person. War, especially a long one, invariably causes the number of medals issued to go up as their value goes down. The Great War, as it was initially called, was no exception. As commander-in-chief of the Wehrmacht during World War II, I did my best to limit the phenomenon. Not, I am afraid, with much success. Inflation notwithstanding, for an ordinary soldier at that time to receive the Iron Cross Class I was quite unusual. Some miscreants, with an eye to discrediting me, have spread all kinds of lies about the way I got it. Let them look at the official citation which accompanied it and is readily available; that is all I have to say.

I passionately loved soldiering. For four years on end I acted as a runner, carrying messages from headquarters to the front and back. It was a dangerous job, the more so because I often volunteered to carry out missions few others wanted and from which my superiors did not really expect me to return. I learned it in the only possible way, i.e. by doing it. I developed map-reading skills, carefully planned my routes, acquired a keen ear for various kinds of enemy projectiles and an equally keen eye for any shelter that might be available on my way, was always alert for the sudden emergence out of some shell hole of enemy soldiers, and became accustomed to crawling, worm-like, on my stomach.

My comrades used to call me the Lucky Linzer. I was wounded twice, once in my left leg in October 1916, and once by mustard gas—yellow cross as it was known—in the very last days of the war. Like so many others on both sides of the front who came under this kind of attack, I lost my sight. Luckily, in my case, the effect was temporary. The claim that my blindness was the outcome of hysteria is so preposterous that I need not bother to answer it. Let me just say that, of all the blockheads who have speculated about this matter and scribbled down their conclusions, not one has gone through what I, along with so many of my comrades, did.

Unlike most soldiers I did not have any people back home with whom I could correspond and from whom I could receive parcels. Unlike them, too, I wanted to keep my body and character clean as, my difficult circumstances notwithstanding, I had always sought to do. I did not join in the escapades which, in Belgium and northern France, were readily available even a short distance behind the front. These facts made my comrades in arms look at me as a rare bird. The more so because, keeping my interest in politics, from time to time I talked to them. Sometimes I met with success as they accepted my position, and sometimes I failed as they made jokes about me. So what? In such things, live and let live is my motto. Then and later, unless there was some political issue involved, I never interfered with the private lives of others. And I expect others to do the same in regard to me.

An oft-asked question is why I, who by every account was a good soldier, never even made the rank of *Feldwebel* (NCO). The question is misplaced. After all, millions of others who went through the war just as I did were not promoted either. That apart, there were three reasons. First, as Wiedemann was later to testify at Nuremberg, I seemed to lack what the Prussians call *Schneid,* the kind of comportment that signals decisiveness and the will to be obeyed. Second, I was not a German citizen. Third, I did not want to be promoted. I felt comfortable in my lowly, if dangerous, position. My commanders did not always act in a responsible manner. At times they sent me, as well as other runners, into the fire simply to deliver a family postcard. However, the job left me with considerable spare time on my hands. This was time which, as I had done in both Vienna and Munich, I used to draw and to reflect.

On the other hand, four years did not pass without teaching me some things. One was minor tactics. In the German Army, as in all others at the time, officers were not normally commissioned from the enlisted personnel. Instead, coming out of high school, they were preselected and put through a special lengthy training course, one which, in wartime, might or might not include a period at the front. Next, assisted by their sergeant-majors, who often knew much more than they did, they were unleashed on their subordinates. Much of this remains true to the present day. Strange to say, I am told that the one major exception is the Israeli Army, which selects most of its officers straight from the ranks. But then who ever said that these Jews, for all their shortcomings, are not clever? Swindlers often are.

In any case, by spending four years in the field I came to understand tactics much better than many senior officers did. Some officers, particularly artillerists on one hand and those wearing the General Staff's trousers with the red stripe on the other, hardly saw the front at all. In part this was due to the peculiar nature of trench warfare. In addition, they did not want to be there. These gentlemen spent the war in comfortable—at times, very comfortable indeed—circumstances, where they were hardly in greater danger than during peacetime. They were always writing, writing, instead of leading, leading. Army Commander in Chief General Werner von Fritsch, Army Chief of Staff General Franz Halder, and Halder's successor, General Kurt Zeitzler, all belonged to one—or both—of these categories. So did the three top officers in the Wehrmacht High Command; Field-Marshal Wilhelm Keitel, his deputy General Alfred Jodl, and Jodl's own deputy, General Walter Warlimont. By far the best of the lot was Jodl. But even he did not have nearly as much field experience as I did. And he never forgot it.

The other—and even more important—thing I acquired was a good understanding of the common soldier. Here again, *not* coming from a privileged background, not having the *Abitur* (high-school leaving diploma), and not having gone to officer school and received a commission, were advantages. I knew, as well as anyone else, how the poor worm, or *Frontschwein* as many called him, felt and thought. I knew the sources of his behavior, his hopes, his frustrations, and his fears. I knew—much more so than many officers, general-staff officers in particular—what he could and could not, would and would not, do, when, under what circumstances, and for what purposes. Later, when I commanded the Wehrmacht in what was and is likely to remain the largest war in history, the experience I acquired proved invaluable to me.

Then and later, I sought to expand my knowledge of military affairs by studying. The works I read included Ernst Junger's *The Storm of Steel*. By common consent, it is one of the best descriptions of life at the front ever written. However, since I knew most of it already, it did not leave a powerful impression on me. Then there were Frederick the Great's various *Werke*, Moritz Arndt's famous *Catechism for the Teutonic Warrior*, *Conquest of the Air*, with an introduction by Count Ferdinand von Zeppelin, Hiegel's *Handbook of Tanks*, a biography of General Schlieffen, the author of the plan named after him, and Colonel Charles de Gaulle's *The Army of the Future*. That is not to mention books on the navies of the world: *Jane's*, (the standard English-language handbook), its German equivalent *Flotten-*

Kalendar, and the current Kriegsmarine yearbook. So detailed was my knowledge of the world's warships that I could often embarrass my admirals by asking them questions to which they did not know the answer. I am told that my volume of Clausewitz's essays, now at the Library of Congress, has never been opened. That may be so, but it does not mean I did not read him. In fact I can quote him by the yard, which is much better than many of my generals, who, uninterested in philosophy and politics, considered him too theoretical for their taste.

The outbreak of war caused the German people to rally behind their Kaiser. No one could have asked for more. Before 1914, he had often struck a ridiculous figure, strutting around, backslapping, and playing practical jokes on his subordinates. But this time he rose to the occasion. His declaration that he no longer recognized parties, only Germans, was magnificent. Amidst immense enthusiasm, everyone was keen "to do his bit," as the English say. This atmosphere lasted for about two months and was stimulated by the immense victories Hindenburg and Ludendorff won in the Battles of Tannenberg and the Masurian Lakes. During the second half of September, though, our enemies, in what they later called "The Miracle of the Marne," succeeded in saving Paris. They even forced us to give up some of the country we had overrun. Much worse, it was becoming clearer every day that the war would not be over by Christmas.

While the armies continued fighting heroically, sustaining losses larger than those in any previous war, back in the homeland discordant voices began making themselves heard. As so often, it was certain sections of the press that took the lead. Some of these gentlemen, pretending to seek nothing but the good of the nation, started doubting whether we should really celebrate our victories. They believed that moderation might make our dear enemies more inclined toward peace. Others were Marxists. To them the fact that, at the beginning of the war, the German worker had risen and offered to give his all for

the Motherland came as a deep disappointment. It showed all their
theories concerning the "international" character of the working class
to be so much rubbish. It put a spoke in their wheel, which they
could not easily overcome. Still, they did not give up. Drop by drop,
they continued to spread their poison. Drop by drop, it did its work.

A proper government would have taken these fellows by their long
ears and hanged them. However, the German imperial government
was a product of the monarchic past. Its roots in the people had
always been weak. As, for example, when it never invited workers'
representatives to attend national events such as the dedication of a
monument or the launching of a warship. On such occasions, all
one saw was a sea of top hats! Being weak, the government did not
dare take the necessary drastic measures. It did not impose effective
censorship. It did not abolish the parties. It did not bring the Reichstag, where the Social Democrats had formed the largest faction from
1912, to its senses. Comparative data on the way these things were
handled in different countries do not seem to be available even in
Hell. However, the statistics show that the German Army executed
incomparably fewer soldiers than the French and English ones did.
Not to mention the Russians, of course.

In any case, as Napoleon said, the pen is mightier than the sword.
At times, persecutions and executions are necessary instruments of
government, never more so than during total war, when every muscle
must strain for the attainment of victory. Nevertheless, they are
no way to overcome a powerful ideology with strong roots among
the people. That is something only an equally powerful counter-
ideology can do. It was the Kaiserreich's greatest failure that it failed
to produce such an ideology. In fact it did not even try to produce
one. Starting right at the beginning of the war, it made little effort
to use propaganda in order to maintain the nation's fighting spirit.
What propaganda it did engage in tended to be timid and apolo-
getic. After first giving our enemies a field day by calling Belgian
neutrality "a scrap of paper," how many times did not Bethmann-

Hollweg apologize for our invasion of that country and even promise to pay reparations? While the life-and-death struggle for Germany's very existence was raging all around us, our dear government did its mediocre best to stay humanitarian—humanitarian! As if war, by its very nature, is not the very opposite of "humanitarian." And as if propaganda were some form of high culture rather than an instrument whose sole purpose is to mobilize and energize people.

Based on such considerations, the truth is that neither our government nor the High Command produced any worthwhile propaganda at all. The little they did produce was aimed neither at the common man nor at the simple soldier but at those eternal doubting Thomases, the intellectuals. As, for example, by reprinting the Allied accusations and then trying to refute them. Much of the time, it was to no avail. Even at the time, it made me want to tear my hair out.

Here as so often, I can only repeat what I later wrote in *Mein Kampf.* The first thing good propaganda must do is to reach the masses. To do that it must be based on a good understanding of them. The idea that the masses are capable of abstract thought is pure illusion. In so far as the propagandists' objective is not to enlighten them but to seduce and inspire them, perhaps it is better that way. Their character is feminine; they respond to emotion, not to the intellect. I strongly suspect that all of this remains true even though the percentage of our people who take their *Abitur* has multiplied many times over in the last hundred years. That is not to mention the vast increase in the number of those who attended a university. In short, the old saying, *vox populi, vox dei* is wrong. It would be more appropriate to say, *vox populi, vox porci.*

Considering these facts, the most important quality successful propaganda has to have is simplicity. It should take a few essential themes and hammer at them, repeatedly and consistently. And it should go on doing so until even the dullards, who in any crowd or population make up the majority, finally get the message. But even that is not enough; relax your efforts for a minute, and they will

quickly forget whatever they have learned. There is, in all this, no
room for subtlety or irony; however, sarcasm, which is to irony as a
trumpet is to a piccolo, can occasionally be employed. There should
be no attempt to present both sides of the picture; no fifty shades
of gray, please! Everything must be presented in strong contrasts of
black and white without anything in between. Posters, too, should
be as simple, as direct, and as easy to grasp as one can make them.
That is why, right from the beginning, we made many of them red.

Propaganda does not have to be true to be successful. Perhaps,
to the contrary. Most people are utterly lacking in imagination.
Consequently, confronted with a really big lie, they assume it *must*
be true. Just look at the mass of lies the enemy produced to cover
us with! By contrast, German wartime propaganda violated all these
rules and then some. One of the worst errors, which affected us
soldiers on the front directly, was the attempt to deride and ridicule
the enemy. We knew perfectly well that our opponent was strong,
brave, and often cruel. To claim otherwise was to belittle our efforts,
as well as the blood we shed so freely.

Some of the things we Germans did, and did not do, were, frankly,
downright stupid. Thus the Kaiser, though no longer having much
influence on the day-to-day conduct of the war, continued to strut
around with his glittering entourage. He would have done better if
he had done as I subsequently did in World War II, i.e. donned a
simple uniform and partaken in the food his troops received from
the field kitchens. But no, his Majesty was too fine for that. Or
is it possible that, after a few months, he felt he would no longer be
welcome? In any case, he much preferred to spend his time chopping
wood at his Luxembourg headquarters.

As it happened, the construction of the residence of the Crown
Prince, Schloss Cecilienhof, in Potsdam continued through most of
the war. That immense building, which has no fewer than 176 rooms,
was shaped like an English cottage. An *English* cottage! Luckily, not

too many people were aware of this particular blunder. But it does show the half-hearted spirit with which the Kaiser, who, after all, was a grandson of Queen Victoria, went to war against his English relatives. Even when he finally permitted his navy to send their Zeppelins and bomb London, he told them to spare Buckingham Palace and other monuments. All this while our soldiers were dying by the hundreds of thousands and their families, in countless cases, literally starving.

The government of England, and later that of the United States, understood all this perfectly well. Right from the beginning they painted us Germans in the most lurid colors. Their lies started with the Kaiser, whom they called "The Beast of Berlin" and "The Spirit of Carnage." They ended, if at all, with the most humble soldier and citizen. Early on, the key man in charge was a certain Lord Bryce. A one-man factory of lies, he invented stories of Belgian nuns being raped and/or having their breasts cut off. He created stories of babies being bayoneted for fun and Allied soldiers being crucified. He told stories of cultural treasures, such as the library at Louvain, being deliberately destroyed. If English caricatures of the time could be believed, even German barbed wire was somehow crueler and less humane than that which the Allies used! And it worked—at least as long as the war lasted. As the English themselves later admitted, once it had ended almost all the stories were exposed for the lies they were. But by then the damage had been done.

As even that Jew and arch-Zionist, Nahum Goldman, admitted, the Imperial German Army was in many ways a superb organization. There was none better! For four years on end it fought, practically alone, against the entire world. Battle by battle, it inflicted more casualties than it took. It brought down our enemies one by one. Romania, which had gone over to the other side, in 1916. Russia in 1917. In the same year, assisted by the Austrians, it all but knocked Italy out of the war. In 1918, had it not been for the Americans, it might very well have defeated the British and the French too. Even the enemy, in rare moments of truth, acknowledged the fighting qualities of our soldiers.

When the war finally ended, on every single front German troops were still fighting on foreign soil. Nevertheless, time took its toll. The longer the war lasted, the shorter manpower became. What few *Ersatz* (replacements) the homeland could still provide us with tended to be of lower quality than those whose places they filled. Only half-trained, and this is one of the few points on which that pacifist scoundrel, Erich Maria Remarque, spoke the truth, they died like flies. Partly because of enemy propaganda, partly because of a growing shortage of food, and partly because the soldiers experienced the overwhelming material superiority of the enemy, discipline deteriorated.

Still the army went on fighting. Until, finally, a *Dolchstoss* (stab in the back) dealt it a blow more powerful than anything millions of enemy soldiers and four years of mortal combat had succeeded in delivering.

Chapter 5

Revolution and Collapse

To repeat, ultimately the only way to defeat a *Weltanschauung* is to oppose it by another equally powerful one. This was precisely the point where the Wilhelmine Reich, for all its glitter, economic success, and military strength, was at its weakest. We front line soldiers started feeling the effects as early as 1915, when the enemy began dropping leaflets over our positions. At first we laughed at them and used them for all kinds of interesting purposes. Gradually, though, the feelings of some of us changed. Particularly effective were the ones that, by blaming the war on "the Prussians," sought to drive a wedge between them and us Bavarians. But there were others, too.

In September 1916 our division went through the Battle of the Somme, an inferno if ever one there was. Later, I learned that, on the first day of the offensive alone, sixty thousand—*sixty thousand*—English soldiers were killed or wounded. Truly, as Ludendorff wrote of them, they were lions led by asses. We, for our part, had a million and a half—*a million and a half*—shells fired at us during the preliminary bombardment alone. The conditions inside our *Stollen,* or fortified underground shelters, where we were constantly under threat of being buried alive, defy the imagination. Yet some of us had to remain in them for weeks on end. Depending on how you define "casualty," how you count, and which historian you believe, the total number reached 660,000 for the English and the French and 600,000 on our side.

It was during this battle that I was wounded for the first time. More or less unable to walk, I was lucky to make my way back to friendly lines. From there an ambulance train took me and the rest back to Germany or, to be precise, a hospital at Beelitz not far from Berlin. The hospital, which had been built just a few years earlier, was magnificent, whereas the change from the mud, dirt, and blood of the front to the clean white linen that awaited us there was shocking at first and took some time to get used to. It was during my stay at Beelitz that I first noticed the gulf which, increasingly, was separating the front from the homeland.

The English historian John Keegan once wrote that the only quality that counts in the field is courage. I didn't need him, who, owing to a childhood disease, never wore his country's uniform, to tell me this. In fact the reason why many self-appointed military historians first start scribbling away is precisely because they want to make up for the fact that they personally did *not* experience the events they try to describe. But he was right: among us frontline troops, whoever did not have courage could expect nothing but contempt.

Here in the hospital things were very different. People were not afraid to boast of their cowardice, whether it was of the kind that had caused them to inflict wounds on themselves or that which had saved them from serving at all. Later, after my wound had sufficiently healed, I was able to confirm these impressions in Berlin itself. It was my first visit to the capital, and the impression it left on me was a sad one. Bitter want was evident everywhere, and the huge city was suffering from hunger. Housewives spent hours every day queuing for the most elementary necessities. Come the next year, more Berliners had died of disease than were killed at the front. I soon discovered that many people shared the views of those I had met in the hospital. Shortly thereafter, the military authorities sent me to Munich, where my regiment recruited is manpower and where its replacement-battalion was based. The situation there was similar yet worse. Avoiding service was not considered a crime. Instead, it had developed into a fine art.

In all this, it was impossible to overlook the role played by the Jews. I know now, as I did not know then, that, in May 1916, Ludendorff, responding to complaints that had reached him, ordered a so-called "Jew-count" to be held. Against expectations, it showed that Jewish soldiers served and died in proportion to their number in the population. This astonishing finding caused the study to be suppressed. And with very good reason. How those who were responsible for carrying it out reached their conclusions I cannot imagine. Or perhaps, on second thought, I can do so all too well. All I know is that, in my firsthand experience in both Berlin and Munich, almost every official was a Jew, and every Jew was an official. Certainly, their proportion in town far exceeded their slender presence at the front.

The situation in the financial world was even worse. As also happened in all other belligerent countries, the war caused the German economy to move toward greater centralization. Large firms with the requisite resources at their disposal swallowed small ones lock, stock, and barrel. In their efforts to do so they were often assisted by the state, which found it easier to deal with a few of the former than with many of the latter.

As so often, those who profited most were the Jews. In 1914 one study, done by a German scholar and publicized much later in a work published in 2011, said that Jews represented one quarter of the businessmen forming "the dense corporate network" that linked large German firms together. One quarter—meaning that, in proportion to their number in the population, they were over-represented by no less than 2,500 percent! More interesting still, Paul Windolf, the author of the study, wasn't an anti-Semitic curmudgeon left over from the Third Reich. Born in 1936, too late to come under the influence of our propaganda, he was a professor of business administration at the University of Trier. The latter is widely known to be one of the

most left-leaning and politically correct in the whole of Germany.
Enough said.

Things reached a nadir in the so-called turnip-winter of 1916–17.
In the summer of 1917 the official food ration only provided 1,560
calories. That was barely half the figure needed to keep an adult in
good health. Yet we somehow held on. In late 1917 the collapse
of Russia freed large numbers of troops for service on other fronts,
causing morale to recover to some extent. The Battle of Caporetto
in October, which came close to driving Italy out of the war, also
helped. Looking across the front, it seemed as if it were the Allies
who were now in a pickle, a fact reflected by the endless conferences
they were holding in Paris. They had good reason to worry. For over
three years they had strained every muscle and tried every trick to
break the backbone of the Reich, only to see every single one of their
offensives repulsed with huge losses. Now the time had come for us
to deliver the final blow; one which, everyone in Germany firmly
hoped and believed, would at long last produce the victory, and with
it the end of the war, we were fervently looking forward to.

It was not to be. In January 1918 our army was busily preparing
for the greatest offensive in history until then. It was one whose
innovative infantry and artillery tactics are still being studied at military academies and colleges the world over. It was just then that
the munitions strike broke out. The strike started in Berlin, where
400,000 workers put down their tools. From there it spread to Kiel,
Hamburg, Mannheim, Augsburg, and other industrial cities. The
total number of those who, demanding "peace and bread," defied
the authority or the state may have been as high as a million.

Fortunately, it did not last for very long, so the immediate impact
on the production of war material was limited. But the psychological
damage it did to our side and the encouragement it gave to the enemy
cannot be overestimated. Was this the monolithic Reich, they asked,
which they had been unsuccessfully fighting for so long? The strike's
acknowledged leader, Kurt Eisener, was a Jew. So was his second

in command, the agitator Rosa Luxemburg. As a typical *Ostjude,* a Jew from Eastern Europe, that was her way of thanking the country which had given her shelter! The rest were a pack of Social Democrats. In 1914 they suffered a debacle when the workers refused to follow their calls to commit treason. Now, practically unhindered, they resumed their treasonous activities. Determined to do whatever it took to ensure that Germany would not win the war, they even went on the road to meet enemy representatives.

By the summer of 1918 the atmosphere at the front was going from bad to worse. From March to July of that year we launched no fewer than three offensives, each one involving every resource we still had. The last of them, known as the Third Battle of the Marne, brought us closer to Paris than we had been at any time since September 1914. Owing to the introduction of the huge "Paris Gun," with its 130-kilometer (81 mile) range, it also caught the public's imagination as few others did. Ultimately, all the offensives came to a halt and had to be suspended. The fact that our advances enabled us frontline soldiers to see the enemy's immense material superiority and the way he fed his troops with our own eyes did not help either.

Meanwhile, with every passing month, more and more American troops were coming to their allies' rescue. Their companies joined into regiments, the regiments into divisions, and the divisions into corps until there were two million of them. Not terribly cohesive and lacking experience, they and their commanders may not have been the best in the world. Had it been a fair one-on-one struggle, we would have made mincemeat of them. Still, they were healthy, strong, well fed, and well equipped. And they were simply *there.*

The *Oberste Heeresleitung (OHL),* or Supreme Army Headquarters, was well aware of these facts. Later, Ludendorff in his memoirs designated the 8th of August as "the Black Day of the German Army." It was the day on which, for the first time, entire units broke and started running in front of the tanks the English had massed against them.

Given how strained our economy was, we did not have a proper answer. As they ran, they were attacked from the air. By this time, the enemy's superiority in that medium had become overpowering. In response, all the poor fellows could do was to climb trees like monkeys!

In September and October the English launched a series of massive attacks on our lines. These were the same ones, incidentally, which my division had held in the fall of 1914 and again in the summer of 1917. Yet so overwhelming was the enemy's strength that they were able to launch a simultaneous offensive on the Meuse, hundreds of kilometers to the southeast, in which no fewer than a million of their troops participated. This was the point at which signs of disintegration, which previously had been few and far between, started appearing in earnest. Red flags began to be lifted over the trenches. Striking sailors from Wilhelmshaven, Hamburg, and Kiel requisitioned trucks and visited us. Led by the usual crowd of Jew boys, they called on us to put down our arms. In the name of the Liberty, Dignity, and Beauty of our National Being, they claimed!

At the time of the armistice on 11 November I myself was in a hospital at Pasewalk, a city in Pomerania, where I had been sent to recover from the injuries gas had inflicted on my eyes. I was just starting to feel a little better when the news broke. We patients got it from an old pastor who had been sent to us for the purpose. He explained that the Emperor had abdicated, that a new government had been established, and that Germany was now a republic. Getting to that point, he could not avoid bursting into tears. Later, he added that we were now helplessly exposed to the enemy's tender mercies and could expect a dark future in front of us.

I too broke down. As I staggered back to my ward, darkness surrounded me. I buried my aching head between the blankets and the pillow. It was the first time I had wept since my mother's death eleven years previously. So our heroism and the unprecedented sacrifices we had made, the indescribable suffering inflicted both on us soldiers and the civilian population, and the millions of dead whom no one would bring to life again—everything—had all been in vain.

Over the next few years, during which I began my political activity, I had plenty of opportunities to analyze the causes of the collapse. In fact, addressing them in numerous public meetings large and small, I did so until I was blue in the face. Some of my conclusions simply continued thoughts that had been with me during the war and even before it had started. The rest were directly related to our defeat.

The Second Reich, as it was widely known, had been born under an auspicious star amidst the thunder of victorious battle. For that we had Bismarck to thank and, coming right after him, Chief of Staff Helmut von Moltke and Minister of War Albrecht von Roon. Nothing symbolized it as well as the Siegessäule, or Victory Column, in Berlin. Originally sixty-seven meters tall, it was wrapped entirely by captured enemy cannons. In 1939, as part of my plan to renovate the city and to turn it into Europe's capital, I had its height increased by another seven and a half meters. I also moved it from its original site at the Königsplatz (now misnamed the Platz der Republik) near the Reichstag to the Grosser Stern. But back to the Reich. Over the first forty-three years of its existence it enjoyed immense prosperity and economic growth. Simple people, who always and everywhere form the great majority, were impressed by that prosperity as well as the evident military strength of the Reich, which was put on display on appropriate occasions.

Having done so, they attributed the sudden collapse of the structure solely to the war, which had brought so much misery to them. But this is absurd. In fact, all the collapse did was to expose weaknesses that had long existed. Chief among them were general suffrage which Germany got before England, misleadingly known as the "mother of democracies," did. On its heels came elections and democracy. All three were non-German elements of government. Initially, they were foisted on us by the professors of 1848, who wanted nothing better than to ape the "ideals" of the French Revolution. Once established, they quickly turned into a morass of useless chatter and corruption.

Next came the failure to properly deal with the liberated provinces, Alsace and Lorraine. As a result, they never truly became an integral part of the Reich. To repeat, Wilhelm II's foreign policy was essentially misdirected. To add insult to injury it was often weak and vacillating as well.

Finally, there was the tolerance long shown for those vile Marxist traitors, the Social Democrats. Starting long before the war and redoubling their efforts while it lasted, they did whatever they could to foment discontent and to incite the people against the army and the government. Their ability to do so was due to the government's inability or unwillingness to rein in the press. Not that the non-socialist press was necessarily better. Only parts of it supported the government in its conduct of the war, and much of it did what it could to undermine them.

Though the war was over, the British blockade still continued. Only in the middle of 1919 was it finally lifted, enabling us to resume our imports and exports. But this happened only to a very limited extent. Partly because of carelessness in August 1914, partly because of enemy action, and partly because no new merchantmen were built during the war, we had lost almost our entire merchant navy. Much of what we still possessed had to be given away gratis as reparations. In any case the enemy had used the war to steal our overseas markets from us. This caused production to come to a halt and unemployment to soar. The demobilization of the armies, which at the end of the war still numbered several million men, added to the problem. That's to say nothing of the hundreds of thousands maimed and crippled men who had to be taken care of in one way or another.

Determined to avenge themselves on us, our enemies took large parts of Prussia and Silesia, which had been German for centuries, if not longer, away from the Reich. This caused hundreds of thousands of our fellow citizens, who understandably were unwilling to live under Polish (mis)rule, to leave their homes to migrate to the west, where nothing had been done to receive them. Nor did the process of drawing the borders unfold peacefully. Throughout 1919, in many places, volunteer units known variously as Freikorps, or the Black Reichswehr, fought heroically, if ultimately unsuccessfully, to retain the lands in question.

All over Germany, wherever one looked, people shivered and hungered. It goes without saying that I detest that self-appointed artist and filthy pornographer, Georg Grosz. Luckily for him, he left the country in a hurry in 1933, or else I would have had him thrown into a concentration camp! Still I must concede that many of his sketches, which show starving workers, fat, evil-looking capitalists with heaps of money, and made-up prostitutes presented a true, if one-sided and perverted, picture of reality at the time. Much later, I learned that the origins of this misery had been explored in depth by the English economist John Maynard Keynes in his booklet *The Economic Consequences of the Peace* (1919). He could hardly have done a better job.

Political conditions naturally reflected the economic situation. The new Social-Democratic government was unable to resist the Allied demands. So weak were the "statesmen" whom the so-called "Revolution" had brought to power that they signed the famous *Kriegsschuld*, war-guilt, article under which Germany assumed responsibility for the war. To be sure, history bristles with occasions when the defeated were not only despoiled but humiliated. However, the *Kriegsschuld* business was something new and unprecedented. Besides preparing the "legal" basis for extracting reparations, it hit straight at the nation's soul, which, of course, was just what it had been meant to do.

Internally, the political situation was even worse. The Social Democrats, having successfully undermined public order, were unable to reimpose it. Everywhere workers, incited by their often Jewish leaders, spat on officers, tore the epaulets from their shoulders, and beat them up. So bad were conditions that many places were reduced to anarchy. That specifically included Bavaria and Munich, where I was stationed at the time and where the Jews set up a "Soviet Republic." The stupidity of these people was truly amazing. During the few days the "Republic" lasted its foreign affairs commissar, Franz Lipp, whose record included several stays in mental hospitals, actually declared war on Switzerland. That was done, he explained, because the Swiss had refused to lend him sixty locomotives! At one point I myself, rifle in hand, had to chase away three scoundrels who had come to arrest me in my quarters.

In the end the Reichswehr, assisted by Freikorps units, re-took Munich and exacted a well-deserved vengeance. Eugene Leviné, the Jewish Communist who had led the uprising, was killed. Not so his uncouth right-hand man and fellow Jew, Erich Mühsam. He was arrested, tried, and sentenced to fifteen years in prison. But he did not have to stay there for long; in 1924 an amnesty was granted, and he was released. After the *Reichstagbrand* on 28 February 1933, I had him arrested and sent to a concentration camp where the boys, seeking their revenge, saw to it that he would expire. Good! As these two gentlemen illustrate so nicely, behind each and every one of these problems stood the Jews.

At the center of the storm stood Erich Ludendorff. Born in 1865, Ludendorff, as his lack of a "von" indicates, was the scion of a bourgeois family. He was educated at a cadet school, one of several similar institutions. So good were they at producing officers that the enemy, in the Treaty of Versailles, paid them a compliment by insisting that they be shut down. Obtaining a commission, he became famous for his skill at mathematics and, even more so, his incredible aptitude for hard work. It was these qualities which in 1911 put him, now a colonel, at the head of the mobilization department. In 1914 he was a major general in command of a brigade.

It was Ludendorff who forced the surrender of Liege, the great Belgian fortress that stood in the way of our invasion of France. For that he got the *Pour le Mérite*. Just a few days later, he was transferred to East Prussia to deal with the Russian invasion of that province. His post was that of chief of staff to Paul von Hindenburg, then an elderly general of no great distinction who had just been recalled from retirement. Together they won the famous victories of Tannenberg and the Masurian Lakes, sending the Tsar's armies reeling back into Poland.

More victories followed in 1915, enabling us to occupy vast territories in that country as well as Russia's Baltic provinces. Though Hindenburg got most of the credit, in every case the real brain was Ludendorff's. Hindenburg's greatest quality was his iron nerves. A story told after the war illustrates this very well. Ludendorff's own deputy, Colonel Hoffmann, used to show visitors over the battlefield. Stopping at one cottage, he said, "Here Hindenburg slept before the battle." Stopping at another he said, "Here Hindenburg slept after the battle." "And this," he would end the tour, "is where Hindenburg slept *during* the battle."

In the summer of 1916 Ludendorff, still with Hindenburg in tow, was appointed first quartermaster-general of the army. In this capacity he went on performing almost superhuman feats, including a vast expansion of armament production and the victory over Russia. But even he, for all his titanic efforts, could not save Germany. Abroad, he was facing a crushing numerical and material superiority. At home he was constantly fighting any number of people who preferred their own interests to those of the state. This included not just the parties and large segments of the press but, all too often, the great industrialists and the trade unions as well. More trouble was occasioned by farmers and peasants who did whatever they could to obtain high prices for their products even if doing so meant starving the cities. The Kaiser, who by failing to exercise his authority had reduced himself to a figurehead, did nothing to help. For over two years Ludendorff, who had lost two sons to the war, stood like a rock. That was just what turned him into a symbol not only of everything the traitors were trying to destroy but also of everything Germany, eternal Germany, had ever stood for.

Somehow or the other, the worst was averted. To a large extent, we had our enemies to thank for that. One, Russia, was involved in bloody civil war. It delivered the country into the tender hands of the Jews and the Bolsheviks, leaving it in an even worse state than it had been in 1917–18. One, the U.S., turned its back on Europe and quickly withdrew its forces to where they had come—but not far enough, as events in 1941 showed. And one, Italy, had not counted for much in the past and did not count for much now. The two most important ones, England and France, were almost as tired of war as we were. As was not yet clear at the time, but became so later on, both had entered the twilight of their power. They also started quarreling among themselves. At times the English on their island, seeking to maintain "the balance of power" as they had done for centuries past, almost reached the point where they saw France as posing a greater danger to them than we did. This only left the Polish attempts to steal even more of our land. In the end, they were somehow thrown back, and the fighting in the east ceased.

The result was that Germany, though truncated, desolated, im- poverished and humiliated, survived. The country was not overrun by foreign armies, as was to happen in 1945. Separatism, though not without support in Bavaria in particular, was overcome and the state prevented from disintegrating. Order was restored, albeit with great difficulty and never completely. Even during the so-called "good years" of the Weimar Republic about forty people each year were killed in political demonstrations and other violent disputations. Conditions remained extremely difficult. Unemployment, poverty, disease, and death stalked the population in a way they had not done since at least the Napoleonic Wars and possibly since the Thirty Years

War. As the phrase went, Germany was *wehrloss, ehrloss, heerloss* (disarmed, dishonored, and defenseless).

These were the circumstances against which I rallied and which formed the background of my first attempts to enter politics. At the time, I had no idea where they would ultimately lead my country and me.

Chapter 6

Entering Politics

To repeat: what caused me to enter politics was the defeat of my country. Contrary to what some of my less intelligent biographers have written, the single sentence in which I summed up my decision does not mean that it was made on the spot or all at once. Much less that, when I wrote it, I was lying. In reality, such decisions are always made step by step, bit by bit. One thing leads to another. And how, I ask you, could it be otherwise? So many factors, quite a few of them unexpected and contradictory, are involved. One has some kind of vague idea. One tries the water. One hesitates, one gets wet, one retreats, one advances. And suddenly one discovers that one has become an artist, or a politician, or whatever.

This is a point I want to stress. Starting in 1945, hardly any of the thousands of historians, both German and foreign, who have written or lectured or made documentaries about my life and times have been sympathetic to me. That is as it should be. The reason why this is as it should be is because only nobodies do not have enemies. Another reason is that they, the historians, did not have a choice. Whoever had the courage to write anything else would surely have been crucified. As the handful who did try to take a more balanced approach, such as David Hoggan in *Der Erzwungene Krieg* were. Let me add that as much as I admire Hoggan's courage, his thesis is wrong. World War II was forced on me, if at all, only in the sense that, in the long run, I saw no alternative. Either the German people had to win fresh *Lebensraum,* or they were doomed. But in the short run it was always I who took the initiative. And *non, je ne regret rien.*

Briefly, the first attribute of any good biographer is his ability to get under his subject's skin. This was something mine, for obvious reasons, either wouldn't or couldn't do. The outcome, a lot of bad history, speaks for itself. Some authors have saddled me with such a long list of mental diseases as to make one wonder how such a person could have existed, let alone succeeded as I did. They cite hysteria, schizophrenia, paranoia, and "dangerous leader disorder," to name but a few. Every time psychiatrists "discover" some new mental disease, it is immediately attributed to me! Others took it for granted that I was wicked, wicked, wicked. Between them they treated almost everything I ever said or wrote as if it were either a product of my alleged perversions or simply a pack of lies. It would be good both for them and for the world if they changed their approach and admitted the truth: namely, that *Mein Kampf* and my other works did no more than reflect the truth as I saw it then and as, to a very large extent, I see it now.

I do not mean that the book does not contain some minor inaccuracies. After all, I did not have access to Wikipedia. Having my attention directed to them, I sought to correct them in subsequent editions or had others do so for me. Furthermore, *Mein Kampf* is a fairly long book. *Any* book of that length is bound to contain some errors. See, for example, the *Iliad,* much shorter though it is. And the Bible has enough errors, misunderstandings, and discrepancies to have occupied thousands of priests over thousands of years. How anyone who does not understand all this can have the gall to call himself a scholar is beyond me.

Once I was discharged from the hospital, I was sent back to Munich by way of Berlin. Returning to my barracks on 21 November, I was reunited with some of my comrades and commanders. I very much hoped to stay in the army. After all, where else could I, now 29 years old, an anonymous figure in the crowd with no family, no home, no recognized profession, no income, and no prospects, go? All around unemployment and misery were widespread. The army offered a steady job, an income of sorts, housing, clothes, and medical care. In some ways, as was indeed recognized at the time, it was the ultimate socialist dream! In the hope of obtaining all this I was no different from millions of others both at the time and throughout history.

In any event it worked out. For a short time I was detailed to help guard a Russian prisoner of war camp at Trauenstein in southeastern Bavaria, very close to Braunau on the other side of the border. By the middle of February—not, as I mistakenly wrote in *Mein Kampf,* in March—my unit was back in Munich, where it was supposed to be demobilized. For days on end we were made to examine old gas masks, the kind of make-work job only the military, in its wisdom, can devise. With plenty of time on my hands, I found the city, and indeed the whole of Bavaria, a seething mess rife with every kind of conspiracy, real and imaginary. Not just in the civilian world but in the military as well, "revolutionary" meetings were held, red flags waved, and "Soviets"—that hateful Russian word—established.

My superiors needed to know what was going on so as to anticipate the next moves and to prepare their own. Why they chose me for the job I do not know. This is not the kind of thing the army tells you, is it? Presumably, they were aware of my interest in, and opinions on, politics. In any case they made me a *Vertrauensmann,* partly an informant, partly a propagandist. My job was to attend all sorts of meetings and to report on them. But also, when the occasion presented itself, to try and influence the participants in the direction the authorities considered desirable.

To prepare me and my fellow propagandists they made us attend some lectures on the three great political movements of the time, i.e. authoritarianism, democracy, and Bolshevism. I need hardly say that, personally, I had long opposed the last two in particular. But neither, especially during the last years of the war, had I been terribly happy with the first, which, in any case, no longer existed. Scant wonder I was a little confused. So, after all, were millions of others. Along with my fellow-propagandists, I tried this and I tried that. Some of my biographers, using accounts written by all kinds of people I had never heard about, did their best to discredit me by claiming that I had briefly flirted with Social Democracy. Hoping to find *some* way out the terrible situation my country found itself in, perhaps I did.

I liked my work. For the first time, I was able to make some use of my extensive political studies. It enabled me to push people in the direction I considered desirable—the national one, of course. It also let me develop my rhetorical skills. My performance was appreciated, as is evident from the fact that people contacted me and asked me for my opinion on the Jewish question. In response I told one of them, a certain Herr Gemlich, that "in his effects and consequences he [the Jew] is like a racial tuberculosis of the nations." The way to get rid of him is not by mounting pogroms; that method, as thousands of years have shown, leads nowhere. What is necessary are systematic legal measures to end his privileges. Later, this one-page letter was described as my "first anti-Semitic writing." More important, I learned that my direct superior, Captain Karl Mayr, whom I met on a daily basis for several months, was very happy with me. He thought I was "a force to be reckoned with, a first-class popular speaker."

It must have been in September 1919 that I was ordered to take a look at some splinter group, previously wholly unknown to me. It called itself the *Deutsche Arbeiterpartei,* or German Workers' Party. Following the Soviet model, the "Revolution" had granted soldiers the right to participate in politics. That was why my superiors took an interest in this and similar groups. So I went to one of their meetings. For two hours I listened to a speech by one Gottfried Feder. An economist by trade, he had written a brochure and now spoke about the need to break the shackles of interest which high finance had imposed on the German people.

The number of those present may have been between twenty and twenty-five. Feder was not the best of speakers, and I was thoroughly bored. I was just on the point of leaving when it was announced that there would be a discussion. At first they talked about all kinds of trivial points. Then, however some professor stood up and argued that Bavaria should secede from the Reich. Instead, he said, it should join Austria! When my turn came, I wiped the floor with him.

Again, I have described what happened next in *Mein Kampf.* A week or so later, I received a postcard saying that I had been admitted to the Party. It was a peculiar method of attracting members, which still amuses me. Nevertheless, I accepted their invitation and went to their next meeting. A more philistine, less interesting one you never saw. They had neither a program nor any kind of written brochure to explain who they were and what they wanted; nor did they have membership cards or stamps. In a way, though, their utter confusion and unimportance spoke in their favor. The reason was that they reflected those of countless people, myself in many ways included. Besides, it seemed a suitable place where I, unknown and without resources of any kind, might make my mark. So I decided to stay and see what I could do.

From then on the seven members of the Party—I was the seventh—met every Wednesday evening in some café. Our first task was to increase the number of participants. To do so, I decided to hold one public meeting a month. When the time came, I personally distributed invitations in the streets or delivered them to certain addresses—with hardly any success, I might add. Switching to mimeographed material, we did a little better. First, we had eleven attendees, then thirteen, then twenty-three, and then thirty-four. At that point we had enough money to put an ad in the *Münchener Beobachter,* the *Munich Observer.* It worked. At our next meeting we had 111 people present. What a colossal success! It was also the first time I spoke to a larger public. It confirmed what I had already begun to suspect: namely, that I had a talent for doing so and could reach people's hearts.

Outsiders who have never taken part in politics may consider all this funny. And funny, in a way, it was; we were a bunch of ludicrous nobodies trying to suggest answers to problems so enormous as to appear altogether insoluble. These detractors have no idea how hard it is to attract people and to keep them interested. Above all, we needed to make them stop complaining and start acting! Nor do they know how much willpower and money doing so demands. We—my comrades and I—had the willpower. But we had practically nothing else.

Encouraged, we increased the number of meetings to one every fortnight. At times it worked; at other times it did not. We made mistakes, as by renting halls located in the wrong neighborhoods, and did our best not to repeat them. On 24 February 1920, by which time we had changed the Party's name to Nazionalsozialisti-sche Deutsche Arbeiterpartei (NSDAP), we felt strong enough to hold our first mass meeting, during which we intended to announce our program. It consisted of twenty-five points, and my comrades thought I was the most suitable person to announce it. So that was what, in front of 2,000 cheering people, I did.

The most important points of the program were as follows.

1. The unification of all Germans in the Greater Germany on the basis of the people's right to self-determination.

2. Equal rights for the German people with respect to the rest, i.e. the abrogation of the peace treaties.

3. The restoration of our colonies.

4. That the right to be a citizen and hold public office be limited to members of the German race alone, meaning that Jews would be excluded.

5. That the state take responsibility for the livelihood of its citizens.

6. Equal rights and obligations for all citizens.

7. The abolition of unearned income and the confiscation of war profits.

8. The nationalization of trusts and a division of the profits of all heavy industries.

9. Land reform and the abolition of taxes on land.

10. The maintenance of a healthy middle class.

11. Educational reform, so as to concentrate all authority in this field in the hands of the state. And

12. The establishment of a strong state capable of doing all this.

Party programs, indeed programs of any sort, are always problematic. Nothing puts people off more quickly than having to listen to, or read, a point-by-point program. One well-known psychologist has claimed that the maximum number of points people can remember is seven. I, who have some experience in the matter, would argue that, with the masses at any rate, the true figure is closer to three. Once a program is formulated, few people ever refer to it again. Yet a program one must have, or else no one will take one seriously. It was in order to be taken seriously, too, that we called ours "unalterable." In this respect as in so many others, we kept our word. Looking back, I think our program was as good as we could make it at the time. This is also proved by the fact that we turned most of our ideas into reality, which is more than the great majority of parties, either before or after us, have done or even tried to do.

It was around this time, too, that we adopted the swastika as our symbol. The swastika is an old Germanic sign going back thousands of years. Symbolizing the sun, it is found in many places all over

the world where people of Germanic people lived and made their
cultural influence felt. During the war and immediately afterward
various groups and units took it up as their emblem. As it happened,
one of them was a German fighter squadron stationed in Palestine!
Having decided to do the same, I used my experience as an artist to
design our flag around it. Computer-assisted design was still in the
future, so the work took time and effort, but what a huge success it
was!

The colors of the flag were those of the defunct German Empire
and, in this sense, a tribute to the glorious past. The red background
stood for the socialist idea of our Party, the white circle for nation-
alism. The black swastika symbolized the eternal Aryan struggle for
survival against other races. The fact that, after 1945, our flag was
prohibited and still remains so in a great many places only shows how
eminently successful, how irresistible, my design was.

This is the place to say a word about some of my earliest comrades with whom I worked at the time. Two of them, a machinist
named Anton Drexler who was the founder of the Party, and the
aforementioned Gottfried Feder, soon fell by the wayside. Drexler
was a serial joiner and joined a variety of other organizations. He
did not participate in the November 1923 Putsch and was elected
to the Bavarian Parliament after standing for another party. He was
present again when the Party was reestablished following my release
from Landsberg, but by then I had little difficulty pushing him aside.

Feder's main problem was that he was an ideologue. Lacking the
oratorical skills we needed so much, he continued to write brochures
on economic matters. Many were quite obscure. But that did not
prevent him from being regarded as the Party's primary economic
expert. He retained this position until after the September 1930
elections, which suddenly turned us into the country's second-largest
party. At that point his extreme Left-wing socialist views forced me
to disassociate myself from him so as to enlist the support, and the
money, of some of Germany's greatest industrialists.

Two others who played a role at the time were Ludwig von Scheubner-Richter and Dietrich Eckart. Scheubner-Richter came to us from the Baltic, where he had spent much of his life and where he had been among those who tried to oppose the Bolshevization of his country. In our march on 9 November 1923 he was in the first rank, walking arm-in-arm with me. Shot in the lungs and dying instantly, he took me down with him to the pavement. I dedicated the first volume of *Mein Kampf* to him, as well as to fifteen others who died on that day.

Eckart was a successful playwright with the outstanding command of the German language such success demands. In 1912 he adapted Ibsen's *Peer Gynt*. Thereupon, it became one of the best-attended productions of the age. In Berlin alone it was shown 600 times. He helped us financially, made me take lessons in oratory and diction, and introduced me to a great many important people. After the Putsch, he was arrested along with me. Taken ill, he was released and died soon after. I dedicated the second volume of *Mein Kampf* to him.

Other comrades dating from those days were Alfred Rosenberg and Julius Streicher. Rosenberg, like Scheubner-Richter, was from the Baltic. Like Feder he was an ideologue first and foremost. He edited the Party newspaper, the *Völkischer Beobachter (Völkisch Observer)*, and wrote numerous pamphlets as well as a book, *Der Mythus des Zwanstigsten Jahrhundert (The Myth of the Twentieth Century)*. Initially, he could not even sell the entire first edition. Later, having been put on the Index, it sold no fewer than 200,000 copies. In 1940–41 I made him the Commissioner for the Occupied Territories in the East, a post for which, given his background, he seemed well suited. Perhaps this is the place to say that, seen from the point of view of propaganda, the value of newspapers and, even more so, books, is limited. It is certainly not zero, or else I would not have bothered with them. But as my entire career shows, it cannot compare with that of the spoken word. Television, which in my time was in its infancy but which, along with its various offshoots, has since grown into the most powerful instrument of propaganda in history, confirms me in my view.

Streicher was a Franconian and as rabid an anti-Semite as I have ever met. By his own account, he had converted to National Socialism after hearing me speak. From that point on he fought for us like a buffalo. On the way he brought us the members of his *Deustche Sozlialistische Partei,* doubling our membership. Had it not been for him, we never would have won Nuremberg for our cause. Later, he became our *Gauleiter* (district leader) of Franconia. A brilliant journalist, his paper, *Der Stürmer (The Attacker)* helped us as much as any newspaper could. No one was better than him at waking up the masses to the Jewish danger! An insatiable womanizer, he often overstepped the boundaries of "good taste," producing material which can only be called pornographic. That, as well as the endless problems he had with women, was why certain Party members disliked him and urged me to get rid of him. In 1940 he was indicted for corruption and convicted. Thereupon, I was forced to strip him of his post as Gauleiter of Franconia. But I never forgot that he had marched with me during the Putsch. He was also one of the very few people whom I allowed to address me with the familiar *Du.* So I left him his paper and did not take any other steps against him.

With so much going on, it was time for me to leave the army and to start working for the Party full time. On 31 March 1921 I was discharged. I spent the next two and a half years organizing and speaking, speaking and organizing. Not just at public meetings— which, on the whole, grew larger and larger—but also at private ones. Particularly important in this regard were some elderly, usually well to-do, ladies of the kind that are always looking for young talent to protect and support. Thanks partly to Eckart's efforts on my behalf, they invited me to their drawing rooms, treated me with tea, and provided me with audiences consisting of people like themselves.

Dressed in a cheap blue suit, all I could afford, I felt like an ape in a zoo, but what other choice did I have?

One of my first female supporters was the widow of a high school principal, Carola Hoffmann. So taken with me was she that she looked after my laundry and baked for me. She also lent us her house, which we used for holding meetings. Others were Viktoria von Dirksen who, starting in 1922, used her salon to put me in contact with the so-called "better circles." So central was her role in helping us during the difficult year after the Putsch that she came to be nicknamed "The Mother of the Movement." Others were Elsa Bruckmann, the wife of the Munich publisher of that name, Helene Bechstein, the wife of the famous piano-manufacturer, and Winifred Wagner, whose tremendous admiration for her father-in-law, Richard Wagner, I shared. Her husband, Siegfried, testified that she "fought like a lion" on my behalf.

Some of their contributions came in the form of cash, of which we had little but could not have too much. The rest took the form of jewels and other precious objects, which I used to pawn. My lodgings, the clothes I wore, and the restaurants where I ate improved somewhat. I even started to be driven around in a used 24-horsepower Selve, one of the countless car models that have since been abandoned and forgotten. So old was it that the seaweed of the upholstery came sprouting out of the seats! Somewhat later, I replaced it with a Mercedes Frau Bechstein had given me. But great luxury? No way. As late as 1928, I was still living in a small rented room in Munich. At 41 Thierschstrasse, in case anyone wants to know.

More important than my personal circumstances was the fact that the Party and I were by no means the only ones in the field. As often happens in the wake of a defeat, Germany at the time was desperately looking for leadership—any kind of leadership, almost, that would tell people what to do, take them out of their troubles, and point to the future. One person who realized this very well was Eckart. He was one of the first who believed that I had the necessary qualities to lead. He also used to say that Germany's future leader had to be single. Only thus, he explained, could he capture the female half of the nation, whose hearts are always stronger than their brains. He was quite correct as it turned out.

Another was Kurt Hesse, a highly-decorated Reichswehr officer of whose existence, however, I only became aware later on. In 1922 he published *The Warlord-Psychologist*. It was one of the few volumes by a German officer that did not content itself with the niceties of strategy such as whether internal lies were preferable to external ones or the other way around. Instead, it showed true insight concerning the psychological needs of the troops as well as the nation at large. Attacking Ludendorff's bureaucratic style of leadership without mentioning him by name, Hesse explained why people in Germany needed a leader and were looking for him as well as the qualities an eventual leader would have to have. Briefly, the field which I had entered and in which I was trying to compete was a crowded one indeed. By one count Germany had seventy-three different *völkisch* movements, all with programs more or less similar to our own. In Munich alone there were at least fifteen.

I will not trouble to list all the countless speeches I held during those years. Nor will I go into the equally countless petty intrigues I had to endure and overcome. That task I leave to my more pedantic biographers, who seem to revel in it. Step by step, and not without an occasional setback, I made my mark in Munich and the surrounding countryside. In July 1921 I was officially appointed the Party's leader. As my fortunes improved, so did those of the NSDAP.

My most important instrument was my voice. This being the case, I will say a few words about the way I prepared my speeches and delivered them. I took every speech very seriously and always came carefully prepared. That does not mean I wrote down every word in advance in order to simply read them to the audience. Reading, rather than speaking, is the prerogative of professors—especially, but by no means exclusively, German ones who do not care as to whether anyone does or does not listen to them. I spoke from brief notes, some of which have been preserved. They were there to remind me of the most important points I wanted to make and help me to transition from one to another. In Germany, this was considered a bold innovation at the time. Much later, the leader of the German Women's Union, Frau Gertrude Scholz-Klink, in one of her speeches specifically thanked me for having taught "us" to speak without notes. Right she was.

Most of my speeches lasted about two hours. I often gave two a week, and occasionally more. The sheer physical effort, often coupled with extensive travel, was beyond belief. After each one ended, I was bathed in sweat and had to change my clothes. I also lost weight. Trying to anticipate objections in advance, I always paid close attention to the kind of audience I was going to address. I also took note of the shape of the hall and my place in it—important matters too many speakers tend to overlook and to neglect. They do not seem to understand the role *mise en scene* can and must play. As time went on, I developed my repertoire by practicing my speeches in front of a mirror. I also made a habit of entering late so as to increase tension and to make the crowd stand on their toes. Meanwhile, we would keep them amused by playing music, having them shout slogans, and the like.

I have often been accused of being an angry man. Yes, I was angry. Or perhaps I should say, furious! Furious at the way my people had been betrayed in pre-1914 Austria as well as ever since. Furious at the way we Germans had been surrounded by enemies who were planning our destruction. Furious because of the deaths of so many of my comrades in the Great War. Furious at the traitors who stabbed us frontline soldiers in the back and brought about our country's defeat. Furious at the way the victors treated us Germans, first by continuing the blockade after the November 1918 armistice and then in the Treaty of Versailles and throughout the 1920s. Furious at the way our *Volksgenossen* were robbed, abused, and sometimes murdered in almost every one of the newly established states of Eastern Europe. Furious at our enemies, domestic and foreign. Furious, above all, at the Jews! The latter stood behind everything unsavory, everything evil, in this world. Apologize for my fury? Never. It was my rage which turned me into the superbly effective speaker I was. So much so that I practiced it. And so much so that, when the mood deserted me for one reason or another, I was able to fake it.

From beginning to end, my fury was precisely the fuel that drove me. I do not mean to say that I was *always* furious. Far from it. Both in Germany and abroad, millions of people owe their impression of me to my rhetorical performances during mass meetings, performances that they witnessed either in person or on screen. They are, however, highly misleading. The great majority of the meetings I addressed during my career were private and relatively small. Early on the audience tended to consist of selected followers as well as society ladies, Later they were joined by professors, high officials, officers, and businessmen. Yelling at such people, or even calling your enemies names, will only make them put you down as vulgar.

It took me some time to learn the trick. Having mastered it, on such occasions I spoke quietly but warmly so as to get them on my side and to carry them along. As my weapons, I used my vast store of general knowledge, the product of years of reading, and an occasional flash of humor. And charm, of course. I well knew how to attract people by taking an interest in the things they did or said. I also pretended to share secrets with them, thus appealing to their vanity and turning them into my accomplices. A good example is my meeting with the elderly and highly respected Finnish Field-Marshal, Carl Gustaf Mannerheim, on 4 June 1942. It is one of the very few of which a sound recording exists; it shows me in a very different light from the one most people are familiar with.

I was beginning to attract notice. Having heard me speak in November 1922, a German-speaking American officer, Captain Truman Smith (who later became his country's military attaché in Berlin) wrote: "A marvelous demagogue! Have rarely listened to such a logical and fanatical man." An early Party member, and my subsequent official photographer, Heinrich Hoffmann, told me that, at that time, the right to publish a photograph of President Friedrich Ebert could be had for $5. For one of mine, though, he was able to charge twenty times as much! As my renown increased, so did the number of hecklers who tried to interrupt me or stop me from speaking. Clearly, I needed some kind of protection. At first the task of providing it fell to Emil Maurice, my chauffeur. He was by no means the first or last man in that profession to add it to his other duties. The meeting of 20 February 1921 was particularly stormy, and it was on that occasion that a few of my men, armed with rubber truncheons, for the first time showed what they could do. Those were the humble beginnings of our SA, or *Sturmabteilung*. I shall have more to say about it later on.

So much has been written about my ideology at this time that I shall refrain from discussing it again. But let me add something most historians have overlooked. There are two faces to the matter. One is the basic *Weltanschauung* whose importance cannot be overestimated. As the demise of the Second Reich illustrated, without it even the most splendid and powerful structure stands on shaky foundations. Another is its day-to-day interpretation for and by the masses. The latter do not like long and convoluted ideological speeches, much less books. What they want and need are concrete targets to vent their spleen on.

Addressing them, I always selected my targets with considerable care. One was the Treaty of Versailles, the most humiliating one ever imposed on a great civilized nation. Others were the miserable economic situation and the traitors who had brought it on our heads.

Yet another was the Jews and the need to combat them without mercy and right to the end. I would often tie several themes together, intertwining and fusing them so as to better employ my hammer while hitting them. Again, different audiences require different forms of address. One does not talk to capitalists as one does to workers, nor to workers as one does to capitalists. That, too, is a fact many professors, always searching for "scientific" truth, tend to overlook.

I do not pretend to know Italian. Nevertheless, I allowed some of our techniques to be inspired by Benito Mussolini. After all, he was in the news—and on the newsreels—practically all the time. He was a great man, without any doubt. He showed us what could be done and gave us hope. His rhetorical qualities came through clearly enough even if one did not understand a word he said. So did the uniforms, the daggers, the salutes, the parades, and much else.

One of his best ideas, which we National Socialists were happy to adopt, was to call his Party a *movimento,* a movement. In that way he, and later we, emphasized that, rather than representing a particular class as parties normally did, we were above and beyond class politics. The Fascists' "March on Rome," which culminated on 28 October 1922 and enabled them to take over the government, gave us hope. We thought that, weak as we initially were, the day might come when we too would be able to do the same. As it turned out, the German government was made of sterner stuff than the Italian one—which, one must admit, is not surprising.

In 1923 I wrote to the newly installed *Duce.* I explained who we were, congratulated him on his achievement, and wished him well for the future. He did not answer. Only in 1931, after I had become the leader of the second most powerful party in Germany, did he finally deign to send me a signed photograph. Our two regimes had many things in common. But there were also some differences. First, Catholicism, with the Pope at its head, was a more powerful force in Italy than in Germany. Second, and even more important, Mussolini never succeeded in ridding himself of those aristocratic clowns, the House of Savoy. One outcome was that, on many state occasions, he was number two and had to take his place behind the king or simply absent himself. That must have been very painful for him, the more so because the king was a midget. Standing up, he looked as if he were kneeling. Especially when in the company of his wife, Princess Elena of Montenegro, who, having been selected to make the House of Savoy tall (as she used to say), had the body of a grenadier. Another more serious one was that his people, and the armed forces in particular, always retained an alternative focus of loyalty to which they could, and in the end would, turn. Perhaps worst of all, during World War II Crown Prince Umberto, "Beppo," as his doting mother used to call him, kept betraying us by passing information to the Allies.

However, in 1923, all that was still in the future.

Chapter 7

The Putsch and Its Aftermath

If the years 1919–22 were bad for Germany, 1923 in many ways was much worse. Our poor country was reeling from the aftereffects of the largest, bloodiest war in history until then. To top it all, our enemies were plundering our exhausted people for all they were (not) worth. In December 1922 the German government, forced by necessity, defaulted on a payment of 135,000 meters of telegraph poles. That, *nota bene,* is almost enough to cover the entire distance from Magdeburg to Berlin or from Philadelphia to New York. In the next month the French and Belgian governments used this fact as an excuse to send in troops to occupy the Ruhr, our most important industrial district by far. On their way they killed approximately 130 German civilians who dared protest. Military resistance was impossible; after all, we no longer had an army. Instead, a general strike was proclaimed.

The occupation did not pass without impacting the rest of the country. Before the war, the mark had been valued at 4.20 to the dollar. By the end of 1919 the figure stood at 32, rising to 800 two and a half years later. With the occupation of the Ruhr all attempts to slow the fall came to a halt. In November 1923 4,210,500,000 marks were needed to buy a single dollar. Countless decent people who had worked and saved all their lives were ruined. So fast did the cost of living index rise that, as noon came, weekly wages paid in the morning no longer sufficed to buy a loaf of bread at noon. People used bank billets to cover their walls or to kindle their hearths.

Unable to trust the Reich, many communities started printing their own *Notgeld,* or emergency money. It took the form of printed bills and cardboard "coins" (many were quite humorous, by the way). But there was nothing funny about large numbers of people who lost their jobs, froze, starved, and were forced to resort to barter in order to survive. Amidst all this misery a few souls were fortunate enough to have foreign currency. Native or foreign, they spent pennies while living like kings at the expense of all the rest.

Economic collapse was accompanied by artistic degeneration. The so-called avant-gardists of 1914 had become the heroes of the day. They called themselves rebels. Rebels, that is, against everything wholesome, healthy, and clean. They attacked the existing social order, covering both Munich and other cities with their filth. Sculptors, dramatists, and musicians, who imitated the American Negro "music" known as jazz, participated in the orgy. Decent citizens, decent Germans, could no longer recognize their own cities. It made me feel sick then just as, looking at the hordes of criminal "refugees" who are again flooding Germany, it does right now.

That, in turn, contributed to, though it certainly did not cause, the prevailing civil unrest. Wherever one looked troops were being made ready, arms stored, and conspiracies hatched. Some originated on the Left, others on the Right. What ought to be done no one knew. That something *would* have to be done everyone knew or thought he knew. The man to whom most people looked in this context was, once again, Ludendorff. As early as February 1919 he was able to return from Sweden, where he had gone after the armistice. Now he lived in Munich, where every sort of right-wing movement did its best to harness him to its cart. It was Hess who, in 1921, introduced me to him. He was, however, no longer the man he had been. One problem was his friend, and subsequent second wife, Mathilde. A feminist she was (she believed the future would prove that men and women were equal, intellectually), as well as a trained mad-doctor and self-appointed philosopher. Dressed in a sort of chiffon tent, she made a strange spectacle. But that did not prevent him from accepting her and allowing her to (mis)lead him into all sorts of bizarre directions. Another more important one was that Herr General Ludendorff, like so many German officers, was very bad at politics. He was too rigid and too concerned about his personal honor as a one-time *Feldherr.* His name was useful and brought us some supporters. But not many. After all, he was a Prussian. And in Bavaria *Saupreussen,* "Swinish Prussians," were not exactly beloved.

Ludendorff or no Ludendorff, amidst the general chaos our Party flourished. By the end of 1923 we had 55,000 registered members. Early in September, joining forces with some veteran organizations, we were even able to hold a rally attended by 100,000 people, no less. Scant wonder I was becoming known, quite rightly, as "the king of Munich." Then and later, we differed from the traditional parties in that we turned to, and succeeded in attracting, people from every class of the population. By my estimate, about a third were workers. They were rough men—I shall say more about the women later— equipped with hard fists they were quite ready to use when necessary. About half came from a petite bourgeoisie background; craftsmen, shopkeepers, teachers, white-collar employees, and farmers. And somewhat more than a tenth belonged to the upper middle and professional classes.

Prominent among the last-named was Herman Göring. Göring was the son of the first governor of German West Africa. He had grown up in a castle, Burg Mauterndorf, not far from Salzburg. Ex-fighter pilot, war hero, and holder of the *Pour le Mérite,* he had ties with "high society" that proved very useful to us. Later on he became my deputy in all but name. We even had a few real blue-blooded aristocrats. If there were proportionally fewer of them than in the general population, then that was due to the fact that, as a rule, I did not like them much. The best-known one was our future youth leader and Gauleiter of Vienna, Baldur von Shirach. Another was Count Wolf-Heinrich von Heldorf, the Berlin chief of police who was later involved in the plot of 20 July 1944 and whom we hanged for his pains.

Who first suggested the idea of mounting a Putsch I can no longer remember. Nor does it matter since in the end it was I, and I alone, who took responsibility and gave the relevant orders. The Bavarian Prime Minister at this time was Eugen von Knilling, a civil servant and parliamentarian who had long served the Wittelsbach Dynasty. He, in turn, appointed Gustav von Kahr General State Commissar with near dictatorial powers. Those powers he could, and intended to, use to put down any kind of civil unrest. To help him do so the government in Berlin put the Reichswehr units in Bavaria, with General Otto von Lossow at their head, at his disposal. Colonel Hans von Seisser, who commanded the powerful Bavarian State police, was the third member of the unholy trio.

Lossow had a reputation for being a "strong man" who would mercilessly crush any opposition he met. True to his image, one of the first things he did was to ban fourteen meetings we had planned for the evening of 27 September. This was a move we National Socialists simply could not take lying down. My close collaborators, including both Scheubner-Richter and the commander of the fledgling SA, Wilhelm Brückner, told me their men were calling for action. But they might also, if nothing was done, turn their back on the Party and slink away. They might even go over to the Communists, who were very active at the time. Given the terrible economic climate, who could blame them if they did?

Our first plan, proposed by Rosenberg, was as follows. On Memorial Day, 4 November, a parade was going to be held. Among the participants would be an SA battalion, which was more or less all we had. To take the salute there would be Kahr and Crown Prince Rupprecht, who had commanded an army group during the war and was considered Bavaria's number-one soldier, as well as several other high-ranking officers. We were going to make our faithful SA men assemble early so as to seize them. Next, it would be my task to approach them and persuade them to join us in marching on Berlin, toppling the government there, and setting up a new one. The SA men did in fact show up, only to find the guests of honor protected by a strong police force. There was nothing we could do except withdraw with our tails between our legs. So bad was the fiasco that our would-be targets never even realized that they had been targeted.

We fixed the next attempt for the night of 10 November. The date was chosen because it was a weekend when all officials would be at home and government would come to a halt. Again, however, our plans were frustrated when Kahr announced that he was going to hold a major speech two days earlier. Rumor had it that he was about to declare Bavaria's independence from the Reich. That was something we could not allow to happen. So we moved the date forward to the night of 8 November. The final meeting was held in Rosenberg's house, but this time we took care not to let him participate in the planning. Instead, we had Captain Ernst Röhm. Röhm was a rough but very competent officer who had fought at Verdun, among other places. In one of those battles he had the upper part of his nose shot off. In 1923 he led a paramilitary organization known as the *Reichskriegsflagge* (Reich-War Banners).

Röhm's connections in the Reichswehr proved invaluable to us. Cajoling and tricking his colleagues, he succeeded in obtaining sufficient arms and ammunition for his men and ours. We were even able to set up a heavy machine gun company under Göring. The total number of fighters was about 4,000, of whom 1,500 were SA men. The rest were provided by other organizations. Kahr's speech was supposed to start at 20:00. The location was the Bürgerbräukeller, the largest of its kind in Munich. It offered enough room for 3,000 people.

When the evening came, the hall was packed to overflowing. In addition, many people, feeling that something dramatic was about to happen, gathered in the nearby streets. Kahr had been speaking in his lackluster way for half an hour when my special bodyguard, with Göring in charge, burst into the hall. Pandemonium broke out, and ere I could reach the podium, I had to mount a chair and fire my pistol into the air. That got their attention and quieted everyone down.

Making use of every ounce of drama at my disposal, I announced that the National Revolution had broken out. We and the Reichswehr were united under a single flag. Together we would march, first to settle accounts with the traitors in Munich and then to do the same in Berlin. I personally invited the three gentlemen, Kahr, Lossow, and Seisser, to meet with me in a private room. There, I asked them to join us, which, however, they proved reluctant to do.

Meanwhile the crowd outside was getting bored and demanded action. Thereupon, I left the trio under guard, reentered the hall, and held a speech to explain what we were going to do. At first people were embarrassed and did not know where they stood. Later, influenced by my words, they repeatedly interrupted me with thunderous applause. The noise must have reached the gentlemen of the government. At any rate, when I reentered the room where they were being held they gave me their word of honor that they would support the Putsch. I did not quite believe them but was unable to stay around because my presence was needed elsewhere. Ludendorff, whom I left in charge, would not hear of anyone doubting the honor of a German officer. He let them go, which quickly proved to be the greatest blunder of the entire operation.

Meanwhile, our commanders throughout the city had mobilized their men. Opening their sealed orders, they started moving toward their designated objectives. Some they captured; others not. The most important among the latter were the engineer barracks and the infantry barracks. In both cases the reason was that both sides were reluctant to open fire on each other. They were, after all, comrades in arms. The outcome was a stalemate. It worked, as stalemates usually do, in favor of the defenders. Still, as the cold, wet night went on, there were two bright spots. First, an entire Reichswehr unit, numbering some 1,000 men and fully armed, decided to join us. The men came marching smartly up to the Bürgerbräukeller, complete with a band playing and swastika banners flying. Second, one of our sympathizers, Dr. Wilhelm Frick, was able to prevent the police, of which he was a member, from acting against us.

When morning came, the reports I received made it clear that we had by no means been defeated. But we were not making any progress either. Meanwhile, Lossow did not rest. From the Keller he went straight to the infantry barracks. There, he was able to assure himself that the commanders of the local Reichswehr, two divisions in all, stood squarely behind the government and were ready to suppress the Putsch if they were called upon to do. Against such a force we had no chance. Later that night he, Kahr, and Seisser met to coordinate their moves. As they did so, a message arrived from the Army Chief of Staff, General Hans von Seeckt, in Berlin. He ordered them to suppress the Putsch, or else they would stand trial as traitors to the nation.

With additional Reichswehr forces converging on the city, by the morning it was touch and go. Here I must hand it to Ludendorff; it was he who suggested that we "march." His call proved disastrous in the short run. But in the long run it saved us and laid the foundation for the future. Informing the various groups of fighters and gathering them together took time. It was not until late in the morning that 3,000 men were finally ready to move.

With Ludendorff, me, and some others at the head, we marched through the city. On our way we changed directions several times so as not to clash with the police, which had sealed off many streets. Wherever we went, crowds lined the pavement, cheering and wishing us good luck. Finally, we reached the Odeonsplatz, where about 100 policemen and soldiers stood waiting. A skirmish with fists and truncheons ensued, and someone fired a shot. Thereupon, the police leveled their rifles and loosened a salvo into us. As always happens in such cases, it seemed an eternity. But in fact it only lasted for about half a minute. When it ended, sixteen of our men, as well as four policemen, had been killed.

With our people taking shelter or running in all directions, the Putsch almost immediately came to an end. I myself was pulled down by the dying Scheubner-Richter and hit the ground hard. My shoulder was dislocated, an injury so painful that only those who have gone through it can imagine it. Somehow I was able to reach Hanfstängl's apartment, which was not far away. He was not at home; to avoid arrest, he had fled to Austria. So had Göring, who had taken a serious wound in the groin and was in even greater agony than me.

The person who opened the door for me was Helene, Hanfstängl's beautiful American wife. Later, he circulated tales that I was in hysterics, threatened to shoot myself, that she took the gun from my hand, and so on. He also said that, on another occasion, I had begged her to divorce him and marry me. All that is pure invention. It *is* true, though, that, in her efforts to cheer me up, she said that, without me, the Party would collapse. That, at any rate, gave me strength to face the future.

Two days later, I surrendered to the police and was arrested. Three months after that my fellow conspirators and I were put on trial. By that time my injury had healed. I was feeling in top form as people often do when things get rough and there are obstacles to overcome. Defending myself, I told the court that we were idealists and had acted out of the best motives. I also assumed full responsibility for everything that had taken place. Should the judges condemn us, I said, history would smile and tear their verdict to pieces.

The trial provided me with my first opportunity to address an audience not just in Bavaria but in the whole of Germany. A large contingent of foreign journalists also attended the proceedings. And it worked. All I was given were five years in prison with a promise of being released in less than a year. My associates got shorter terms; Ludendorff, the only one in our ranks who had not dropped to the ground but marched right into the police cordon and through it, was acquitted. He stormed and ranted, claiming that the verdict had insulted him and demanding to be re-arrested but to no avail. By letting the trio go, he had committed the worst blunder of the entire episode. From this point his influence declined very rapidly and he left the stage of history. To console him, in 1935 I offered him the rank of field marshal. But he, apparently still under the influence of his wife's nutty ideas, refused.

I shall not describe the time I spent at Landsberg in detail. As I said, it bore some similarity to my life here in Hell. Then, as now, there were no dogs around. Alas, but it seems the loyal creatures can only be found in Paradise. The guards were uniformly kind, and I bore them no grudge. Later, some of them even joined our movement. As to the cell in which I was held, it became an object of pilgrimage for *Hitler Jugend* and others. There is, however, one amusing detail I want to mention. The prison authorities allowed me to see about as many visitors as wanted to come. A great many of them were women. In fact it was a woman, Winifred Wagner, who gave me the paper on which first Maurice and then Hess took down my dictation of *Mein Kampf.* Asked who they were and why they had come, the ladies would come up with all kinds of fictitious blood relationships. One of the wardens, I am told, commented that never had he met anyone who had so many mothers.

Have you ever listened to Beethoven's *Egmont* Overture? I have done so many times, both during my sojourn on earth and here in Hell. The story is about a sixteenth-century Dutch nobleman, Count Lamoral of Egmont. In 1568 he rose to liberate his country from the Spanish yoke, was caught, and died on the scaffold. His spirit, though, did not die with him. Instead, it rose from the grave and became much more powerful, much more inspiring, than it ever had been during his life. All this Beethoven, our ur-German Beethoven, captured in his music. Not for nothing did I fund a new monument for him in Bonn! Similarly, our Putsch, precisely because it had failed and because some of our men had sacrificed their lives for the cause and died, became a symbol and legend.

Legends have their own way of developing. Ours having been born, year by year our own propagandists and others embroidered on it and added to it. The swastika flag we had carried was salvaged. Later, someone had the idea of calling it the *Blutfahne,* or blood banner. Year by year, whenever a new SA unit received its colors, I, as the Führer, used to consecrate those colors by touching them with one hand and the *Blutfahne* with the other. Next, looking the commanders straight in the eye, so as to impress them with the seriousness of the moment, I would shake hands with them. After our seizure of power, we started re-enacting the march year by year. And I would address my old comrades at the Bürgerbräukeller just as I had done in 1923.

The Putsch also taught us, or at any rate me, a few important things. Some historians have described my SA men, as they were at the time, as a well-disciplined, heavily armed force. In fact they were neither. By their looks, they had escaped from a concentration camp! It is true that Röhm, thanks to his ties with the Reichswehr, had been able to obtain arms for them. But on no occasion were they used to open fire on the representatives or order. That apart, many of them were raw youths—rowdies, to call them by their proper name— who had never received any real training. Quite a few would not have known how to use a rifle if they had tried. Except for that one occasion at the Odeonsplatz which proved decisive for all of us, the police did not use their weapons either. Whatever else, civil war was averted.

Taking a wider view, it was clear that we had underestimated the strength of the Republic. It might not have taken strong roots among the people, many of whom were looking back in nostalgia. How could it, given that it was led by a bunch of traitors and mealy-mouthed democrats who, to quote Eckart, where always shivering in their wet pants? But neither were they ready to fight it, let alone risk their lives to replace it with some other regime.

One reason was simple fatigue. Nine years after the outbreak of the World War I and five after it had ended, the only thing most of our countrymen wanted was stability so that they could finally start repairing the immense damage they had suffered. Another was the outcome of the presidential election which was held, for the first time, in March 1925. It resulted in the election of Field-Marshal Paul von Hindenburg, the man who, starting in 1915–16, had been venerated like no other person in the whole of Germany.

I do not want to imply that Hindenburg was some sort of super-competent genius. He was not. During the World War a gigantic statue of him had been erected in Berlin. In return for a few pennies, people were invited to take up a hammer and drive nails into his body. This led one of his English biographers, John Wheeler-Bennet, to call him the Wooden Titan, a name that suited him very well. A monarchist at heart, he never thought he would play the role he eventually did and always resented having had to do so. And it was no wonder because, at the time he assumed office, he was already seventy-eight years old. His great strengths were iron nerves, unflap-pability, and the kind of courage a person in his position needs to appear in public without a bodyguard. Even more important was his willingness to accept responsibility. Always somewhat slow, though, a leading intellectual light he had never been.

To return to my proper subject, what I learned from the attempted uprising was that Germany was not Italy. As the Blackshirts marched on Rome, the Italian army and police stood aside and did nothing. That was not what happened in our case. I therefore concluded that, in the future, we would have to limit ourselves to legal methods. Many of my colleagues did not like the decision. That was especially true of our SA fighters. They felt we were a revolutionary movement and were always thirsting for action. Recalling the history of the

French Revolution and punning on the words equality and legality, some of them used to call me *Adolph legalité!* I, however, held firm. As I used to tell my colleagues, we should hold our noses and enter the Reichstag, always with the objective, of course, first of using that institution for our own ends and then blowing it sky-high. There simply was no other way.

Finally, in all modesty, the Putsch, the trial, and the time I spent in Landsberg taught me a lot about myself as well as the role I might play in the history of my country. I had, after all, come from humble origins. Though I had always had a feeling that there might be something special about me, even as late as the trial that followed the Putsch I was still thinking of myself merely as a "drummer." As I told the court, my task was to call the minds together in preparation for the great national leader to come. Early on, I even thought that the name of that leader might be Herr General Erich Ludendorff. That was one reason why I courted him as much as I did.

As I said earlier, though, Ludendorff proved a deep disappointment. A great soldier he had been. But a great popular tribune capable of rallying the masses he was certainly not. Or perhaps, having been born in 1865, he was simply getting too old for the role he would have loved to play but could not. It was during my stay at Landsberg that the consciousness first dawned on me that I myself might have been selected by Providence to lead the nation in its time of crisis. The coming years were to provide ample confirmation of that understanding.

Chapter 8

My Happiest Years

As Nietzsche wrote, whatever does not kill me strengthens me. For me, that proved to be the case. I emerged from Landsberg much stronger and more self-confident than I had ever been. The months I spent here provided a welcome period of rest after the excitement, exertions, and dangers of the previous ten years. They also gave me the leisure one needs to think and to plan ahead.

I left prison on 20 December 1924 after thirteen months inside. Ere I did so I gave all my cash, 282 marks, to my comrades who had to stay behind. What a feeling, being free! Not expecting a hard hand on my shoulder took some weeks getting used to. My first destination was Hanfstängl's brand-new villa in Munich. His son, four-year-old Egon, was very glad to meet me again. In days past I had imitated the sounds of every kind of artillery for him. Now I obliged him by doing it again. I asked Hanfstängl, who was a very fair pianist, to play for me. Listening to Isolde's *Liebestod* relaxed me. It was just the kind of music that used to bring tears to my eyes! Landsberg had made me put on weight because our wealthy visitors brought us so much good food that our dining room resembled a delicatessen shop. That same evening, when dinner came, I told Hanfstängl of my decision to stop eating meat and drinking alcohol. This was a decision I kept until the end of my days.

Coming up for air, I soon discovered that the Party, which I had created almost single-handedly and in which I had invested so much energy, had more or less gone to pieces. I had appointed Rosenberg as my successor during my absence. After all, most of the rest were either in prison or else had fled across the border. Unfortunately, he proved totally unable to do what had to be done. He had always been primarily a man of words, not action. His haughty manner and tendency towards *Besserwisserei* (knowing everything better) also drove away many supporters. The heads of the various local organizations spent their time fighting each other tooth and nail. Meanwhile, what little funding we had trickled and dried up. In the end it was the women—Frau Bruckmann, Frau Bechstein, and a few others—who somehow prevented the worst. For that the Party, and I personally, are eternally grateful to them.

Officially, my status was that of an ex-convict with a criminal record. Therefore, my first care was to rehabilitate myself. I was able to arrange some meetings with the Minister-President of Bavaria, Heinrich Held, a Center (Catholic) politician who had taken over from Knilling. I convinced the elderly gentleman that, from now on, I would only use legal means in my quest for power. That too was a promise I rigorously kept. True, the tactics our SA used in dealing with opponents were not always exactly delicate. How could they be, given the nature of the Red opposition? But at no time thereafter could anyone accuse me of planning anything similar to the 1923 escapade, let alone trying to carry it out.

The meetings went well, as is made clear by the fact that, shortly afterward, most of my imprisoned comrades were also released. The Party, which in the aftermath of the Putsch had been banned, was once again permitted to exist and act in the open. With Hoffmann's help, I rented a suite to serve as our headquarters. As early as 16 February, even our *Völkischer Beobachter,* whose masthead I personally had designed in such a way as to distinguish it from the rest, was able to resume publication. It provided Rosenberg with a field of activity for which he was much better suited than for leading any kind of organization. The next step was to reestablish my control over the Party. I was, after all, their greatest asset by far, being the only person able to attract large numbers of people and make them join our cause. I was holding the trump card, and I made sure they never forgot it.

Still, it was anything but easy. Dealing with the heterogeneous lot who had used my absence to fish in troubled waters demanded all my energy and my powers of persuasion. The fact that I was banned from speaking to assemblies of non-Party members—until 1927 in all of Germany and until 1928 in Prussia as the largest German state by far—did not make things any easier. In Berlin and elsewhere the ruling gentlemen, when they spoke of freedom, only meant their own! Swallowing my rage at this insult, I did what politicians do. I gathered supporters. I cajoled, I charmed, and, yes, I flattered leaders. I built coalitions. I got rid of some comrades who, often claiming to act in the name of this or that crackpot program, did not want to listen to me or accept my authority as Führer. Who first used that title, incidentally, I have no idea. It just floated about until more and more people took it up.

The climax of my campaign arrived on 27 February 1925 during a meeting at the Bürgerbräukeller, the very same place in which we had mounted our Putsch. Some of my most important collaborators re- fused to attend or were unable to do so. One of them was Rosenberg, who was in a funk. Others were Göring, who was still convalescing, and Röhm, who was trying to reestablish his own National Socialist Freedom Party. That old foggy, Drexler, was present and still trying to prove that he was somebody. In the end the chair was taken by my trusted business manager, Max Amman. Three hours before I arrived the hall was already packed to capacity. Others crowded the streets outside. I spoke for two hours. I explained the reasons for the plight Germany was in, demanded that all of them forget their differences and unite so as to save her, and predicted that the road ahead would be long and hard. I also demanded full authority—I would brook no opposition—and ended by having all the various leaders meet and swear undying loyalty to me as the leader of the

Party. That ceremony having been performed, the applause simply would not come to an end.

The elections that gave Hindenburg the presidency also finished off Ludendorff. Influenced by his dear Mathilde, Ludendorff had been assuming a more and more anti-Catholic stance. Doing so in Catholic Bavaria was a foolish move that could not and did not take him anywhere. Not surprisingly, he got just one percent of the vote. He promptly threw in the towel and retired to a villa in Tutzing, near Munich, where he and Mathilde went on spouting their drivel. Our own results were no better, but I did not let that trouble me too much. My main task now was to further consolidate the Party. Again, it was anything but easy. The most important obstacle was Otto Strasser's older brother Gregor. A Bavarian by birth and a pharmacist by trade, this Strasser was a gifted speaker second only to myself. Previously, as a member of the Freikorps, he had taken an active part in the suppression of Communism in Munich. He also participated in our Putsch. Tried and sentenced to prison, he was elected to the Reichstag as a representative of the *Völkisch* Block. In May 1924 he was freed.

When the Party was reestablished, I put Strasser in charge of our propaganda department and sent him to build up our organization in the north. He did so with considerable success. He was so successful, in fact, that at one point his part of the organization counted more members than mine did. The trouble with Strasser was that, then and later, he did not strictly follow the Party line. Along with many members of the SA, he developed radical socialist ideas that I could not and would not accept. He even wanted to replace our 25-Point Program! It took a national meeting of our Party, which was held in Munich in February 1926, to more or less paper over the differences. Though the future was to show that my problems with him had by no means ended, I was able to draw his associate, Dr. Joseph Goebbels, then a young man with an outstanding gift for propaganda, over to my side. It was easy; all I had to do was send my chauffeur-driven

Mercedes to pick him up at the railway station. Later, too, rarely did he ask for anything but a pat on the head.

There things rested, more or less. Over the next few years I lived for the Party. For twenty-four hours a day I spoke and organized, organized and spoke. While I always took care to tailor my speeches to the occasion and to the audience, more and more I focused on the essential points. They were, not necessarily in that order, the need to reverse the Revolution of November 1918; to oppose Marxism with all our might; to oppose the Jews by disenfranchising them and removing them from all public posts (a sentence or two in *Mein Kampf* notwithstanding, the idea that all of them would have to be killed only came much later); the need for casting off the shackles imposed on us at Versailles and rebuilding our armed forces; and, finally, the need for additional territory to secure our daily bread. I presented these ideas as I saw fit, now in one way, now another, and always adding new examples to illustrate them. I must have been convincing, for over time there grew around me a veritable cult. It was one Goebbels, who tended toward hero worship, encouraged as much as he could.

Exercising leadership is a gift one must be born with. But it is also an art that must be studied and mastered. A talent for speaking and organization apart, it demands two contradictory things. First, one must be, or appear to be, easygoing and accessible. The days when the Kaiser sought to make an impression by means of his glittering uniforms, of which he had a vast collection, are gone. Nor will plumes, gilded carriages, or high-stepping horses do the trick. One must, at all costs, present oneself as a man of the people. For me doing so was not very difficult. After all, a man of the people I was and have always remained.

But popularity must not be confused with familiarity. No one, they say, is a hero to his servant. Nor has anyone has ever become a successful leader while wearing his heart on his sleeve. That is why it is necessary to keep one's own council, something I was always very good at doing. It is also necessary to maintain a certain distance and to create a certain mystique of the kind that will attract followers and give one a certain advantage in dealing both with friends and opponents. That, and not shyness, as so many people thought, is one reason why, in my entire adult life, I allowed very few people to address me with the familiar *Du*.

In the modern world, one of the key tools leadership can and must use is photography. My right hand in doing so was the afore-mentioned Hoffmann. Hoffmann's father, like mine, prevented him from becoming an artist, a fact that created a bond between us. He was also something of a buffoon in whose company I could relax; I never made him address as me as *Mein Führer* as almost everyone else did. I used to visit him at his home and liked him and his wife, Lelly, very much. She was a much more ardent National Socialist than he; in this respect she resembled the wives of several other of my collaborators. Unfortunately, she died in 1928. Though Hoffmann did remarry, he never quite got over the blow and ended up drinking far more than was good for him.

In October 1923 I appointed him my official photographer, a position he held for the next twenty-two years. How many pho-tographs of me he and his assistants took only God knows. Initially, I demanded that he publish none of them without my permission. Later, as our acquaintance deepened, I could trust him to do what had to be done. Accompanying me everywhere, he was the only press photographer permitted to operate without the appropriate armband. As I once told him, his armband was me. In time, his monopoly over my pictures made him a very wealthy man. For me the arrangement had the advantage of enabling me to avoid the error of some senior Weimar politicians, who allowed themselves to be caught in their bathing trunks playing Neptune in the water. Instead, I only presented myself to the public the way I wanted, i.e. properly clothed and in dignified poses suitable to the occasion. As for those pushy pests, the so-called paparazzi...what else are bodyguards and concentration camps for?

Our success in the various election campaigns remained modest enough. But I did not allow this to discourage me. Hard as doing so sometimes was, I always looked on the bright side. In this I was assisted by Goebbels, whom I had made our Gauleiter in "Red" Berlin. He had to be content with a tiny little flat in Caputh near Potsdam, yet no one could be more inventive in devising ways to advertise us and to play tricks on our opponents. Another encouraging factor was the SA. The dedication and self-sacrifice of our brown-uniformed men, all of them volunteers and all of them serving for very little pay indeed, cannot be praised highly enough. They always gave me hope and inspiration.

Personally, too, these were among the happiest years in my life. My income from the sales of *Mein Kampf* was fairly modest, especially after the first year or two. It would, of course, pick up later on. And how! However, in 1928 that was still *Zukunftsmusik,* future music, as we Germans say. Meanwhile, Amman and Rosenberg paid me generously for the articles I wrote. Above all, there were the funds which the Party put at my disposal and to which I helped myself as I saw fit and as my task demanded. Once way or another, the financial cares that had clouded so much of my previous life were gone. In fact I was growing rich. But wealth did not turn me into a miser, as often happens to people who have known poverty as I did. If anything, to the contrary; I always insisted on paying those who performed services for me even when, as sometimes happened, they themselves refused to take a fee.

I was able to rent, and later to buy, a villa at Berchtesgaden, a village not far from the lovely Königssee and very close to the Austrian border, to which I had originally been introduced by Dietrich Eckart. The house had the advantage of being located on the north side of a hill, meaning that it was always in the shade. I renamed it the Berghof, meaning, Mountain Court, redesigned it myself, and filled it with the kind of beautiful objects that elevated the mind and inspired me in carrying out my great task. It served me well on weekends, and in time it became my favorite place to stay. Foreigners who visited it before the war, such as the English journalist George Ward Price, also liked it. I asked my widowed half-sister, Angela Raubal, to come and run the place for me, and she did. I also had a succession of valets. After all, someone had to select and prepare my clothes, collect them after I used them, choose the diet of the day, clean my rooms, make doctors' appointments, and look after a thousand similar small but indispensable details. In 1929 I also rented an elegant nine-room apartment at the Prinzregentenplatz in the center of Munich.

But beauty and show are not the same. As the same visitors noted, never at any time did I live in any but modest luxury of the kind, let us say, a prosperous businessman might enjoy. I did not change my uniforms several times a day or cover myself with orders and jewels. Unlike a certain English degenerate whose name I shall not mention, I always opened my own tube and put my own toothpaste on the brush. Nor, for that matter, did I ever tell any woman that I wanted to be her feminine hygiene product. My villa did not, by a long shot, compare with the magnificent houses that some of my associates, such as Göring and Amman, later built for themselves. Nor did it compare with the lifestyle of the imperial Hohenzollerns, who, at the time they were finally deposed, owned well over a hundred castles and palaces all over Germany. Just taking the Kaiser's loot across the Dutch border took up entire trains, with a total of 59 wagons, I am told.

Working as Party leader and political journalist during the late 1920s, I used to stay in fairly modest hotels. For example, the room I regularly took at Weimar's Haus Elephant had running water but neither a bathroom nor a lavatory. Leaving my room or returning to it, people on both sides of the corridor would line up to salute me, obliging me, an embarrassed smile on my face, to walk the gauntlet while doing the same! Others would gather in the adjoining square and chant:

Lieber Führer
Komm heraus
Aus dein Elefantenhaus!

Which is to say, Dear Führer, do come out, of your elephant house. Later, I had the hotel modernized.

Traveling the country, I used a Mercedes which I changed every few years. We were often accompanied by another car or two carrying bodyguards, guests, and friends. How often did we not find some nice spot, spread a blanket on the ground, and have a picnic in the open! My schedule, though quite busy, was not nearly as crowded as it became later on when I rose to be, first the leader of a large mass party and then Chancellor of the Reich. And it was not nearly as stiff and formal; since my entourage was small, I had little difficulty changing my plans at a moment's notice. It was small enough, too, to mislead stalkers by taking one route while my entourage took another. Best of all, I was not yet obliged to meet an endless number of snobbish officials, diplomats, and high-ranking officers. They are the sort of people whom I have always disliked and who, however much they were obliged to fawn on me, have always disliked me.

I also met any number of women. During my youth in Linz I had been too shy to approach them. All I had ever dared do was send poor Stephanie a letter in which I promised her to become an architect and asked her to wait for me! In Vienna, Munich, and the army things were different. Particularly in the former, *not* to notice the existence of any number of half-naked prostitutes was impossible. That was just why my main concern during those years was to keep my body pure.

Some idiots, reading *Mein Kampf,* have claimed that I had all sorts of sexual hang-ups. That even applied to the NKVD officers who, not long after the war, prepared a report on me for Stalin to read. Others alleged that I was fascinated by syphilis and the prostitution that spread it. Supposedly, I ranted on and on about the subject. As if they themselves, by taking me up on it, did not do the same! What these gentlemen overlook is the plain fact that the disease was rife in large cities in particular. It was no wonder, for the Jews were deliberately spreading it as part of their campaign to weaken the German race and to establish their own dominion over the world. They also forget that, in the age before antibiotics, there was no real cure. That is why, according to some American figures, seventy percent of those who did not get treated within three years of contracting the disease were "doomed." Briefly, syphilis was to society what AIDS is today. Only, since it was much more widespread, it was worse.

During the war, in spite of all the precautions taken by the High Command and its attempts to deal with the issue, about a million— one in twelve—of all those who wore the German uniform contracted venereal diseases. At any one time, the equivalent of entire divisions were incapacitated. Proportionally speaking, the English Army suffered even more. Serves those hypocrites right! How serious the problem was can be gauged from the following episode. A few weeks before his country was attacked at Pearl Harbor, the U.S. Surgeon General, Dr. Thomas Parran, said to be "among the most revered figures in the history of sexually transmitted diseases," went on the record as saying that, in 1917–18, the U.S. had waged two wars. One was against Germany, which it had won. And one was against syphilis, which it had lost. That was why, during the 1930s, the Federal Government, through its Work Projects Administration (WPA), produced more posters addressing this problem than any other public health issue. As for me, no one can say that I have ever shirked away from battle, either military or political. When it came to VD, though, I chose not to be a combatant.

As far back as I can remember, I have always liked women. What real man doesn't? The more so because, in the person of my own mother, I had the best possible example of what true womanhood is. Had her name been Mary rather than Klara, she could have played the part. I cherished women and was always polite to them. I also did what I could to protect them from the hardships of life. Above all, I knew exactly how to charm them. It was easy: a hand-kiss here, a little compliment there. I made them feel important and desirable. Jewesses apart, I never treated them nearly as harshly as, when the occasion demanded, I did men.

A rich man can support a woman and offer her a comfortable life. But the best aphrodisiac is not money. It is power, physical or social. Physical power is what at least two Roman empresses, Agrippina and Faustina, looked for when they took up with gladiators. It was also what Princess Stephanie of Monaco, supermodel Heidi Klum, and, according to rumor, Princess Diana of England sought when they started liaisons with their bodyguards. Social power, meaning the kind that involves wielding authority over other men, is even better. A powerful man makes a woman feel safe to surrender herself, conceive, and bear the children which, if she is normal and not some sort of unnatural creature, are her greatest wish in life. Such a man is like a piece of outsized jewelry. A woman can put him on and show him off to her friends, making them jealous. Look what I've got! Last, but not least, he is someone she can look up to. A real woman, meaning one who obeys her instincts and does not allow herself to be brainwashed by feminists, *wants* to be governed and restrained. She even desires, under some circumstances, to be punished. How else can she feel her man's strength?

In short: every woman adores a Fascist. That even includes most feminists, of course, however much they may deny it. As to the few exceptions—who said they are women? They are nature's blunders, that's what they are. What organ they have they do not use as they should; what organ they do not have they unconsciously crave. No sooner had I started making my mark in the world than women be-gan buzzing over me like maidens around a maypole. For the society ladies who invited me to speak in their drawing rooms I played the role of Mr. Savage—precisely the one they wanted.

Another excellent example of the way these things work is provided by Göring. His first wife, Baroness Karin von Kantzow, was married to a very rich man indeed. She fell in love with Göring after he flew her brother home during a snowstorm when no other pilot dared take off. Nor is it an accident that she was Swedish. Sweden has not seen a war for a very, very long time. As a result, so weak are Swedish men that their women keep running away. To cap it off, the men do not even get angry at the women. Instead of giving them a sound thrashing as they deserve, they forgive them, as Karen's husband also did. No wonder Sweden's divorce rate is among the highest in the world. Göring, of course, was as rapacious as any man in history. But he was basically monogamous and never had more than one woman at a time; both his marriages were extremely happy. In that he differed from a great many others in his position or similar ones.

Liking women as I did, I surrounded myself with artwork that depicted them in all their glory. That included works by the sculptor Eugen Henke as well as the painters Anselm Feuerbach, Franz von Stuck, and Adolf Ziegler. The latter's famous *The Four Elements*, each represented by a young, nude woman, hung in my Munich flat. Women themselves were well aware of my weakness for them and often asked me for favors. Here and there I probably allowed them to exercise too much influence over me. Doing so is always a symptom of weakness and, therefore, a mistake. One example was the admirable Frau Troost, one of only two women whom I ever allowed to visit my military headquarters. So fast did she talk that I could hardly get a word in! On several occasions she intervened on behalf of Jews. Once she went so far as to ask me to read a letter written by one of them in her presence. She had some cheek.

Another was Winifred Wagner. English-born, highly intelligent, and enterprising, for several years after 1924 she, along with her husband Siegfried, were the closest thing to a family I had. Driving from Munich to Berlin and back, I used to spend the night at Villa Wahnfried in Bayreuth. Later, they even built an annex to their house to lodge me and some of my people. Their young sons, Wieland and Wolfgang, used to call me Uncle Wolf. I told them many a story and have nothing but pleasant memories of them. But she kept complaining about how weak Siegfried, who, incidentally, was a homosexual, was. Perhaps that is why, after his death in 1930, there were rumors that I was going to marry her. What nonsense.

I often attended the Bayreuth Festival and can testify that Frau Wagner managed it well enough. More than once I helped by making the necessary funds available to her. My very presence of course, was one factor that attracted a crowd. The problem was that she tried to meddle in politics, about which she, like most other artists, did not have a clue. She was, it is true, an enthusiastic National Socialist. And she was one of the few with sufficient courage to remain so not only to the end but, in some ways, beyond it. But she was also very kindhearted and kept pressing me to do favors for all sorts of people, including, I am sorry to say, quite a few Jews. That was why, after 1941, I no longer saw her or answered her letters. She could count herself lucky. Making use of the fact that few people knew about the breach between us, she went on helping Jews as much as she could. I knew this full well but decided to turn a blind eye. In so far as running the festival was concerned, though, more and more often I dealt with her sons rather than with her. They proved to be good choices.

A third woman I liked very much was Henriette von Shirach. I first met her in the house of her father, Heinrich Hoffmann. She was nine years old, and I used to call her "my blonde angel." Much later, I introduced her to Baldur, and they got married in 1932. She was very pretty and lively. However, like Frau Wagner, she did not know her proper place. At some point in 1943 I invited her to have tea at the Berghof. She had just been to Amsterdam on a shopping spree.

There, she had the misfortune of witnessing a raid during which some
elderly Jewish women were rounded up and loaded onto trucks on
their way to the transit camp prior to resettlement in the east. Young
and tender, she was deeply affected. There were some of my men in
the company, and I had no alternative but to stand firm. So I told
her that, with thousands of our best German soldiers dying every day,
the biological balance in Europe was being upset. Whereupon what
had to be done had to be done. After that, I refused to see her. It was
not because I did not care about her but because I cared too much.

Before proceeding with this theme, I want to put it on record that,
at the time, sex did not receive nearly as much public attention as,
in large part "thanks" to Dr. Freud, it did later on. Educated people
did not boast about the "openness" with which they discussed it. To
the contrary, as Streicher ended up by learning to his cost, doing so
was considered to be in very bad taste indeed. My assistants here in
Hell, using Google N-Gram as their source, tell me that even the
word itself was much less current than it later became. Instead, all
kinds of euphemisms were used. Nor were public figures praised for
the number of affairs they had, as they so often are today. To the
contrary, *not* becoming involved in them, at least not openly, was
considered not only a plus but a prerequisite for success. Decency
had to be preserved. The press, which today has nothing better to do
than expose the leaders' peccadilloes, was more or less cooperative.
The days when tots in kindergarten are obliged to learn about sex,
specifically including all its sickening variations, were, thank God,
still in the future.

Back to the 1920s. So many female admirers did I have that it was
necessary to keep most of them away from me. Some knew that I
liked to go around armed with the kind of whip one sometimes uses
to teach a dog what is what. I never used it for any purpose but for the
one it had been intended for; it was part of my image, so to speak. As
if to confirm Nietzsche's famous saying on the subject, they competed
to see which of them could give me the fanciest one. I ended up

with quite a collection! Many of the women in question were *not* elderly and did not try to mother me. Some were very good looking indeed. Helene Hanfstängl apart, chief among them was Fräulein Leni Riefenstahl. Riefenstahl started her career as a dancer but later switched to film-making. She hovered over me and repeatedly tried to seduce me. But I was not interested.

After my death Soviet doctors, claiming to perform an autopsy on what they claimed were the charred remains of my body, claimed to have discovered that I only had one testicle. Let me say, once and for all: that is pure hogwash. The more so because several extant doctors' reports explicitly testify that such was not the case. And the more so because similar things have been said about Mao Zedong, Stalin, and Franco as well. One might think monorchism is some kind of occupational disease twentieth-century dictators suffer from! How about that great womanizer, Mussolini? How about Pinochet? How about Saddam Hussein? Did they have the same problem? To be sure, I kept myself to myself. I never allowed others to see me as I was washing or carrying out my natural functions. In my eyes, and I think in those of most people, any leader who does that instantly disqualifies himself.

I did, however, have another problem. Germany enfranchised all women in 1919, ahead of both England and the U.S., and long before the great home of democracy, France, did the same. Women form fifty percent of the population. But for them, we National Socialists could not win. But how to go about it? I knew exactly how. I used to flatter them by speaking tenderly about my mother and the role she had played in my life. But I could also take the opposite line. On one occasion I told a female audience that I had brought them *The Man*. With great success; they were always prominent among those who cast their votes for the Party and me. At meetings they used to occupy the front ranks (which we reserved for them). As I spoke, I often heard and saw, in front of me, a sea of harsh breathing, heaving bosoms, and strangely contorted, half weeping, faces. Their expressions combined extreme concentration with ecstasy. Many seemed about to melt as if they were made not of flesh and blood but of jelly. Obviously my words, and even more so my personality, touched them to the marrow. Not because I tried to turn them into second-rate men, as most modern feminists and their decadent "male" fellow travelers do, but because I took them for what they were: women.

Very early on I realized that their support was absolutely dependent on my remaining single. At all costs, they had to be kept in a position where they could retain their pretty little dreams. This was made evident, for example, on my birthdays, when they used to send me acres of presents, such as porcelain, clothing items, cushions, bed covers, table clothes, and what not. Many had my portrait, initials, and/or swastikas lovingly embroidered on them! The rooms in which they were stored looked like department stores. Some of my associates and I used to have fun going over them. Afterward, they would go to all kinds of welfare organizations.

So I never married. I was not Mussolini, who always had his pockets full of mistresses as well as one-night lovers. And my people were not Italians; had I followed his example, they would have appreciated me less, not more. That does not mean I did not have a number of women friends. Beside those I have already mentioned, there was Maria Reiter. Ours was what is called a *Hundenbekantschaft*—our dogs met when she, accompanied by her younger sister Anni, went walking in the park in Munich. The rest followed of its own accord. This was 1926. I liked her and took her and her younger sister Anni out a few times. But that was all. She was, after all, only sixteen years old. I was in my mid-thirties, and with the best will in the world found it impossible to take her seriously, let alone marry her as she wanted. In 1928 we parted, and two years later she married. Unhappily, as it turned out. She divorced and remarried an SS officer. Later, when he was killed at Dunkirk, I sent her 100 red roses.

The case of my niece, Angela ("Geli") was very different. She was a bit older than Maria, an artless, lively, quite curvaceous girl. Quite unlike the bones, ribs, and nipples one sees hopping about the stage today, who are always starving, always frowning, and always complaining about one thing or another! I loved her very much, and regularly took her to the cinema, the theater, and on trips. For her sake, I was even prepared to set aside my aversion for shopping! She, for her part, called me Uncle Alf. As my protégé, she used to harmlessly amuse herself by lording it a little over my entourage and flirting with some of its members. Yes, I did a few nude drawings of her, but not nearly as many as any art student is being made to do every day. To repeat, all other details about our relationship were spread by Hanfstängl, who picked them out of his filthy imagination. Next, they were taken up by my enemies, such as Otto Strasser, and eagerly collected by my sensation-hungry "biographers," such as the half-Jew Konrad Heiden; who in turn served many of the rest as their source.

Geli ended up shooting herself with my gun in my apartment. She left no note, so I never knew why. This was 19 September 1931, when I was already the leader of the second-largest party in Germany and famous the world over. I was traveling to Berlin and received the news on the way; that fact prevented my enemies from claiming that I had killed her. They did, however, leave no stone unturned in their search for all the bad things I might have done and not done to her and which supposedly had driven her to commit the terrible deed she did.

It is true that, busy as I was, I could no longer give her the sort of attention she had become used to. It is also true that I broke up her relationship with Emil Maurice. Maurice was a good man who had worked for me for quite a few years. However, at one point I found out that his great-grandfather had been a Jew. Could I, and through me Germany, afford to have a Jew in my family? Much to my regret,

I had to let him go. But this did not prevent him from staying in the SS, where he eventually rose to full colonel. Much later, Himmler wanted to dismiss him and his brother from the organization. But I have never been ungrateful, so I intervened and prevented him from doing so. Finally, it is also true that Geli wanted to go to Vienna to study singing. However, it is not true, as has been claimed, that I opposed the move. All I did was watch over her and make sure she would not lose her heart to an unsuitable man.

Her death left me prostrated with grief, so much so that I did not have what it took to attend her funeral and thought about leaving politics altogether. Later, I ordered her room in my apartment to be kept just as it had been. I also had bronze busts of her placed in all my residences. But life goes on. We bear what we have to bear. This was a critical juncture in German history, and I had no choice but to proceed along the road Providence had laid down for me. Our relationship was no one's business but ours, and I do not want to go into any more detail about it. Suffice it to say that, while the lying stories told about me caused me much pain, I was not the only leader to be surrounded by similar ones. Far from it! Stalin, according to his daughter Nadezha Alliluyeva, had a very low sex drive. Frederick the Great's intimate life remains a mystery to the present day. So does that of Alexander the Great. And how about Achilles and Patroclus? Were they bosom-friends, or were they more?

In brief, it seems to be the fate of great historical figures that both their supporters and their enemies want to know everything about what is, after all, the aspect of their lives that is the least important and the least differentiated from that of other people. Meaning, what they do and don't do in the bedroom. Never more so than today. They are welcome to their prurient fantasies. But I am not going to oblige them.

Chapter 9

Into the Storm

Volume I of *Mein Kampf* dealt with my early life and my rise as a leader. Volume II dealt with the ideology and structure of the National-Socialist State my associates and I wanted to build. In the summer of 1928, having a little spare time on my hands, I decided to add a third volume, one specifically directed toward foreign policy. The immediate background was an ongoing public debate about the future of South Tyrol. South Tyrol, as a separate geographical and administrative district, was a new entity. It only came into being in 1918–19 when the Allies tore it off the southern part of the County of Tyrol and handed it to Italy. The county itself had been part of Austria-Hungary since 1867, part of the Austrian Empire since 1814, and part of the Holy Roman Empire since the days of Emperor Maximilian I in 1504.

That the population of South Tyrol, or the Alto Adige, as it pleased the Italians to call it, was almost entirely German no one could deny. The question was what to do about it. The Austrians strongly resented the loss of part of the province and its people. And indeed, according to the Allies' own loudly-proclaimed principle of nationality, they had every right to do. But Austria was a rump state that barely survived the multiple amputations it had suffered in 1919. Small, poor, and in disarray, on its own it was powerless in front of the power Mussolini possessed or seemed to possess. What ought the Reich to do? At the time of writing in 1928 it, too, was powerless to do anything. Still, most people believed we ought to support Vienna, as our common blood demanded. I disagreed. Recalling the World War, when we had been encircled on all sides, I thought an alliance with Italy was essential for the future. The problem of our *Volksgenossen* in South Tyrol would have to be solved by other means.

Another major point was the need to form an alliance with England. As I wrote above, I considered the Kaiser's policy toward that country one of the greatest, if not the greatest, blunders in his entire career. Basically, it was determined by the fact that he liked sailing so much! I did not begrudge him his fun. However, that is no basis on which to build the foreign policy of a great power or, indeed, a small one. The plain fact is that there were no fundamental issues dividing us from our racial cousins, the English. They were a naval power; we were a continental one. They were the Leviathan; we were the rhinoceros and should have never tried to learn to swim as well. They could have their empire, provided that we could have a free hand on the Continent.

The war had enabled the English to add vast spaces and millions of people to their empire, both in Africa and the Middle East. However, as the outcome of the Irish struggle for independence proved, under the surface both the empire and the home country were already showing clear signs of decline. Had the English had any sense, or, which is more or less the same thing, had they not fallen under the influence of the Jewish plutocrats such as the Rothschilds (who day-by-day fixed the gold-prices in London and continued to do so until 2004), they would have welcomed our offer with open arms.

Another advantage of an English alliance was as follows. It would do away with any possibility that the U.S. might come across the Atlantic and wage war on us, as it had done in 1917–18. Many Germans have tended to underestimate American power, none more so than the Kaiser's admirals. In 1917, hoping to win the war before the U.S. could intervene in force, they decided to declare unrestricted submarine warfare. They persuaded Ludendorff, and the rest is history. American democracy was and remains a source of weakness. It is nothing but a device for plundering the nation and dividing what the Americans themselves call the pork barrel. What passes for American "culture" is even worse. It is a repulsive combination of plutocracy, Fordism, and all sorts of scraps dug up from the garbage heap by Indians, Negroes, and Jews.

The U.S. was hardly a military nation. Americans, proud of their "individualism" and lacking a strong sense of duty, have never made very good soldiers. Referring to the Civil War, our good old Moltke said that it consisted of "two mobs chasing one another." Yet do not delude yourself. Some small minorities apart, the population's racial makeup was (in 1929, not today) excellent. It consisted of Englishmen, Irishmen, Scandinavians, and Dutch along with a very large and potentially very powerful German element. And America's industrial power was far greater than that of anyone else. This became clear in 1917–18 and, much more so, in 1942–45 when we faced the GIs first in Africa, then in Italy, and finally in France. Every time our brave troops saw an American tank, they shot it up. Not too difficult, incidentally, because their Shermans burned like lighters and were, accordingly, nicknamed Ronsons. The problem was that we ran out of shells before they ran out of tanks.

There would be nothing better, therefore, than to put the English Navy between them and ourselves. That would leave us with France and the Soviet Union, and those we could very well tackle on our own. The former was in an even greater mess than England. Its birthrate was sinking like a stone, its public life was characterized by corruption and low morale, and socialism was on the rise. The French were also cursed with a defensive mentality intent on avoiding casualties at all cost—one that later led to the expensive fiasco known as the Maginot Line. The Soviets had been devastated by years of war, revolution, and war again, to say nothing of the idiotic inefficiencies of Communism. The Jews and Bolsheviks who ran the place, presiding over as many as a 160 million Slav *Untermenschen,* only made everything that much worse.

I also used the opportunity to repeat my views on foreign policy in general. The struggle for existence among states, nations, and races was not something a few kings and aristocrats had invented for their own amusement. Instead, it was an unalterable law of nature that made the strong prevail and the weak go under. Nor, contrary to the views of some good souls both in Germany and abroad, had it ended in 1919. That was what the English and the French, in an all-too-transparent attempt to legitimize their possessions, claimed; in fact, though, it was an exercise in hypocrisy second to none. From our German point of view, adopting this idea meant resigning ourselves to our current weak situation without any prospect of improving it. The best we could expect was the quiet life. The worst we could expect was slow—and perhaps not so slow—strangulation. Hence the need for an active foreign policy based on risk taking of the kind, I might add, that few, if any Germans, or Europeans for that matter, even dare think about today.

In the event the book was never published. But not because there was anything secret about it as some people, hoping of make money out of it, later claimed. Rather, following the radical improvement in the Party's fortunes around this time I simply did not have the time or the inclination to complete it as it deserved to be. Eventually, the manuscript was "discovered" by an American-Jewish historian named Gerhard Weinberg. This was in 1961, and he used it to "prove" what a thoroughly wicked man I had always been, did remain, and would forever remain. In fact the book was an abortion. But it was no more so than thousands of others, and it did help me clear my mind, as writing one's thoughts down often does.

Another document which had its origins during these years was Hermann Rauschning's *Hitler m'a dit (Hitler Told Me),* the original French title. Rauschning was a right-wing conservative politician from Danzig. The city which, in violation of the Allies' own loudly proclaimed principles, had literally been torn out of Germany's living body so as to allow Poland an outlet to the sea. After flirting with various local parties, he joined the NSDAP. Representing us, he was even able to win the local elections and became President of the Senate. However, his loyalty to Germany and the Party was always somewhat dubious. In 1935 he went so far as to start writing articles about the need for closer cooperation with the Poles as well as the Catholic Church. Subsequently, he felt his life was in danger. If so, he must have known why. He sold his property and fled the country, finally landing in the United States.

Between 1932 and 1934 I did in fact meet Rauschning on a number of occasions. He and I talked a little, but definitely not over a hundred times as he later claimed. Where would I have found the time? Thus the book he wrote rests on rather shaky foundations. Subsequent research revealed that he had plagiarized *Mein Kampf* as well as many of my speeches. Add some passages from Nietzsche and Ernst Jünger, stir well, and boil over a slow fire. The outcome is a broth ready to be eaten, or rather, slurped. Much in it is true; much false. However, considered from a literary point of view, the book is a real *tour de force*. That, of course, accounts for its success.

Rauschning's other book, *The Revolution of Nihilism,* also sold well. But it is not nearly as good. It is not true, as he and others after him claimed, that we National Socialists believed in nothing and were out to destroy all the values of Western civilization. In fact nihilism is an essential characteristic not of the German race but of the Slavs and the Jews. The former are like horses. Unless one rules them with a strong hand, they tend to fall back into the state of nature. The latter are ready to sacrifice anyone and anything for the sake of Mammon. Our own objective was just the opposite. We wanted to return to the old, pure, heroic *Völkisch* values of our own people. Values which Jews, Catholics, socialists, and freemasons had buried under mountains of pornography and other filth and were doing their best to destroy. And which, we hoped would enable us to restore the health, unity, and, yes, power of our people.

That was not the end of the matter. Starting in the early 1960s, entire shoals of historians, both German and foreign, have spilled oceans of ink in an attempt to separate my "real" objectives from the chaff of my various tactical maneuvers. A. J. P. Taylor (as he was known), Hugh Trevor-Roper, Eberhard Jäckel, Ernst Nolte, Volker Ulrich, the lot... The main texts they used were *Mein Kampf,* my "secret" book, and Rauschning. To these they added two other "secret" documents. One was the so-called Hossbach Memorandum. It got its name from a certain Colonel Friedrich von Hossbach, who took notes of a talk I held on 5 November 1937 in front of several dozen senior officers and high officials. It was indeed secret, but only in the rather limited sense in which a speech delivered to so many people can be secret in the first place. As Hossbach, whom I later promoted to general, himself said later on, had the meeting been pronounced secret, he never would have written down its contents. After the war, his notes fell into the hands of the Allied prosecution at the Nuremberg "War Criminal Trials." It used an "edited" version of them—the notes themselves have disappeared—to "prove" that Göring and others were guilt of preparing and launching an "aggressive" war. From there it passed into the hands of the historians, who kept copying one another in saying the same. Big deal.

The other document consisted of my "Secret Conversations" of 1941–44. In fact they were simply a record of the small talk with which I used to entertain my female secretaries and, from time to time, some other guests. They owe their existence to my former secretary and subsequent Head of the Party Chancellery, Martin Bormann. Starting in the summer of 1941, Bormann was the closest to me of all my associates. When my workday ended, his began, with the result, as he once told his son, that for years on end he never slept more than five hours a night. Brutal—he readily did all kinds of jobs others had no taste for—but highly efficient, I used to call him my mole who moved mountains overnight.

One and all, Bormann's aides hated him and kept complaining about him. One even claimed that he was as he was because, growing up in the countryside, his early contacts had been mainly with animals! I laughed but kept him nevertheless. He acted as a useful barrier between me and them, enabling me to take unpopular measures without assuming the guilt for them. At one point he decided that my every word was immensely valuable and had to be written down so posterity could seek enlightenment in it. In fact I liked talking about all kinds of things, related and unrelated. Doing so was a form of relaxation. And I could see no reason why he shouldn't do as he proposed. But *secret* conversations? Anyone who makes this claim simply has not read a single word of them. In truth, the conversations are a bit like the present book. Only, perhaps, not as well organized.

Thus four of these five "basic" documents were rather dubious. That did not prevent historians from lifting entire paragraphs from them and throwing them at one another in the hope of reconstructing the path I had taken. They just could not make up their minds: Were all my objectives present from the first? Or did some of them at least develop later on? How consistent was I? What was real? What was make-believe? What was strategy? What was tactics? Did I really hate the Jews? (Of course I did and with very good reason, too.) Or did I simply use them as scapegoats, a target I could present to my countrymen for them to unite against and to shoot at? Entire libraries were written about these questions. As if anyone, least of all a statesman, is born fully grown and armed like Minerva emerging from Jupiter's brow. As if flexibility and the willingness to use the opportunities that come one's way are necessarily the opposite of long-term consistency. And so on. All these are academic debates whose true significance, if any, is limited. Better leave them to the universities, where they belong.

Nevertheless, at the risk of repeating myself, I want to put the essence of my *Weltanschauung* on paper once more. Yes, I put Germany first. *Deutschland, Deutschland über alles.* Yes, I believed that in order to harness the masses to the national chariot, any modern political movement worth its salt had to profess and practice some kind of socialism. But the socialism I had in mind was not of the Marxist variety. Marxism was disqualified by the fact that it was, or claimed to be, international and by its desire to do away with private property. Plus, it was Jewish. Yes, I came to hate Jews with all my heart; even if that hatred did not have its first roots in my childhood in Linz but a few years later in Vienna, right before World War I. Yes, I loathed democracy and insisted on the *Führerprinzip* as the only sound way on which to base a polity. Yes, I despised the kind of reactionary ideology on which the Second Reich was built. Yes, the state I wanted to build was going to be of a completely different kind. Not reactionary, but revolutionary. Not democratic, but totalitarian. And not international, but national socialist.

No, I did not believe in individual freedom of the liberal sort. No, I did not believe all men (and women, but that is a different story) were created equal. For this there were two reasons. First, mankind originated not in one race but in two or more—this being a point which the most recent anthropological discoveries, which are based on DNA, seem to confirm. Some of the races into which mankind is divided are valuable and create culture. Others are inferior and can do nothing but destroy it. Among the latter, the most prominent and the most dangerous, dangerous because of their parasitical nature, are the Jews. Working now in secret, now openly, but always in unison, their true goal is world domination.

Second, nature has decreed that life should be a struggle—*vide,* on this point, the great Charles Darwin and our own Ernst Häckel. In this struggle the strong emerge on top whereas the weak are pressed to the wall. And those who do not take part lose. That applies both to the lives of private individuals and to foreign policy as it is conducted among states. For us Germans, the supreme goal of that policy ought to be the acquisition of living space in the east. To do so we had to use every ounce of military force at our disposal. Am I, my dear professors, making myself clear?

Meanwhile, the Party was not doing well. That, in fact, was the reason why the various state governments lifted the ban on my public speaking. Miserable worms that they were, they firmly believed the Party and I were finished. They could not have been more wrong! The event that triggered our ascent was the financial crisis of late 1929. I am no economist, and my interest in economics has always been limited. Instead, I believed that, if the will is there, the means will follow. I can say, in all modesty, that my own career itself provides the best possible proof of that.

My secret in gaining adherents was to do the opposite of what most politicians, especially in democracies, do. I neither tried to put voters to sleep nor to reach them by way of rational arguments. Nor did I promise them, say, cheaper kindergartens, subsidized housing, better railway service, and free birth control. Except perhaps in the U.S., as the land of the dollar, and among the English, the nation of shopkeepers, such promises will seldom get a leader very far. Look at Switzerland. It may well be the most democratic country in the world. But it is also the most tepid and most uninteresting one. There is nothing there but banks, cheese, chocolate, and cuckoo-clocks! When the Swiss are in doubt, which, owing to their immense wealth, rarely happens, what they do is sit down for dinner.

No. To enthuse the masses, to infuse them with the kind of spirit with which great deeds are performed, one has to do two things. The first is to make them feel that they are the victims of an injustice, to point out those responsible, and to turn them into the object of hatred. The second, which follows naturally from the first, is to demand purposeful work and sacrifice so as to bring about a better future. There is nothing like purposeful work, even such as is hard and/or dangerous, to pull people out of their lethargy and to make them happy. Sacrifice makes them feel better, nobler, than they are. Blood, toil, tears, and sweat. The imams who are currently busy radicalizing Europe's Muslims and turning them against the native Aryan majority understand this all too well. Like me, they are using democracy against itself. Like me, they have taken the position of the underdog. Arousing sympathy and making them, the imams, hard to hate; when people started to realize the truth, it was too late.

Anyhow, the years from 1925 to 1929 were relatively prosperous. But the prosperity, based on huge American loans as it was, was artificial. When Wall Street collapsed in October 1929, the first thing the banks did was to call in the loans. The effect was to make the entire structure, which people like Gustav Stresemann had built so painfully from 1925 on, disintegrate like a house of cards. First in the U.S. and then in the rest of the world as well. Governments did what they could—or thought they could—do in order to cope with the crisis. As, for example, by raising interest rates in an attempt to maintain the value of their currencies and to prevent money from fleeing abroad; slashing budgets; reducing salaries; and believe it or not, increasing taxes so as to leave people with less spending power than they had. All this only made things even worse than they were.

In the post-2008 world, when people speak of "an economic recession" or even "an economic depression," what they normally mean is that GDP goes down by a few percent and that there are some more unemployed. A bank or two may go under; but the system, thanks to massive injections of money like the one provided by President Obama in 2009, survives more or less intact. In my time things were very different. Banks, having had the stuffing knocked out of them, collapsed *seriatim,* taking along the hard-won savings of millions. By 1932 our industrial production had fallen by over forty percent. The plight of our farmers was, if anything, worse still. Unable to compete with cheap American, Argentinian, and Australian imports, many of them went into debt and had to sell their farms. The effect of all this was to drive up the number of unemployed from 1.5 million to 6 million, just over a quarter of the entire workforce. All this was at a time when, since relatively few married women worked outside the home, families were much more dependent on the earnings of the male breadwinner than they later became.

All over Germany, men got up in the morning, ate whatever little there was to eat, and did not know what to do next. They gathered on the street corners. They talked. They collected cigarette butts others had thrown away and smoked them. They begged for work—any kind of work, however nasty or low paying. Those among them who had families to feed lost their self-respect as well as that of their dependents. One outcome was a sharp drop in the marriage rate. In view of the fast-breeding hordes in the east, that was the last thing we needed.

Some people lived more or less illegally in huts or shacks erected in the so-called *Schrebergarten,* small garden plots surrounding many German cities which people work in on weekends. They were the lucky ones. Others rented—listen to this—ropes strung out by café owners. For ten pfennig a night, they were allowed to rest their backs against them! Last not least, entire classes of young university graduates, the flower of the nation, were unable to find jobs. That was why, once in power, we started cutting down on academia.

At the end of October 1929, all these troubles began to work in our favor. Not that it happened of itself or was easy going. There was plenty of opposition, some of it very violent as the Communist Red Guards challenged our SA in the streets. Our allies, Hugenberg's Conservative German National People's Party, played their own games. Now they joined us; now they coyly withdrew. Most galling of all, Gregor Strasser's younger brother, Otto, chose this moment to challenge me with his radical Left-wing views. I met with him but could not find common ground with him. Even his brother agreed that his agitation against the Party was pure lunacy. In the end he left me no choice but to expel him, whereupon he founded his own "Black Front."

Somehow we overcame all the difficulties. We worked like men possessed. Mindful that Germany's future was at stake, and sensing our opportunity, we *were* men possessed. We, a small fringe party, held as many as a hundred propaganda meetings *every day* to such effect that, in a private letter I wrote in February 1930, I felt confident enough to prophesy that we would gain power in two and a half to three years. That estimate proved to be spot on.

In March 1930 the Social Democratic Government of Hermann Müller collapsed, and he himself resigned. Some historians have blamed Hindenburg for not allowing him to continue to govern with the aid of the famous Article 48 of the Constitution; the one which enabled him, the President, to ignore the Reichstag and to govern without it if necessary. They forget that, by the time Hindenburg dismissed him, Müller was already a sick man. Deeply disappointed, he no longer had what it took. In his place Hindenburg appointed Heinrich Brüning of the Catholic Center Party. Brüning, who assumed office in March 1930, governed, or at any rate tried to govern, Germany for a little more than two years. A few historians, seeking to belittle my role, have claimed that some of the economic measures we National Socialists later took, such as the *Autobahn* (motorway) program, originated during that period. If so, Brüning must have kept them well hidden, for the crisis only became worse and worse. By the time he finally left office in mid-1932 the situation had reached nadir.

The first half of 1930 brought us some successes in local elections. That was encouraging, but the real test was still ahead of us. Once more, our will strengthened by our realization that it was now or never, we pulled out all the stops. In Franconia alone, a district made up primarily of small towns and villages, we held over one thousand meetings. The total number of meetings we organized in anticipation of the elections of September of the same year during the last months of the campaign was no fewer than 34,000. People, the authorities specifically included, were astounded by our energy, our determination, and our willingness to take risks. For example, we entered "red" working-class districts in which we were not exactly welcome and where our brave SA men were often attacked and beaten up.

Traveling from one meeting to another, I myself gave twenty big speeches in six weeks. Each one was attended by 10,000–20,000 people. As I did so, I deliberately downplayed the Jewish card. Not, of course, because I had suddenly concluded that the Jews were or could ever be decent, law-abiding citizens of the Reich. But because voters, enveloped in misery or desperately worried that they might lose their jobs and, with it, their standing in society, were, at that moment, not terribly interested in them. Instead, I hammered away on Germany's collapse. Blaming the Treaty of Versailles and parliamentary democracy, I announced that, with the voters' help, we would build something different and much, much better. But I also had to attend to the usual party routine: conferring, organizing, raising money, appointing, and occasionally dismissing those who did not fall into line or failed to perform as required. Standing for hours in my open car, right arm extended, I took the salute in God knows many SA march-pasts. To be sure, I trained with the aid of springs; but how I ever did it I can no longer imagine. Over time it affected my physique, leaving me with my right shoulder slightly higher than the left one.

This was before public opinion polls, a typical American invention dating to the 1930s, started being used in Europe. Not that it mattered much. As we know, polls are very often wrong. Knowing, as I do, something about the way states and politicians steer public opinion, I could easily point out the reasons for this. Polls can even be dangerous. Told that party so-and-so is either going down to defeat or to win big-time, many people will not bother to cast their vote. Polls, in other words, can nullify their own results in advance. Basically, all we had to gauge how well we were doing was our intuition. My intuition, above all: going from strength to strength, as I did for many years, I showed that I understood the German people better than anyone at the time or, perhaps, at any time.

To this must be added the fact that such polls are not exactly suited for a strong Führer regime such as mine. I never believed in transparency, freedom of information, and similar drivel people today value or, in a great many cases, pretend to value. My collaborators and I wanted to control public opinion, not just to find out where it was blowing. As a result, it was only after World War II had ended that the first surveys were held in our Motherland.

The elections took place on 14 September. When the results were announced, it was as if Germany had been shaken by an earthquake. Just a decade earlier, we National Socialists had set out as a ridiculously small club of fewer than ten cranky people. Now we succeeded in making over six million Germans vote for us. Consequently, the number of our representatives in the Reichstag grew six-fold, to 107 seats out of a total of 577, making us the second strongest party after the Social Democrats. On our heels came the Communists, who had also made big gains, and the trusty old Catholic Center, which had registered a small loss.

All the rest suffered, and suffered badly. That was particularly true of the traditional Right—people who, their minds frozen in 1914, had learned nothing and forgotten nothing. Listening to them, one would have thought the economic crisis had never existed and that millions of their countrymen were not suffering! Several factors accounted for our success. Among them were our ability to attract people in the small cities of the north, with the result that the number of Protestants who voted for us exceeded that of the Catholics for the first time. In addition, many young people, whose first election this was, cast their ballots in our favor.

My associates and I were beside ourselves with joy and made the most of our triumph. But our real work, I knew very well, was just beginning.

Chapter 10

Reaching for Power

As if to confirm my poor opinion of democracy, the Reichstag that emerged from the September 1930 elections included the representatives of no fewer than fifteen different parties and micro-parties. Several of the latter only held three seats. It was a true Babylon of conflicting programs. If, indeed, the miserable ideas most of them claimed to represent deserved that term.

As always, since the years before World War I, the strongest single party was the Social Democrats with 143 seats. That figure represented just under a quarter of the total, meaning that building a coalition would be extremely difficult. This was particularly true because we and the Communists together held 184 seats. This left the theoretical possibility of a Social-Democratic *cum* Catholic Center coalition, except that the Right did not go along. The outcome was a stalemate, and it was into that stalemate that Brüning, citing Article 48, stepped.

The next twenty-eight months, ending on 30 January 1933, were, for us, a period of frustration. It was not that our momentum had been spent. To the contrary; almost until the last moment, we went from one triumph to the next. So great was the number of those who now flocked to join the Party that the latter's character was totally transformed. The fact that many of the new members were not idealists committed to helping Germany out of its difficulties but opportunists eager to join our bandwagon hardly requires mentioning. This problem, incidentally, plagued us throughout the years of the Third Reich. At times it obliged us to close the lists so as to gain breathing space, to clear the air, and to prevent ourselves from being flooded.

I myself had been *Staatloss* (stateless) since 1925. That was when, to avoid being deported, I gave up my Austrian citizenship. Thus I could not have run for the Reichstag even if I had wanted to; but in spite of the advantages membership conferred, such as a nice salary and free railway travel, I most certainly did not. Instead, I had Göring lead our faction, a task he undertook not only with success but with considerable gusto. Nevertheless, as the leader of the second largest party, it was inevitable that I should be widely regarded as head of the opposition. That is why, when the presidential elections came up in early 1932, I saw no way I could avoid campaigning against Hindenburg even though I knew I would lose. To enable me to participate I turned to my old associate Frick. At that time he was serving as Minister of the Interior and of Education of Thuringia, the first state in which National Socialists set up a government. He made me a German citizen, and that was that.

Once again, my collaborators and I gave everything we had. The fact that we had the backing of one of the biggest German industrialists, Fritz Thyssen, certainly helped. Another key figure was the managing director of Lufthansa, *Parteigenosse* (since 1929) Erhard Milch. He put one of his aircraft, a Ju-52, at my disposal. That not only enabled me to travel around much more quickly and more easily than before but gave one of my collaborators the idea behind the famous campaign poster called "Hitler over Germany." The implication, namely that the movement and I formed a dynamic force, as opposed to the staid, if respectable, Hindenburg, was clear.

In the first round, which was held on 13 March, Hindenburg fell just short of obtaining the absolute majority he needed. I came in second with 30 percent of the vote. A slight disappointment, I admit. But still a vast improvement over our performance in September

1930. The rest of the ballots were divided between the Communist Ernst Thälman and the Right-wing nationalist Theodor Düsterberg.

Having come in last, Düsterberg wisely withdrew. So the next round was contested only by three of us. This time Thälman went down to ten percent whereas I went up to 37 percent. That was more than twice what I had gotten in 1930. But Hindenburg got 53 percent. It was not the great triumph he had looked for, perhaps, but is was enough to make sure that Germany would be stuck with him for another seven years. At the time he had already passed his eighty-third birthday. In Germany and elsewhere, life-expectancy was much lower than it is now; the chances that he would survive until his ninetieth, let alone be able to function as he should, seemed quite slim. That was why, no sooner had he been elected than everyone started speculating as to what would happen after his death.

To repeat, Hindenburg had never been a great intellectual luminary. Had it been up to him, he would have retired years earlier. The more so because, as he readily admitted, he was unable to comprehend the complicated economic bills Brüning kept submitting to him for his signature. All they did was frustrate him and make him long for his estate at Neudeck in faraway East Prussia. Not that I blame him. There is nothing economists like better than to obfuscate and to confuse; in this respect, they are almost as bad as lawyers! But he had a strong sense of duty and was as unshakeable and as dignified as any man can be. He was just the kind of oak the German people, in their misery, were looking for.

He and I met for the first time in January 1931. The occasion was a high-level conference held to decide what to do with us, the National Socialists, who seemed to be sweeping all in front of them. It was mutual dislike at first sight. I considered him an old fogey, which, by this time, he undoubtedly was. He for his part called me "The Bohemian Corporal." Historians have often puzzled over the expression. However, to anyone who has followed his career the explanation is simple. In all probability he was confusing my birthplace, Braunau-on-the-Inn, with Braunau, now Broumov, in northeastern Bohemia. As he wrote in his memoirs, *that* Braunau was where, as a young lieutenant during the Prussian–Austria War of 1866, he had smelled powder for the first time. That, as I can testify, is an experience one does not quickly forget.

One of the characteristics of senility is obstinacy, even obtuseness. Whether Hindenburg was senile in the full sense of the word I leave it to the mad-doctors to decide. But he was certainly determined to have his way in not appointing me Reich Chancellor. Since the Reichstag did not function, everything came to depend on the coterie which surrounded him. Perhaps the most important person involved was his son Oskar. Acting as the President's amanuensis, he had a greater influence on him than any of the rest. Yet Oskar von Hindenburg had none of the qualifications needed for holding high office. As a matter of fact, few people had even heard of him before his father was elected President in 1925. Once Hindenburg Sr. had died in 1934, Hindenburg Jr. did Germany and me the inestimable favor of proclaiming that his father had designated me as his successor. With that he disappeared from history; no great loss.

Another figure who played a key role was General (ret.) Wilhelm Gröner. Gröner was a brilliant organizer, railway expert, and logistician. During the war he had been close to Ludendorff. By the time it ended he was able to mitigate some of the effects of the *Dolchstoss* by organizing the army's orderly retreat into the Motherland and preventing its disintegration. Later, he did much to build the Reichswehr. Marrying for the second time in 1930, so quickly did he and his new wife produce a child that it was nicknamed "Nurmi" after the famous Finnish long-distance runner and Olympic champion. He served as Minister of Defense under Müller. When Brüning assumed office he appointed him Minister of the Interior as well.

A much less savory character was another general, Kurt von Schleicher ("Creeper," in German). Schleicher was a political officer *par excellence.* Immediately after World War I, he had been instrumental in negotiating the "pact" between Gröner and the Social Democrats that secured the Reichswehr's support for the Republic while at the same time enabling it to function and develop. Having found his true *métier,* from this point on he never ceased intriguing. This was made evident, for example, by the fact that he brought down Seeckt, the man who, along with Gröner, had done more than anyone else to ensure that Germany should still have any kind of army at all. He also had a hand, a big one, in building up some other military units with the self-explanatory name, the Black Reichswehr. It was Schleicher who first suggested to Hindenburg that the answer to Germany's constitutional crisis was a presidential government under Article 48. And he, having suggested it, did as much as anyone to bring it about.

The fourth member of the cabal was Franz von Papen. A conservative nobleman and a member of the Center Party, Papen was a no one, really. During World War I he had served in our embassy in Washington. As he was being expelled, he committed a blunder that enabled the U.S. authorities to capture all German agents in America. During the 1920s he started dabbling in politics. As late as the first half of 1932, few people had so much as heard his name. But he was suave, not to say, slippery. And he knew how to talk to Hindenburg, which was what really mattered. Their intimacy started in 1925 when Papen, defying his own Party's wishes, decided to vote for the latter as president. This intimacy in turn made him dear to Schleicher, who hoped that, using Papen as a figurehead, he would be able to govern Germany. In the end it was Papen, having turned his back on Schleicher, who persuaded Hindenburg to appoint me.

For a period of some two and a half years these four men, steering Hindenburg now in one direction and then in another, played poker with Germany's fate. Notwithstanding the fact that none of them was very well known or had any number of voters behind him. And notwithstanding the fact that none of them had anything even remotely resembling the qualities a great popular tribune, let alone a statesman of world stature, must have. So far behind the times was Papen himself that he really thought that the masses could be excluded from running the state and "depoliticized," as his speechwriter, Edgar Jung, put it! Contrary to his wishes, though, politics was not limited to the cabal's deeds and misdeeds. All over Germany the leading members of the various parties met, negotiated, horse-bargained, and struck alliances, only to break them as soon as they thought they might profit from doing so. Not being a member of the Reichstag, I did my best to stay above the fray as Hindenburg also tried to do. But others in the Party, especially Göring, kept splashing in it. His extensive ties to the so-called "better circles" made him well suited for the task, one which he greatly enjoyed and, by taking bribes right and left, profited from.

Our own immediate task was to bug the Social Democrats as much as we could. They were, after all, the largest party. They were also the one that, having overthrown the Kaiser in 1918 and held a majority for so long, were mainly responsible for Germany's plight. The Communists apart, we were prepared to cooperate with anyone to carry out this task. That included the Center and, above all, the conservative Right. In October 1931 we even joined the latter in forming the so-called Harzburg Front. Some subsequent German historians, seeking to discredit that Right as well as their own fathers, who had been very much a part of it, have exaggerated its role out of all proportion. Not only did it share much of our ideology, those historians claimed, but it made a decisive contribution to our victory.

But that is nonsense. It is true that, like ourselves, Herr Alfred Hugenberg and his cronies were nationalists. They demanded an end to reparations, the reestablishment of a powerful army, and the restoration of Germany's 1914 borders. In every other respect, though, they were very different from us. We were revolutionary; they were reactionary. We came from, and turned to, the people; they were a bunch of millionaires and snobs who looked down on everyone else and could only appeal to other millionaires and snobs like themselves. We were anti-Semitic—rabidly so, our enemies claimed. They, while not liking Jews very much, did not give the racial problem nearly as much attention as it deserved. All this limited their electoral appeal. In the words of a man whose name I do not wish to mention, they were useful idiots. One of them, the abovementioned Fritz Thyssen, having fallen out with us and left Germany, even admitted as much! They brought us some votes in the Reichstag and quite a lot of money to use to pay the SA and to conduct our propaganda. But that was all.

Nor was politics limited to the smoke-filled rooms where these and other men—there were, as yet, no women among them—met. More, much more, was going on in the streets. Better than anyone else, we understood how important the streets were and that they had to be conquered. "He who rules the streets rules the country" could have been our motto. Our principal instrument in achieving this goal was the SA. The first small unit, which was charged with making sure that hecklers could not disrupt our meetings, was established in February 1920 with Emil Maurice as its commander. In 1921 I replaced him with Hans-Ulrich Klintzsch, a former army officer who knew more about military organization than Maurice did, and then by Ernst Röhm. The term *Sturmabteilung* dates from the same period.

We put our fledgling troops into brown mustard-like uniforms. Not because I liked brown, as some idiot of a psychologist, eager to put me down and to make a name for himself, claimed. In fact, brown was one color conspicuously missing from all three of my homes, the two private ones and the flat in the *Reichskanzlei*. But because, early on, there happened to be on sale a large contingent of uniforms, originally destined for our African colonies, of that color. Armed with chair legs, beer mugs, truncheons, and occasionally knives as well, oftentimes the men engaged in more or less massive *Saalschlachten* (hall battles) against our opponents. I personally taught them to concentrate their forces and to attack one table after another. That, after all, is what Clausewitz also recommended. A fight is a fight, regardless of its size! Using those tactics, they normally emerged on top, enabling me and the Party's other speakers to perform without too many interruptions. Besides, nothing impresses both opponents and bystanders as much as a show of force does. That was the purpose of the uniforms, the parades, the bands, and so on, Our Putsch having failed, the Bavarian Government banned the SA. But it continued to exist under different names.

After we reestablished the Party in 1925, the SA resumed operations. It tackled our opponents, the Communists in particular, not only at meetings but in the streets, too. Now commanded by Franz Pfeffer von Salomon, another former officer, the number of its members grew slowly but surely, from a few dozen at first to tens of thousands at the end of the 1920s, and much more than that after our victory in the 1930 elections. Shortly after those elections Pfeffer fell out with me, however, compelling me to dismiss him. Thereupon, I placed a telephone call to Röhm, who had gone to Bolivia to train the local army. He came.

History, and the historians who write it, often perform strange somersaults. Before 1933, a great many of those who wrote about the SA described it as a bunch of uncouth rowdies. From 1933 to 1945 we saw to it that they would change their tune. Goebbels in particular, by glorifying our dead comrade Horst Wessel, contributed heavily to this. By the late 1930s there probably was not one city, town, or village in the whole of Germany that did not boast its very own *Strasse der SA,* SA Street. Then came 1945, and things changed again. In Babelsberg, which thanks to its villas and the fact that it was the center of movie production became Goebbels' favorite stomping ground, the *Strasse der SA* was renamed after Karl Marx. Imagine that!

Here, I want to put it on the record that the SA were not just a band of rowdies. To be sure, they were a rough bunch, addicted to drinking and brawling. They liked beating up people, including

Communists, socialists, Jews, and similar swine. Who would begrudge them that pleasure? And how, given their low social origins and the nature of their opponents, could they be anything but what they were? The day-to-day lives of many of them were desperately hard, so much so that, at times, we had to organize soup kitchens for them. No wonder they looked forward to the moment when they could put on their brown shirts and take action. Almost any action.

Some of them were homosexuals. But it was not we National Socialists who enacted the notorious so-called "Pink Paragraph," which made it a crime for people of the same sex to have it. That had been done as far back as 1871. I personally did not care much about the matter. Whom they did it with, and how, was their own affair. What I *did* do was to use it retroactively to persuade the German people that my 1934 purge of the SA leadership had indeed been necessary and justified. In 1935, to prevent more of the same, we passed a law broadening the legal definition of punishable homosexual offenses. The rest I left to Himmler in his capacity as chief of the German police. He was far more puritanical and far keener on uprooting homosexuals than I was; even so, they only ever formed a very small minority of those incarcerated in our concentration camps.

More important, right from the beginning the SA were not always as disciplined as they should have been. That was particularly true in Berlin, a city which, then as now, had strong socialist and even communist leanings. In 1930 the local commander, Walter Stennes, called for an SA strike against their own party. A year later, his men even had the gall to storm our offices! This was the kind of thing that ultimately forced me to settle accounts with them. It was painful, but it had to be done.

However, there was another side to the SA, which subsequent historians have done their best to deny. Starting at a time when our Party's prospects looked anything but bright, they joined us and did their duty week after week, month after month, sometimes year after year. All this, for very little pay indeed. Those of them who

were employed gave us their leisure hours. Many also brought along
their wives, girlfriends, and sisters. They distributed rolls, ran soup
kitchens, looked after the men's uniforms, dressed their wounded,
and mourned their dead. Dead they had eighty-six in 1931 alone,
and wounded plenty more. After all, their opponents often gave as
good as they got. Under their rough exterior, many of them were
idealists. Their contribution to our eventual victory was much greater
than that of some others I can think of.

We were, in fact, going from strength to strength. In May 1932,
two months after he was reelected, Hindenburg made Papen Chancellor. Not having the support of anyone else, it's no wonder he
steered a zig-zag course. In an effort to appease us, one of the first
things he did was to rescind the ban Brüning had imposed on the
SA. Not that it made much of a difference, given that the ban had
never been effective. His next move was to dissolve the Reichstag
and to order new elections to be held. Once again we mobilized
all our forces. Once again we campaigned as hard as we knew how
to. I personally held so many speeches in so many cities that I lost
count. My audiences, which ten years earlier could be counted in
the low thousands, now grew to tens of thousands. Entire trainloads
of people came to see and hear me speak. And the results more than
justified our efforts. The number or our seats in the Reichstag almost
doubled, reaching 230, which made us the largest party by far. In fact
we now had more seats than did the Socialists and the Communists
combined. Power appeared to be well within our reach.

First, however, it had to be paid for with blood. In the summer
of 1932 461 street battles took place in Berlin alone, leaving eighty-
two people dead. But it was to no avail. Hindenburg and his advisers
refused to see the light. Instead, they blamed the growing number of
casualties on us. They were strengthened in their determination to do
whatever they could to prevent me from becoming Chancellor. On
13 August, Hindenburg personally told me so. To rub salt into our
wounds, he let it be known that he had advised me to steer my politics

and those of the Party into kinder, gentler channels! So obstinate was
their opposition that some of my followers started giving up. Others,
to the contrary, redoubled their efforts to push me into mounting a
coup.

I, however, was determined to stay the course. Not, Heaven
knows, because I had a particular love of democracy. But because
I knew that Hindenburg would have been all too happy to use the
Reichswehr against us. So, in case we tried to use force, would the
Reichswehr's commander, General Kurt von Hammerstein-Equord.
Known as "the Red General," Hammerstein was as left-leaning as
any German officer has ever been. My boys in the SA, for all their
dedication and courage, did not stand a chance against him. Much
later, it transpired that both Marie-Luise and Helga, Hammerstein's
daughters, were members of the German Communist Party's secret
intelligence service. That explains how, no sooner had I addressed
the Reichswehr High Command 3 February 1933 than the gist of
my words was passed to Moscow.

At the end of 1934 I forced him to resign, thus ridding myself
of his presence. But that did not prevent him and his family from
remaining what the Americans, bluntly but accurately, call a pain in
the ass. Until his death, which took place in November 1943, he
never ceased his treacherous activities. First, he resigned his membership in Berlin's *Herrenklub*, "The Gentlemen's Club," because it
had expelled its Jewish members. As if, given how prestigious the
club and how important the matters that were discussed there, the
presence of members of "the chosen race" could be tolerated! Later,
he and his family joined Brüning in an attempt to save some Jews
from the gas chambers.

He also took an active part in some of the plots against me and
would certainly have assassinated me if only the opportunity had
presented himself. When he finally died, his family refused an official
funeral. The reason, I am told, was that they did not want the
Reichskriegsflagge with the swastika on it to cover his coffin! But that

was not the end of the matter. Both of Hammerstein's sons, Ludwig and Kunrat, were involved in the attempt to kill me on 20 July 1944. After that conspiracy failed, they fled abroad. Unfortunately so, for I would have loved to have them hanged like the rest.

Back to 1932. On 12 September von Papen, to preempt a motion of no confidence by the Communists, dissolved the Reichstag and ordered new elections. When the results were announced in November, it turned out that the Communists, mounting their strongest showing in the whole of German history, had gained eleven seats. Our dear nationalist allies gained four. As for us, we went down from 230 seats to 196. That still left us the strongest party by far; but it was nevertheless a stinging blow to our comrades' morale, especially to that of Goebbels, who was being sued by the Jew Bernhard Weiss, deputy chief of the Berlin police, and did not see a way out. Worst of all, our funding was drying up. All of a sudden people who had supported us in the past no longer wanted to have anything to do with us. It may be true, as they say, that nothing succeeds like success. What is certain is that nothing fails like failure.

Still unable to command a majority, on 17 November Papen, confident that his friend Hindenburg would reappoint him, resigned. However, the old gentleman surprised him, and everyone else, by appointing Schleicher in his place. As it turned out, Schleicher was no more able to form a coalition than his predecessors Papen and Brüning had been. He would, however, not have been up to his reputation as an accomplished intriguer if he had not had a plan up his sleeve. A Plan B, as people say, which, in reality, was Plan A.

First, he offered me the vice-Chancellorship, knowing perfectly well that I would refuse to accept it as I had similar offers in the past. Next, he turned to Gregor Strasser. Strasser no longer served as my chief of propaganda. That was a post I had given to Goebbels. But he still remained number two in the Party. Now Schleicher was hoping to lure him away from it, splitting it and providing him, Schleicher, with some kind of parliamentary base to build on. In return he would get the vice-Chancellorship which Schleicher had just offered me! Discovering this double treachery, I was beside myself with rage. I immediately forced Strasser to resign from the Party and made him take his supporters with him. I also seized the opportunity to make all remaining officials to swear a loyalty oath to me. From that point on, all new appointees had to do the same. Even so, this was the worst crisis the Party had gone through since our Putsch nine years before. It was one whose originators I neither forgot nor forgave.

Later, after he had lost power, Schleicher was heard to complain that he had been Chancellor for fifty-seven days and that, on each of those days, he had been betrayed fifty-seven times. Look who is talking! He held on desperately, but to no avail. The chief intriguer against him was Papen. Though no longer in office, he still retained the confidence of Hindenburg. He also remained High Commissioner for Prussia, a post which, with Hindenburg's support but in direct violation of the Constitution, he had grabbed for himself during his time as Chancellor. Almost as adept at intrigue as Schleicher, his next step was to approach his master with a new proposition. The Right would join the NSDAP and form a government with me at is head. But he himself, acting as deputy chancellor, and his conservative friends, would see to it that I remained a prisoner in their hands. Hindenburg still did not like the idea very much. But he did not have a choice. What was needed was a strong man able to command a majority and restore order. And I was the only one who fit the bill.

The news that Hindenburg had finally agreed to make me Chancellor reached my associates and me as we were gathered at Goebbels' new luxurious flat on the Reichskanzlerplatz (today's Theodor Heuss-Platz) on the evening of 29 January. Our reaction may well be imagined. But not all the news was good. We were told that Schleicher and Hammerstein had put the Potsdam garrison on alert. Between them, they were going to pack Hindenburg off to his estate and, using his name, mount a military Putsch in a last-ditch effort to prevent us from taking over. Hindenburg, for his part, summoned General Werner von Blomberg, who was representing Germany at the Geneva disarmament conference, to come home by the first train to take over from Gröner as Minister of War, a move whose significance was by no means clear. In response, I immediately alerted the Berlin SA. In the event it turned out there had been no coup attempt. But better safe than sorry.

The meeting with the President was scheduled to take place at 10:30 the next morning. There were some last-minute difficulties. Hindenburg had finally given way and was prepared to make me Chancellor. But he was adamant that he would not let me have Papen's post of High Commissioner for Prussia as well. In the end, I had to concede that point. That having been settled, I was sworn in. At 12:00 I emerged from the Presidential Palace on the Wilhelmstrasse to be congratulated by my associates, acclaimed by my supporters, and photographed by the press.

Much later some historians, such as Hans Mommsen, created a veritable cottage-industry by identifying and denouncing all those who, in their opinion, had supposedly "levered" us in our bid for power. Who haven't they blamed? The Right, the Left, the unions, the middle classes, the intellectuals, Hindenburg Sr., Hindenburg Jr., Hugenberg, Papen, Schleicher… Supposedly, all these, and many others, had either failed to resist us or were happy to join us. I want to put it on the record that this is rubbish. Almost to a man, anyone who was somebody in Germany at the time opposed us to the best of his ability and for as long as he could. Why should they have done otherwise? They had their own interests in mind, not ours. We, with myself at the head, did everything, or almost everything, ourselves. In this, as the fact that, even after the setback of November 1932, we were easily the largest Party in the Reichstag, we had the support of the German people, and that was that.

For that evening Goebbels organized a parade of the Berlin SA to celebrate our victory. The men marched past me by the tens of thousands, carrying torches and singing the *Horst Wessel Song* until they were hoarse. Hindenburg too watched, tapping out the rhythm of the march with his cane on the floor. A new era had begun, and I was absolutely determined to make it the greatest in the whole of German history.

Part II

The Years of Peace

Chapter 11

Gleichschaltung

Taking power is one thing. Wielding it effectively, quite a different one. A visitor who did not know my collaborators and me might have considered our, and my, chances of doing so quite poor. Not only was my experience zero, but Hindenburg, on Papen's advice, had appointed me specifically so that I would *not* be able to do as I pleased. And even after I had become Reich Chancellor, he still remained a factor to be reckoned with. Apart from myself, out of twelve ministers only one, Frick, represented the NSDAP. All the rest were either conservative or apolitical and were determined to go their own way.

True, together with my right-wing allies I commanded a majority in the Reichstag. However, it was fairly slim and could not be depended on to carry out the radical, and much-needed, reforms I had in mind. Most of the senior members of Germany's old, venerable, institutions—the army, the bureaucracy, high finance, industry, the churches, and the universities—regarded us National Socialists as *arrivistes*. Not to say *canaille*. After all, with very few exceptions we had neither been born in noble houses, nor raised under privileged circumstances, nor attended the best universities as, almost to a man, they had. Nor did we carry dueling scars on our cheeks. An idiotic fashion bearing witness to an equally idiotic custom, and one which, after a fight in which one of our best-known journalists was killed in an even more idiotic quarrel over a woman, I did my best to abolish.

Two other forces stood in our way. One was the trade unions, most of which were associated with the Communists and the Socialists. In the past they had proved capable of enforcing their will. As, for example, they had done during the well-intentioned but incompetent and ill-fated Kapp Putsch of 1920. To go against them, or rather against the millions of workers they claimed to represent, was madness. We needed them; who else was going to build the new Germany we were planning and fight for it when the time came? Others were the *Länder,* or states, which made up the Reich. In fact the Reich had never been a centralized entity. That had been true of the so-called First Reich—the most decentralized political entity in Europe, much more so than countries such as Spain, England, Italy, Russia, and, above all, France. It was almost equally true of the Second Reich. At that time each *Land* had its own ambassador in Berlin; several of them even had their own armies.

Briefly, our political tradition was, and after 1945, once again became, federal. To be sure, federalism has its advantages. It is one reason why, in Germany, cultural facilities of every kind, such as universities, palaces, museums, theaters, and opera houses, are not concentrated in a single city as, to a very large extent, is the case in England and France. Instead, they are scattered all over the country. Personally, I always felt that the various dialects, dresses, customs, and traditions of each district represent the very essence of Germandom. It was through them that the spirit of the people, bubbling up as it were, manifested itself. As such they were worth preserving and fostering. Politically, though, federalism is and remains problematic. It makes it very hard for the central government to enforce its will.

I did not wait until my hundred days' grace were over. In fact, I did not have even a single day's grace. Holding the first Cabinet meeting just a few hours after my appointment, I moved to dissolve the Reichstag and to hold new elections. My purpose in doing so was to allow us to pass an Enabling Act, which would give us the right to govern by decree, without the Reichstag. As I had expected, our right-wing allies and the Catholic Center raised some objections. I won them over by promising that I would govern constitutionally.

That, incidentally, is a promise I kept. During our years in power we National Socialists, and I personally, were presented with plenty of ideas for a new constitution. By none more so than by Herr Professor Carl Schmitt, the famous jurist and political scientist whose often incomprehensible tomes are still being hotly debated in Germany and abroad. In the end, though, we preferred to keep the one we already had. Changing it would have brought down on our heads every single jurist in the country. Personally, I dislike jurists. They are cretins, always hiding behind their paragraphs in the hope of disguising their utter lack of common sense. I would have loved to create an *ambience* in which no right-thinking German man would lower himself to the point of studying law. But I admit that, for any large organization, they are a necessity. An evil one, to be sure, but one which unfortunately we cannot do without; witness our top-level SS, SD (*Sicherheitsdienst,* Security Service) and Gestapo organization, all of which were full of them.

Instead, we undermined the Constitution until all that was left of it was essentially a hollow shell. We also modified it when necessary. As, for example, we did in 1934 when we amalgamated my position as Chancellor with that of President. But we never replaced it. In any case, after some quibbling I got my way. The elections would be held on 5 March. We, my colleagues and I, immediately threw ourselves into the fray. This time, as one may imagine, money was not short. Not only did we receive large sums from the industrialists, but we generously helped ourselves to the state's resources as well. As usual, the SA played a key role. Enjoying greater freedom of action than ever before, some of its men actually wore armbands designating them as auxiliary police. It protected our meetings, broke up those of our opponents, and ransacked the offices of opposition newspapers as, owing to their lies, they deserved to be. It also plastered the walls with propaganda posters, held marches and popular concerts, and briefly did what it could to impress voters and to attract them to our side.

A week before the appointed date we had an unexpected stroke of luck. On the evening of 27 February I was dining with Goebbels, Hoffmann, and some others when Hanfstängl called and said that the Reichstag was going up in flames. At first I thought he was drunk! It was, however, all too horribly true. In the aftermath four people were arrested: three Bulgarian Communists and one Dutch Communist, Marinus van der Lubbe. The Bulgarians were tried and acquitted. One of them, Georgi Dimitrov, later ended up as his country's first Communist dictator; that showed what our justice system was like in those days and what a long way we still had to go before it, too, was *gleichgeschaltet* (coordinated) with the other elements of the state and made to work smoothly with them. As for van der Lubbe, who, unlike the others, was caught torch in hand, by all accounts he was something of an oddball. He was found guilty and beheaded. How, considering the size of the building, he could have set the fire single-handedly remains a mystery to the present day.

Not that it mattered. Having dealt with the Communists for years, we National Socialists knew very well who was responsible for the dastardly act. We leaped at the opportunity and did what had to be done. As to the claims that we ourselves had set the fire, they are too ridiculous to merit an answer. Supported by Moscow, which like an octopus was sending out its tentacles in all directions, the Communists were dangerous enemies. The reason was that, as I knew from my days in Vienna, they were the only ones who possessed a *Weltanschauung*, one which, however perverted it might be, had the power to carry the masses. "Arise, ye wretched of the earth!" I did not want to take any chances. That is why, on the very next day, I had Hindenburg sign a decree that abolished certain civil liberties—freedom of speech, freedom from non-judicially-ordered search, the whole rotten liberal rigmarole—and imposed the death penalty for certain crimes. It also authorized the central government to take over from those of the states in case a national emergency demanded doing so.

For all our campaigning and occasional intimidation of opponents, the elections themselves did not go quite as well as we had hoped. Our efforts notwithstanding, we National Socialists did not obtain an absolute majority. Even with the help of our allies we still fell far short of the two-thirds majority needed to pass the Enabling Law. In a way, it did not matter. We were determined that there should be no more elections for a long, long time to come. Partly because we did not believe in counting noses as a method of government, and partly because we had no intention of giving up our hard-won power. Not then, not ever. As Goebbels put it on the very first day, we would have to be carried out first. That, too, was a promise we kept.

My next problem was to do away with the state governments and to centralize all power in our hands. On the evening of 9 March, just four days after the elections, our forces swung into action. Our key man on the spot was General (ret.) Franz von Epp, another *Pour le Mérite* holder who had joined us almost immediately after the war. A Bavarian by birth, in 1919–20 he had played a prominent role both in the border fighting with Poland and in the suppression of the Munich Communist "government." Now I appointed him Reich Commissioner; he took over the government facilities and functions in Bavaria, and that was that. His move gave the signal for similar ones in the remaining, smaller states. Thus within twenty-four hours, we National Socialists accomplished what not even Bismarck, the greatest German statesman of all time, had been able to do: namely, take power away from the *Länder* and concentrate it in the hands of the Reich, where it properly belongs.

Personally, I was not at all sorry to see the Reichstag gone. It had been, and in spite of its new glass cupola still remains, a big, ugly lump of a building typical of the pompous period during which it was built. But its destruction made us look for a proper setting to open the new one. As so often, it was Goebbels who came up with the idea and oversaw is execution. We would hold the meeting not in Berlin but at Potsdam's Garnisonkirche; the 200-year-old church King Friedrich Wilhelm I had built for the local garrison where the bones of King Frederick II were resting at the time. In the whole of Germany, no other building had such long and strong links with the Prussian/German military tradition.

The date chosen for the opening of the first Reichstag of the Third Reich was 21 March. That too was a happy choice, because 21 March 1871 had been the day on which Bismarck opened the first Reichstag of the Second Reich. I shall not go into the details, which were shown in every newsreel in every movie house all over Germany. Suffice it to say that so successful was the ceremony that even Hindenburg, who for over two years had done what he could to prevent my appointment, was visibly moved. The high point came at the end. Making a deep bow, I shook Hindenburg's hand—a symbolic union of the new Germany with the old. From that point on our relationship improved. The better he understood what my collaborators and I were trying to do, the easier he found it to get along with me.

Two days later, we passed the Enabling Law by a vast majority. How did we do it? Simple: by making sure the Communists would not attend. A few of them were already dead, killed by our brave, if unruly, SA boys as an act of spontaneous revenge for everything that they had gone through during the previous years. Some were interned in the new, improvised, concentration camps we were setting up, and some were running for their lives. That only left those old windbags, the Social Democrats. To a man, those of them who succeeded in getting into the building voted against us. However, as I was not slow to tell them during the meeting itself, their time was past.

With that, the legal basis we needed for taking decisive action had been put in place. Our next targets were the trade unions. Against them, I used deception—yes, deception. Deception in the service of a great national cause is no vice, especially if your opponents are a bunch of mendacious Marxists. I made my first move as early as 20 February. In a talk to some twenty of Germany's biggest industrial magnates, I made them understand that I was absolutely not the Red bogyman some of them thought I was. To the contrary, I was going to do what they wanted most: to wit, keep private enterprise intact, make sure proprietors retained control over the property by destroying the Communists once and for all, and rebuild our armed forces on an unprecedented scale. All this would enable them to realize their dream of making lots and lots of money, the only thing those rich creeps care about.

Having covered my rear in this way, I turned around. First, I made the 1st of May into a national holiday. That was something no previous German government, not even those headed by the Social Democrats, had done. The move took the unions totally by surprise, filling them with euphoria and lulling them to sleep. It was a nice birthday present for them, so to speak. I personally, in a speech held at Berlin's Tempelhof Airport in front of 100,000 people, honored the German worker and promised that May Day would be celebrated forever. On the very next day I sprang a surprise on them. I had the SA and the police occupy the trade unions' headquarters throughout Germany. The unions' leaders were arrested, their assets confiscated, and they themselves dissolved. Collective bargaining, that scourge which can and often does paralyze entire countries for weeks on end, was abolished. So, in effect, was the right to strike. We expected no resistance. And none materialized.

All this having been accomplished, the time had come to deal with the last obstacle to our rule, i.e. the parties. On 10 May 1933 I had the police seize the assets of the Social Democratic Party. The operation went off without a hitch. Ten days later, the remaining Social Democratic representatives in the Reichstag—those who had not yet been arrested or fled—obliged me by voting in favor of my foreign policy. How much spittle can a man take while pretending it is rain? On 22 June Frick, as Minister of the Interior, abolished the Party, for so long the largest and strongest in Germany, by means of a simple decree. The rest took the hint. Over the next fortnight they shut down without any need for further action on our part. On 12 November we held yet another election which confirmed all this. With that, the corpse of democracy was not only buried but had an epitaph erected over it as well.

That did not prove the end of the matter. It is said that revolutions devour their children. Unfortunately, ours was no exception. Starting as early as 1920, the SA had been one of the strong pillars on which our movement rested. But for it, our progress and ultimate victory would have been inconceivable. Expanding year by year, on the way it spawned various subordinate organizations. Chief among them were the National Socialist Motor Corps, known as the NSKK, and, above all, the SS. Having absorbed other paramilitary organizations, such as the right-wing Stalhelm, by late 1933 it had a paper strength of three million men, thirty times as many as the Reichswehr. More than any other party organization, the SA had always been permeated by socialist ideas. That was especially true of the rank and file. Our seizure of power, far from ending their revolutionary impulse, reinforced it. They felt they could do much, much more. And, of course, they were looking for their proper rewards in the form of jobs for themselves and bread for their families.

Many of their commanders shared these feelings. However, with them much more was at stake. They hoped and expected to take the place of the Reichswehr, thus turning themselves into the army of the Reich. Röhm personally thought in these terms. He refused to accept that the National Socialist Revolution had largely ended. Nor did he make a secret of his belief that the old officer corps was no good and of his hope to be appointed chief of staff. But for all my sympathy for the ordinary SA-men who had worked so long and so faithfully on our behalf, that was something I could not allow.

There were two reasons for this, both of them of the utmost importance. First, the army at this time was the one major institution which we National Socialists had not yet been able to bring under our full control. As the Putsch of 20 July 1944 was to show, in a sense we never did. The gentlemen with their monocles, gold leaf, breeches, red stripes, and colored ribbons formed a cohesive caste that had to be treated with some caution. Or else, probably using Hindenburg as their rallying-point, they might have turned against us and taken over. Needless to say, we ourselves would not have taken such a move lying down. The outcome would have been civil war and chaos, perhaps even foreign intervention. Second, with all respect to Röhm and his men, they were not the army. Only the latter had, or could develop, what it took to prepare Germany for war and to fight it if and when necessary.

There things remained for the time being. In early 1934 I tried to find a compromise between the two organizations several times. A greater contrast could scarcely be imagined. On one side stood my newly appointed Minister of War, General von Blomberg. He was aristocratic, tall, elegant, and very handsome. Too handsome for his own good, as it turned out. His family had provided more than one German state with officers and civil servants for generations past. On the other stood Röhm, a former captain, man of the people, and swashbuckler.

Several times, I personally drew up documents defining their respective sphere of action. Military training and preparation for the army, which was to remain our nation's only organization entitled to bear arms; and political tasks for the SA. Much to my annoyance, all my attempts failed. In the spring things went from bad to worse. Göring, drawing on material obtained by his secret, newly established, *Forschungsamt* (wire-tapping service), started forwarding me reports that the SA was acting like a state within a state. It was setting aside money—some of it, apparently, provided by the French embassy in Berlin—collecting arms, training its men, and preparing to launch a coup. More evidence of the same sort was brought to me by the Army High Command, which had its own intelligence organization.

I felt obliged to Röhm. He and I had gone through so much together; but for him we would never have been able to mount the 1923 Putsch, unsuccessful though it was. Later, in 1930, when I needed him, he came with no questions asked. Among all my subordinates, he was the only one whom I allowed to address me by my first name. But now, as he apparently prepared to take the route Napoleon had taken in 1799, I felt I had no choice. As I had done with the trade unions, I started by protecting my rear. To this end I arranged a meeting with the commanders of the armed forces aboard the newly commissioned armored cruiser *Deutschland.* I promised them that, whatever Röhm might say and do, they would remain Germany's only armed organization. I also stated that they would have a free hand in rebuilding Germany's military power.

In return, I demanded that they should not interfere while I was dealing with the SA as I saw fit. I additionally promised them that they would not have to interfere and that, in consequence, their hands would be kept clean. They were, after all, "men of honor." Few things interested them more than that. The bargain having been struck, in June I turned to Hindenburg and explained the situation. The old war horse was clearly dying. His mind was already more or less in Valhalla; nevertheless, he gave me his blessing.

This time my main instrument for doing what had to be done was Heinrich Himmler, commander of the SS. The SS, short for *Schutzstaffel* or defense squadron, dated back to 1925, when I ordered the establishment within the SA of a small force that would be loyal to me alone and do anything I ordered them to. I called them *Verfügungstruppe*—roughly translatable as "troops at [my] disposal."

In 1929, the year in which I appointed Himmler as its head, it numbered just 290 men. Two years later, Himmler himself set up the SD within the SS. It soon joined the others in providing me with intelligence about Röhm's deeds and misdeeds.

In time Himmler, "Heinrich you make me shudder" as, like Goethe's Faust, he was sometimes known, acquired a sinister reputation for terror. Peopled hated seeing him come and were happy to see him go. This was rather curious, for he always looked and behaved like an inoffensive little clerk. And at heart, a petty little clerk is exactly what he was. Born in 1900 as the son of a high-school principal in Munich, he had missed the World War because of his age. Consequently, he developed a life-long romantic view of what war was all about. His greatest dream was to become a general and to command an army in the field, a post for which, it turned out, he was totally unsuited. Meanwhile, he studied agriculture and at one point tried his hand at raising chickens! A photograph taken during our 1923 Putsch shows him standing near a roadblock, with a vacant expression on his face, holding a standard. Later, he married a woman several years his senior of whom, it was said, he was absolutely terrified.

Appearances can be misleading. In his case they certainly were. Mouse-like as he looked, during the war Himmler surprised everyone by starting a second family with his secretary with whom he had an illegitimate daughter. More important, behind the polite façade, the pedantic demeanor, and the pince-nez with its thick glasses, there was a first-class administrative brain. No one knew better how to acquire power, expand it, and maintain it even if it meant going against other, equally ambitious and equally ruthless men such as Göring and, later, my Minister of Munitions, Albert Speer. He also had a strong sense of the theatrical. That quality helped him and his black-uniformed myrmidons put on some of the most impressive shows—tattoos, parades, and the like—in the whole of history.

It was Göring and Himmler who, happy to see the SA cut down to size, secretly prepared troops, weapons, transport, and lists of people who were to be executed. I myself once again resorted to deception. First, I summoned the most important SA leaders, with Röhm at their head, to a meeting at the resort town of Bad Wiesee on the Tegernsee, some fifty kilometers south of Munich. Next, I took Göring and Viktor Lutze, an SA general whom I knew I could trust, along with me to the much-publicized wedding of one of our Gauleiters in Essen. It was during that ceremony that the news arrived that Papen, acting by way of his dear friend Oskar, had prevailed on Hindenburg to see him.

Pygmy though he was, Papen had in fact been causing some trouble. Speaking at the University of Marburg on 17 June, he expressed his dissatisfaction, and that of his conservative friends, with the way things were going. He even dared criticize the way we dealt with the Jews, whom he called "helpless segments of the people"! Parts of the speech were printed in the press. Faced with opposition from both left and right, I knew it was now or never. Any further delay could only make the situation worse.

The appointed day was 30 June 1934. 29 June found me at Bad Godesberg, where Goebbels and the commander of my personal bodyguard, SS General Joseph ("Sepp") Dietrich also arrived. That evening we and several others flew to Munch. The sun was just coming up when we entered the Bavarian Ministry of the Interior, where the local SA commanders had been summoned. I personally tore the epaulets from the traitors' shoulders and had them arrested. Next, we drove to Bad Wiesee, where we stormed into the hotel. One by one, Röhm and the rest were rounded up. At least one of them, SA General Edmund Heines, was found in bed with a youth.

I ordered six of the miscreants to be shot on the spot. Röhm, who was arrested but baited me by refusing to use a pistol that was handed to him, had to be shot as well. But that was only the beginning. In Munich and Berlin the SS execution squads received their orders and went into action. A few dozen other top SA officers apart, the dead included Jung, who had written Papen's speech for him, Gregor Strasser and General von Schleicher, the traitors who had tried to break up the Party and take it away from me, and General Ferdinand von Bredow. The latter was a trusted collaborator of Schleicher's and almost as great a traitor as his master. I also took the opportunity to deal with Kahr and Seisser, the men who ten years earlier had given me their "word of honor" and subsequently broken it.

Not all the killings were ordered from above, i.e. by me, Göring, Himmler, and Himmler's second in command, Reinhard Heydrich. Several were carried out by individuals out to settle accounts with their personal enemies. At least one, that of a Munich music critic named Willi Schmid, was due to a mistaken identification. One cannot make an omelet without breaking eggs, can one? However that may be, by the evening of the 30th the operation, later nicknamed "The Night of the Long Knives," was essentially over.

Abroad, the reaction was as we had expected. Incited by the Jews, both officials and the press did what they could to blacken our image and to denounce us as the new barbarians. Not so inside the country, where the reactions were almost uniformly positive. Not just those of the press, which were orchestrated by Goebbels, but those of Hindenburg and Blomberg, both of whom congratulated me for what I had done. Later, I learned that even some future participants in the conspiracy of 20 July 1944 had expressed their agreement. On 3 July 1934 I went on the air to explain myself to the German nation. Then and later, it was the only community to which I felt myself accountable. The SA leadership, I told them, had conspired with a foreign power to betray the Party. They had planned a Putsch against the Reich Government. They were within hours of going into action when my lieutenants and I discovered them. Given the situation, I had no choice but to appoint myself supreme judge of the German people and to do what had to be done. For this I took full responsibility.

Just how many men (no women, incidentally) died on that day, not even I have ever been able to find out. Subsequent historians have put their number at anything between 76 and 1,000. However, the last-named figure seems to have been picked out of empty air. It is certainly a vast exaggeration. Taking the unauthorized killings into account, the true one might be around 200. Here I want to put it on record that, street and beer hall brawls apart, our National Socialist struggle for power, though not without some violence, fell far short of civil war. Over ten years or so, the total number of those who died was probably under 2,000. This was not the Chinese Revolution in which, by some estimates, six million died. Nor was it the Russian Revolution, nor the French one with mademoiselle guillotine standing in the city square and waiting for the cartloads of aristocrats who were brought to have their heads cut off. Even the Paris Commune of 1871, a relatively minor episode as such things go, claimed many more.

On 2 August, just a month after these events, the news arrived that Hindenburg had died. He had certainly not been without his shortcomings. He was slow and obstinate and could be as obtuse as any man has ever been. In his last years he surrounded himself with worthless advisers, whom I shall not name again. It took him a long time to realize that the National Socialist Movement was more than a bunch of rednecks and I, not merely a Bohemian Corporal.

To repeat, politically, he was a monarchist. Throughout the period from 1919 to 1934 he wanted nothing so much as the restoration of the Kaiser, whom he saw as his only legitimate sovereign, or, if that was impossible, of one of his sons. Only at the last moment did he change his mind and told his son Oskar that he wanted me as his successor. But it must be granted that he also had tremendous courage, strength, and dignity. It was these qualities that, during the war, made him a good counterpart to Ludendorff's more nervous nature and enabled them to form the excellent team they did. He certainly deserved the place he has taken in German history.

As had been decided in advance, I now assumed his duties in addition to mine. On 19 August forty-two million German citizens, both men and women, went to the polls. Outside the U.S., which in this respect has always formed a class of its own, it was the largest occasion of its kind in history until then. When the results came in, it became clear that ninety percent of the voters cast their ballots in favor of my fusing both functions and exercising them. For our country, a new dawn was coming.

Chapter 12

It's the Economy, Stupid

How many historians have written that the Party and I owed our rise to the 1929 economic crisis? The claim is undoubtedly correct, but it is also trivial. One does not need to be a *Herr Professor Doktor* or write learned books in order to understand that bad times demand new leaders and new solutions. In addition, unless a leader can come up with such solutions, he will quickly lose the trust of the people. That is why, just two days after I assumed office, I addressed them by radio. I made it crystal-clear that I understood the situation and sympathized with the enormity of their sufferings. And I promised action—quick, decisive action.

In fact we were in an awful mess. Nor, looking around, could we see anyone to help us get out of it. Certainly not the so-called "international community" as represented by the League of Nations, which kind- but feeble-minded people talked about so much. To the contrary, it did everything it could to make us sink deeper still. The victors in the World War still insisted that reparations be paid, though their ability to extract them in practice was declining fast. Among the most nefarious measures they took was the 1931 Smoot–Hawley Bill. It raised customs-barriers over 20,000 imported goods to their highest levels in American history. The outcome was to cut German, and European, exports to the U.S. by three quarters. One trading company after another was forced to close. Half a century later, President Reagan himself said that the bill "made it virtually impossible for anyone to sell anything in America and…spread the Great Depression around the world." Right he was.

To help me to get the economy moving again I turned to Dr. Hjal-
mar Schacht, a banker of international reputation, He was also a
liberal-conservative and a terrible snob. No man was ever haughtier
or looked down more on ordinary people, us National Socialists
included. The feeling was heartily reciprocated. But he had a strong
record; in November 1923, at the height of the inflation, President
Ebert and Chancellor Stresemann appointed him special commissioner for currency. So successful were his efforts to stabilize the mark
that he was made President of the Reichsbank, the Central Bank. He
remained at that post until the spring of 1930.

Over the subsequent three years, recognizing that there really was
no alternative, he drew closer to some elements in our party. Using
his links with his conservative friends, he helped us obtain funds.
The aforementioned meeting with Germany's leading industrialists
was held in his house. In March 1933 I reappointed him President
of the Reichsbank. Later, I made him Minister of Economics as well.
To be sure, the man was never quite filled with the kind of National
Socialist élan I valued most. He was much too elitist for that. Nevertheless, he proved a good choice. I provided the indomitable driving
will; Schacht provided the technical and administrative details of
the program that we now started putting into place. Essentially, it
consisted of spending, spending, and spending. The objective was to
generate work and to put money into people's pockets. They, in turn,
would spend it to buy what they needed, and so on. Once given a
push the avalanche would start rolling, growing ever larger as it did
so. At the time all this represented a revolutionary policy. It was the
very opposite, I should add, from the one Brüning, as well as Ramsay
MacDonald in England and Herbert Hoover in the U.S., had been
implementing from 1929 on. With them the response to the crisis,
and the fiscal deficits to which it gave rise, had been to cut and save.

The way Schacht explained it to me, two obstacles stood in our
way. First, rearmament was illegal under the Treaty of Versailles. At
the time we were too weak to resist the Allies, so we would have to

find ways of raising money without drawing the attention of foreign experts to what we were doing. Second, the same Treaty, specifically with a view to preventing such rearmament, prohibited our government from borrowing more than 100,000,000 marks from the Reichsbank. The time was to come when we could safely ignore both issues; for the time being, though, we had no choice but to avoid provoking our enemies.

Schacht neatly solved the problem by forming a limited liability company named *Metallurgische Forschungsesellschaft* (Metallurgical Research Company), or MEFO for short. The company itself only existed on paper, and its capital amounted to no more than one million marks. Building on these slender foundations, during the six years leading up to World War II he used it to issue no fewer than 12 *billion* marks' worth of bills. The bills were convertible into marks after five years. Until then they were guaranteed by the Reich government. Industry, pressed by us of course, used them to pay its suppliers. As a result, there came into being an economy within an economy. The vast majority of ordinary Germans never put their eyes on a MEFO bill. Most of them probably did not even know they existed. Nor, going about their day-to-day business, was there any reason why they should. Using this device, we were able to increase our deficit by two thirds, no less. Other measures included high corporate taxes, curbs on shareholders' rights, limits on dividends, and increased taxes on profits derived from the sale of stocks. All of this encouraged long-term investment and growth.

To stimulate our foreign trade Schacht, making full use of the fact that we were Europe's largest importers of foodstuffs by far, negotiated a series of reciprocal agreements with a number of other countries, chiefly in Eastern Europe and the Balkans. They enabled us to use our industrial products to pay for our imports of food and raw materials. All calculations were made in marks, and any surpluses our trade partners enjoyed were held in German banks in special accounts created for the purpose. All this enabled us to keep our scarce dollar and sterling reserves. To make sure we did, we imposed strict control on all non-government foreign transactions. Later, in 1939–41, we put in place somewhat similar arrangements with Russia. To such effect that the last train, carrying supplies, crossed the border fewer than twenty-four hours before we launched our attack on that country.

I do not pretend to understand every detail of the financial wizardry involved. But it certainly worked. By 1935 the English magazine *Economist* was praising our economic recovery, noting that it was proceeding faster than anywhere else in Europe. By 1939 our gross national product had increased eighty-one percent—eighty-one percent—over the 1932 figure. Even if one subtracts the forty percent we had lost in 1929–32, a forty-percent increase in seven years still represented a substantial achievement. Our interest rate had been halved, and the stock exchange had responded accordingly. Thanks partly to the measures just described and partly to my refusal to go on paying reparations, our foreign debt had also been stabilized.

Last, not least, unemployment, that great scourge of the period 1929–32, disappeared. By 1936 everyone who wanted to could easily find a job. For those who did not want to, meaning the *Arbeitscheu,* or work-shy, we had our concentration camps, complete with their famous slogan, *Arbeit Macht Frei.* There was nothing like a stay in one of those camps to teach people what was what! Starting in 1937–38, indeed, the place of unemployment was taken by a shortage of labor, especially skilled labor of the kind our factories needed. We achieved all this without devaluating our currency and without leading to any inflation worth mentioning, measures which, though they were often urged on me, I always refused to use because of the negative impact they would have on public opinion. After all, for countless ordinary people my integrity, *Erhlichkeit,* was the ultimate guarantee that their hard-earned savings would not be taken away from them as they had been after 1918. "An absolutely unique achievement," as the famous American economist John Kenneth Galbraith wrote much later.

To be sure, here and there people grumbled. Don't they always? They specifically mentioned long hours, poor working conditions, and some shortages of consumer goods such as poultry, fruit, and clothing. This, in turn, led to the creation of a black market. It reflected the fact that we were hard pressed to produce both guns and butter. Choices had to be made. And we, unlike so many of our predecessors and successors both in Germany and abroad, had what it took to make them and stick to them.

Take the problem of motorization. At the time we Germans had far fewer registered motor cars per head of the population than England and France did. That's not to mention the U.S., which had about as many cars as the rest of the world put together. But that was a problem we had inherited from the Republic. Even without taking into account the enormous Volkswagen project, which would have provided every family with a car but had to be put on ice at the outbreak of the war, we multiplied production over and over again. On the way we forced some firms to merge, thereby driving prices downward and making sure that the share of foreign-built cars on our roads would fall from forty percent in 1928 to under ten percent just six years later. If we still did not have quite as many cars as some critics thought we should, then one reason for this was that our railway system led the world in terms of both size—it was the largest single public enterprise—and quality. On the whole, our countrymen were enthusiastic about the measures we put in place. Recalling the situation as it had been just a few years earlier, they had every reason to be.

I well understood that only political and military means can create a great power. To last, though, it also needs artistic expression. That is why, defying the naysayers and the bean counters, we built and built and built. We weren't building just weapons, on which I will say more in a moment, but everything we could think of and then some. New housing projects for our population which, owing to the measures we put in place, was starting to grow again; new factories, new ministries, new theaters, new barracks, and new airports; new railways, new canals, new bridges, new theaters—especially open-air ones—and new museums; and new sports facilities, of course, in order to help us achieve the Graeco-Germanic ideal of *mens sana in corpore sano.* Of those, the largest was the Olympiastadion in Berlin. Originally it was constructed for the 1936 Olympic Games. It was so successful that, renovated after more than half a century of neglect due first to the war and then to the Communist government of the GDR, it was used again for those held in the same city in 2000.

In Augsburg, Bayreuth, Breslau, Dresden, and a dozen other cities new buildings shot out of the ground like mushrooms. My own principle was that money was no object. I simply assumed that the necessary funds would be found, and, almost invariably, they were. On one occasion I encouraged a certain mayor to build something— I think it was a new community center, or whatever—for his town. He hesitated, said that he did not know where the money would be coming from, etc. etc. Finally, he asked me to assure him—in writing!—that the bill would be paid. What he got, by return mail, was his dismissal.

The crowning glory of our efforts was the system of *Autobahnen,* or motorways. I myself was descended from simple folks. I could appreciate the beauty of horses, and even commissioned several gigantic statues of them for Munich and other cities. However, I had never cared for them as so many of my self-appointed "betters" did. Instead, starting around 1920, I had taken an interest in motor cars, talking to my Mercedes dealer and reading manuals until I became quite knowledgeable about them. Campaigning for the party, I had driven all over Germany many, many times. That is how I learned to appreciate the advantages of this means of transportation over the railways and to enjoy the incomparable beauties of our German Motherland.

The idea of building special roads for our automobiles and trucks, as *the* most important form of twentieth-century transport, was in the air. It had been discussed by the various ministries even before our rise to power. Against the background of the economic crisis, though, my predecessors did not have the determination and the *esprit* to carry it out on anything like the scale needed to make a difference. I, by contrast, wasted no time. As early as 11 February, fewer than two weeks after I entered office, I spoke to a gathering at the Berlin International Motor Show. I told them that, in the future, the state of the roads would act as the principal yardstick by which a country's prosperity would be judged. Like so many of my prophecies, incidentally, this one turned out to be spot-on.

My man in charge was Friedrich (Fritz) Todt. Todt had joined the party as early as 1922. Thus he had every right to consider himself one of my oldest fellows and followers. By trade he was a civil engineer; in fact his dissertation dealt with the construction of roads. Now he threw himself into the job, designing and building roads right and left. By his own estimate, directly or indirectly, the project would provide work for no fewer than 600,000 people. In September 1933 I personally turned the first sod on the Hamburg-to-Basel motorway. By that time, so much did the workers on the project admire, not to say worship, me that, no sooner had I turned my back, than they took away the little earth I had shoveled as souvenirs.

But that was just the beginning of my involvement. I wanted to make sure that my *Autobahnen*, far from spoiling the natural beauty of our Germany, would enhance it. That is why, in this case, as in that of many other construction projects, I saw to it that the constructors were not just engineers but architects. I myself looked into the building materials used and the way in which contours, bridges, rest areas, and so on were built. Decades before anyone else started doing so, we even paid attention to the impact on wildlife! At that time, the project was by far the largest of its kind undertaken by any country. As our propaganda never tired of saying, it could be compared to the construction of the pyramids or the Great Wall of China. And it worked. To this day the German *Autobahnen* are often considered a model of their kind.

The overall objective was to get the gears of the economy running again and to modernize the country's transportation system. I remember how, at one time, we were considering building a motorway from Munich to Augsburg. Someone told me that there was little traffic between the two cities. Do you think, I answered, that such will remain the case after the road is built? But it also goes without saying that the *Autobahnen,* running all over Germany as they did, served military ends as well as civilian ones. Indeed, *not* having them do so was just the kind of stupidity only our bourgeois could think of! They made it much easier to move our troops from one theater of war to another.

It is one of my deepest regrets that, owing to the outbreak of war, construction of the *Autobahnen* had to be interrupted. I planned to renew it as soon as circumstances would allow; unfortunately, that only happened during the 1950s. At that time I was no longer around to provide direction. But most of my people were. Of course they did their best to disassociate themselves from me. But there is no denying that they continued the work in my spirit.

As we rebuilt the economy, there were growing complaints about corruption. As long as we stayed in power, they remained muted. After all, ours was not a liberal state. We did not believe in permitting every Tom, Dick, and Harry to say whatever he thought about everyone and everything without distinction or regard for the consequences. Later, though, some historians made a fetish of the issue. They could say little against me. Everyone knew I had no gang of hungry relatives to feed and that I lived abstemiously enough, so much so, in fact, that there were many jokes about the subject. Goebbels, who always had his ear to the ground, saw to it that I was told about them, and I quite enjoyed them. The worst thing my critics could accuse me of was that, upon entering office, I made sure the tax authorities got off my back. So I did, but only to avoid distractions and to enable me to concentrate on my proper work. Better that than not understand my own tax bill, as Reagan later said was the case with him. In any case, this was decades before many other heads of state, including the kings and queens of England, started paying income tax either.

Another much-repeated claim was that not only did I close my eyes to what was going on but that I actively encouraged it. That is an exaggeration. However, it is certainly true that I wanted to reward those who helped me on my way. The worst error any politician can make is to suppose that people are better than they are. Whatever Napoleon may have said, to maintain their loyalty, especially over time, one must give them more than just colored ribbons. He himself set the example. So much so that, in his last years in power, he complained that his marshals had turned into *grands seigneurs*. Instead of leading their men in battle, they would much rather enjoy their estates! I followed in his footsteps. As, for instance, by giving large (and tax-free) sums of money to some of my senior officials and generals who, through their efforts on Germany's behalf, deserved them or who had fallen on hard times.

Some of the things we did, such as giving old party members priority when they were looking for work, did not really represent corruption at all. We were not liberals and did not believe in *their* kind of distributive justice. In fact the system had been copied, lock, stock, and barrel, from the pre-1918 Prussian/German *Rechtstaat* (state based on law) on which both our own scholars and foreign ones have lavished so much praise. In particular, I saw to it that NCOs should get the gravy. Rightly so, because it is the NCOs, men who have reenlisted, who form the indispensable backbone of any army. And also because they make the best low-level civil servants and elementary teachers of all. Nor were we National Socialists exactly the only ones to provide jobs for the boys. If, in Germany and abroad, some effete intellectuals did not like the system, then that was their problem.

But such things are small potatoes and are hardly worth mentioning. I realized very well that many of my associates were helping themselves to state money and/or took massive bribes and/or found other ways to enrich themselves. The champion in this game was Göring. Others included trusty old Wilhelm Frick; Robert Ley, my Minister of Labor; Joseph Goebbels, whom I appointed Minister of Propaganda; my old comrade Alfred Rosenberg; my one-time lawyer, Hans Frank; my Foreign Minister (from 1936 on) Joachim von Ribbentrop; my Party Secretary, Martin Bormann; most of the Gauleiters; as well as countless smaller fry. Some I knew; others not. All of them accumulated more or less considerable fortunes, often in the form of country houses and valuable works of art as well as money in the bank. First in Germany and then in other countries, too, some of the property they confiscated or bought at ridiculously low prices had been expropriated from Jews. Serves the latter right.

Among the few exceptions known to me were Speer, the *haute bourgeois* architect whom I made my Minister of Munitions, Himmler, the incorrigible romantic, and his deputy Heydrich. In fact the importance they attributed to *Anständigkeit,* best translated (I am told) as a combination of decency, incorruptibility, and reliability, was one of the things that kept the last two, who in other respects were ill matched, together. But even in their cases that only meant that they refrained from amassing property and displaying it, not that they did not live as opulently as they wished at the expense of the organizations they led.

During the last few years before the war our emphasis shifted. Our initial objective of doing away with unemployment and getting the economy moving had been accomplished. So we got to the stage where we could start preparing for war in earnest. I decided to place overall responsibility on Göring as Plenipotentiary for the Four Year Plan. To be sure, Göring's qualifications as an academic economist were dubious to nonexistent. But for all his immense bulk, he had proved himself a dynamo able to get things moving. He did not, to use an expression not yet current at that time, stop at the red light. As he put it later during his "trial" at Nuremberg, he did not simply provide us with arms; he did so until we were positively bristling. His only regret, he neatly added, was that he had not provided us with more of them still.

In keeping with my promise to the industrialists, we did not carry out any large-scale nationalizations as the Communists in Russia had done. However, we *did* get rid of some owners, such as the aircraft fabricant Hugo Junkers, who did not cooperate. We also forced some companies to sell their patents to the Reich so that other larger companies active in the same field could use them as well. Instead, we put in place a whole series of regulations to ensure that industry would be doing what we wanted it to do in the national interest. That included very stringent controls on imports and a strong drive towards autarky.

I personally had learned from our errors during the Great War. At that time the government had done almost nothing to alleviate the plight of the masses, particularly the urban masses. The outcome was immense, almost indescribable, suffering. People starved; people froze. People lost their immune systems and died of disease, especially the very young and the very old. Perhaps worst of all, the fertility of many young women was threatened. I was determined that no such thing would happen again. By hook or by crook—one of my favorite expressions by the way—we had to make sure that our population remained at least tolerably well fed, clothed, and housed. This included, of course, heating. We did all this even as we engaged in large-scale hostilities against our neighbors.

Another pressing concern we had was our supply of strategic raw materials. Again, this was a field where the lessons of the Great War were only too clear. The imperial government of those days had been hopeless. Before the war, they did not even consider that, to produce explosives, we needed nitrogen; but nitrogen was something we did not have. In the event we had to turn to a Jewish scientist, Fritz

Haber, to help us produce what we needed.

I myself, humble as my position was, remember how, during the
last months of the Great War, the prevailing shortage of copper
caused us to be issued cartridges made of steel instead of brass. Now
heat causes the former to expand much more than the latter. The
outcome was jammed weapons that just would not fire, often at the
most critical moment. How many brave German soldiers lost their
lives as a consequence no one knows. So desperate was our need for
rubber, which at that time could be had only in the Far East, that
many of our vehicles and aircraft actually ran on wooden wheels.

Even more serious was our need for oil. Our indigenous production of that commodity was very limited. Experience taught us that
no sooner would war break out than our maritime communications
would be cut. At that time no one knew about the vast reserves of
high-quality oil buried under the sands of Italian-owned Libya. Had
we known, the war might have ended differently. In the event, except
for some wells in Hungary, the nearest sources of any importance
were located at Ploesti, Romania. From there the oil could be transported to Germany by way of the Danube. Even so, we only had
at our disposal about two percent of the world's "proven reserves."
Moreover, experience had taught us how unstable, to put it mildly,
Romanian politics could be. No one could know where they would
end.

To make ourselves autarkic, large investments were needed. But
industry, fearing for its profits, would not make those investments.
Thus we had no choice but to depart from our declared policy of
relying on private enterprise. Instead, we made the state step in. By
the beginning of the war our scientists had solved the problem of
producing synthetic rubber, which was known as Buna. Its quality
was not as good as that of natural rubber; but it met our needs,
more or less. Synthetic oil, which could be produced from coal, was
also available. However, the necessary installations were complex,
delicate, and, when the time came, vulnerable to bombing. We never

succeeded in building a sufficient number of plants to meet all of our needs in that field; synthetic oil was also considerably more expensive than its natural equivalent.

Finally, there was the problem of steel, the most important raw material of all without which no modern society, let alone modern war, is conceivable. So much so, in fact, that it was customary to rate the relative power of countries by the annual amount of steel they produced. Here we were lucky in that, at Salzgitter in Saxony, we had plenty of ore. Albeit it was of a low quality not normally considered suitable for exploitation. Göring's solution was to build, at state expense and under state ownership and management, a vast new industrial complex. Named after himself, of course. After we annexed Austria in 1938, the company, by taking over some Jewish property, expanded into that country as well. As a result, steel was one commodity of which we did not suffer any serious shortage until late in the war when Allied bombing destroyed both the factories and our transportation system.

Meanwhile, Schacht, who had managed our economic recovery so well, started causing problems. At his post as President of the Reichsbank Schacht had remained faithful to his liberal-conservative principles. Increasingly worried about our deficit, he suggested that we slow down the pace of rearmament and rely on trade to fill our needs. As if peace would last forever! By contrast, we National Socialists saw war and territorial expansion as the solution to our present and future economic problems. That is why we were determined to extend the state's control over industry so that it would serve our purposes.

Adding to the difficulty was Schacht's opposition to our Jewish policies. It was not that he had any particular liking for Jews. He did not. But he saw our policies as economically disruptive and sharply attacked Streicher and his paper. As I could not know at the time, from 1938 on he was also in sporadic contact with the bunch of traitors whose activities culminated in the attempt on my life on 20

July 1944. That suited him fine. In the event, the outcome was a breach between us. In November 1937 I took his post as Minister of the Economy away from him, and in January 1939 I also dismissed him as President of the Reichsbank. His successor in both capacities was Walter Funk. To be sure, he did not have Schacht's stature. With war approaching, though, I had more important things to worry about.

Chapter 13

A New Kind of State

Having done without, I learned to appreciate both how important money is and what it can do for you. Nevertheless, I always saw economics as a means to an end. Like all truly great leaders, I had a vision. I wanted to create a new kind of state, not just to increase the GDP of the existing one so that people would be able to buy larger houses, go on more expensive vacations, or dine in fancier restaurants. Much later, I accidentally learned how one German novelist, Hans Carossa, saw these things. "There is," he wrote to a friend who had chosen exile, "a lot going on here in Germany. We are being laundered, purified, scrubbed, disinfected, separated, nordicized, toughened up…" This was in 1933, and he could not yet know how spot-on he was. Appointed head of the European Writers' League by Goebbels, within a few years he was writing odes to "the brave…fighter and leader who bears all our destiny."

By the mid-thirties our most important problem, i.e. providing our people with work and bread, had been largely solved. Watching the country wake up and buzz with activity was a joy indeed. I now felt free to turn my attention to other aspects of our Party program. The first, and in some ways most important, was the wish to build a *Völkisch* state. Let me explain what I mean. Our German political tradition had long been authoritarian, meaning that it worked from the top down. Definitely in the case of the smaller states, it had even been patrimonial. Even after Napoleon reduced their number by nine tenths, so small did many of them remain that, down to the end of the World War, separating the rulers' private affairs from those of their states often remained all but impossible. In all this we differed from many others who, starting with the English Revolution of 1688 and proceeding through the American one of 1776, and the French one of 1789, had turned to democracy and liberalism.

That does not mean I wanted to make our country more democratic in the usual sense. Far from it. My experience, first in Vienna and later during the years from 1919 to 1932, had thoroughly immunized me against any such idea. What it *did* mean was that, unlike the Italian Fascists, we were not *étatists*. It was not the state, imposing itself on society like a steel helmet on a head, which was the shining goal of our efforts. It was the racial community; specifically including all its varied forms of life, constantly bubbling up from below like mineral springs at the bottom of a pool. Endowing it with color and making it come alive. I wanted to make the state, that coldest of all cold monsters as Nietzsche once called it, shed some of its pomposity and grow closer to the people. It and the bureaucracy that represented it should be made to serve them rather than the other way around.

Such being the case, I did not seek to imitate Napoleon by creating a body of law to be named after me. After all, such a body, if enacted, would have served little purpose except to limit our moves. Instead, I used other methods that seemed more appropriate. Among the most important ones was propaganda. By that I mean the unceasing drumfire, ably orchestrated by Goebbels, which sought to convince people that they and the state were not two separate entities but one. As the famous slogan had it, *ein Volk, ein Reich, ein Führer.* No translation needed! It was to make sure that this propaganda—and no other—would reach the masses that we imposed censorship on all papers, magazines, books, theaters, and films. Not only did we tell them what *not* to publish and to show, but very often we gave them explicit orders as to what to write, on what page to put it, and even what size the letters comprising the headline should be. Editors

who disobeyed our instructions soon learned who was boss, by being
fired if they were lucky or sent to a concentration camp if they were
not.

We, the government, also assumed complete control over that
most accessible means of modern communications, radio. I myself
hardly ever listened to any of its programs. However, I fully understood how important it was and was determined to use it to the
best advantage. Our *Volksempfänger,* or people's receiver, was a great
help in this respect. It could only be tuned to German stations and
no others; nevertheless, being cheap, it sold by the millions. For
those who did not have a set we installed loudspeakers in public
squares as well as at schools, clubs, factories, and so on. To quote
Goebbels, in National Socialist Germany the only time people could
avoid what we wanted them to hear was during their sleep. At the
time television only existed in a rudimentary form. In fact the first
experimental broadcasts were made during the Berlin Olympics. But
had the technology been mature and available for mass production
and use, we surely would have taken control of that as well. As to the
Internetz, I shall leave you to think what we could, and would, have
done with it.

A considerable part of our propaganda took the form of mass
ceremonies, rallies, and political theater in general. Probably no
regime has ever made greater use of them than we did. Those of
Fascist Italy were paltry by comparison whereas Soviet ones, though
as large as ours, lacked imagination and tended to be boring. The
meetings started at the village level, where they became a regular
part of life (this was at a time when electronic media and electronic
communications had not yet begun to close the gap between cities
and the countryside as they later did.) They went up all the way to
the gigantic Party rally held in Nuremberg each year from 1933 on.
Effectively covered by radio and film—think of Leni Riefenstahl's
masterpiece, *The Triumph of the Will*—they lifted both participants
and observers out of their day-today existence. Making them feel

part of an entity much greater, much more powerful, than their insignificant selves. Once again, we had a nice slogan which summed up all this: *Du bist nichts, dein Volk ist alles* (you are nothing, your people are everything). Often we invited foreigners to watch the ceremonies. Others attended of their own accord. Almost to a man, they came away impressed by our display of unity, order, discipline, and power. Sheer power.

Another method we used was to hold plebiscites. Plebiscites were frequent in the ancient world, especially in Greece. Since everyone had one vote, and since no one had heard of representation and parliaments, in a sense the whole of political life consisted of a continuous series of plebiscites. In Athens, classical scholars say, they were held about once every three weeks. Napoleon used them, and so did his nephew Napoleon III, in both cases to very good effect. Not so German emperors, kings, grand-dukes, princes, or whatever they called themselves. Claiming to be God-appointed, they had always been somewhat afraid of what a plebiscite might bring. Article 73 of the Weimar Constitution allowed them. However, only one was held—in 1926, to decide on the thorny question of whether the various former royal houses should be expropriated. (They were, but only in part.)

I myself saw plebiscites in a completely different light. To me they were a method to draw people and government closer together by making the former feel that they were participating in the affairs of the latter. Our opponents and subsequent critics have claimed that, ere we put a question to the nation to decide, we made sure that the nation would come up with the answer we wanted. Of course we did! But so did everyone else since the beginning of the world. A plebiscite held without proper preparation is both foolish and dangerous. Look what happened to de Gaulle in 1969. As the voice went against him, he was forced to resign, thereby depriving his country of the one outstanding statesman it has produced since at least 1945. In any case there was hardly any need to do so. Time after time, the overwhelming majority of people were happy to say yes. At most, here and there, a little intimidation was needed. But not much. In November 1933, when we asked voters whether Germany should or should not remain a member of the League of Nations, even the inmates of concentration camps voted in our favor.

But what *is* a plebiscite? Does the term always and necessarily refer to a formal process whereby the government puts a question to the people, sets up neat little voting boxes, and then proceeds to count the number of those who respond with a yes or a no, as in the case of BREXIT, for example? Can't it also refer to acclamation, as in ancient Sparta? And how about the Germanic Middle Ages, when it was known as *Huldigung?* One of my better-known biographies is called *A Study in Tyranny.* But that is typical petit-bourgeois rubbish. As Joachim Fest quite correctly said, I did not tyrannize the German people. I seduced them. Not because I had come from Mars, but because they and I had grown out of the same roots and were made of the same material. Hence the acclamation I received and the outcome of the plebiscites I held; in more ways than one, I was the most democratic ruler in the whole of German history. And not just German history either. Wherever I went, tsunamis of people came to see me, listen to me, identify themselves with me, and *experience* me. Just as, four hundred years earlier, they had done with Luther! Considered in this light, wouldn't it be true to say that the entire history of the Third Reich—certainly until July 1940, when we celebrated our victory over France—was one long plebiscite, one which got me the confidence of the people not once, or twice, or thrice, but day by day, a thousand times over?

The wish to close the gap between the government and the people also caused us to tackle the bureaucracy. I in particular, since personal experience had taught me both what the lack of the *Abitur* could do and the way bureaucrats treated those who did not have it. Too many of them really believed that, as the German proverb goes, "He to whom God gives an office He also provides with the necessary wisdom." This, it must be admitted, is not very great! Our efforts to change this state of affairs had two prongs. First, we wanted to open the way to talent—to create equal opportunity, as it is now known. The situation whereby only the scions of the upper classes, properly groomed, polished, and schooled, could rule had to be altered. During our early years in power in particular we did our best to identify young working-class people with leadership potential to prepare them for important tasks without putting too much emphasis on any formal education they might or might not have.

Second, and perhaps even more important, we wanted to make it, if not exactly more populist—an oxymoron, that—at least more flexible and more responsive to the demands of ordinary people. To that end, decentralization would have been essential. The situation, so characteristic of Germany, where every petty *Rat* (Councilor) hid behind the regulations and looked down on those who needed his services, had to be terminated. Instead, we wanted to encourage initiative and to make people take responsibility for their actions. In addition, we wanted to modify the system of promotion by seniority so as to make way for talent. As part of this, we started using the term *Genosse*, roughly translatable as "fellow participant." We also abolished old-fashioned forms of address such as "most humbly." In the event, our attacks on rank and privilege proved quite popular. Unfortunately, though, they remained limited, partly because many of the new candidates were just not up to the job and partly because the existing bureaucracy, with its tradition going back hundreds of years, resisted us tooth and nail.

Closely related to our attempts to establish the *völkisch* character of our state was the socialist part of our National Socialist program. This takes me back to my years in Vienna. I myself came from a petit-bourgeois family. However, keeping track of what Lueger was trying to do taught me that, in the modern world, no political program that does not promise an improvement in the condition of the workers stands the slightest chance of success. Not even my difficulties with Röhm and his associates, who wanted to go much further than I did and paid the price, made me forget that lesson. Like the Italian Fascists, our entire intent in governing Germany was to find a "third way" between capitalism on one hand and communism on the other. We wanted the advantages of both systems, but without the concomitant disadvantages of either.

We were not going to follow the Communists by nationalizing industry. But we *were* going to remind it of its duties toward those who worked for it and were largely responsible for generating its wealth. Though we prohibited strikes, we did put in place an organization charged with mediating between owners and workers and finding solutions to any problems that might arise. We sent our officials to talk to industrialists and to press them into making all kinds of improvements to their factories, such as adding safety devices, lighting, cafeterias, shower rooms, and gardens where the workers could relax during pauses. Nor did we limit our efforts to industry alone. We also looked into the shipping business, where we made sure that the crews would have proper lodgings. Ditto with respect to domestic help and other workers not previously included in the social security system.

Nothing is perfect, but by and large our efforts in this direction worked out very well. This happened partly because industrialists and other employers realized the benefits that would accrue to them. And partly because they understood that the officials in question enjoyed the backing of the state and, ultimately, mine. Had it not been for the war, we surely would have made our factories not only the most efficient but the most pleasant in the world. Far more so than English ones, where early industrial conditions still prevailed in many cases. And far more so than Americans ones, where the dehumanizing practice of *Fordismus* reigned supreme.

Thus the dissolution of the unions in 1933 did not mean that every worker was left to face his employers, and the market, on his own. To the contrary: with Ley in the lead, we went ahead and organized all our German workers in a single gigantic union known as the *Arbeitsfront*. Membership in the organization and the payment of dues were compulsory for most categories of workers. In return the *Arbeitsfront*, working through one of its subsidiary organizations, *Kraft durch Freude (KdF)*, organized a vast number of different activities. Such as sporting events, hikes, concerts, film shows, plays, day trips, you name it. We even reorganized the entire structure of football leagues, making them far more competitive and exciting than before.

The best-known measures of all were vacations, which could be spent either in the country or in neighboring ones such as Austria, the Netherlands, and Scandinavia. At a time when few workers even knew what a vacation was, this was an innovation. In 1934 2.3 million people took advantage of the holidays on offer. By 1938 that figure had gone up to 10.3 million, about one in seven in the entire population. By the time the war broke out the total had gone up to over 45 million packages. My goal was to make sure that every worker should be able to have one or two trips to the sea during his life.

Even this does not exhaust the list of "socialist" measures we put in place. Among the most important ones was the *Arbeitsdienst*, the Labor Service. The organization conscripted several hundreds of thousands of youngsters each year and put them to work. By so doing it helped carry out all sorts of projects, reduced unemployment, and welded together different parts of the *Volksgemeinschaft*, or popular community. It did all this on top of teaching future draftees the rudiments of discipline and order even before they joined the armed forces. Both men and women participated. However, we soon discovered that the latter, assisted by their parents, were very good at finding all sorts of excuses as to why they should *not* serve.

Another measure we introduced was the *Eintopf*. It was a sort of national solidarity day, held several times a year, during which people, taking meals consisting of one course only, used the savings to help the poor. Yet another, *Winterhilfe* was a system for helping poor folks by collecting goods for them and distributing them. There were some others, too. To be sure, they were essentially symbolic by nature. However, that does not mean they were not important in helping generate the kind of spirit we National Socialists wanted to infuse the community with.

And then there was education. As has been said, it is not old opinions that die. It is those who hold them who do. That is why, as I personally said in at least one of my speeches, we would see to it that the coming generation would be ours. It was also why, right from the beginning, we laid our hands on the schools. In Germany, as in other countries, there was not one type of school but many. This was a situation we National Socialists could not tolerate and to which we soon put an end. The only important exception were the Catholic schools. The issue played a major role in the talks that led to the Concordat of 20 July 1933. As expected, the representatives of the Church proved to be tough and shrewd negotiators. In the end, we had no choice but to allow the schools to continue to exist and to function.

That point having been settled, we left the outline of the school system with its division into elementary school, intermediate school, and high school more or less as it had been. The same applied to the system of mostly separate education for boys and girls; co-education only became the rule in Germany after 1945. Whether that was a good idea, incidentally, was and remains undetermined as yet. But we did modify the curriculum. We added more physical training and military exercises for boys and put a greater emphasis on housekeeping and handiwork for girls. We also made sure that students should be familiar with the origins of our Party, its principles, and the heroic struggle through which it came to power. Another very important innovation was teaching students the basics of racial science. Both sexes had to master them, but girls in particular. Given that, without their willing cooperation in their roles as wives and mothers, keeping our race pure was impossible to begin with.

To the existing school system we added the so-called NAPOLA (National Political Institutes of Education). It was in them that our future leaders were to be put through their paces. Students, all of them male, were selected on the basis of both mental and physical tests. Among the latter was a requirement that candidates swim ten meters under the ice. True to our ideology, they were selected regardless of social origin or class. No gifted youth should be barred from school because his family did not have money. NAPOLA students had to wear full military-style uniforms. The curriculum was less classical and more modern than that of regular high schools. This was especially true at the gymnasiums. The schools were a great success, as a collection of memoirs, written long after by their grateful former students, proves.

Above the NAPOLA we had the so-called *Ordensburgen.* Their purpose was to take the place of the universities in educating the crème de la crème. Students were in their early to mid-twenties. To gain admission they had to be in perfect physical health as well as show proof of Aryan descent. To these requirements were added full military service and a period of probationary party work. The curriculum emphasized National Socialist ideology, racial science, geopolitics, and sport. Three campuses were built, and the first students arrived in 1936. Unfortunately, the outbreak of the war did not allow us to sustain the program after 1939. As a result, from then on the buildings were used for a variety of other purposes.

The female equivalent was *Glaube und Schönheit,* Faith and Beauty. The program aimed at developing young women who, through healthy bodies and balanced minds, would embody the beauty of divine creation. They would believe in Germany and pass that belief on to their future children. It was not without some success, as I was often able to observe at first hand. We also planned schools for *hohe Frauen,* elevated women. The term originated in the Middle Ages when it referred to the women of the nobility. Goethe used it, too. For us it meant well-bred women of the kind our elite would be able to marry and take pride in as they, the women, deserved. Himmler, who dreamed of turning his SS officers into the nucleus of a new racial community, was particularly interested in this subject. Selected from among those with pure Aryan backgrounds, the women would have to know how to dress, how to make themselves up decently, how to behave, how to entertain, and how to cook. And they had to learn languages, of course. Some desultory efforts in this direction were made. Much to Himmler's regret, though, they did not get very far, and even became the object of some ridicule.

True to its name, modern "liberal" society puts far too much emphasis on the rights of the individual versus his duties to the *Gemeinschaft,* the community, to which he belongs. It also overemphasizes theoretical knowledge at the expense of what the English used to call "character" as well as practical experience and physical development. From my seat in Hell, I can observe the outcome in almost every one of the wars that have broken out since 1945. In almost every case, whenever Western troops met non-Western ones, they were defeated. Think of Iraq (post 2003). Think of Afghanistan. Think of Somalia. Think of Vietnam. Think of Cyprus. Think of Algeria. Think of Malaysia and Indo-China. Think, too, of the handful of Jews—Jews, of all people—who threw the English out of Palestine in 1947–48. Truth be told, the troops in question are not soldiers at all. They are pussycats, helpless nerds. Instead of training, they are made to listen to lectures about sexual harassment, its nature, and the need to avoid it. Instead of fighting, they complain about PTSD. And that specifically includes the *Bundeswehr*—the "army without pathos," as it has been called.

We National Socialists did not want our youths, the greatest treasure any society can have and the sole support of its future, to grow up as pussycats. That is why, especially in the Hitler Youth and its equivalent for girls, the BDM, of which every young person had to be a member, we de-emphasized *Bildung* and diplomas, precisely the things which the bourgeoisie treasures so much. Much to the chagrin of some of the teachers, we preferred to stress physical training on the one hand and a sense of community on the other. Boys wrestled and boxed; girls did calisthenics. Youngsters of both sexes went on hikes, swam, rowed, and marched. They also played the kind of rough field games where everyone depends on, and has to cooperate with, one another. They spent evenings engaged in singing in front of the campfire and slept on the hay in primitive lodgments. It was for them that we expanded our network of youth hostels, perhaps the most extensive there has ever been. All under instructors who, unlike the ridiculous adults who run the U.S. Boy Scouts and are occasionally caught abusing their charges, were themselves young. Not only did they enjoy it, but it worked. As one important Israeli historian has written, in the whole of history it is impossible to find soldiers who fought better than our German ones in World War II.

As always, we put the community ahead of the individual. Hence our slogan, "It is your duty to be healthy." No state before us had ever invested so much in the field of preventive health. Few have done more since, least of all the great and humane US of A where, to this day, some thirty million people are without any medical insurance at all. We put great emphasis on anti-smoking campaigns, though ultimately without success. But that was because the war put much of our population under such tremendous stress that they simply could not do without cigarettes. We taught them the principles of a healthy diet. In fact, doing so was one of the main tasks of the *Nationalsozialistische Frauenschaft* (National Socialist Women's League) with its millions and millions of members. We did our best to make people reduce their consumption of meat. We actively fought diseases such as breast cancer (the disease that had killed my mother) and colon cancer. We distributed leaflets and produced films on those subjects, calling on people to undergo annual and even biannual tests. We did so much more that entire books could be, and have been, written about that issue alone.

Finally, it is a fundamental principle of education, at any rate, education as we National Socialists understood it, that it should not be limited to the young or to the schools. It is, instead, a process that goes on, or should go on, throughout life down to old age. Perhaps it should focus particularly on old age, which is when people, having little to do, may end up poisoning the minds of youth, as, for example, Socrates was accused of doing. We did not want to bring people to culture as philistines so often try to do. To the contrary, we wanted to bring culture to people. Again, my ideas on the subject had started forming during my years in Vienna and Munich. Learning to know those two cities, I could not help noting how much of our national culture was shut up in museums. Many were splendid indeed, and no one enjoyed visiting them more than I did. But working people and their families, who along with farmers formed the mainstay of the nation, had no use for them and rarely bothered to do so. That, incidentally, remains as true now as it was then.

I do not mean to say I wanted to close the museums, which certainly have a role to play. Indeed, the art I myself collected in such huge quantities was never meant for my own use. How could it be? Both at the *Reichskanzlei* and in my private residences I had enough and more to spare. My intention was to build a vast new museum in my favorite city, Linz, to which I hoped to retire after the *Endsieg* (final victory). It would be something like the British Museum and the Louvre combined! There the German people would be able to enjoy it and be inspired by it. That is why I had my agents, the most important of whom was Dr. Hans Posse of the Dresden Gallery, acquire art left and right. A lot was confiscated from the Jews, first in Germany and then throughout occupied Europe. Nor, their postwar denials notwithstanding, were those in charge unaware of that fact; quite a few of them used to boast of it.

I was determined to make sure that members of the lower classes should also have access to art. It was to this end that I initiated a series of vast and very expensive programs meant to employ talented artists such as Josef Thorak, Arno Breker, and a host of others. Their task was to beautify—I deliberately do not say decorate—our buildings, city streets, avenues, squares, and what have you. That is why many of their creations are as large as they are. Going further still, I wanted people to enjoy art, not just on special occasions but as a self-evident and omnipresent part of their daily lives. And I wanted this to happen not just in the big cities but in small provincial ones as well. The people were to be immersed in an artistic environment, so to speak, as if in some kind of perpetual bath. It would be something like the medieval Fountain of Life, perhaps. Another method of achieving this result was to put art on display during reviews, parades, sports events, and so on. As, for example, when we added an amphitheater to the Olympiastadion in Berlin. Unfortunately, not all the art we brought to the people in this way was of the highest quality. But that problem we would have solved in time.

No country, not even ancient Athens, has ever done more in its attempt to merge art with politics and politics with art. But what kind of art? Nineteenth-century German art had often been magnificent. Think of Caspar David Friedrich, Franz von Lenbach, Arnold Boecklin, Adolf Menzel, and many others no less good. Or, later, of Hermann Gradl, who captured our German landscapes as no one else before or after him did. He, however, was an exception. As I said before, starting around 1910, Munich in particular turned into a hothouse for all kinds of half-demented experiments in this field. After the war, with chaos reigning all around, things became even worse. Not only in Germany but over much of the rest of Europe as well. The more grotesque and perverted an image, the louder the applause it drew. Expressionism and Cubism were joined by Dadaism, a "style" whose idiotic name speaks for itself and whose symbol, appropriately enough, was a urinal with its neck turned upward. It was enough, more than enough, to make one ashamed of being called an artist! Then there were Abstractionism, Brutalism, Constructivism, Fauvism, Supremacism, Surrealism, Vorticism, and entire hosts of other isms only sick minds could come up with. Even Italy, once home to da Vinci, Michelangelo, and Titian, was not spared some association with this "modernist" trash.

Most of those responsible for producing this junk would have been unable to paint a decent picture if they tried. But they did not try. Instead, they deliberately produced all kinds of abominations. From Otto Dix to Kate Kollwitz, many went out of their way to undermine the national spirit, the will to fight and sacrifice. Not to mention women's desire to have healthy children! Others, often taking their inspiration from the quack Freud, were simply pornographers. All they had on their brains was sex. I did not care about what foreigners said or did. Throughout my years in power I was quite happy to have them provide us with hard cash in return for all kinds of junk we unloaded on them. Normally in Switzerland, and sometimes with the help of Jewish middlemen who had left Germany for safer havens. Jews are constitutionally unable to create culture. But that did not prevent them from hovering about like birds of ill omen, cawing and trying to make a profit at our expense.

What I *did* care about was the kind of art our own countrymen would experience. I wanted sane art. Healthy art, Aryan art, German art. Aryan, in the sense that it drew on Greek and Roman prototypes. German, in the sense that it should be the opposite of Jewish, meaning international, and rootless. The kind of art our ancestors, starting over a thousand years ago, used to produce and we, having inherited it from them, could be proud of. The kind ordinary, decent people, ordinary, decent Germans, could relate to and which would lift them, however temporarily, out of their humdrum existence into the higher realms of the spirit.

I well knew how to reward outstanding artists by means of commissions, awards, and appointments to juries and offices of every

kind. As, for example, when I made both Frau Troost and her fellow
designer, Leonhard Gall, professors. I also knew that the supply
of truly talented artists, not only painters and sculptors but singers
and actors and writers as well, is always very limited. That is why,
once the war had broken out, I personally made sure that the dumb
military machine would not treat them as cannon fodder. But that
did not mean molly-coddling them. Those of my favorite city of
Linz, for example, were drafted into the SS; believe it or not, some
ended up as concentration camp guards at Mauthausen.

To show people what I meant, I allowed Goebbels to organize an
exhibition of "Degenerate Art" in Munich. A gathering of uglier,
more revolting, monstrosities you never saw; no wonder that, wherever it and its various offshoots were shown, it attracted masses of
people. The total number of visitors was said to have been in excess
of two million. We also put into place a system of censorship aimed
at preventing certain "artists" from painting or sculpting and certain
"writers," from covering the rest of us with their *Dreck*. Or from playing and listening to the kind of degenerate Judeo-Negroid "music"
known as jazz. Those who disobeyed their orders were sent to prison.
Or else, if they persisted, they were sentenced to be reeducated in a
concentration camp, where harsh living conditions, strict discipline,
and forced labor sometimes did wonders. Usually, though, the threat
was enough.

Ironically, the term "degenerate" *(entartet)* owed its popularity to
a Jew, Max Nordau. A physician by trade, a Zionist and close friend
of Theodor Herzl, back in 1892 he published a famous book by that
title. This did not prevent our policies from coming under sharp
attack by foreigners. After 1945 native Germans, eager to lick the
victor's boots, also chimed in. Some went directly from praising our
art to denouncing it, showing you how hypocritical people can be!
Nazi art was bad and did not merit serious attention or study, they
claimed. Nazi art was Nazi propaganda, they claimed. As if the same
had not been true of ancient Egyptian, Greek, Roman, Byzantine,

ecclesiastical, and Renaissance art, in fact almost any kind of art from the earliest times on. All except "art for art's sake," of the kind first invented by bourgeois philistines in the nineteenth century and later misused by so many lunatics in our own.

That is why, sitting here in Hell, I was gratified to learn that thousands of paintings and sculptures dating to the Third Reich are being kept under lock and key both in museums and private collections. Not necessarily, as some people both in Germany and abroad frankly admitted, because they are unsightly. But out of fear that "ordinary people" everywhere, rejecting the critics and following my lead, would like them too much! If so, no wonder. Whatever else one may say about our artistic productions, at any rate they were of such a nature that the man on the street could understand what he saw without a need for all kinds of learned, and often fraudulent, intermediaries to teach him. Some objects, traded in a sort of underground market, fetch very high prices indeed. Serves those snobs, our critics, right.

In sum, what we wanted was to extend the rule of our *Weltanschauung*, not just over the realm of politics but over every aspect of the community's life. Even more, we wanted to amalgamate politics with the community and to return the former into the bosom of the latter, where they originated and where, by right, they belong. In a certain way, what we wanted was politics as reflected in that famous American painting of a town hall meeting, all in an environment kept as pristine and healthy, and rendered as beautiful, as we could make it. And, yes, we were going to shut up anyone and anything that stood in our way in reaching toward these high ideals. "Totalitarianism" is what our critics, and we ourselves following Mussolini, called this. But they and we used the term in different ways. To them it was the denial of individual caprice, the worst thing anyone could do. To us, on the contrary, it was the immersion of the individual into the community so as to give meaning to his life and to make him an integral part of it, the best thing there is.

I did not attend a gymnasium, and I am no classical scholar. But I am told that, turning in this direction, we could claim, as one of our predecessors, no less a philosopher than Plato. He, too, was an enemy of individualism. Not only did he precede us in trying to abolish the struggle between richness and poverty, but his whole purpose was to eliminate the difference between "mine" and "thine" even to the point that children were taken from their parents and reared by the community! He, too, opposed what a famous twentieth-century scholar called "the open society." Using every technological means available at the time, we made our regime as all embracing, as totalitarian, as we could. My only regret is that, not having enough time, we did not make it more totalitarian still.

Chapter 14

The Racial Question

To serve the people, as I tried my best to do from the beginning of my political career to my last hour on earth, is a good and noble thing to do. But which people? The obvious answer is, my people. That, incidentally, was the answer given by good old Kaiser Franz Joseph. Early in the World War, some of his advisers wondered why he had allowed some Jewish refugees from Galicia to camp in the *Hofgarten*. He answered that they, too, were his people.

But he was wrong. Whether his words constituted deliberate treason to the German race, as was so often the case on other occasions in the history of the dynasty to which he belonged, or were the outcome of misplaced kindness, I shall not try to judge. The important point is that the host of lesser breeds—Czechs, Slovaks, Ruthenians, Poles, Slovenians, Croats, Bosnians, the lot—over whom it was his fate to reign were *not* his people. Nor were they the people of anyone else. As they never ceased telling anyone who would and who would not listen, they were their own and their own alone. The Czechs in particular were notorious in this respect. And the Jews! As even some Israelis complain, in the whole of history no one has ever been more racist than the rabbis. Compared to their millennia-old efforts to maintain the purity of their race, we were babes in the wood. In the words of one well-known Zionist agitator, Zeev Jabotinsky, whose name I came across for the first time here in Hell, "My love is reserved for my own people alone." To be sure, he did not say this because they were good and noble. In fact he devoted much of his life to a hopeless attempt to make them so. He said it simply and solely because they were *his* people.

My case was entirely different. I did not serve just any people. Let alone a people made up of subhuman criminals. Rather, I served the noblest people—race, to use that much derogated term—that has ever appeared on the face of this planet. Namely, the Nordic-Germanic-Aryan one. The salt of the earth. The only one capable of producing high culture. The only one that was human in the full sense of the word. This was the race Providence had called me to protect and to lead to new heights of splendor. I for my part was going to do my duty. Right to the end, without any ifs, ands, or buts.

As I wrote earlier, the beginning of my understanding of how big the problem was went back to my days in Vienna. It was there that I first encountered Jews and recognized them as a separate race. As a result, all efforts to "integrate"—at that time, we used to say, Germanize—them were doomed to failure. The Jews, I now understood, were bound to remain what their biology had made them. The more rights we gave them, the more insolent they became.

Starting as early as 1919, the Jewish question also played an important part in my political efforts. I did not just rant away as so many others did. The better I understood what we were facing, the better able I was to tailor my exertions to the occasion and to the audiences I was addressing. As Schacht's differences with me indicated, there was no point in raising the issue with industrialists and financiers. There were quite a number of Jews among them, and they understood the problem. But they had, or thought they had, more important issues to deal with. Ditto the officer corps, especially the senior officers. Many never quite understood what I was trying to do.

As Jewish "social scientists" themselves have often said, many Jews were *Luftmenschen,* "air men," or transients. Very few worked with their hands either in the towns or, much less, the countryside. So few were capable of manual labor that it became one of the objectives of the movement that calls itself Zionism to force more of them do so! To no avail, it is needless to say. This being the situation, few workers had much to do with them. A few hotheads apart, the workers did not care much about the Jews either. Those among whom anti-Semitism was most useful, politically speaking, were the petit bourgeois: small farmers, shopkeepers, salespeople, white collar employees, and so on. They were the ones, in other words, with whom the Jews competed and whom they exploited. After the 1929 economic crisis, large numbers of people who had experienced down-ward social mobility or feared doing so in the near future started taking the same line. It was they who bore the full brunt of what one president of the State of Israel, Shimon Peres, speaking of his own country, called "swinish capitalism." He ought to know.

It is my unalterable conviction that race provides the key to history. I also believe that race alone can provide a sound basis on which to build a community, large or small. That is why, having seized power, we lost no time in dealing with the problem. Our goal was simple: to neutralize people of foreign blood and to get rid of them. We wanted to do this not only because they were swine but because we feared the corrupting influence of miscegenation. Early on, our attempts to do so were clumsy and amateurish. SA men and *Hitler Jugend* members, acting more or less on their own initiative, beat up or humiliated Jews they met in the streets. Here and there they also plundered and destroyed shops, took care of Jewish men who had slept with Aryan women and Aryan women who willingly polluted their bodies by sleeping with Jewish men, and the like. The police stood by, watching the goings-on but doing nothing to stop them. What these spontaneous attacks did prove, though, was that the racial instincts of those who perpetrated them, the young in particular, had remained sound.

But they did not usually meet with the approval of the majority of our *Volk*. We ourselves learned this during the boycott of Jewish businesses Goebbels organized for 1 April 1933. We had expected foreigners to criticize us. After all, that was what they were doing most of the time. What we did not expect was the reaction of many ordinary "good Germans." They felt ashamed; they looked the other way. Some even tried to argue with the brave SA men who were guarding the shops and preventing clients from going inside. A few—very few—went so far as to defy the boycott and to go on with their business in spite of it. The situation on the night of 10–11 November 1938, the so-called *Kristallnacht* (Night of the Broken Crystal) was broadly similar. Again, the first target was not people but property in the form of synagogues, shops, and other businesses. All over Germany they were looted and burned. About 1,000–2,500 Jews were either killed or died as a result of being rounded up and sent to concentration camps. The rest of those arrested, about 30,000 in number, were released after a relatively short stay on the condition that they leave Germany immediately.

We had every right to do what we did. After all, we were avenging the death of one of our diplomats, Ernst von Rath, who had been shot by a Jew-boy in Paris. Here and there bystanders cheered our actions. However, the German people as a whole remained aloof at best and adverse at worst. From Göring down, our economists and financiers were also aghast. They thought they would have to compensate the owners of insured property—that, in the end, we were able to prevent—and also that the pogrom would put obstacles in front of our foreign trade. All in all, the operation was not a success. That is why we did not repeat it. Nor did I overlook the fact that, both in 1933 and in 1938, the organizing brain had been Goebbels. I continued to trust him, but made sure he would not repeat the same error.

Sobered by these experiences, we changed our methods. Spontaneous, unorganized anti-Semitic actions by individuals were brought under control, though they were never completely eliminated. In their place, we mounted what must surely have been the most intensive, most sustained propaganda campaign in the whole of history. It started in kindergarten and never let up; among the means we used were graffiti, leaflets, posters, and newspapers. Particularly noteworthy in this respect was the *Stürmer*. Much as the self-proclaimed "better circles" despised our campaign, in this respect it did an excellent job, as did magazines, books, every sort of game, radio, film, public addresses, and popular rallies. All showed the Jews for what they were: greedy hogs out to swindle the German people and to corrupt it as much as they could. Here I must hand it to Goebbels. Hating Jews as much as any man alive, he made sure that much of his propaganda was directed against them.

The other tool we used was legislation. No sooner had we seized power than I had Frick, as Minister of Internal Affairs, start drafting what later became the Law for the Restoration of the Professional Civil Service. Directed against the Jews as well as other non-Aryans, it enabled us to fire not only professional civil servants but professors, teachers, and judges as well. Shortly thereafter we extended the law to include lawyers, notaries, physicians, and tax consultants. Most of these were professions in which the number of Jews was proportionally much greater than in the population. They had weaseled their way in; now it was our task to ferret them out. At the last moment Hindenburg gave us a little trouble. He insisted that those who had fought at the front during the World War should be exempted. The same applied to long-term civil servants and to those who had lost a father or son in combat. We had no choice but to accept these compromises. Not, however, for very long.

The law was passed on 7 April 1933. It was, I am proud to say, the first official attempt in a hundred years to resist what has since become known as "integration." What it is, in reality, is the bastardization of the Aryan race. But it did not go nearly far enough. The most difficult problem was to determine who was a Jew and who was not. That is why we made every member of the population fill in a so-called *Ariernachweiss* (proof of being an Aryan). The form listed each person's parents and grandparents and had to be accompanied

by the appropriate documentation. We took great care to distinguish
between full Jews, half Jews, and quarter Jews. A separate category
included Jewish men married to non-Jewish women and the other
way around.

At the time, the population of the Reich was a little short of seventy
million. Obtaining all this information, sorting it, and registering it
represented a gigantic task. The more so because, especially in comparison with the U.S., our civil service was somewhat backward. It
hardly used business machines, so everything had to be done by hand.
At one point we even had to turn to IBM in order to administer
our concentration camps! And because, owing to the need to keep
the population on our side, we could not afford to make mistakes
as to the identity of our target. Still, by the end of 1935 we had
sufficient confidence in the quality and quantity of the information
at our disposal to pass the famous Nuremberg Laws.

The most important articles of the laws, and the supplements
which followed them, were as follows. First, Jews ceased to be citizens
of the Reich and were reclassified as its subjects. That meant they
could no longer vote, carry any public office, or have the honor
of serving in the military. Second, marriage and sexual relations
between Jews and German women under forty-five years of age were
prohibited. To make sure, Jews were also prohibited from employing
Aryan housekeepers and cleaning ladies. Third, a whole series of
professionals—lawyers, physicians etc.—were forbidden from representing or treating anyone except their fellow Jews. Fourth, all Jews
and Jewesses had to add the names "Israel" and "Sara" to their given
names.

The reactions to the laws varied. Abroad, they were almost uniformly condemned. But that did not prevent several Eastern European countries from passing similar legislation. Hungary did so
before the war; Romania, Slovakia, Bulgaria and Croatia did that
after it had started. All of this shows how urgent, how much in
need of a solution, the problem was; it was not simply a figment

of my imagination as has so often been claimed. In Germany itself some organizations anticipated our laws. They started expelling their Jewish members even before we ordered them to do so. However, the vast majority of citizens only cared about whether it applied to them. What a relief to learn that one was not Jewish! What a burden to have to report that one was! Here and there was some hanky-panky. Some women married to Jewish men swore that their children's official fathers were not their biological ones. Some of them even found Aryan men who were prepared to support their testimony. It's a pity we did not have the kind of DNA tests that are in use today.

The most interesting aspect was the Jews' own reaction. They certainly did not welcome the laws. Had they done so, then we National Socialists should have been ashamed of ourselves. The National Representation of the Jews in Germany described them as "the heaviest blow to the Jews in Germany." Excellent! But the Jews did find some consolation in the fact that, as they believed, from this point on their status and their rights were defined in such a way as to leave little room for error or misunderstandings. This included the right to hoist Jewish colors, which was specifically protected. The outcome, they hoped, would be "a tolerable relationship" between them and the Aryan population of Germany.

To forestall any problems with respect to the coming Berlin Olympics, we only started implementing the full rigor of the law during the second half of 1936. That apart, the remaining three years until the outbreak of the war saw comparatively little change. We took some additional steps. For example, we prohibited Jews from owning or driving motor cars and from using public facilities such as park benches, swimming pools, hotels, and the like. We also started Aryanizing the economy by persuading companies to fire their Jewish directors, by bringing pressure to bear on individual Jews to sell their assets to Aryans, and so on.

All in all, the combination of occasional violence, propaganda, legislation, and economic pressure worked as we had hoped it would.

It was not always easy. Quite a few countries were no more eager to have the Jews than we were to keep them. One reason for that was that, the more time went on, the more successful we became in making sure they left their assets behind. In 1938 the Anschluss with Austria, which had proportionally far more Jews than Germany did, caused a major delay. But that problem too, was dealt with—largely, I later learned, thanks to a certain SD lieutenant-colonel by the name of Adolf Eichmann. He set up a most efficient office in Vienna. It worked like an assembly line, taking just eight days to shear Austria's Jews of their property before providing them with a visa and booting them away to wherever they could go. Later, the same model was used in Germany itself. I am not sure whether Eichmann was ever properly rewarded for his efforts. He should have been.

The Jews, who formed a little under one percent of our population, were the largest and most important component of the racial problems we faced. But they were by no means the only one. Two others were the gypsies and the mixed offspring of black French soldiers with German women who were conceived as a result of the occupation of the Ruhr in 1923–24. The former we treated more or less as we did the Jews. The latter we tried to register—by no means an easy task, since they were very good at making themselves inconspicuous and hiding. Those we caught we sterilized. Typical of us Germans, entire bureaucracies developed, and a vast correspondence ensued, to decide who should be sterilized, by what methods, and, above all, at whose expense. This operation was still ongoing when the war broke out.

But getting rid of non-Aryan blood was just part of the story. Our aim was not merely to purify the race and to maintain it unsullied, but to improve it as much as we could. In this we were anything but unique. The idea of breeding people in the same way as we breed, say, pigeons and horses goes back at least as far as Plato. Darwin had something to say about it, as did his half cousin, the famous polymath

Francis Dalton. Starting around 1880, it was very much in the air. Not only in Germany, but in all West-European countries as well as the U.S. Two different paths were available for the purpose. The first was to mate superior males with superior females so as to produce superior offspring. The second was to sterilize or, if necessary, destroy life unworthy of living.

We never went very far in the first direction. In fact, we did much less than the government of Singapore, which at one point set up a state-run marriage bureau to encourage women with academic degrees to marry. The prohibition on mixed marriages apart, essentially all we tried to do was to ensure that people would not marry partners with hereditary diseases. Thus the process of artificial selection, to the extent that it worked at all, was essentially negative. The other part of our program was more successful or, at any rate, more active. We set up special committees whose task was to identify all sorts of inferior people suffering from incurable hereditary diseases. As experience accumulated, the exact nature of the regulations changed; we included feeble-mindedness as well as alcoholism. Such people were sterilized so they would not pass their problems to their offspring. Over a period of twelve years, the total number is said to have been around 200,000. Nor, once again, were we by any means the only ones who carried out such measures. Others included the U.S.—who were actually the pioneers—and Switzerland. Proportionally speaking, the largest program was the Swedish one. Ere it was terminated in 1975, it took care of 63,000 people, all under the auspices of those great humanitarians, the Social Democratic Party.

It was shortly before the outbreak of World War II that one of my physicians, Dr. Karl Brandt, drew my attention to a related problem. A married couple had sent him some horrible photographs showing a horribly deformed baby they, through no fault of their own, had given life to. In the letter they wrote they begged me, as Führer and Reichskanzler, to help them deal with the problem. In addition to

Brandt I consulted Philip Bouhler, the Chief of my Party Chancellery. Thereupon I gave my consent to the campaign later known as T-4, after the address of the building in Berlin's Tiergartenstrasse, which housed the headquarters in charge.

The procedure was similar to the one we used in the case of sterilization. Teams were sent to mental asylums, homes for the feeble-minded, and, where appropriate, the homes of families with problematic offspring. But not all the work was done by officialdom from above. Far from it! As I just said, the original impetus was created by two unfortunate parents. In many other cases people told on their neighbors. Quite a few of those who did so were Protestant priests; that was typical of them, I should say. Next, special committees made up of physicians, psychiatrists, lawyers, and social workers decided who should live and who should die. The patients were gathered, loaded onto buses with sealed windows, taken to specially prepared centers far from populated areas, and given a merciful death by gas or injection. Later, their families would be informed that they had died of this disease or that.

Besides, we had little choice. This, after all, was wartime. Our best efforts notwithstanding, food was in short supply, and its quality was deteriorating. The same applied to hospital beds and medical supplies. Doctors and nurses had their hands full looking after the wounded. Should we really have allowed them to go short just to keep all kinds of monstrosities alive? Still, we worked to find better solutions. One promising line of research was meant to discover methods to identify all kinds of birth-defects while the fetus was still in the womb. That, of course, would lead to an abortion; though whether it should be voluntary or obligatory was a question we never got around to discussing.

We did our best to proceed in secret. Nevertheless, T-4 encountered considerable opposition on the part of the people and, even more so, the Catholic Church, whose German heads voiced their antiquated, rather maudlin, doctrines concerning the "sanctity" of human life. Any human life, except, until a few centuries ago, that of people who opposed its doctrines and were executed as heretics! The strongest voice was that of the Bishop of Münster, Clement August von Galen. His sermon was picked up by the English. They reprinted it and had the Royal Air Force drop it over Germany in the form of leaflets. Many of my men wanted to hang him. I, however, decided that the resulting outrage would be more than the man was worth. First, because the issue was relatively minor; and second, because he never attacked National Socialism as such. Instead, I would settle accounts with him after the war. Meanwhile, so strong was the opposition that we had to suspend the campaign until greater precautions to preserve secrecy could be put in place. To us, however, this was a matter of principle. In the *heile Welt* (wholesome world) we were building there was no room for all sorts of degenerates.

Some of the relevant research was done in the concentration camps. In them our physicians enjoyed unlimited access to every kind of human flotsam and jetsam. There were people whose lives were expendable if not actually harmful to the community. Prominent among the physicians in question was the excellent Dr. Josef Mengele in Auschwitz. Like Eichmann, Mengele has been demonized after 1945. Consequently, he had to spend the last decades of his life in hiding from the Jews and their agents. In reality he was small fry, never rising any higher than SS Captain. During my life on earth I never heard of him. Judging by what I later learned about his medical experiments, though, he seems to have been on the right track.

Nor did the end of the war and the destruction of National-Socialist Germany bring the enterprise to an end. To the contrary, I am told that, partly building on our efforts, over the last few decades physicians have made very great progress in this direction. The number of tests, and of the birth-defects they can uncover, now runs into the dozens. Scarcely a week passes without some new one being announced. Whatever people may say about me in other respects, my contribution to this work is something of which I am, and have every right to be, proud.

As well as enhancing the quality of the race, we also wanted to increase its numbers. Most of what I have to say about the ways we tackled that problem will be found in the next chapter. Here, however, I want to mention two programs we put in place. Both were designed and managed by Himmler, who was always very interested in this kind of thing. Neither was very important in terms of the numbers affected. But both pointed to the way in which I, and even more so he, hoped to shape these things in the future. The first was *Lebensborn.* In the overheated popular imagination, *Lebensborn* was a sort of supervised brothel system where young unmarried German girls could have themselves impregnated by selected SS studs. That, however, was nonsense, possibly spread by Himmler for his own ends.

The real nature of *Lebensborn* was very different. Himmler was what we Germans call a *Prinzipenreiter,* a man very much concerned with principled behavior. I suppose it was the teacher in him; throughout his life, there were few things he liked doing more than lecturing his subordinates. One thing he always worried about was the fate of illegitimate children born to healthy German women who would, as a result, be lost to the nation. He wanted to ensure, as far as possible, that every drop of Germanic blood would count regardless of whether or not its mother wore a wedding ring. The idea met with a lot of opposition. Most of it came from decent married women who feared that the distinction between them and unmarried mothers would be lost. Their fears were not without reason. Beginning with the introduction of the pill during the 1960s, so loose has sexual morality become as to make one wonder whether there are still any decent women who are not sluts left.

But those things were still to come. Beginning in the late 1930s, Himmler set up a number of centers where "girls in trouble," as the euphemism goes, could turn, provided, of course, they and the fathers were of healthy racial stock and free of hereditary diseases. They would spend the last weeks of pregnancy in a safe environment where, contrary to legend, no strange men were admitted. There they would give birth and be taught the rudiments of child care before being sent on their way. Himmler, in his capacity as Chief of the German Police, would also provide them with the necessary papers and the like. Later the program, having been extended into the occupied territories in the West, set up homes where women pregnant with the offspring of German soldiers could turn. Subsequent historians have estimated the total number of children who were saved in this way at 12,000 or so. Of those, two-thirds were born to German mothers and the rest to Aryan women of other nationalities.

The second program was much larger. It consisted of taking away Aryan, but non-German, children from their parents and having them raised as Germans by German families. On 15 May 1940 Himmler prepared a memorandum for me on the topic. I cannot remember it—at the time I had a few other things on my mind. But he claimed it had my "full approval." The title was "Racially Pure Children of Foreign People in the East." That meant, at that time, chiefly Poland. They would, provided their parents agreed and as a condition for receiving a good education unavailable in their native lands, be removed to Germany and brought up as Germans. "Cruel and tragic as this may be in each individual case," Himmler reasoned, "if, from inner conviction, one rejects the Bolshevik method of physical extermination as un-German and impossible, then this method is still the mildest and the best." I am not sure what happened next. But I am told that, as the war went on, several hundreds of thousands— the figures differ—of racially fit children were in fact taken away from their families, placed with German ones, and raised as Germans. Good for them, I suppose.

Some years ago, an American historian published a book about my "willing executioners" that generated a lot of noise. In it he put forward his thesis that the German people as a whole were permeated by what he called "eliminationist anti-Semitism." He also stated that they gladly cooperated with our racial program, especially its Jewish component. I wish things had been that simple! In fact, the program *did* meet with considerable assent among broad swaths of the nation. But by no means did everyone approve. And even those who agreed that the Jews had to go were often reluctant to get involved in the dirty work which alone could lead us to that goal. Or else why does the worthy historian think we had to put in place a gigantic propaganda machine and run it for years on end? We had to proceed carefully, step by step, lest we should find ourselves saddled with the kinds of problems that attended both the 1933 boycott and the 1938 Crystal Night.

Those two were just the tip of the iceberg. Every time we wanted to do away with this or that Jew, some good German nobly stepped forward to defend him. All the other Jews, he would readily admit, were swine. But this one was a first-class Jew, and therefore deserved to be exempted from the measures we had in mind. One of the Jew-defenders most active in this field was none other than Frau Wagner. Another, it turns out, was Göring's brother Albert! Göring himself was also involved to some extent. It was not that he liked Jews—he did not. But, accomplished extortionist that he was, he saw many opportunities to make a profit. In one notorious case, in return for some valuable paintings, he allowed the widow of a Jewish art-dealer in Amsterdam to get away to Switzerland. Another family he helped was that of Moritz Ballin, the founder and owner of a famous furniture-producing firm in Munich. He probably did that because one of its female members had helped save his life when he was wounded during the 1923 Putsch. I myself made up my mind to ignore all of the appeals of which I was made aware. But even I did not have one hundred percent success, I must confess.

Chapter 15

The German Woman

I am, as everyone knows, an incorrigible racist. A racist, as everyone knows, is the worst thing anyone can be. That, of course, does not disturb me in the slightest. Though tactically flexible, I have never surrendered one iota of my principles. Not when I was a penniless semi-vagabond in Vienna. Not when I was on trial for treason. Not when I was one of the most powerful men in the world. And I have no intention of doing so in the future either. But racism has one implication which, we National Socialists apart, only a few people seem to have grasped in full measure. To wit, the fact that it all depends on, and revolves around, women.

Women are the mothers of the race. *Any* race, including the one to which my people and I belong. Only women can make sure that a race should keep itself pure, multiply, and develop so as to fulfill the destiny Providence had laid down for it. Or why else did the Jewish rabbis always count descent by way of the mother? Without women, their readiness to love and to conceive and to bear and to deliver and to suckle and to raise and to sacrifice and to suffer, a race is doomed to be overcome by its neighbors, fall behind in the struggle for existence, and disappear.

That is why the women of any race, and the German race more than any other, are the most precious treasure of all. As the mathematics of reproduction shows all too clearly, compared with them, men always have been and still are expendable. At all costs, women must be sheltered and protected from the full harshness of life. How else can they perform the task nature has designed them for? If nothing else works, this must be done even against their own will, by barring them from the activities, fields, and professions for which they are not suited.

Watching the world from Hell, I still believe the best a woman can do is to have children. She should preferably do this in conjunction with a husband, but if necessary without one—a point on which many feminists seem to agree with me. Doing so, she will benefit both herself—recent experiments with other mammalian females confirm the mental and physical boost that pregnancy gives them—and the people to which she belongs, without which she is nothing. For confirmation, just look at what is happening in Europe and, more recently, the U.S. So low is the birthrate in both that they are flooded with immigrants, almost always ones of inferior stock. Once admitted, they breed like rabbits. As history shows, these people are entirely incapable of creating anything that passes for culture. What they call their language is simply a series of grunts; their only contribution to the community is to rape native women and to kill one another as well as members of the surrounding society which, through its thoroughly mistaken policies, has given them shelter.

In contrast, a childless woman is the most superfluous, least needed, creature in the entire world. So much so that she is in more than slight danger of going entirely off her head unless, of course, she can find satisfaction by looking after the children of some other woman. Quite a few women have always done this, and many still do. Often, the childless woman is also the unhappiest one. Ask the English writer Virginia Woolf who, not having children and being a lesbian to boot, named her cottage "Mad Misery" and ended by drowning herself in a river. Or even recall, if you are willing to go back that far into the Old Testament, the Jewish woman Rachel telling her husband, Jacob, "Give me sons, or else I will die." Women's tendency, so prevalent in today's "developed" world, to postpone the birth of their first child until they are well past their thirtieth birthday only benefits the fertility clinics on the one hand and the adoption agencies on the other. Everyone else pays and suffers.

We National Socialists have always been aware of these problems. In part, that was because no Party's program was more deeply rooted in biological reality. Not for nothing did proportionally more physicians join our ranks than did the members of any other profession. Partly it happened because, for us, nothing was more important than strengthening our nation and our race as much as we could. That is why, almost from the beginning, one of our most important objectives was to protect women—racially fit women, needless to say. We wanted to empower them—not by turning them into second-rate men, but by providing them with the opportunity to have children and to raise them as they deserved to do and as the children themselves deserved to be. Doing so does not mean to belittle, or to despise, or to discriminate against, or to exploit. To the contrary, it means to respect and to cherish and to adore and to worship women as proper men should. As I, for example, did my mother.

So what was the real position of women in the Third Reich? To answer this question, let me briefly explain the state of German feminism before we took power. We had a very wide variety of feminist groups: a Catholic *Frauenbund,* a Protestant *Frauenbund,* as well as conservative, liberal, socialist, communist, colonial, and Jewish *Frauenbünde,* to name but a few. The total number of women's organizations has been estimated at no fewer than 230.

Some of these organizations were liberal and campaigned in favor of "equal rights" for women. Others opposed such rights in the name of motherhood and even blamed the Republic for having enfranchised women. Some supported abortion rights; others opposed them. Others still advocated the compulsory sterilization of unfit people. It was interesting to watch how, during the last years before 1933, the socialist and liberal women's movements, the same which demanded "equal rights" for women, lost power and adherents. Conversely, those promoting motherhood and demanding greater attention to the needs of mothers gained them. At that time, the term "feminist" itself was becoming anathema to many women.

The organization that claimed to speak for all the rest was the *Bund Deutscher Frauen* (BDF), a loose confederation of many different groups. Its head was Fräulein—not Frau—Gertrud Bäumer, a veteran campaigner for women's rights. Nowadays she even has a school named after her! Under the Kaiserreich she had anticipated us by opposing both abortion and contraception. In 1919 she helped rewrite the program of the BDF, injecting it with a right-wing, nationalist ideology that suited us quite well.

Bäumer's organization was never terribly important. Still, by 1932 it was advocating the abolition of democracy and the establishment of a corporate state modeled on Fascist Italy. It also called on women to help undo the consequences of the Great War by giving our nation as many children as they could. They were just the things we National Socialists also wanted. Conversely, the social ills associated with the Weimar Republic, such as sexual libertarianism, pornography, abortion, and the spread of venereal diseases, were to be combated and defeated.

To these objectives we National Socialists added our racial consciousness. It was the one feature, I am proud to say, that formed the greatest difference between us and many other totalitarian regimes both at the time and since. Translated into concrete terms, that meant the need to save women from being debauched and corrupted at the hands of Jews and other enemies of true Germandom. Healthy family values, the kind that had prevailed throughout German history, had to be restored. The most important objective of girls' education should be to prepare them for motherhood. Marriage was merely a means for multiplying and maintaining the race. We definitely saw childless women (and men) as harmful to the *Volk*. Ultimately, though, all we did was tax them more heavily. That was a measure a great many other governments have also adopted and still adopt. Briefly, nature had made man for the world, for society, and, last, but not least, for politics and for war. As for woman, it had made her for her husband, her family, her children, and her home.

Our program did not repel women. To the contrary, right from the beginning it attracted them. And no wonder. The Weimar Republic was headed by pacifist cowards. Not to say criminals and traitors. We, and in their different way, the Communists, were the only real men prepared to fight for the future, including the future of women and their offspring. Women donated money to the party (and to me personally, but that is another matter). Women kept the party running when I was in prison. Women helped us organize meetings and conduct propaganda. Always by means of hard work, and sometimes by taking risks in the streets. After all, a brick thrown at a demonstration does not always hit its intended target. Above all, growing numbers of women voted for us. In the decisive elections of September 1930, almost half of those who did so were women.

Women, it should never be forgotten, are governed by emotions rather than the intellect. I knew exactly how to talk to them. They, in turn, cheered me as loudly as anyone, often while weeping uncontrollably. If anything, women's adoration—I can think of no better word—of my person intensified during the years after 1933. The crowds that followed me wherever I went were made up in large part of women. Other women made the pilgrimage to Berchtesgaden. They waited for hours to give the German salute or to hold out their children for me to touch. Nor did the flow cease even during my absences. So numerous were they that, come 1938, I had Bormann forbid the practice and fence off the place where they used to wait for me. Nothing could disturb the love affair between German women and myself. And until the end, nothing did.

Women were as opportunistic as men. In 1933 alone, 800,000 new members joined the *Nationalsozialistische Frauenschaft*. To be sure, the NSF wielded little real power. However, as its head, Frau Scholz-Klink, said much later, it enjoyed as much autonomy as any other organization in our totalitarian state did. Compared to similar organizations in other countries, the funding it received was generous indeed. We also gave it substantial leeway in its own areas of activity, such as women's welfare and health. There was hardly a single German woman whom it did not reach in one way or another.

I well knew that, by punishing women too harshly, one risks rousing sympathy for them. That is why we treated female opponents of our regime with kid gloves. Out of the numerous concentration camps established before the war, only one was earmarked for women. It was not until 1938 that we executed the first female political criminal, the Communist agitator Lieselotte Hermann. She was arrested for passing classified information to the headquarters of the banned German Communist Party in Switzerland. Convicted of treason, she and three of her male colleagues were guillotined. That served them right.

We instituted and celebrated Mother's Day. We awarded medals to fertile women. At the time, similar measures were common in other countries too; in France, they persisted until the 1990s. But we went considerably further than most. Long before most other countries, we allowed working women to deduct a certain sum used for child care from their taxes.

In principle, though, we did not want mothers to work. To encourage them to stay at home we instituted the famous marriage loans. Provided a woman did not work during the first two years after her wedding, with the birth of each additional child a quarter of the sum was written off. Later, the regulations were quietly changed so that she would receive the benefit even if she did work. Much as subsequent feminists might rail against them, most of these measures proved to be immensely popular. The leader of the Catholic German Women's Association, Antoine Hoppman, called the loans "a stroke of genius," which, in their own way, they were.

We also tried other ways to help women. By their very nature, women are unsuited either for the rough and tumble of politics or for the kind of dirty work lawyers often do. The more they try to be like us men, in fact, the less we, and I, personally, like them. That, not any desire to oppress them or humiliate them, is why we banned them from both professions. At all costs, we wanted to protect them and to keep them pure. Female professors—unhappy creatures, most of them, working in fields for which they were not suited—were also dismissed. Jewesses apart, all those who lost their jobs received full pensions. Many also found other kinds of work. In any case the number of those affected only amounted to less than one percent of the female workforce. Whatever critics may say, all these measures received the full support both of the Frauenschaft and of the *grande dame* of German feminism, Fräulein Bäumer. A greater tribute to our policies would be hard to find.

In December 1933, we took our one and only measure against female students by establishing a *numerus clausus* of ten percent for them. Once again, Fräulein Bäumer welcomed the decree to the best of her mediocre ability. For many years past she had supported higher education for women. Now, however, she felt that declining academic standards called for a partial retreat. Our enemies have often cited the decree as an example of our "hatred" for women, particularly intellectual women. They overlook or conceal the fact that, as early as February 1935, the decree was rescinded. Thus the only female students affected were those in the graduating class of 1934. And even those could earn retroactive credit provided they wanted to and provided they had been registered with the university as "listeners." Later, during the war, the fact that practically all young men were serving in the armed forces enabled women to take over and to form the majority of students, even in faculties such as law, from which we had initially tried to remove them.

Contrary to the legend concerning "oppression," in 1933 proportionally far *more* German than American women worked outside the home. With the Great Depression in the background, many countries sought to alleviate the situation by dismissing women in double-income families. Austria, Belgium, Britain, France, Italy,

Luxembourg, the Netherlands, Spain, Sweden, and the United States all either passed such measures or contemplated them at some point. Brüning had tried them as well, but to no avail. Whatever the situation abroad, in practice few, if any, German women ever lost their jobs for this reason.

From my time in Vienna and Munich I knew how little dancing girls were paid. They earned so little, in fact, that many were driven to make a living on the streets, selling their bodies. It made me furious! That is why, as soon as I had the opportunity, I personally saw to it that their wages should be raised. As the economy started picking up, we found ourselves in a position to provide employment to any woman who wanted a job. The number of those who took the opportunity rose and rose. By the end of the 1930s, proportionally more women worked in Germany than in any other European country except France. Step by step, too, our welfare state expanded. By the late 1930s it had come to embrace almost all working women. As someone said, five years of National Socialist rule in some ways did more to help German professional women than a decade of feminist pressure in the Republic had.

Not only did we not refuse to employ women, but we did more to protect female workers than any other country did. One law prohibited employers from requiring women to work on pedal-operated machinery. Others prohibited women from working underground, dealing with poisonous materials, or carrying heavy weights. Nor could they be employed for shift work or night work. In the late 1930s, moreover, the developing shortage of labor forced employers to woo their female employees. As a result, their wages rose faster than those of men did. In industries such as textiles, mining, metal, electronics, and bricks, women began receiving equal pay with men. Of this achievement, our National Socialist trade union was very proud.

We also put in place arrangements designed to help working women. Among them were special facilities for mothers at work,

a "birth premium" and a "breastfeeding premium" as well as free
nursing services, medical treatment, and medicines for themselves
and their babies. Many of these measures proved so advanced that
they remained part of German law long after 1945. Some were so
advanced that a great many other countries are still debating whether
they should or should not be adopted.

As preparations for war started in earnest, and also during the war
itself, I came under intense pressure to make greater use of our female
labor force. Among those who tried to persuade me were Göring in
his capacity as Plenipotentiary for the Four Years Plan; Fritz Sauckel,
who was responsible for labor; and General Eduard Wagner, the
Chief of the Army General Staff Economic Department. Later, they
were joined by Speer in his capacity of Minister of Munitions. I, however, always refused. My reason was that our long-limbed German
women were not suited for the kind of physical work our factories
demanded; this, after all, was long before the production of steel was
automated and robots took the place of men at the assembly lines.
German women could undertake such work, if at all, only at the cost
of very great physical and psychological hardship. I also wanted to
protect them against the kind of sexual harassment which, working
in the factories side by side with men, they were bound to suffer.
That was something, I felt, we owed them as well as their fathers,
husbands, and brothers who were serving in the armed forces.

Against the advice of some, I did not encroach on family life by
ordering children to be evacuated from the cities. Voluntary evacuation, of course, was something else. I did not want to imitate
Russia where, during the Second World War, women formed the
majority not only in the factories but even among miners. That was
the only time in history this happened. As a result, they died like
flies. Instead, to take the place of our men at the front, I had Sauckel
bring in millions of foreign workers, both male and female, from
all the occupied territories. That was why he was later hanged at
Nuremberg. I personally made sure that many of the workers were

employed in the countryside so as to lighten the burden our peasant women were bearing.

We ensured that, in proportion to their absent husbands' income, German women received *twice* as much money as English and American women did. Not to mention the fact that we National Socialists were the only government in the entire world which paid the widows of fallen soldiers for any illegitimate children they had by them. Unfortunately, the war prevented me from protecting German women as much as they deserved to be and as much as I wanted to. Some compromises had to be made. But I never lost sight of my long-term goal: namely, to make sure that, in the not-too-remote future, no German woman would have to do hard work in a factory.

As part of his declaration of "total war" in 1943, Goebbels wanted to close down all kinds of factories and facilities that catered to women, such as fashion houses, the plants where cosmetics were produced, beauty parlors, and the like. The way he saw it, the objective was not just to save labor and resources but to raise the nation's spirit by showing that waste was being eliminated. When Eva heard that, she was appalled! I stepped in and made sure it would not happen. Most women—real women, not feminists—are content with home and family. Politics only interest them on the margins. But will a maiden forget her ornaments? Never. Women are very addicted to their little luxuries and vanities. Grant them those, and they are content. Deny them, and they will become, if not dangerous, sullen and resentful.

Necessity knows no bounds. No one was a stronger opponent of using women as soldiers than I. As the war went on and our sources of manpower were exhausted, though, I gradually dropped my objections to using women as auxiliaries in all kinds of defense-related work. Toward the end those who served may have numbered as many as half a million. And that figure does not include 400,000 Red Cross auxiliaries. They did a sterling job as civil defense organizers, air traffic controllers, telephone operators—at that time, they were not yet known as "communicators"—and the like. But when Goebbels, shortly before our final defeat, came up with the idea of issuing them weapons and sending them into combat, I sent him packing. In any case most of the weapons in our arsenal were too big and heavy for them to use. Nor could women stand the physical demands of combat itself. As is shown by the fact that, in their silly attempts to turn women into warriors, all modern Western forces have done is to vastly increase the number of injuries they suffer.

Rather than denounce me for somehow mistreating them, women ought to thank me. At a time when German men, including Hitler Youth boys not yet eighteen years old, were dying in masses, I saved the lives of God knows how many young women who might have otherwise been sent to the front. My objections rested on three principal considerations. First, personally I have never been able to overcome the feeling that it is women's task to give life, not to take it in a variety of mostly horrible ways. Call it romanticism; call it sexism; call it male chauvinism; call it whatever you wish. Once again, *honni soit qui mal y pense!* Second, for women to fight and suffer large numbers of casualties goes against the very purpose of waging war, which is to preserve the nation and strengthen it for the future.

Third, as someone who has been to war and seen more of it than all the world's feminists put together, I feel entitled to say this: for a man to be made to participate in combat alongside a woman is the ultimate insult to his manhood. The desire to defend women is very thing that makes him fight in the first place. A handful of women around can do no harm. They may even help motivate the men, as women have always done. However, beyond a certain point an army that has too many women in its ranks will simply fall apart. Once again, look at the armies of developed countries which, tamely surrendering to the idiotic claims of ignorant academics and half-demented feminists, have taken this road. They are nothing but hopeless crybabies.

None of this means that we prevented women from using their talents in the service of the community. Far from that being the case, it was one reason why they felt attracted to us. Frau Wagner apart, the best known was Leni Riefenstahl who produced the most famous propaganda films ever made for a political movement. I personally patronized her, made sure she got the resources she needed, and thanked her for her efforts. I did the same for the writer and poetess Agnes Miegel. In 1933 she was among eighty-eight writers who, on their own initiative and without being asked, swore an oath of allegiance to me.

Frau Miegel owed her fame to the numerous poems and short stories she wrote about East Prussia. In them she grieved about the separation of that province from the rest of the German Motherland, praised motherhood, glorified war, and preached hatred for the Poles. Knowing them as she did, she rightly suspected they were trying to steal her native land from us. As, to our eternal shame and regret, they ultimately succeeded in doing. Two of her odes were specifically dedicated to me! In return, I publicly listed her among the twenty-five people who were Germany's greatest national assets. And she was by no means the only female artist for whom I publicly expressed my appreciation; far from it.

Two other talented women with whom I often consulted were Elsa Bruckmann and Frau Gerdy Troost. The latter in particular acted as my interior decorator, advising me on every detail of my domestic arrangements from the rugs to the cutlery; when it came to these topics, no one was as knowledgeable as she was. Following in my footsteps, some of my collaborators also engaged her. Nor was our support for outstanding women limited to the arts. During the war British and American female pilots were only permitted to fly aircraft on transport missions behind the front. Not so our German ones. At least three of them became test pilots, a dangerous and very responsible job. One, Hanna Reitsch, flew the world's first helicopter in 1937. Later, she was involved in a crash which she only barely survived. Another, Melitta Schiller, flew no fewer than 1,500 missions testing Stuka dive-bombers as well as test-flying the world's earliest jet and rocket planes. A third female test pilot who flew jets and rockets was Flight Captain Beate Köstlin. After the war, she took on the name Beate Uhse. I was amused, but also a little piqued, to learn that, under that name, she became rich and famous by establishing a very successful company dealing in pornography and sexual aids.

Our movie industry also produced numerous female heroines and held them up as examples for the German people. In return most German women, to their everlasting credit, gave our National Socialist cause their unqualified support. Some feminist organizations, aware of where the wind was blowing, started expelling their Jewish members even before we required them to. Others, especially middle-class ones, had long favored the compulsory sterilization of their inferior sisters. When we finally implemented that policy, they were ecstatic. Here it is important to remember that the program in question depended almost entirely on denunciation; we did not have the manpower needed to screen every household. Had it not been for our brave women, who kept an eye open, it never could have been carried out.

Female doctors sat on the courts which examined candidates for sterilization and carried out some of the operations. Others performed compulsory abortions on female concentration camp inmates. It was mostly female nurses who killed tens of thousands of mentally and physically handicapped people of all ages. Unpleasant, but necessary. Women, whom the SS recruited by means of simple newspaper advertisements, even took on the rather unfeminine duty of guarding concentration camps. Some of them belonged to the General SS, others proudly displayed the special *Totenkopf* insignia, featuring the famous, fearsome skull-and-bones. When Bernhard Schlink in his 1995 novel, *Der Vorleser,* described them as a bunch of heartless bitches, he was not far from the mark. A few were even put in charge of concentration camp brothels, where they supervised the prostitutes' activities! In brief: there was hardly any field of activity in which German women did not participate to the best of their ability. Often they did so with considerable enthusiasm as well.

To sum up, it is simply not true, as feminists and other *Sitzpinklers* (people who pee sitting down or squatting) have so often claimed, that we National Socialists were the enemies of women nor that we did what we could to discriminate against them, put them under all kinds of restrictions, and oppressed them. To the contrary, when we called on them they came, almost always out of their own free will and in ever-growing numbers. The reason why they came was that they understood what we were trying to do: namely, help them direct their lives into the channels most suitable both to their own nature and to the needs of the community. Well aware of how precious they were, we pampered them and protected them as best we could. To be sure, the war prevented us from bringing all our projects to a successful conclusion. Nevertheless, both in peace and in war, in many ways we did more for them than the leaders of any country before and since. They rewarded us, and me personally as their Führer, with what one post-1945 magazine called *Nibelungengtreue*. The highest form of loyalty there is.

Chapter 16

My Private Life

Can a leader such as I was have a private life? In theory, the answer is yes. After all, my body and physical needs were no different from those of other people. Like everyone else, I also had my preferences in day-to-day life; what to eat, what kind of *ambience* to surround myself with, what to do during my leisure hours, and the like.

One might think that all this was no one's business but mine. But that was by no means the case. It only took a surprisingly short time after I took power for a large market for consumer goods, such as busts, postcards, porcelain, and embroidered articles with my image on them, to emerge. That forced me to pass a special law ("The Law for the Protection of National Symbols") to regulate them and to make sure they would not be used in an inappropriate manner. But there was more. If I publicly expressed my approval or disapproval of this or that, countless people followed my example and/or tried to profit from doing so. That even applied to the kind of mustache I grew! At one point someone floated the (false) rumor that my favorite flower was the Edelweiss. No sooner had the news spread than the Edelweiss, with a little help from Goebbels' Propaganda Ministry, became the favorite flower of half the nation. The same happened with clothing, music, and everything else you could think of. The opposite was also true. If I fell ill, then the consequences not just for me but for the German nation could be very serious, especially if the fact became widely known.

My long experience in politics made me well aware of all this even before January 1933. Such being the case, perhaps my greatest problem was to make sure that my image as a man of the people would stay intact. Others too have found out how difficult that is. Before I became Chancellor, out of every ten men I met, nine belonged to the people and one to the elite. From that point on it was the other way around. Moreover, high society has its customs. At the risk of my being looked down upon as a boor, I had to respect them, antiquated and ridiculous as many of them were and are. Just imagine me wearing a cummerbund!

Some leaders have sought to solve these problems by having themselves filmed while they engaged in various popular activities. Think of Mussolini fencing or riding horses, Fidel Castro playing basketball, Reagan riding a horse at Quantico or on his ranch in California, or Vladimir Putin riding a motorcycle, fishing, and throwing opponents in judo. I, alas, did not have the physique to do as they did. I did, of course, attend the Berlin Olympics as my position demanded. And I was proud of our team which, on this occasion, garnered more medals than any other. However, my interest in sports has always been limited.

Most of the time I had to use other methods. One was wearing a simple uniform coat whenever possible. Decorated solely by my Iron Cross, First Class, and contrasting sharply with the glittering uniforms of my generals, it served the purpose very well, as is evident from the fact that any number of subsequent leaders have imitated me in this respect. Another was my custom of sitting or standing in the front seat of my open cars. Rather than relaxing in the rear one, as so-called VIPs, communist ones included, almost always did and do. I wanted to show my people that, eschewing luxury, I was no soft simpering ninny but a strong, hard man. I also wanted to show that I trusted them, was not afraid of them, and, in fact, was one of them. That none of this precluded the most stringent security measures hardly requires saying. An entire book has been written about that subject, to which I have nothing to add.

All my life I went to bed late and got up late. During the daytime
there were a public agenda and a secret one known only to those
who had to know. I also liked springing surprises on my people; it
kept them on their toes. Keenly aware that I could be assassinated
at any moment by some criminal or lunatic, I used to change my
plans frequently and unexpectedly. On at least two occasions, doing
so saved my life. One was in November 1939. A bomb was planted
in the Bürgerbräukeller, where I held a speech to commemorate our
Putsch. I, however, left the meeting early so that the explosion took
place when I was no longer there.

The other was in March 1943. I was scheduled to greet an officer
by the name of von Gersdorff during a weapons review held at Army
Group Center Headquarters. He was carrying a bomb and was ready
to blow himself up along with me. However, something told me to
walk right past him. Next, by cutting my visit short, I did not give
him a second chance. I suppose that, on both occasions, what saved
me was my intuition. Or perhaps it was Providence. Having lost my
faith during my schooldays, I am not religious in the ordinary sense
of the word. Starting at quite an early age, though, I have always
believed that there was a mysterious force guiding and protecting
me.

Anyhow, I received reports, and I issued orders. I read memoranda,
during the war I had them presented to me on a special typewriter
with large characters. I signed all kinds of decrees and directives.
And I made plans, and I held meetings. Not, however, of the whole
cabinet, where we National Socialists were initially a minority. Even
after that problem had been rectified, I preferred to govern by dealing
with each minister separately rather than with all of them together.
After the beginning of 1938, I held no cabinet meetings at all. More
than one of my ministers, visiting the new chancellery Speer built
for me in 1939 and looking over the cabinet room with the chair
with his name on it, felt sorry he would never take his place at the
table! I appointed people and, when the occasion arose, dismissed

them from their posts. I received all sorts of dignitaries, both of the home-grown variety and foreigners. Briefly, I did everything rulers have always done and will always do.

But there were also some differences. To repeat, these were the times before television. Yet my rule was as personal as personal can be. Seldom, if ever, in history did the charisma of a single man matter so much as mine. The more so because Goebbels never ceased extolling me, almost turning me into a god on earth. At Hitler Youth ceremonies they went so far as to compare me with Christ! National Socialism was me, and I was National Socialism. But for me, no party, no Third Reich, no concentration camps, no World War II, no Holocaust. And no *Götterdämmerung* either; no one else could have inspired the German people to follow him practically to the end.

Yet such ties, far from being self-evident, must be constantly refreshed and renewed. I wanted—I had to—show myself to as many people as I could as often as I could. And I had to address them, of course. That is why, during the six years before the war, I traveled much more than most contemporary rulers did. By air, by train, by car, whatever. Unlike Stalin, who owed nothing to oratory but governed Russia from his Kremlin office, I addressed countless meetings, large and small. I also devoted more time than most to the problems of art, as by opening exhibitions and talking to artists. I also regularly attended the Wagner Festival at Bayreuth. So, I am told, does Frau Angela Merkel.

To repeat, one reason for putting so much emphasis on this field was that I considered art to have a vital role in the education of a people. Another was that I always remained an artist at heart. There were few things I enjoyed more than meeting Paul Troost, my first architect, and his admirable wife, Gerdy. After his premature death in January 1934, the same applied to his equally able and gifted successor, Albert Speer. Together, we would lay down plans for the grandiose building projects I had in mind. We exchanged views about the things we had done and would do, examined models, made changes, etc. Some of our sessions took place in the studio and others on the spot. All this took me through moments when I regretted the fact that, carried by circumstances, I had not realized my youthful dream of becoming an artist. *Mais c'est la vie.* One cannot always consult one's own preferences. Least of all if one is in a position like mine.

Regardless of whether one's field is politics, the easel or the drawing board, to be an artist means that leisure is absolutely essential. Right from the beginning I was determined not to be taken over by, or to drown in, affairs of state as has happened to so many others before and after me. I wanted—I very much needed—time to relax and to think. In fact I always considered my ability to do so to be one of my greatest strengths. That is why I often exasperated my collaborators by postponing meetings and delaying decisions. It was not that I could not make them; Heaven knows that, when circumstances called, I could and did. But it was because I soon learned there existed lots and lots of issues which, given enough time, tended to disappear of their own accord. So I simply turned my back on them.

I also continued my long-time habit of rising late and going to bed late. Evenings were often spent talking to close associates or else watching some movie selected by Goebbels. Both German and foreign ones were included in the program. I was particularly interested in American ones. I hoped they would enable me to form at least some idea of what that country, known to me principally from the writings of Karl May, which I had read in my youth, was like. Seen from the point of view of their ability to attract viewers and to feed their lessons to the people, many were better than ours; good as the people at Babelsberg were, we never found a German equivalent to Walt Disney. But that was not the end of the matter. Each night, before going to sleep, I would spend some time reading a little about things completely unrelated to those that had been preoccupying me throughout the day.

On Fridays I would take the train to Munich, and from there travel by motor car convoy to Berchtesgaden. There I would remain until Sunday evening, when the night train would bring me back to Berlin. In the meantime I had redesigned and enlarged the Berghof to suit my tastes. The centerpiece was a very large living room. Originally, it was furnished simply in the Bavarian style. Later, when I sometimes used it for representative purposes, I had it redecorated with costly furniture. There was a bust of Wagner as well as some exquisite paintings done by German, mostly nineteenth-century, artists. It also had a huge picture window that provided an unexcelled view of the Obersalzburg. On fine days it could be lowered into the ground, allowing in fresh air. There was a dining room, a study with a library, a large marble-top table for maps, and a big terrace. Upstairs, there were several more rooms, including two interconnecting bedrooms for Fräulein Braun and me.

I always found the mountain air invigorating. It was at the Berghof that I had my best ideas and made my most important decisions. In 1937 a tea house was built about a kilometer away. Accompanied by a guest or two, during my stays I used to walk there and back almost every day I was there. Himmler in particular used these walks, and the privacy they afforded, to discuss some of the most sensitive subjects of all, to receive his orders, and to report on his progress in carrying them out. For my birthday in the spring of 1939 Bormann had another tea house built for me higher up the mountain at Kehlstein. Access was by means of an elevator whose shaft was hewn right into the rock. Constructed at breakneck speed, technically it was a magnificent achievement. However, the thin air—it was located 1,800 meters above sea level—did not agree with me. Consequently, I only went there a handful of times.

As I said, the person in charge of the Berghof was my stepsister Angela, Geli's mother. She had some experience in the field and did as good a job as I could have wished for; unsurprisingly, though, she did not get along with Fräulein Braun. So I eventually had to let her go. The place was run like the small resort it had originally been, complete with housekeepers, gardeners, cooks, waiters, and so on. The overall responsibility for it was in the hands of Bormann and, coming under him, a Frau Mittelstrasser, who acted as hostess. I used to entertain guests there every weekend. Himmler apart, among the most frequent visitors were Goebbels, Speer, Hoffmann, Hess, Ribbentrop, Otto Dietrich (my press secretary), and my physicians Theodor Morrell and Karl Brandt. Also, before he was assassinated in 1942, Heydrich. At times their wives were also invited; so, less often, were figures from the world of art.

Having gone over my mail, I used to come down from my upstairs apartment around noon or even later. I would talk to the guests a little before inviting them inside for lunch. Since I was busy, on such occasions it fell to Bormann to look after Eva. The food was normally quite light. Though I did have something of a sweet tooth, I never pretended to be a gourmet. No fancy dishes with incomprehensible French names, no twelve-course dinners for me! Soup, baked potatoes, and rice or pasta served with asparagus or some other vegetables were quite enough. Though I myself was a vegetarian and a teetotaler, I did not object to others consuming meat or drinking a glass of wine. However, the terrace apart, I did not allow them to smoke in my presence.

I also used my stays at the Berghof to play an occasional game of bowling—there was an alley in the basement—and to train my dog, among other activities. On occasion I held a little party to which one of my associates' children were invited. I did that because I liked children and they liked me. Hoffmann and Eva, who was an enthusiastic photographer and a good one too, made sure some of our idyllic existence was captured on film. The resulting images were in greater demand than any of the rest. People, it seems, were eager to see me as one of them. It lay in the nature of things that my paladins wanted to be as close to me as possible, mainly to compete for my favor and to have my ear, of course. But I flatter myself that some of them also did so because they valued the relaxed, informal, *ambience* I provided them with.

As the years went by, each of them felt obliged to build his own place nearby. The paths, originally covered with pine needles, were paved over. The entire complex was fenced in and guarded by an SS company, whose troops, in turn, had to be provided with living quarters, a dining hall, exercise facilities, and so on. As each addition led to others, year by year the number of people who lived or worked on the mountain increased. Ultimately, it almost became a small city, complete with shelters and underground corridors that would allow the occupants, and me of course, to escape in case of an emergency. The moving spirit in much of this was Bormann. In this and other fields, to get what he wanted he was not above using rather brutal methods, such as, for example, evicting the original residents and acquiring their property. A few spent time in concentration camps before they understood what he expected of them. Personally, I would rather have left things as they had been early on. Again, though, one cannot always consult one's own preferences.

From time to time I used to invite foreign guests I wanted to honor. Among them were former British Prime Minister David Lloyd-George, the man who probably did more than any other to bring down Germany during the Great War. Hoffmann, who was present as usual, later told me that he had said that Germany should thank God for having sent it such a leader. Others were the Agha Khan, the Duke and Duchess of Windsor, Austrian Prime Minster Kurt von Schuschnigg, British Prime Minister Neville Chamberlain, Pierre Laval, and Benito Mussolini. Not to mention various smaller fry. I also sometimes invited the top officers of the armed forces to Berchtesgaden to discuss my plans in the privacy the place afforded.

Those of my German visitors who frequented the Berghof were aware of the existence of Eva, on whom more in a moment, and kept the secret. But I just could not afford to have the nation know about her. Any public shows of affection were strictly out of bounds.

Simple, affectionate soul that she was, that was hard on her. But it could not be helped. She would mix with my paladins, especially Speer, with whom she sometimes used to go hiking. But when foreign visitors arrived, I had to ask her to stay in her room. "Up there," she once commented, "there is something people are not allowed to see—me!"

Speaking of Mussolini, he kept "changing the guard," as he used to put it. I, by contrast, considered myself lucky in my choice of my senior and mid-level associates. As long as they did not commit major blunders, they normally stayed with me for years, as Göring, Bormann, Speer, Himmler, Keitel, Jodl, and any number of Gauleiters did. They understood my power, of course. But they did not fear me the way Stalin's subordinates were absolutely terrified of him. Only during the very last months of the war did I have to prohibit some of them from presenting me with their defeatist ideas. To lend weight to my words, I had Ernst Kaltenbrunner, Heydrich's successor as Head of the Reich Central Security Office, sit in on a few of our meetings. The traitors of July 1944 apart, only very rarely did I bother to put any of them on trial. Nor did I lock them in concentration camps or have them taken from their homes and shot.

I did not want people to question my decisions. Nor, much less, did I desire scandals among my close collaborators that would reflect on the regime. That is why, rather than dismiss senior officials who at one point or another were no longer up to the job, I would take part of their power away from them and give it to someone else. Needless to say, I didn't inform the loser of what I had done. For example, I did this in 1943 when I backed Milch, Galland, and Kammhuber against Göring, effectively ending the latter's control over the Luftwaffe. And again in late 1944 when I promoted Speer's assistants, Xaver Dorsch and Karl Saur, at his expense. This method had the added advantage of forcing my subordinates to compete for my favor. Right to the end, that competition prevented them from uniting against me.

Other dictators have often made the personnel around them—

valets, secretaries, communicators, messengers, even physicians—
tremble with fear. Apparently, that was how Stalin died. It was
nighttime when, alone in his room, he was felled by a stroke, but
his people, not daring to disturb him, left him alone until it was
too late. My situation was entirely different. Contrary to what one
might think from watching the film, *Er ist wieder da* (Look Who is
Back), I did not treat those people harshly, yell at them, or threaten
to fire them. Though life was becoming harder and harder for me,
right to the end my relations with them were uniformly cordial and
occasionally even light hearted. For example, I was once informed
that a former orderly of mine had not one but two ships on which
he served (he was a sailor) go down under him. Thereupon, I sent
for him, told him I could not afford to have him sink my entire navy,
and took him back. Those who were closest to me did not hesitate
to have a little fun at my expense. Hoffmann once served me juice
colored in such a way that I started berating him before I realized it
was not alcohol. Once, one of my adjutants suggested that the blood
Morrell took from me might be mixed with a little salt and sold as
Führer black pudding!

I saw to it that those of them who yielded to temptation would
be severely punished. For the rest, though, I did not care about their
rank but used to address them simply by their surnames. Unlike
today's great democratic leaders, until after the Putsch of 20 July
1944 it never occurred to me to humiliate them by having their
persons searched, their bags checked, and so forth. I made sure I
remembered their birthdays, and I gave them small presents. To
express my appreciation I also had my staff keep a ready supply of
more expensive gifts, such as gold watches inscribed with my initials,
to hand out to people as the occasion demanded. Staying at my
various headquarters during the war, I made sure that my female
secretaries, who were surrounded by men, most of whom had not
been home for a long, long time, would not be sexually harassed.

Those of them who were unmarried, such as Walter Hewel, my liaison officer with the foreign ministry, I gently tried to provide with mates. Quite often, my efforts were crowned with success; that having been accomplished, I was happy to act as best man. If I sometimes inadvertently hurt their feelings, I was quick to apologize. I distinctly recall doing so both to Hewel and Traudl Junge. Above all, I knew how to talk to them when, as did happen from time to time, their husbands, fiancés, or other relatives died or were wounded or killed.

Many, if not most, of the personnel in question were aware that they were living through extraordinary times and kept diaries. Not only didn't I check on them or stop them, but here in Hell I took the time to read several of their accounts. This includes not just the published versions but the unpublished ones as well. None seems to have had any serious complaint about me. To the contrary, amongst themselves, they often called me USA. Meaning *unser seeliger Adolf,* our blessed Adolf. Some remained devoted to my memory for decades after my death, notwithstanding the way I am remembered and notwithstanding the problems this stance sometimes created for them.

This brings me back to Fräulein Braun. As I said earlier, the more famous and powerful I became, the more women competed for my attention. Don't they always? They are a strange lot, these women. The more one shows one's contempt for them, the more they run after one. They take contempt as a sign of strength. Among the women who ran after *me* were some who were very beautiful indeed. The English aristocrat Unity Mitford in particular was a model of Germanic womanhood. Unfortunately, she was also as crazy as a bat and a danger to herself; after she tried to commit suicide in 1939, I had her packed off to Switzerland so that no one would know. In any case, I first met Eva in 1929. At the time she was working in Hoffmann's studio in Munich. I was forty, she seventeen.

Nothing unusual about that. When the aforementioned Kershaw maintained the opposite, he was simply jealous; the same applies to other historians, both male and female. The truth is that great men have always turned to younger women for relaxation. Caesar was 31 years older than Cleopatra. Napoleon was 17 years older than Maria Waleska, Goethe was 54 years older than his last love, Ulrike von Levetzow. Does that mean he was incapable of relating to mature women?

The attraction is often mutual; for example, Gerdy Troost was 26 years younger than her adored husband. To return to Eva, I liked her from the start but only began seeing her regularly in October 1931 after Geli's death. From that point our relationship blossomed. Early on she and I used to meet in my flat in Munich. She was what people call a nice girl, blonde—with a little help from peroxide, to be honest—quite good looking, cheerful, modest, and unassuming. She was of lower-middle class origin and neither terribly intelligent nor very well educated. And she was totally uninterested in politics. She did not understand my anti-Semitism, and my speeches bored her. All that was just as I wanted it to be. Having spent so much of my life fighting—first at the front, then in politics, then in the international arena, and finally as warlord—absolutely the last thing I needed near me was a philosophizing Brunhilde à la Mathilde Ludendorff. Much less a gold-digging vixen like Jacqueline Bouvier-Kennedy-Onassis, of whom de Gaulle once said that she would end up on the yacht of some tycoon—as she in fact did—or some half-demented feminist fury always complaining about being discriminated against, oppressed, and "objectified." Knowing the world as I do, I believe that ninety-nine percent of real men agree with me on this point.

What Eva did have was a soft heart for dogs, children, and people. I called her Tschapperl, which is Austrian slang for "little girl." To protect her, I had a small air shelter built in the garden of her house. Rather than use it, though, she would invite her neighbors to come in. She herself used to go up on the roof to see if any incendiaries had fallen; no coward was Fräulein Braun. She also had a sense of humor and would poke occasional fun at me, even in the presence of others. She kept herself trim—a bit too trim, if you ask me—by hiking, swimming, and skiing. Had it depended on her, she would have gone out even when it was snowing heavily. But I, considering it too dangerous, prohibited her from doing so.

As I said, one of her hobbies was photography. Another was fashion. She knew how to dress tastefully, though not grandly, and kept a meticulous record of the clothes she wore on each occasion. I encouraged her by giving her pocket money to buy jewelry and other trinkets. To keep her company I got her two dogs. They were Black Scottish terriers, which she named Negus and Stasi. In the mornings they used to wait for her, sitting like bronze statues at her door. I used to tease her by saying they weren't dogs but dusting brushes; she retorted by claiming that Blondi was not a dog but a calf. Her dogs and mine could not stand one another, with the result that, when I wanted to bring Blondi to some place where she was present, I had to ask for her permission first! Those—I shall not name them—who say I kept her in a "golden cage" at the Berghof are lying. Partly in order to get her away from her parents' house, which she hated, as early as 1936, I gave her a house in Munich. There she lived with her younger sister Gretl, continuing to visit Hoffmann's shop when she felt like it. She also had an apartment in the *Reichskanzlei,* where she stayed from time to time and where one of my orderlies, Rochus Misch, once accidentally caught her in my bed. She also had her own car. During my absence, which was most of the time, she did as she pleased. That included going on long walks, which, when I was around, she could not do.

What *is* true is that I could never think of marrying her. I could not even take her around openly. Partly, this was the case because our relationship had to remain secret. And, sweet thing that she was, she was totally unsuited for acting like a *grande dame* at public functions such as diplomatic receptions and dinners. That is another reason

why so many great men have two (or more) women. One is for show
and the other for love. This is what German Chancellor Helmut
Schmidt did. How much of her life did Anne Pingeot sacrifice for
President François Mitterand! The most I could do for Eva was to
have her attend the Nuremberg Rally in the company of Morrell and
his wife. On other occasions she went with Hoffmann, her former
employer. Even so, we had to be careful and could not sit closely
together. Add the fact that I was, after all, a rather busy man, and
her feeling that I neglected her becomes readily understandable.

Twice, in 1932 and 1935, she tried to put an end to her life. The
first time she used a pistol I had given her, but the bullet merely
grazed her neck; the second time, she used sleeping-pills of a kind
that were unlikely to kill her. Thus neither attempt seems to have
been terribly serious; after all, she was neither the first nor the last
woman to try to make her man feel guilty so as to bind him to her. It
worked, and our relationship became closer. Partly because I could
not help but sympathize with her, and partly because, after what
had happened to Geli, I simply could not afford to have another
dead woman around me. She was fiercely loyal. While not above
criticizing me to my face, even in the presence of others, woe to
anyone who dared to criticize me in front of her. I shall not satisfy
people's curiosity by going into detail except to say, *"Für die Liebe,
hatte ich eine Mädchen in München."* For love, I had a young lady in
Munich.

Absent a representative wife, I turned to Göring's second wife
Emmy, a former actress. And, above all, to Magda Goebbels. Born
Magda Ritschel, she attended some of the best available schools for
girls before marrying Günter Quandt in 1921. Quandt was one of
Germany's richest men, whose offspring still owns a large part of
BMW. By him she had one son, Harald. However, the marriage was
not a happy one. She, being twenty years old, wanted to dance and
dazzle while hosting parties at their villa in Potsdam. He, eighteen
years her senior, wanted to do business. In 1929 he divorced her,

leaving her a well-to-do woman. In 1930 she joined the party and
started doing volunteer work for Goebbels in his capacity as Chief of
Propaganda. In 1931 they married, with me acting as a witness.

She and Josef had six children. I am, however, sorry to say that
the marriage was no happier than Magda's previous one. Repeatedly,
they cheated on one another, quarreled, and were reconciled. She
even claimed he beat her; though how, given his dwarfish body and
the metal brace he had to wear, he could have done so remains a
mystery. At one point he wanted to divorce her. Next, he was going
to marry the Czech actress Lida Baarova, with whom he had a steamy
affair, and remove himself from the scene by taking up a post as our
ambassador to Japan! The idea was ridiculous, and I curtly forbade
him from going through with it. Ordinarily, I did not much care
much what people did and with whom they did it. But scandal in
high quarters was something I could not and would not tolerate. It
might give our good, decent Germans some undesirable ideas as to
who we, their rulers, were.

Frau Goebbels was everything Eva was not. That, as well as the
obvious way in which they competed for my attention, was why the
two women developed a strong dislike for one another. Magda was
highly intelligent, very well educated, and one of my most fervent
admirers. When she was in my presence, one could hear her ovaries
rattle. One of the last things she told me before we both died was that
she could not imagine living in a world without National Socialism.
Above all, she was every inch a lady. It was this last quality which
attracted me to her and made her useful to me. She knew how to
dress, how to use makeup, how to present herself, and how to talk.
And not just in German either. Her excellent education and manners
enabled me to take her as my companion during official events. And
yes, during the 1930s I liked to drop in on the Goebbels family home
at Schwanenwerder on the Havel when the opportunity offered. But
no, a thousand times no. It is not true that I was what we Germans
call a *Hausfreund*. And I did not have an affair with her.

Nor was I the sick man I have often been portrayed to be. Had I not enjoyed robust health, I never could have summoned one tenth of the stamina needed to acquire the allegiance of millions and reached the position I did. To be sure, as I approached my fiftieth birthday, I could feel my age. There were some minor complaints, chiefly concerning my intestines and digestion. At one point I suffered from severe stomach cramps as well as eczema. I cannot say that I did not worry about them a little. These problems were handled by my physicians, principally the invaluable Dr. Morrell. I was well aware that many of my associates, Fräulein Braun included, did not like him. Neither did some of my other doctors. Motivated by professional jealousy, they were always intriguing against him. He was, in fact, somewhat unsavory—during mealtimes, you could hear him enjoying his food. And he was so fat that he had difficulty getting out of the bath and through the doors of railway carriages. He was almost a German Rasputin, I would say. But to me and Goebbels, whom he cured of dermatitis after twenty-two other doctors had failed to do so, he was a godsend. So effective were his injections that I often started feeling better even before he took the needle out of my arm. Whatever my problems, they certainly did not prevent me from carrying out my duties and presiding over some of history's greatest military triumphs in 1939–41.

From that point on things became very difficult. At times the war went well for us; at other times less so. So great was the strain that people who have not gone through it can hardly imagine what it is like. More than once, I felt like Atlas carrying the world on my shoulders! I worried and worked and worked and worried—the latter often at night while lying in bed and plagued by insomnia. I also slowly developed heart trouble, which gradually limited my physical activity. All this was just the opposite of the kind of life I had always thought was the best for me and tried to create for myself. The worst part of it was being unable to share my worries with anyone.

At all costs, I *had* to appear young, healthy, sprightly, and ready for anything. Even during the most difficult moments, as when 6. Army was encircled at Stalingrad and all of us at headquarters were worried half to death. I could not even draw up my last will and testament; doing so would have had a depressing effect on everyone around me. That is why I postponed doing so to the last possible moment. Still, considering the circumstances, my health held up tolerably well. I was still able to do sustained work day in and day out. At no time was there any question of a loss of control, let alone an incapacitating physical collapse.

Only after the *Attentat* on my life, which took place on 20 July 1944, did I really start to suffer from all kinds of symptoms. Prominent among them were partial deafness; eyes that, instead of being simply somewhat protruding, seemed to jump out of their sockets; a body which began bending itself forward; and an uncontrollable trembling in my left arm and right leg that my doctors attributed to Parkinson's. That's not to mention sleepless nights and the kind of nervousness that reflected the unbearable stress under which I was living. But I did not permit even that to wear me down. To the contrary, I felt that, the more vulnerable I became, the more Providence was holding its hand over me for its own purposes. One way or another, life was hard. At times it was only my sense of duty that kept me going. I held out as best I could right to the end.

Like all VIPs, I attracted visitors as a flame attracts moths. Everyone and his brother wanted to be introduced to me and be photographed with me. And yet I was a lonely man. Many of my biographers have traced my loneliness to my youthful experiences or else to my alleged mental peculiarities, not to say pathologies. My subordinates also took note of how lonely I was. Here is what Ribbentrop, not always the most sensitive of men, had to say about the matter during his trial at Nuremberg. "If I am asked today whether I knew him well—how he thought as a politician and statesman, what kind of man he was—then I am bound to confess that I know only very little about him; in fact nothing at all. The fact is that although I went through so much together with him, in all the years of working with him I never came closer to him than on the first day we met, either personally or otherwise."

General Jodl, my closest military aide with whom I used to meet twice a day for several years on end, said similar things. Then there was Speer, my architect and subsequent Minister of Munitions. In his memoirs he wrote that, if I had any friends, he was my friend. And he was right; he *was* my friend—up to a point, at any rate. With him I could discuss my artistic plans as with no one else. Until, that is, the very end of the war when he disobeyed my "scorched earth" order. At one point he even tried to kill me by feeding poison gas into my bunker. Or so, fighting for his life at Nuremberg, he claimed. Some friend.

Another close "friend" was Goebbels. Goebbels was a giant locked in a pygmy's body. As he proudly noted in his diary, with him I talked "man to man" as I did with no one else. True enough. But part of it was calculation, not sentiment. It was a way to keep him absolutely loyal. And it worked. In any case, can a man in my position really have friends? True friendship requires total mutual trust. But could I really trust people all of whom, without exception, wanted something from me? A favor, perhaps? Greater authority to help them against one or more of their rivals? A promotion? Or simply to bask in my glory? On one occasion, during a lunch at the Berghof, I lent Speer a jacket of mine, complete with the emblem I alone was entitled to wear. Thirty years later, in his memoirs, he still recalled the incident. With pride! Friendship, true friendship, is only possible between equals. But I, in all modesty, did not have an equal. How could I when I was still the party's greatest asset? It was even more impossible after I became Reich Chancellor and was holding the fate of tens of millions in my hands.

Nor did I have a family as so many other rulers, especially, but not exclusively, hereditary ones, did. For a ruler, a family is by no means always a good thing to have. The number of them who had to kill their relatives, or were killed by them, is legion. Neither Shakespeare in *Hamlet* nor Schiller in *Don Carlos* invented anything; in fact my own nephew, William Patrick Hitler, the son of my half-brother Alois, tried to blackmail me. Even if things do not go that far, family, official or unofficial, means obligation. Obligation, in turn, means nepotism, favoritism, and corruption. Look at Napoleon, who was always appointing his worthless brothers to this office or that. Mussolini, whose mistress Clara Petacci became the stalking horse her relatives rode to riches, could also tell a pretty tale in that respect.

The fact that I did not have a family did not stem from the inability or, especially during my last years, even the inclination to find a mate. It was the outcome of a conscious, politically motivated decision. Had I won the war, I would have resigned all my posts and left Berlin, a city I never liked. Let someone else look after government affairs, especially war! I would have spent the rest of my life with Eva in quiet retirement. I would not exactly have been trying to repair clocks, but I would have been reading, talking to a few friends, listening to records, writing my memoirs, enjoying art, designing buildings, walking a little, and training my dog without once having to see a uniform or meet a dunderhead of a bureaucrat or an officer. After years and years during which I suffered nothing but vexation at their hands, what a relief it would have been!

Everything considered, was I really lonelier than others in my position? More, say, than Julius Caesar, who ended up by being assassinated by Brutus—the very Brutus whom, in an act of unparalleled generosity, he had forgiven for siding with Pompey during the civil war? Or than Henry VIII with his six wives, two of whom he executed, two of whom he divorced, and two of whom died on him?

Or than Frederick the Great, who, as he grew older, increasingly preferred dogs to men and finally asked to be buried with them? Isn't loneliness always and necessarily the price one pays for power?

In brief, my private and public lives were in many ways one. I was what I was, and I did what I thought I had to. Even if the road was long and hard. Even if, especially toward the end, it gave me no joy. Even if I had to go against my own nature and use the most brutal available means. Not so much for myself, perhaps, as for the love I bore my people. Here is what one of our national poets, Ernst Moritz Arndt, had to say about the matter:

> The God who made the iron grow,
> Didn't want slaves.
> So he gave saber, sword and spear,
> The man in his right hand.
> So he gave him the brave courage,
> The wrath of free speech.
> That he consisted to the blood,
> Till to the death the feud.

Chapter 17

Rearming the Reich

Right from the beginning, I was absolutely determined to cast off the shameful shackles of Versailles and rebuild our German military power. Nor did I waste any time in starting to work in this direction. Within seventy-two hours of my appointment I met with the chiefs of the armed forces. I told them in no uncertain terms what I, with their help, was going to do. And I promised them a free hand in doing it.

But we had to proceed carefully. First, our enemies, meaning mainly Britain and France, were watching. Instigated and bribed by the Jews, some of their generals and politicians would have liked nothing better than to cut off our heads when we were still small and weak. And weak we were. In 1914 Germany had a standing army of 750,000 men with another 3,750,000 trained reservists ready to join the ranks and be thrown into battle within a couple of weeks or so. We also had a navy which, at that time, was the third most powerful in the world after those of Britain and the U.S. Our defeat changed all this, leaving us essentially disarmed.

The Reichswehr was as well trained as any other army in the world. But with just 100,000 men in nine small divisions, including two cavalry divisions, in truth it was little more than a frontier guard. Nor did it have any trained reserves on which it could draw. As some wargames held during the 1920s showed only too clearly, so weak was it that it could never have stopped even a Polish attack, let alone resist a full-scale French invasion. The navy had a couple of so-called pocket battleships. For their time they were true technological

marvels. But they were no match for the numerous *real* battleships
our opponents had. Nor, as we later learnt, were our ships a challenge
for the carriers they were already developing.

We did not have submarines, another weapon that would be essential for waging any kind of future war. We did not have military
aircraft. We did not have heavy artillery, the only weapon capable of
knocking out fortifications. And we did not have tanks. Tanks had
proved their worth during the last months of the Great War, and it
was becoming clearer every day that they would dominate the future
battlefield. That was why the Allies did not allow us to build them.
Those we used for training were cardboard constructions mounted
on the chassis of trucks. So weak was their "armor" that children
used to amuse themselves by sticking pencils into it! How our men
felt about *that* may readily be imagined.

I do not want to say that we took all this simply lying down. We
did our best to keep abreast of the most recent technological developments. Throughout the 1920s we sent officers to Russia, where
they taught themselves and the Russians how to use tanks. Come
Operation Barbarossa in 1941, some of them put their knowledge of
Russia to good use, especially von Manstein and Model, of whom I
shall have more to say later. We also had some companies working
for us in Spain, the Netherlands, and Sweden. They produced a
few experimental submarines and aircraft. To train our future pilots
we put a great deal of effort into gliders. Both our pilots and our
gliders did in fact become the best of their kind in the world; to
that extent the effort paid off. On the whole, though, our situation
with respect to the most modern and most powerful weapons was
not unsatisfactory. It was disgraceful.

The other problem I faced was more serious still. Ever since we
had won our victories over Austria and France in 1866–71, the world
had looked up to our General Staff as a model of its kind. Foreigners
such as the Englishman Spenser Wilkinson and the American General Emory Upton studied it and wrote books about it. Under the

terms of the Treaty of Versailles, its existence was prohibited. That fact, of course, did not disturb us too much, since the General Staff continued to exist under the name of *Truppenamt*. In a way it even assisted us, because the army's small size allowed us to select and train our officers more rigorously than ever before. The real problem was different. Under the Kaiserreich, our top commanders had a reputation for always pressing for the most extreme political and military measures. As, for example, General Moltke Jr.—who, at that time was Deputy Chief of the General Staff—did in 1905. He told his wife that, if Germany failed to use Russia's defeat to push through its demands, it might as well fold its tail, place itself under the protection of Japan, and concentrate on making money! When I came to power, I expected them to adopt a similar attitude.

It did not turn out that way. I very soon learned that my generals were not the bloodhounds everyone thought they were. They did not growl, they did not bare their teeth, and they did not have to be put on a leash. In reality, they were pussycats. To be sure, they were delighted with my promise that the Treaty would be abrogated and rearmament started as soon as possible. For them it meant more resources, greater power, and, in many cases, promising prospects for promotion. Colonel-generals wanted to become field-marshals, lieutenant generals wanted to become colonel-generals, and so on down the ladder all the way to the second lieutenants. Quite natural, I suppose. But war? No way. The more senior the officers, the more convinced they were that they had drawn a lesson from 1914–18. And the lesson, they thought, was that Germany should never again go to war against a powerful coalition of other countries.

Not only were they pussycats, but they were totally lacking in vision. In their very first meetings with me they asked for an additional 50 million marks for the Reichswehr. They also wanted, as someone timidly said, another 43 million earmarked to start a fledgling air force. As I said before, I am no economist. My strong point has never been numbers and equations but my ability to reduce

complex problems to their simplest components. And I also had
something even more important: vision. I knew full well that the
sort of rearmament *I* had in mind would cost billions, not a few
paltry millions. This tendency of theirs to think small continued to
plague me right down to the end. Each time I proposed some bold
measure or operation, it reappeared.

Like all other bureaucrats they were also parochial. They neither
understood the broader historical context in which our national life
necessarily developed nor cared for it. Their intellectual horizons
were limited to Europe from the Ukraine to the Pyreneans. Anything
beyond that might as well be on the other side of the moon. The
Japanese attack on the U.S. provided a very good example of this.
When the news arrived, I turned to the great military minds in my
headquarters and asked where Pearl Harbor was, only to learn that
none of them knew the answer. Not even my naval adjutant, Rear
Admiral Karl-Jesko von Puttkamer! As to General Halder, four days
later he did not even bother note my declaration of war on the U.S.
in his diary. Geniuses, each and every one of them.

The most important single actor was General Blomberg, whom I
have already introduced. As a member of the Reichswehr, he could
not join the party. But in all other ways he was very close to us
National Socialists, so much so that he was nicknamed Hitler Youth
Quex after the juvenile hero of a novel by that name! Others were
General Werner von Fritsch, known as "The Iceberg," whom I made
Army Commander in Chief in 1934, and General Ludwig Beck, who
took over the post of Army Chief of Staff in the following year.

The Commander of the Navy was Admiral Erich Raeder, another
iceberg (though he did not carry that name). Strangely enough for
a native of Protestant Hamburg, Raeder was a practicing Catholic
who sometimes carried his faith to ludicrous lengths. Later, during
his trial at Nuremberg, the American prison chaplain called him the
best lay Bible student he had ever encountered! He too was firmly
opposed to war, at least until he could build up his miniscule force

so that it would be a match for the English Navy. In practice, that meant more or less forever. I, however, had been born in Austria and served in the trenches. Naturally, I knew much less about naval affairs than about land warfare. So I had no choice but to respect his views, up to a point at any rate. That was why, unlike the rest, he survived until 1943.

My next move was purely symbolic. I took Germany out of the disarmament talks in Geneva. The talks, which had been dragging on since 1931, were simply nonsensical. Some representatives talked about offensive arms. Others, especially America's oafish President Franklin Roosevelt, focused on defensive ones. As if there were really a difference. As the Egyptians proved in October 1973, "defensive" anti-aircraft missiles can very well be used to cover an attack. Ten years later, the same applied to America's "Strategic Defense Initiative." Some thought gas was a civilized weapon—having experienced it, I could tell them some stories about that—and should be allowed. Others believed that it should be not be.

The most difficult problem was our situation in all this. Having been prohibited from having proper armed forces, we were determined to gain equality. That could mean either that others should reduce their armaments to our level or that we be given permission to build and expand until we were level with theirs. The other countries, primarily France, refused to accept our demands. So we went round and round until I finally said, enough is enough.

Now that we had burned the bridges behind us, it was time to step on the gas so as to get through the "risk period" as quickly as we possibly could. As early as 1934, we drew up a production schedule for military aircraft with the objective of having 17,000 by 1939. To assuage Allied suspicions as much as we could, many of them were to be disguised either as transports or as trainers. On 17 March 1935, Heroes' Memorial Day, I announced that, as far as Germany was concerned, the Treaty of Versailles no longer existed. I also announced that we had just reintroduced conscription, thus providing the framework for a vast expansion of our armed forces. The initial goal was thirty-six divisions with many more to come. To accentuate the change we dropped the term Reichswehr and introduced a completely new one: the Wehrmacht.

We restarted production of infantry weapons, artillery barrels, tanks—at first they were disguised as tractors—and naval vessels. Firms such as Borsig, Mauser, Thyssen, Krupp, and Rheinmetal made huge profits, reinvested them, and made even greater ones. The impact on unemployment was dramatic. In just two years employment in aircraft manufacturing increased by no less than 1,800 percent! As early as the end of 1934, we were able to suspend the various work-creation programs we had inherited from our predecessors.

The impact on the public mood was even more dramatic. We Germans have long been denounced for being "militarists." The accusations go back to the first half of the eighteenth century, when people used to call Friedrich Wilhelm I, the father of Frederick the Great, the "soldier king" of Potsdam. As sayings such as "the soldier is the first man in the state" indicated, we carried this attitude into the nineteenth and twentieth centuries. No nation was better served by its soldiers; no nation held them in higher honor. None loved reviews, tattoos, and parades more than we did. Our uniforms, many of them designed by the well-known firm of Hugo Boss, were the best in the world. They were tight, snappy, and gaudy with numerous multicolored badges and ribbons. In the judgment of one former Wehrmacht soldier who had worn them for years on end, "No other uniform [was] so deliberately designed as the German to turn a man into a soldier, absolute and united with his fellows, and not just a civilian in special clothes." At least one famous American writer, Kurt Vonnegut, agreed; having spent several months with us as a prisoner of war, he should know.

But that was just the beginning. Even in the eighteenth century the spectacle of Frederick the Great's goose-stepping grenadiers had deeply impressed onlookers. So popular were some of our marching songs, especially Schiller's *Cavalry Song, I Had a Comrade,* and the famous *Erika,* that they were translated, played and sung in several other languages as well. To this day the Netz bristles with "clips," as they are known, showing our troops either on parade or in action. Just one version of *Erika* was watched over four million times! Our reintroduction of these traditions affected the nation like a tonic. It was one of the things they and I, being German myself, had in common. Alas, after 1945 all of this was *verboten.* Nowadays, to watch *real* soldiers on parade, you'd better turn to China or North Korea.

In June 1935 Ribbentrop, who was serving as our ambassador in London, negotiated a new agreement with England. We dressed it in diplomatic language, of course, but what a defeat for our rivals and what a triumph for us! It enabled us to embark on a vast program of ship construction. At the same time, it did away with any fear that the English would try to Copenhagen us, as they did to the Danes in 1807 and as they would subsequently do to the French at Dakar in 1940. In March 1936 I took another daring step. Though we really did not have the forces to back it up, I decided to take a risk and re-militarize the Rhineland. The accretion to our strength and ability to defend ourselves against the West as a result of that successful action was very great indeed.

Needless to say, most of my generals opposed the move. They worried about this and were afraid of that. Truth be told, so did I. For two nights before the move I didn't sleep a wink. However, unlike them I could not afford to show my feelings or to tell anyone about them. After all, the enemy's military superiority was crushing. Had he decided to use it, there was precious little we could have done. He could have marched straight to Berlin! That is exactly what I would have done! But I did not let my fears govern my actions. Instead, I bluffed, threatening to send in additional forces I did not have. And I proved to be right, increasing the confidence of the German people in me and making it a little harder for my opponents to criticize me.

We also gave a lot of thought to what the next war would look like. During the World War the tremendous firepower of modern weapons—magazine rifles, machine guns, quick-firing artillery—as well as devices such as barbed wire and mines, had caused the defense to dominate the offense as perhaps at no time before or since. The outcome was *Stellungskrieg*, trench warfare and a prolonged war of attrition. It was a type of war which, owing to our limited human and material resources, even the magnificent performance of our troops could not win.

The solution had a political aspect and a military one. Politically, I wanted to make sure we would never again have to fight on more than one front. In this, unfortunately, I did not succeed. Militarily, we had to find some method of breaking the stalemate and restoring mobility to the battlefield. We were lucky in that it was a time of tremendous technological progress. New tanks, new aircraft, and masses of other kinds of new equipment were coming from the factories in mighty streams. I was no Mussolini who piloted his own plane and who, on one occasion, boasted that he personally used to check the repairs of his country's military aircraft. But always having taken an interest in military technology, I was probably more aware of the way things were changing than many of my opposite numbers in other countries. But how to organize them? How to combine them? How to keep them battle ready and supplied? How to enable them to communicate with each other? In what ways, and against what targets, to use them? For these questions each general and each pundit had his own answers.

For me, personally, the decisive moment came in September 1937. We were holding our usual autumn maneuvers. The scale on which we went to work was nothing short of gigantic; no fewer than 160,000 troops, 25,000 horses, 21,700 motor vehicles, and 830 tanks participated. The way our forces were organized at that time, the last-mentioned figure was the equivalent of about two armored divisions. German soil was never to see their like again. Nor, after

1941, did that of any other country. The spectacle of our Panzers in action was enormously impressive. As I watched them, I had what religious people like to call a revelation. I saw, in a flash, what future wars would be like and what we ourselves needed and wanted. I turned to our tank expert, General Heinz Guderian, and told him so. The rest is history.

At that time we were deeply involved in Spain. Our intervention in the Civil War was motivated principally by political considerations, not military ones. Having France surrounded on three sides by Fascist regimes looked like a good idea. That is why, no sooner had Göring suggested that we provide the Nationalists with aircraft to fly their troops from Morocco to Spain, than I agreed. The operation, the first of its kind in history, jump-started the rebellion which eventually got Franco to power. However, unlike the Italians we never sent ground troops. Our main contribution consisted of the Legion Condor, an improvised Luftwaffe force that never numbered more than 5,000 men at any one time. Its first commander was General Hugo Sperrle, a typical monocled Prussian whose experience as an air force officer went back to World War I and who always looked as if he was getting ready to swallow someone whole. Later I had him replaced by General Wolfram von Richthofen, a younger man and a distant relative of the famous World War I ace.

It was the Legion which carried out the bombardment of Guernica in April 1937, an incident whose real extent was vastly exaggerated by the world press. However, it certainly served a useful purpose in putting the fear of God into our enemies' hearts. The Legion's contribution to Franco's victory was great. It also served our own purposes well. Having had no air force for so long, we were lagging behind the remaining powers. The war in Spain enabled us to prepare our commanders, to train our men, to test our equipment, and to devise doctrines, including, among other things, the "finger four" formation later adopted by all other air forces as well. Returning from Spain, many of the men were given training assignments. Their contribution to the further development of our Luftwaffe was invaluable.

Inevitably, the vast sums we were spending on armaments had a negative impact on our economy. Instead of exporting our products, we built weapons. As one story had it, one customer, having bought one of those baby prams meant to be assembled at home, was surprised to find himself handling a machine gun instead. Seriously, rearmament caused our balance of trade to go from bad to worse. As our wealthy Western opponents caught on and started to rearm, time was working against us. In November 1937 I summoned my generals to what later became known as the Hossbach Conference, after the aforementioned officer who took notes. I explained the point, saying that they could get the details from Göring, as the man in charge of the Four Year Plan, if they wanted to. I do not recall that anyone asked. Military technicians that they were, doing so would have been totally out of character.

Based on this, I announced my unalterable determination to go to war. Not immediately, but by 1943–45 at the latest. Any further delay would find me too old. It would also work against us by making our equipment obsolete. It, might however, be possible to open hostilities at an earlier date. One scenario I mentioned was the outbreak of civil war in France, which would enable us to tackle Czechoslovakia. These, after all, were the years of the Popular Front Government; there seemed to be a real possibility that France would follow in the footsteps of Spain. Another was a war between France and Italy that would lead to the same result. In any event, neither of these eventualities materialized. When we went to war in 1939, we did so against an enemy, Poland, whom the memorandum did not even mention as a possibility.

The generals did not like the speech. Once again, they raised objections. France might do this and Britain that. Clearly, it was time to get rid of the old, reluctant horses and hitch my carriage to some new and more highly spirited ones. Here fortune came to my aid. In January 1938 Blomberg, who was a widower, remarried. Both Göring and I were present at the wedding. But then it turned out that his new wife, a shorthand typist by the name of Erna Gruhn, had a criminal record. In fact she was registered as a prostitute in no fewer than seven different cities! When the file was brought to my attention, I offered Blomberg the chance to annul his marriage. After all, the man, though not terribly bright, had acted in good faith. He refused and decided to stick to his wife instead. Under such circumstances, and if only because his fellow generals would no longer tolerate him, I had no choice but to fire him for conduct unbecoming an officer and a gentleman. But he had always been loyal, and his fate made me feel sorry for him.

Hardly had this affair ended then another one burst on us. This time the problem was von Fritsch. As stiff as a stick and speaking with a grating, unpleasant voice, Fritsch had never been married. In 1936 Heydrich, in his capacity as Chief of the Reich Security Service, prepared a file on his alleged homosexual activities and presented it to me. Personally, I have never liked denunciators or denunciation. This time, too, my response was to order him to destroy it. But Heydrich being Heydrich, he never did. Now he put it into the hands of Himmler, as his superior, and of Göring. They turned it over to me, and the fat was in the fire. Previously, Fritsch had been one of those who demanded that Blomberg resign. Now he himself came under similar pressure. Later, a court discovered that the man who had denounced him, possibly acting on the instructions of the Gestapo, had consciously lied by mixing him up with another man by the name of Frisch. By then, though, it was too late to repair the damage.

Decades later, the entire business remains shrouded in mystery. Göring, it was said, may have wanted to prevent Fritsch from taking over from Blomberg as he wanted to take the post of Minister of War for himself. Perhaps so, but the accusation has never been proved. I want to put it on record that I myself was not involved. Why should

I be? Hindenburg was long gone. The military had sworn a personal oath to me as Supreme Commander of the Armed Forces, promising to obey me and to sacrifice their lives "at all times" if ordered to do so. My position in Germany was as strong as that of any ruler in the whole of our history. Probably stronger. I did not need to stir up a scandal to let both of them go. On the contrary, throughout my years in power, I did what I could to prevent public scandals as far as I could.

If Göring had hoped to take Blomberg's place, he was up for a disappointment. As was to become abundantly clear later on, he simply did not have the necessary stamina and capacity for hard work. Instead, I took on the post myself. To help me I chose General Wilhelm Keitel. Keitel, whose voice bore an astonishing resemblance to mine, always made an impression by standing ramrod straight. But his behavior belied his appearance, so much so that his fellow generals nicknamed him *Lackeitel*. No translation needed! As a strategist, he was not exactly famous; neither on that account nor on any other did he ever cause me any problems. On one occasion he even said that, every time he thought of opposing me in any way, he wetted his pants. But let's give him his due: he was a first-class organizer. And no one, but no one, worked harder than he. If the Wehrmacht survived and fought on for as long as it did, then part of the credit belongs to him. In May 1945 he had the painful duty of signing the capitulation of Berlin to the Russians. In the next year he and his deputy, Jodl, were both hanged at Nuremberg.

My replacement for Fritsch was General Walter von Brauchitsch. A hero he was not. No sooner had he been appointed than he expressed his opposition both to our annexation of Austria and to the intervention in Czechoslovakia. That was not because he disagreed with the principles behind my policies; he did not. He did so out of sheer cowardice. Later, he used to hide behind the back of his chief of staff, General Franz Halder, about whom more presently. Brauchitsch was obliged to me. First, I made an exception for him by allowing him to divorce his wife. Next, I personally saw to it that he should survive the trial without financial disaster. In return for 1,300 marks a month paid out to his wife, I had him in my pocket, After the Polish campaign, he caused me some minor difficulties with respect to our treatment of the Jews. During the Russian one he proved totally worthless. He was a man with over-boiled macaroni for nerves. At the end of 1941 I got rid of him and took over his post myself.

Important as these changes were, they were merely part of a larger reform. Like most countries at the time, Germany had never had a single high command with authority over the two, and later three, services. One outcome was that, in 1914–18, the only formal link between the army and the navy had been the Kaiser himself. How weak *that* link was hardly needs to be retold! In 1938–39 I tried to change this situation by putting Keitel in charge of a new organization, the OKW (*Oberkommando der Wehrmacht,* Wehrmacht High Command). The OKW, in turn, was supposed to coordinate the operations of the Army, Navy, and Air Force *(Luftwaffe)* High Commands.

In theory it was a good solution, well ahead of its time and one which most other countries adopted after 1945. In practice it never worked very well. In part the reason was that both the Army and Navy High Commands were much older and better established than OKW and unwilling to take its orders. In addition, Göring, as commander in chief of the Luftwaffe, refused to obey anyone but me. Göring's squabbles with the Navy High Command were even worse. As I shall explain later on, his declaration that "everything that flies belongs to me" was to cost us dearly. Thus the relationship between the four organizations always remained somewhat shaky. Our attempt to make the officers of the services less parochial and to facilitate cooperation among them by setting up a new *Wehrmacht-akademie* common to all three services did not work out well either. Jealous of their independence, the services hated it and never made their best officers attend it. That is why it only graduated three classes consisting of ten officers each before it was closed. Its impact on the Wehrmacht was next to zero.

In March 1938 we annexed Austria. For me personally it was the realization of a dream I had had ever since my time as a schoolboy in Linz; I shall have more to say about it later. There was neither resistance nor bloodshed. Wherever our troops went, they were received with unparalleled enthusiasm. But militarily, the operation was a mess. Driving the 400 kilometers from Munich to Vienna, Guderian's Panzers could neither be kept supplied nor properly repaired. So many of them broke down that the highway became littered with them. In Guderian's defense it must be said that it was the world's first operation of its kind. He and his men learned their lesson, and a similar debacle did not take place again.

My problems with my senior commanders continued. This time the troublemaker was General Beck, the Army Chief of Staff. Dour faced—no one had ever accused him of having a sense of humor—he had the reputation of being an intellectual. He had been responsible for, and had signed, the famous 1936 regulations, *Truppenführung*. But that seems to have been the limit of his soldierly achievement. Like so many others of his caste he shared our National Socialist objectives, especially with respect to the need to rearm and to reclaim our lost provinces. In 1930 he had even testified on behalf of some of his subordinates who, acting against the law, had joined our Party. However, like so many others of his caste he was, at heart, a coward. How so many weak-kneed men ever came to command our armed forces, the army in particular, is beyond me. Judging from what I hear and read and see, the situation in the *Bundeswehr* is even worse. In Berlin nowadays, cowardice seems to be not an obstacle for reaching high command but a prerequisite for doing so.

When Beck learned of my plans for dismantling Czechoslovakia, he was aghast. He immediately put together a number of wargames. All were expressly designed to reach the conclusion that, in a war with Czechoslovakia, France, and England, Germany was doomed. He sent me the results. I thought they were childish and told him so. In July 1938 he resigned. At that time, it later turned out, he was already in touch with some officers and diplomats who were hoping to overturn the regime. In 1944 he was part of the conspiracy against me. When that Putsch failed, he was forced to commit suicide. Not by me—I would have loved to have seen him hang—but by his own dear comrades who hoped to save their necks in this way. Serves him right. In 1938 his replacement was General Halder, another artillerist who had made his mark primarily as a trainer. He was an improvement, but hardly a big one.

As I had predicted, we succeeded first in occupying the Sudetenland and then the rest of Bohemia and Moravia without shedding either our own blood or that of others. They represented a considerable addition to our strength. The most important single acquisition was the Skoda Works at Jungbunzlau. Founded in 1895, they had originally produced arms for Franz Joseph. That included the world's second largest howitzer after the one Krupp built. Now they worked for us and continued to do so without any problems up to the end of the war. At that point, though, March–April 1939, it was increasingly clear to me that further triumphs would only be possible by the use of armed force. To explain what happened next, I have to retrace my steps to explain how our foreign policy worked.

Chapter 18

Foreign Policy

In the nuclear age, defense and foreign policies tend to revolve about picayune issues. As everyone but a few academic do-gooders understands, the reason is not that the better angels of our nature have taken over or are about to. It is that the most important powers either already have nuclear weapons and their "delivery vehicles" or can build them quite quickly. Consequently, they skirmish—"fight" would be much too big a word—over problems that are almost invisible. A glacier here, an oil well there. Some godforsaken reef fit only for goats in an out-of-the-way place. Certainly in the so-called "developed" world, so much time has passed since the last existential conflict that the vast majority of people there no longer even understand the meaning of the words. Relative to the global population, far fewer people have died in war each year since 1945 than was the case at any other time in the whole of history.

What *I* would have done if fortune had caused me to live and act in a nuclear world, I find it very hard to say. Here I want to put it on record: like anyone else, I sometimes got very angry. When necessary, I also knew how to intimidate people by acting out my rage. Both in public and in private, I sometimes did just that. Nevertheless, and regardless of what some of my less intelligent biographers have said about me, I was, and am, no raging maniac. I did not foam at the mouth. I did not fall down to the floor and eat the carpet as some people have alleged. Nor was I a drunk or a slave to my passions as quite a few heads of state, both before or after me, have been. No Mademoiselle de Poisson, no Monica Lewinsky scandal, was ever tied to my name. Nor did I molest any attractive female who was presented to me, as Chairman Mao regularly did and as President Trump claims to have done. I was as much in control, as rational, as capable of "strategic" calculation, as any ruler in history, let alone any historian, political scientist, or "game theorist" who has prattled about such things. And I did not come to destroy the world. I came to increase my people's share in it and to help them dominate as large a part of it as they deserved and I could.

Had I been the first and only one to possess nuclear weapons and their delivery vehicles, I probably would have used them. Not against small fry, for doing so would have served no purpose. Why bomb a country such as the Netherlands, which we intended to annex, if equally effective but less destructive methods were available? But use them to force my most powerful enemies to see reason and, if necessary, utterly destroy them? Yes, I would have done that. After all, that is what Truman, true-man, did even though victory over Japan was already assured and not far away, and even though the Japanese were already putting out peace feelers. Some historians say his real objective was to impress Stalin. In any case it did not cause him to be execrated nearly as much as I have been. But I would not have used them in a world where other countries also had them and might very well have reacted by turning Germany, our beautiful, densely populated Germany, into a radioactive wasteland fit only for grasses and cockroaches.

I must, however, admit that, seeing how that Germany of ours was being literally demolished during the last months of the war, the idea of *Götterdämmerung* began to have some appeal to my mind. The more so because some of my principal collaborators were starting to betray me left and right. I was furious but also completely helpless. Yes, under such circumstances, I probably *would* have used the bomb if I had it. Who could blame me? I certainly would have *threatened* to use it. And I would most certainly have known how to use my theatrical talents to make the threat "credible," as strategists like to say. By so doing, I might very well have saved my country, my people, and myself from the fate that overtook us.

Back to reality. Unlike today's *Gutmenschen,* bleeding hearts who are always kvetching about peace on earth and goodwill among nations, I did not believe that foreign policy was based on some kind of justice or right. Except, of course, the right of the strong to take what he needed. Even if it meant crushing the weak, and even if it meant that many frail flowers had to die in the process. I did not come just to readjust our frontiers or to reacquire our colonies. Let common, or garden variety, politicians amuse themselves with such things. To repeat, my fundamental goal in foreign policy was to gain more *Lebensraum* for the German nation. Not overseas, which is what Wilhelm II wanted, but right here in Europe. To be precise, Eastern Europe with its enormous, fertile, but badly neglected, spaces.

My plan had an economic aspect and a strategic one. Economically, I wanted to make sure that we would never, ever again suffer from blockade. Strategically, I wanted to make sure that Germany would remain a world power. Not just for five, ten, or twenty-five years, but for a thousand years to come. And this was a field in which the future did not look at all bright. We could, as we later proved, take on France and Britain combined. However, in terms of size, population, and resources Germany could not compete with those two giants, Russia and the U.S. Thus to procrastinate and postpone was to court disaster.

Even a journey of ten thousand kilometers starts with a single step. The more so because, owing to our initial weakness, we had to tread carefully. That is why, in some of my early speeches as Chancellor, I told everyone that I wanted peace. They lapped it up. It soothed their worries and encouraged their hopes. As late as 1938, long after the belligerent nature of our regime and our preparations for war had become obvious for all to see, quite a few people still retained their illusions. Their eyes were open, but they did not see. Their ears could hear, but they did not listen. As, for example, when that stiff little prig, Chamberlain, returned from Munich with his umbrella, waving a little piece of paper and speaking of "peace in our time."

Again, I have to qualify my words. I enjoyed soldiering as much as anyone ever did. But I had been through war. I knew what it is like more than ninety-nine percent of today's "strategists." I did not see it as some chivalrous contest. Instead, I recognized it for what it is: a chancy business for those who launch it, a brutal hell on earth for those who fight in it, and a source of want, pain, and sorrow for the fathers, mothers, brothers, sisters, and children at whose expense it is fought. Often, that is almost as true for the victor as it is for the vanquished. Briefly, up to a point I would have much preferred to attain my objectives without war. By maneuver, by trickery, by threats, by bluff. Wasn't that just what I did during my first six years in power? And not without success either. But there are limits. All good things must come to an end. If only because, if they do not, they will usually take on a different character and become bad.

When I came to power, Germany was isolated. We did not have a single ally in the world. True, in 1925 we had signed the Treaty of Locarno, which stabilized the situation in the west. But that did not prevent the French from preparing for war against us by maintaining a system of alliances with the smaller countries to our east. Fortunately, at a time when they could still easily have done so, they chose not to use their forces. Instead, totally misunderstanding the direction in which military developments were moving, they focused on the defensive and started building the Maginot Line. Nor did the Treaty prevent the British, some of whom still believed France was their most dangerous potential enemy, from trying to play off the French against us, as had been the policy of "Perfidious Albion" for centuries past.

The other Powers mattered a lot less to us. As our rearmament got under way, we no longer needed the Russians to conceal our moves. So one of the first steps I took was to put an end to our cooperation—

a cooperation which, hopelessly backward as they were, may well have benefited them more than it did us. For example, it enabled them to lay their hands on our 75-millimeter flak gun, whose range was almost twice that of their own primitive contraption. Russia, or the Soviet Union as it called itself, had lost vast territories in the Great War. As a result, it was quite far away and still in no position to threaten us.

Considering all this, as late as the Munich Conference in 1938, we were able to proceed almost as if Moscow did not exist. Japan was located on the other side of the world and could do little to help us. The U.S. was in an economic depression and in an isolationist mood. Here it is worth mentioning that we had a lot of trouble with the American ambassador, Herr Professor Doktor William Dodd. First, he was he an imbecile. Second, he was strongly against us National Socialists and did not bother to hide that fact. His daughter, Martha, was even worse. Running about Berlin, she pulled up her skirt for every pair of trousers in sight. She even tried her charms on me! The only ones who did not enjoy her favors were our own diplomats. They should have subjugated the girl and taken advantage of her for intelligence purposes. But no, not they; they were too snobbish for that.

The last remaining Power was Italy. In reality it was not a Power at all but merely a gaudy circus with much pomposity and no substance. For all the bombastic slogans that decorated walls throughout the country, the only real Roman south of the Alps was Mussolini himself. All the rest were mere Italians. But that was something we only learned too late. In my so-called *Second Book* I had written in favor of an alliance with Italy even if it meant either abandoning the inhabitants of South Tyrol to their fate or, if necessary, resettling them.

In July 1934, my plans were frustrated by some of my own over-eager supporters in Austria. They assassinated Chancellor Engelbert Dolfuss. It was a stupid move on their part. Had I known the full details of what they were planning, I definitely would have stopped them. To be sure, Dolfuss was strongly committed to Austria's independent existence. But he was also the kind of ruler I appreciated. He had shown his mettle when, five months earlier, he put down his native Social Democrats and established a Fascist dictatorship with himself at its head. We could have gotten along with him, at least for a time.

In any event, Mussolini saw himself forced to bring troops to the Brenner in case I was planning an Anschluss. I, however, was much too weak militarily to try anything of the sort. What a triumph for him! What a humiliation for me! It was a bit like Austria's triumph over Prussia at Olmütz in 1850, I suppose. In the autumn I went to Venice in an attempt to save what could be saved, but it was to no avail. We simply did not see eye to eye—not only over foreign policy but over the Jewish question as well. Proportionally, the Italians only had one tenth as many Jews as we did. Good for them! Yet Mussolini's own government included some Jews. He did not like them much but decided to close his eyes to the real problem they presented. At one point he even had a Jewish mistress, Margherita Sarfatti. After he got rid of her, she wrote a book about him under the title *Sawdust Caesar*. To this day, how he could lower himself to such an extent remains beyond my comprehension.

Far from mending his fences with me, Mussolini joined England and France in setting up the so-called Stresa Front. This was April 1935, and the objective was to save Austria from falling into my hands. But *il Duce* was already making plans for the occupation of Ethiopia or, to use the name people called it at the time, Abyssinia. Eventually, his troops conquered it, enabling him to proudly proclaim the reconstitution of the *Impero Romano*. As soon became clear, though, in reality the war did more to reduce Italy's power than to increase it. Abyssinia could only be reached by way of the Suez Canal, which was firmly in the hands of the English. As a result, when World War II came, they had very little trouble occupying both Abyssinia and the neighboring countries of Eritrea and Somalia. The entire miserable episode did little but prove my point about the worthlessness of overseas colonies.

But it also provided us Germans with an opportunity. Responding to the invasion, the League of Nations slapped sanctions on Italy. To be sure, since they did not include either coal or crude oil, they were not terribly serious. Even if those two products had been put on the list, the Italians could always have bought what they needed from us (coal) and the United States (oil). But the sanctions did worry Mussolini. To the extent that opposition under a totalitarian regime such as his is possible at all, they also helped strengthen his domestic critics.

Next, the Spanish Civil War broke out. Forming an informal alliance, the Italians and we fought against the Spanish Republicans and Communists as well as some of Stalin's gangsters. And, less directly, England and France. Doing so brought our two countries together even though, operationally speaking, there was hardly any coordination between Mussolini's "volunteers" and our men. And even though the latter thought very little of the former.

When Mussolini and I met in Venice in 1934, he had treated me as a junior partner and looked down on me. Two years later, in November 1936, things had changed sufficiently for him to start speaking about the Rome–Berlin Axis. A year later, we got him to the point where we were able to ask him to come over for a state visit. When he arrived in September 1937, we pulled out all the stops to welcome him. Never in history was a foreign leader given a more cordial reception! First, I personally came to greet him in Munich, where we laid commemorative wreaths in memory of the sixteen heroes who had died in our attempted Putsch. Next, we held a grand parade in his honor. From there he went to Essen for a tour of the Krupp Works, and from there again I took him to Mecklenburg

to watch the aforementioned autumn maneuvers. He had never seen
anything like them, and they made a tremendous impression on him.
As well they might.

He visited Karin Hall. There Göring, behaving like the big child
he in many ways was, showed him his pet lion and his miniature
railway system. By way of the crowning glory, we had him address
a million of our people at the Olympiastadion. Unfortunately, they
found his heavily accented and not quite grammatical German hard
to understand. To make things worse a thunderstorm interrupted his
speech, soaking his notes and causing the loudspeakers to creak and
squeak. Finally, having lost touch with his escort, he was forced to
seek his car on his own! Yet the better I came to know him, the more I
appreciated him as a true friend. All in all, the visit was a great success.
So much so that, upon turning home, he insisted that his military
introduce their own version of the goose-step. He changed its name
from the *passo dell' oca* to the *passo Romano* and explained that the
goose was a perfectly respectable Roman bird. On one occasion, he
said, a flock of them had even saved the Capitol.

Just how successful the visit had been became clear five months
later when we annexed Austria. I need hardly repeat that the Anschluss, which incidentally had been specifically prohibited by the
Treaty of St. Germain, had long been one of my most cherished
dreams. It was all Schuschnigg's fault. Schuschnigg was a practicing
Catholic. So stiff was he that some people thought he was dead!
Having taken over from Dolfuss, for several years he did all he could
to suppress our National Socialist supporters in Austria. He even
put many of them in so-called internment camps, the polite name
for concentration camps. Incidentally, it was not us who invented
them. The English had used them in South Africa and the Italians
in Libya. And that's not to mention the Russians, who put together
the largest net of them of all.

Schuschnigg's camps may not have been as bad as ours. But the
principle, that of arresting opponents without trial and keeping them

under arrest for as long as was considered necessary, was the same. I responded by imposing economic sanctions. They brought the country to the brink of ruin. As early as the summer of 1936, Schuschnigg told his protector, Mussolini, that he would have no choice but to seek some kind of accommodation with us. In fact he did sign an agreement with our Ambassador in Vienna, Papen. Typical of him, Papen called it a gentlemen's agreement. It was the first time that absurd phrase made its appearance in international diplomacy, and it proved to have a great future ahead of it. But it did not satisfy me. On 12 February 1938, Schuschnigg came to Berchtesgaden, cap in hand. By loudly calling out Keitel's name, I bullied him a little. Then I forced him to set free all the National Socialists he had arrested and to increase the number of our people in his cabinet.

The key appointment was that of Arthur Seyss-Inquart as Minister of Public Security. A lawyer by trade, highly intelligent, Seyss-Inquart had served us well in the past. As he joined the cabinet, Schuschnigg realized that the game was up. His Austria, the Austria the Allies had built to keep us Germans apart after the Great War and which Dolfuss had converted from a democracy into an authoritarian state, was doomed. By way of a last desperate gamble, he decided to hold a referendum in which his people would be asked whether they wanted a free, independent Austria. Having acquired some experience in using referenda of this kind, I immediately realized that this was something I could not allow. On 11 March I sent him an ultimatum demanding that he resign. He did so almost immediately, appointing Seyss-Inquart in his place.

On the very next day Seyss-Inquart invited me to come to restore order. Needless to say, I was very happy to send in my troops to do so. He and I met at the Hotel Weinzinger at Linz, whose owner had given me his best suite. Strangely enough, it was decorated with paintings of naked women, including, I remember, a framed gravure of Josephine Baker, the degenerate, if well-known, Negro dancer! Entering, I kept stumbling over carpets made of the skins of animals.

That was just the thing for me, who has always detested blood sports of every kind.

Only one problem remained. By this time we had grown strong enough to defy France and England, separately or together. Or so at least London and Paris, both of which were impressed by our rearmament and neither of which was exactly eager to go to war, felt. But we did not know what Mussolini would do. His attitude remained a riddle to the last moment. I cannot describe how relieved I was when Prince Philip of Hesse, who was married to a daughter of Italy's King Vittorio Emmanuelle, and whom I was using as my emissary, called. He said that the Duce had received the news in a friendly spirit and declared that he would not interfere with what we were doing. I myself grabbed the phone and told the Prince to thank the Duce in the strongest terms he could find. Tell him, I said, that I would never, ever forget and that he could count on me even if the entire world should gang up against him. That, too, was a promise I kept.

With the Anschluss a *fait accompli,* two months later I paid Italy a return visit. Mussolini treated me even better than I had treated him. Rome was thoroughly scrubbed. The Italians called a newly built street the Via Adolfo Hitler in my honor. Protocol demanded that, as a head of state, I spend time with the king. I even had to share a horse-drawn carriage with him; as Mussolini pointed out, the House of Savoy had not yet discovered the internal combustion engine. I found His Majesty a tiresome little man of no great interest. All he could talk about was the number of nails in an Italian infantryman's boot! He himself, being a midget, never could have served in the infantry. At most, he might have made a good batman. Later, I used to mimic his high-pitched laughter, much to the amusement of my associates.

There were the usual meetings, dinners, and parades. In Naples, my entourage and I witnessed a sort of underwater parade by no fewer than one hundred submarines. Not having anything of the sort, I could only envy our hosts. Goebbels, who had come along, used his sharp wit to make fun of the Italians and their uniforms. They made them, he said (quite rightly) look like clowns. Their attempts to imitate the goose-step were not exactly a great success either. But I greatly enjoyed the beautiful Italian women. There was nothing like them! And I took the opportunity to visit some of the world-famous museums in Rome and Florence. So impressed was I that I almost wished I could have restarted my life and become an anonymous young artist in Italy, wandering about and painting what I saw. What a lovely country! What wonderful works of architecture! Neither London nor Paris, much less Berlin, had anything of the sort. Mussolini, for his part, trudged along dutifully enough. But I did not feel that he really appreciated the opera or the plastic arts, for that matter. With his jutting jaw, on some of the photographs Hoffmann took on that occasion, he looks almost like an orangutan! That very month we signed an offensive alliance which obliged each signatory to join the other in case of war. There was also a clause in which we promised that, fighting shoulder to shoulder, neither of us would make peace without the other's consent.

Mussolini called it the Pact of Steel. Ever since the Abyssinian adventure, when the League of Nations had prevented Italy from importing iron ore, he had had steel on the head. Unfortunately, there were limits to what he could do to augment his country's resources. When the time for action came in the summer of 1939, he declared that Italy was not ready. In doing so, he may well have made a decisive contribution to the Allied decision to come to Poland's aid and to declare war on Germany. Next, he had his experts prepare a list of all the weapons and raw materials he needed to make it so. His Foreign Minister, Galeazzo Ciano, wrote in his diary that the list was big enough to kill an ox if an ox could read it.

This Ciano was the son of an Italian war-hero (assuming there is such a thing) who had been one of Mussolini's first followers. He was married to Mussolini's daughter Edda, an exceptionally courageous woman whom Göring admired so much that he named his own daughter after her. But he himself was a worthless fellow. A sharp dresser, slick, suave, all talk—gossip, really—and no action. Except in bed. Accompanying the Duce in 1937, he used this opportunity as well as subsequent ones to visit Berlin's most expensive brothels. Or so Heydrich, who had set up a special one for the purpose and provided it with hidden microphones, claimed. His idea of showing his martial qualities was to shoot rabbits! During the Anschluss he tried to steer the Duce into mending his fences with England so as to form a united front against us. In July 1943 he took a central part in the conspiracy that brought Fascism down. A year later, at my insistence, the Duce had him tried for treason and executed. Unfortunately, Ciano's diary, or rather the heavily "edited" version of it he left behind, had been taken by Edda, who smuggled it into Switzerland. Later, it was published, providing historians with lots of unsubstantiated gossip about the Duce and me.

Up to this point I had achieved all my foreign policy aims. Not only had I done that without bloodshed, I should add, but I had done so without making too many enemies among the Great Powers. Even Churchill, speaking in Parliament, said, "I have always said that if Great Britain were defeated in war, I hoped we should find a Hitler to lead us back to our rightful position among the nations." Impressed by my successes, America's right-wing *Time* magazine appointed me its 1938 "Man of the Year." The one important objective that remained beyond my reach was the forming of an alliance with England. Whatever some of my countrymen might feel, I myself had never been anti-English. I did not repeat the words of the popular song, *God Punish England.* I had fought them in 1914–18 and learned to respect their qualities. They were courageous, cold blooded, and tough. And they knew how to put on airs. 100 percent pure pomposity! As I said in both my books, I saw them as our racial cousins. I would have liked few things better than to draw them to our side. Combining their fleet with our army, we could hold our own against both Russia and America and win.

Ribbentrop, who knew the country well from the years he had spent in England, shared my views. So did Himmler. In molding his SS officers, he even tried to turn them into his own version of the English gentleman, for example, by having them learn to box, ride, and eat porridge for breakfast! Alas, it was not to be. The English remained suspicious of me. They followed their traditional policy of always opposing the strongest Power on the Continent so as to prevent the latter from being united. That was a pity, for it ended by costing them their empire and triggering the ongoing decline of the white man which we can see all around us.

I could not, did not, want to rest on my laurels. Partly, because my ultimate objectives were much broader. And partly because I knew I would not live forever. I only had a limited amount of time. No future German leader was likely to enjoy the trust of the people or to wield authority as I did. That, incidentally was why I had Speer build the new Chancellery. Not because I wanted that kind of luxury—God knows I did not. I was not Louis XIV, and I was not trying to construct a new Versailles. Let alone Romania's boss Nicolae Ceauşescu who, in order to make room for his palace, demolished half of Bucharest before his people overthrew him and executed him.

Personally, I much preferred the Berghof and tried to spend as much time there as I could. What a relief, compared to both Berlin and my various military headquarters! But I wanted to have a building that would impress visitors as much as possible. And one, which was even more important, that would be filled by my spirit so that my successors, at least some of whom were likely to be mediocrities, might be hallowed by it, so to speak. The building was a great success, so much so that I told Speer I wanted the "diplomats' walk" extended from 150 to 300 meters. It was, however, utterly destroyed during

the last weeks of the war. Much later, the nearby site was occupied
by the so-called "Holocaust Memorial." If anything shows what utter
cowards and traitors my successors have been, this does.

With Austria in our hands, I turned my attention to the next problem: Czechoslovakia. In the whole of history, probably no person
had less belief in the role of international law than I did. But this time
I felt our case was excellent indeed. After all, President Wilson had
personally proclaimed that national borders ought to be governed by
the "principle of nationality." There was no doubt that the Sudetenland was German and that its inhabitants had always been German.
Nor was it in doubt that the vast majority of them wanted to join the
Reich (albeit that we helped them a little by stirring up trouble and
making their wishes clear to the world). In fact, there were actually
more Germans in Czechoslovakia than there were Slovaks. So why
should they be treated as second-rate citizens? Previously, I had been
able to guide our policy in such a way that international intervention
was not required. Now, however, so hostile were France and England
that I had no choice but to bring them into the game.

Throughout the summer, as I demanded that the Czechs cede
the Sudetenland, our relations with them went downhill. And they,
meaning President Edvard Beneš, obstinately refused to give us our
due. In this tug of war, for the first time, our principal opponents
proved to be the English. But for them, the French, shaking in their
pants for fear and busily working on their Maginot Line, would not
have lifted a finger. By alternately threatening war and promising
peace if my demands were met, I was able to arrange for an international conference in Munich. To make sure Germany would not
be outvoted two to one, I insisted that Mussolini should be present
as well. He, Chamberlain, Daladier, and I agreed that the Russians
should be left out. At the time Stalin was busy arresting and executing huge numbers of his own officers. Besides, who needed him?

The conference went as well as I could have expected. Poor Beneš,
who had not been invited, had no choice but to bow to the inevitable.

He signed on the dotted line, resigned, and went into exile. From there he emerged after the war, our bitter enemy, to preside over the expulsion of three million of our *Volksgenossen*. But that is another story. The conference over, our troops marched into the Sudetenland as they had gone into Austria. Some actually hailed from Austria, or the *Ostmark* as we, wishing to eradicate its previous identity, called it. They were greeted by a rain of flowers thrown at them or strewn at their feet by a cheering population. Again, I had triumphed not only over my foreign enemies but over my domestic critics too: principally, the generals who, as so often, were trembling with fear.

Even the London *Times* agreed that the change was "both necessary and fundamentally just." The Czechs apart, perhaps the only man who was not completely happy with the outcome was me. Generals or no generals, somewhere in the back of my mind, I *wanted* war. Not against the West, of course. However, and if only because too many bloodless triumphs tend to demoralize an army, a campaign against Czechoslovakia, something on the lines of our subsequent invasion of Poland but on a smaller scale, would have suited me just fine. In any event Chamberlain's surrender at Munich robbed me of the opportunity to show the generals and the world what Germany, my newly constructed Wehrmacht, and I myself could do.

And so, on the Ides of March 1939, we took over Bohemia and Moravia. First, I summoned Beneš successor, Emil Hácha, to my brand-new Chancellery in Berlin. Built to intimidate, it served its purpose well. Just the sculptures by Arno Breker, two powerful, nude, stern-looking male figures that I dubbed the Party and the Wehrmacht, respectively, and put on both sides of the main entrance were enough to make one shiver. I made Hácha wait for hours before finally receiving him at 0130. Ribbentrop and I explained to him that our forces were already marching. He could sign, in which case the occupation would follow peacefully. Or else. Several hours passed during which Ribbentrop actually had to chase him around the table and put pens into his hand. Next, he suffered a nervous breakdown so that we feared he might die. Dr. Morrell was summoned and administered an injection which revived him, but with unexpected results: so lively did he become that I feared he might not sign after all.

In the end the old gentleman surrendered. Having made him swear an oath of loyalty to me, I kept him in office. Naturally, that did not mean I left him with any power to wield. Over him I appointed, as Protector of Bohemia and Moravia, my former Foreign Minister Konstantin von Neurath. The dismantlement of the Czechoslovak Republic also gave the Slovaks their long longed-for independence. Their leader, Jozef Tiso, a former clergyman turned nationalist, was grateful to me. Slovakia became part of our zone of influence. During most of the war it remained faithful to its alliance. In some things, such as the need to exterminate the Jews, the Slovaks were even more on the ball than many of my own subordinates were.

Chapter 19

The Road to War

There could be no doubt about my next objective. First, I had Ribbentrop ask Lithuanian Foreign Minister Jozuas Urbšys to hand us back the town of Memel, which he immediately did. On a silver platter, as they say. Next, I trained my sights at Poland. I offered them an anti-Soviet alliance, but they rejected the idea. Their refusal to join me left me with no option but to beat them. The lever I used was the town of Danzig. Danzig itself was a relatively small and unimportant city. It had, however, turned into a symbol of everything that had been unjustly taken from us. I wanted it. I needed it back.

No sooner did we make our intentions clear than we found ourselves confronted with a problem. Until then it had been His Britannic Majesty's government's aim to prevent us from expanding while at the same time keeping the peace. So foolish were they that they turned over to us $100,000,000—present value, approximately $3 billion—worth of Czech gold that had been stored in London! But on 30 March, just two weeks after our occupation of Bohemia and Moravia, Chamberlain, the same Chamberlain who had promised "peace in our time," changed his mind. Following a series of consultations with France and speaking in the latter's name as well, he personally drafted a note for the Poles. In it he promised them that, should they feel obliged to use their armed forces in order to fight for their independence, the two countries would go to war to assist them. His intention was to surround and intimidate us. The mouse, for that is how he had impressed me at Munich, had roared. Who would have believed it?

This was a challenge I could not ignore. I had just started wondering how to go about it when Roosevelt, with his usual American naiveté, sent me a telegram. In it he asked me whether I would be willing to guarantee that I would not use my armed forces to either attack or invade an attached list of thirty-one countries! Both Göring and Mussolini, who had also received the telegram, thought it was a piece of stupidity not worth answering. I, however, immediately understood what a great opportunity had come my way. I summoned the Reichstag for a meeting on 28 April. Normally, I liked to speak more or less freely. But this time I prepared very carefully indeed. I also had Ribbentrop send a short questionnaire to the countries in question. They were asked, first, whether they felt themselves threatened by Germany, and second, whether they had asked Roosevelt to speak for them.

When the day came, I started by listing, for the nth time, all the wrongs Germany had suffered under the Treaty of Versailles. I painted our situation as it had been when I took over power and provided a brief overview of all the great things my colleagues and I had done to put matters right. Second, I expressed, also for the nth time, my genuine admiration for England and my wish to improve relations between our two countries. Third, using the Poles' new alliance with England and France as my excuse, I declared the 1934 non-aggression pact we had signed with them null and void. At the time it had been a useful device to assuage people's suspicions concerning our intentions and, to some extent, to end our isolation in the international arena. Five years later, though, it no longer served any purpose.

My next move took everyone by surprise. We had used the previous two weeks or so to contact the countries on Roosevelt's list. Some of them were a bit dumb at first and did not understand what we expected them to say. In the end, though, all answered as we wanted them to. Now I slowly read the answers, all of them negative, needless to say, one after the other. I did not forget to add that some of the countries we had asked could not really provide an answer, given that they were not independent but occupied by the English! Next, I turned to Roosevelt personally, assuring him that, in case he was worried, I would gladly give my word to him, too. The Reichstag roared with laughter, and so did millions of other people both in Germany and abroad. I ended with a peroration to the German nation, a paean to their great qualities and my own burning love for them. And on both counts I was perfectly sincere.

As I had expected, my fellow Germans loved the speech. And with good reason: it addressed their self-esteem like few others I have ever delivered. As so often, foreigners were less impressed, particularly because I had been careful not to name Poland. But that was just a small detail. My task now was, first, to prepare German public opinion for the likelihood that war with Poland might in fact break out. And, second, to isolate the latter as much as I could.

To put muscle behind my word, I also had my generals prepare plans for an invasion. Given the way geography and topography were configured, it was not a very difficult task. Some ancient plans for the campaign were dusted. That done, the brass came up with a large-scale offensive. One army was to advance from the east. Another one would come from the north and one from the south. They would meet at Warsaw, and that would be that.

The date I gave them was 1 September. I did not choose it with an eye to the next Party Day at Nuremberg, as some historians, with no evidence whatsoever to back them up, imagined. I did so because it was the traditional date on which we finished bringing in the harvest. In addition, at that time, the rains would not yet have turned what it pleased those Polish *Versager* (failures) to call "roads" into quagmires. Planning went ahead and made good progress. But nothing had been decided yet.

England and France well understood that, by giving Warsaw the guarantee they did, they had effectively enabled the latter to rule over war and peace. They also realized that, in view of the geographical facts, the only way they could make good on their promise was to call in the nice people at the Kremlin. During the mid-1930 there had been some attempts to set up an English–French–Russian alliance. Typical of the age, it was called "Collective Security." Its obvious purpose was to surround us and to stop us in our tracks. Memories of pre-1914 days, no doubt.

In any event, mutual suspicion prevailed and nothing came of the project. One reason for this was that the Poles, on whom everything depended, had just signed the aforementioned non-aggression pact with us. It caused them to reject any proposals to join a united front against us. England's Prime Minister, Stanley Baldwin, tended to disparage Russian military power. The French plutocrats, worried to death about what their own working class might do to them, openly said that they preferred me to Stalin. Stalin, for his part, was convinced that his two presumptive "allies" were trying to embroil him in a war with us. One from which, acting as the proverbial *tertius,* they would emerge as *gaudentes.* As far as England was concerned, he may very well have been right in being suspicious.

Now, in the spring of 1939, negotiations between the three Powers resumed. The great stumbling block was, once again, the Poles. Chamberlain's guarantee to them had been given without mentioning the name of any other country. All it said was that London and Paris would guarantee Poland's independence in case anyone would try to put an end to it. If post-war accounts are to be believed, Poland's Foreign Minister at the time, Jozef Beck, received it without batting an eyelid between two flicks of his cigarette! But it did put Paris, and behind it London which was looking over its shoulder, so to speak, back into the dilemma they had faced in respect to Czechoslovakia. They either had to keep their word and fight or break it and lose their credibility. Or, at least, lose whatever part of it that, following first the Munich Conference and then our occupation of Bohemia and Moravia, they still possessed.

But there still was no way they could help Poland without bringing in the Russians as well. In plain words, to fight us the Red Army would have to cross Poland first. Let me put it on record that no one hates and despises the Poles more than I do. One and all, they are Slavs, fit for nothing but being slaves. Still, one cannot blame them for not relishing the prospect. If the Poles, as we Germans like to say, are *Versager* (blunderers), then the Russians are twice as bad. Starting in 1756–63, when they occupied Berlin for a short period of time, their drunken, uncouth peasant hordes were notorious for the way they smashed up everything in their path. Plus, once the Russians had got in, there was no knowing when they would get out again. If they ever would.

Back in the 1920s General Seeckt had said that Poland was like a small drop of sweat. When its two strong neighbors shook hands, as was bound to happen sooner or later, it would disappear. Now, however, the situation was just the opposite. The Poles behaved like a canary that had swallowed not one cat but two. And what enabled them to do so was precisely the guarantee they had received.

Throughout the spring of 1939 negotiations between London and Paris on the one hand and Moscow on the other proceeded rather sluggishly. On the whole it was Stalin who seemed to be in a greater hurry to come to an agreement. He was probably hoping to recover territory Russia had lost in 1915–18. That explains why, whereas the Western Powers often took weeks to reply to a note, he would answer almost immediately. Only at the beginning of August did the English and the French finally announce that they were going to become serious. Even then, they only sent, as their envoy, a certain Admiral Drax, of whom no one had ever heard before and of whom few heard anything later on. The brave man had no authority to sign anything. To add insult to injury they had him travel to Leningrad by sea! Mysterious are the ways of Whitehall. Had they wanted to convince the hard-nosed men in the Kremlin that they were useless and/or insincere, they could have found no better way of doing so.

Stalin had been taking note of all this. Tentative contacts between some of his diplomats and ours had been going on for several months. At first, they were limited to economic issues. Later, they extended to cover political problems as well. The decisive turn came on 3 May when the Man of Steel let go of his Commissar for Foreign Affairs, Maxim Litvinov. "Let go" is really too mild a term for the drama that took place. First, Litvinov, who was Jewish, had his dacha surrounded and his telephone cut. Next, Malenkov, the man in charge of the Party bureaucracy, and Beria, the head of the Secret Police, arrived on the scene and told him what was what. NKVD troops surrounded the Commissariat. They arrested Litvinov's aides and beat them up in an attempt to extract compromising information about him.

Somehow, Litvinov managed to survive. Later, he went on to become his country's envoy in Washington, where he did what he could to incite the Americans against us. But many of his collaborators were purged. Quite a few of them were also Jewish, so their departure was no great loss either to Holy Mother Russia, to us, or to the world at large. Litvinov's replacement was Vyacheslav Molotov, a veteran Bolshevik. His colleagues in the Politburo used to call him "Iron Ass." By rank and position he was the second most powerful man in the country after Stalin. But this did not prevent him from being as terrified of the latter as any of them. With good reason, as it turned out, since Stalin later had his wife, Pauline, arrested and sent to a concentration camp in Siberia. In his dealings with us he proved to be a tough and wily negotiator.

Litvinov's sudden dismissal hit me like a cannon shot. I knew I could act—and also that I would have to do so quickly. Serious negotiations between us and the Russians started almost immediately. Again, my point man was Ribbentrop. Ribbentrop, an officer's son, had married a rich woman and worked for her father, the manager and co-owner of Germany's largest manufacturer of champagne. Unable to stand up to her, he allowed her to exercise far more influence on policy than she should have. Addicted to pomp—he even added a "von" to his name—he was haughty and arrogant; more than once, he went so far as to keep me waiting on the phone. Talking to people, he liked to close his eyes and turn his face upward. Next, when it was his turn to speak, he would ask his interlocutor what he had said! He was a coward, and during air raids, he set a bad example. No wonder he was unpopular with his fellow bosses as well as his staff, who were terrified of him, and whom he treated like lackeys. After the Anschluss he took over beautiful Schloss Fuschl, near Salzburg, by sending its owner to the Dachau concentration camp, where the man later died.

Unpleasant company as he sometimes was, Ribbentrop was one of the few among my senior associates who was always more radical than I was. I knew I could count on him in this respect, and that, in turn, made him useful to me. In 1935 he had been instrumental in negotiating the naval agreement with England. Much later, on the occasion of one of his birthdays, his staff presented him with a magnificent casket containing copies of all the treaties he had signed. They had been somewhat embarrassed because, by that time, we had violated almost all of them! When I heard the story, I laughed until there were tears in my eyes.

Seriously, Ribbentrop had not succeeded in realizing his original ambition and bringing about a further rapprochement between our two countries. That made him bitter at the English and strengthened his determination to try his luck elsewhere. Whatever his shortcomings, he proved to be a good choice for the mission at hand. The talks were not easy. As late as 4 August, our ambassador in Moscow, Count von der Schulenburg, still believed that a Soviet–Western alliance was about to be signed. Acting in concert with Ribbentrop, I proved him wrong. By 22 August the details had been settled, and everything was ready.

On the same day, 22 August, I had a meeting with my top generals at the Berghof. Having dealt with them for years, I well knew whom I was talking to. Many were afraid of war and were looking for all kinds of reasons why we should not wage one. And almost all were still sticking to ridiculously old-fashioned ideas concerning chivalry, honor, and the like. My aim was to put some backbone into them; but, obviously, I cannot remember every word I said. Clearly, though, some of what my listeners took down, or claimed to have taken down, is pure invention on their part. For example, at that time our triumph over the West, let alone its magnitude, was still so far in the future as to be inconceivable. Hence even I, endowed with supernatural foresight as I supposedly was, could not have threatened to send my "death head squads" to kill men, women, and children in those countries. In fact the record shows that I never did.

Judging by the several different versions of the speech available here in Hell, I must have explained that our strength consisted of our speed and brutality, just as was the case with that great conqueror, Genghis Khan. I did not care what a rotten European civilization would say about me. I had issued my orders and would deal ruthlessly with anyone who dared say a word of criticism. And I was not merely trying to change our borders so as to get our own back. That was simply petit-bourgeois thinking. As I had said so often before, my ultimate goal was to gain the living space we Germans needed. History would forgive us—just as, for example, it had forgiven the Turks' massacre of the Armenians back in 1915.

That very day Ribbentrop flew to Moscow, where he found the airport decorated with swastikas. On the 23rd he and Molotov signed the agreement in Moscow. Stalin, pipe in hand, was present. He looked on with as benign a gaze as he, half-god, half-monster that he was, was capable of. The agreement consisted of two main parts. First, we undertook not to attack each other. Second, we arranged for an economic exchange under which we would provide them with all sorts of industrial products whereas they would pay us in raw materials and food. There was also a secret protocol. Under its terms we agreed to divide Eastern Europe between us. In case war broke out we would get most of Poland; in return, we recognized his right to annex that country's eastern provinces, the Baltic States, and part of Romania. This part of the agreement came to light when our archives were captured in 1945. Still, that did not prevent the Russians from denying its existence for another forty-five years.

The agreement was the greatest diplomatic coup we Germans had succeeded in pulling off since the time of Bismarck. Chancellor Helmut Kohl's success in making the Russians accept the *Wende* (unification) of 1989–91 and get the hell out of our country notwithstanding, it remains so to the present day. It struck the world like a thunderbolt. For six years the Russians and we had done nothing but oppose each other by every conceivable means short of open warfare. Some even claimed that Heydrich, by feeding Stalin false documents, had played a major role in triggering the great purges of 1937–39 which had decapitated the Red Army. True or false, all of a sudden our two countries turned around. Seen from the German point of view, the most important point was the first. It did away with any hope the English and the French might still have had to make Stalin pull their chestnuts out of the fire for them.

One would expect that the news of the pact would have made the Poles think again and agree to our modest demands so as to escape destruction. However, even at this late hour, they still did not— or would not—understand what was coming at them. At that time we had set the beginning of our invasion of Poland for early in the morning of 26 August, five days earlier than originally planned. Everything was ready, except that all kinds of mediators now presented themselves and tried to find a diplomatic solution. One of those most in favor of such a solution was Göring. Increasingly addicted to morphine, a habit dating to the wound he had suffered during the

1923 Putsch, he had grown so fat that he would never have fitted into a Volkswagen—or a trench, for that matter. And he much preferred life at Karin Hall to fighting.

It was because they had realized this fact that the Italians had contacted Göring in September 1938 to arrange the Munich Conference and, by doing so, to avoid war. Now, in August 1939, Göring himself turned to a Swedish friend of his, Birger Dahlerus. The latter engaged in what, much later, would become known as shuttle diplomacy. His efforts were to no avail. The English, with the French in tow, proved pigheaded. Having convinced themselves that I could not be trusted, they refused to understand and to give way. To the contrary, on 25 August they converted their unilateral declaration into a fully-fledged political and military alliance with Warsaw. Thus encouraged, the Poles, or rather, Herr Beck, were determined not to give an inch. They really believed they could take us on. Chamberlain personally at one point called them "a great and virile nation!" If this was not cloud-cuckoo land, what was?

But that was not the only piece of bad news. Accidentally or not, Mussolini's announcement that Italy would not honor its word and join us arrived on the very same day. Somewhat shaken, I found myself forced to postpone the invasion in order to consider what to do next. In fact some of our troops had already started moving to their starting positions. It was only with great difficulty that we succeeded in recalling them at the last moment.

Dahlerus, a businessman by trade, loved nothing better than playing at diplomacy. With Göring behind him, he had still not given up. On 27 August he flew to London. There, astonishingly, he was able to see both Chamberlain and his Foreign Secretary, Lord Halifax. He brought with him Göring's proposal that Danzig be handed over to us. The fate of the corridor was to be decided by a plebiscite. In return, we would guarantee Poland's truncated borders. I myself hesitated. First, having been robbed of a military triumph in the previous year, I did not want something similar to happen again.

Second, the World War had brought Poland not just the corridor but parts of Silesia, too. A new war now had the advantage that it would solve that problem as well. Why content yourself with a slice if you can have the entire sausage? Nevertheless, if only because I knew that the German people wanted peace and to show them I had done what I could to keep it, I gave Göring some leeway. In the event, the English resolved the issue for me. They consulted the Poles and told them to refuse my very decent offer. Or perhaps it was the other way around.

Still, negotiations of a kind continued. On 29 August Ribbentrop, flush from his triumph in Moscow, met with the English Ambassador, Neville Henderson. He presented him with a list of our proposals to Poland, consisting of sixteen points. Our reason for choosing Henderson was because we knew that he had always been in favor of an accommodation with us. This time he claimed that Ribbentrop had spoken too fast and that he himself had not been given a written copy. Supposing the story was true, it would have been typical of Ribbentrop. So Göring, on the next day, gave a copy to Dahlerus who passed it to Henderson. Henderson, in turn, obligingly passed it on to Poland's Ambassador in Berlin, Jozef Lipski. Lipski said that he had never heard of Dahlerus and that he had received no instructions from Warsaw. But by then I had recovered my nerve. I had also decided that I had had enough of the Poles' procrastination and would go ahead under any circumstances. One of our sixteen demands was that a Polish plenipotentiary should present himself in Berlin before 1 September. The Poles refused.

Dahlerus did not give up. He proposed that Göring meet Henderson for the second time. That he did at 1700 hours on the 31st, but to no avail. At 2100, to prove to the German people that I had done everything I could to preserve the peace, I had all German radio stations broadcast my proposals. I also had Heydrich stage some "Polish" attacks along our border with Poland. The principal one was launched on a small broadcasting station of ours at Gleiwitz in Silesia.

The objective was to convince the world, and our own people, that we were acting in self-defense. And no, I did not worry about "the truth." In the event the affair did not go very well. "Polish" irregulars dressed in Polish uniforms did in fact take over. They broadcast a few anti-German slogans, fired a few shots, and withdrew, leaving behind a "Polish" corpse. However, someone had blundered: at the time the station was not linked to the main network, with the result that few people knew what had happened. Still, it enabled me to tell the Reichstag the next morning that there had been shooting and that we were shooting back. In other words, that we were at war and that the invasion of Poland had gotten under way.

Even that did not prove to be the end of the attempts, if not to preserve peace, then to prevent the war from spreading. In spite of all their aggressive attitudes, both England and France were desperate to do so. The last thing they wanted was *mourir pour Danzig,* as the phrase went. Chamberlain in particular moved heaven and earth to get some kind of "negotiations" going. Provided I stopped shooting and withdrew my troops, he told Parliament, he was even prepared to reconsider some of our demands! At this point, for the first time, he met with opposition. The members of his own Conservative Party forced him to desist and to declare war on us, as he and his French colleague did on 3 September. It didn't matter, of course. I never would have considered what London and Paris asked me to do. Had I given way in this matter, both my regime and I myself would have been done for.

I shall have more to say about our military situation as it was at the time in the next chapter. Here, I want to put it on the record that the German people were not enthusiastic about what was happening. Far from it. In 1914 masses of people, myself included, had celebrated the outbreak of war on every city street and square. This time I was a little disappointed to see that the atmosphere was subdued. To be sure, the reception of my speech in the Reichstag was as enthusiastic as always. But no number of Goebbels' tricks, no censorship even, could conceal people's anxiety. My collaborators and I, especially Göring and Ribbentrop, also understood that, with England and France arrayed against us, the road ahead was going to be longer and harder than if we had had our way and waged war on Poland alone.

Whatever does not kill me strengthens me. After all, our entire National Socialist existence since 1919 had been one long struggle, often against what others, and we ourselves, saw as impossible odds. And so, looking into the future, I felt confident that, whatever the difficulties, we would eventually emerge on top.

Part III

The War Years

Chapter 20

Baptism by Fire

When war broke out in 1914, our armed forces had been ready to the last gaiter-button. In 1939 that was much less the case. Germany is a land power, so I shall start by sketching the condition of the ground forces first. In 1933 we only had 4,000 officers. Even that figure included 450 medical and veterinary personnel. True, the Reichswehr had been constructed with expansion in mind. Consequently we had plenty of excellent NCOs whom we could and did promote.

But that was a stopgap measure. Six years is enough to train a captain, more or less. But we had a problem with our majors, lieutenant colonels, and colonels. In other words, the field-grade officers and regimental commanders whose roles in the system were vital. The more so because, owing to the breakneck pace at which the Wehrmacht expanded, our *Kriegsakademie,* or Staff College, suffered. Less qualified candidates had to be accepted, and the course itself was diluted. The generals were something else again. The most senior ones, as I have already said, tended to be former staff officers with little personal experience of combat. Those directly under them had served as subalterns, but not one of them had heard a shot fired in anger since 1918. To make things worse, the war we were planning bore an entirely different character from the *Stellungskrieg,* position warfare, of 1914–18. All exercises notwithstanding, how our commanders would adjust to it remained to be seen.

The condition of the rank and file was hardly any better. The quality of the new recruits we inducted was as good as ever, perhaps better. Our NCOs in particular were wonderful; they were tough, professional, and capable of making independent decisions which, in some other forces, had to be made by subalterns. However, the "white" years from 1919 to 1935 had prevented us from making full use of our manpower. As a result, in 1939 approximately 3,250,000 men between ages of twenty and forty had not received any training at all. The proportion of men aged twenty-one to thirty five—those in the prime of life, forming the best human material of all—who *had* received such training was particularly low. When we went to war, we had an active army of 730,000 men organized into fifty-two active divisions. By calling in the reservists, as, of course, we did, we raised these figures to 3,700,000 and 103, respectively. But of those reservists only about 500,000 were fully trained and fit for frontline service. The value of the rest was limited at best. It was only during the period after the Polish campaign that we were able to resolve this problem.

At the time, our Panzer divisions were the best in the world, but not necessarily because our tanks were technically more advanced. That was the case, if at all, only during the second half of the war. And even then they were not without their problems. But we had a better understanding of the way they should be organized, supplied and maintained, how they should be combined with other arms, and what auxiliary equipment, principally optics and radio, they needed to be effective while on campaign. Perhaps it was no accident that Guderian had started his career as a signals officer. Above all, we knew exactly what we wanted to do with them whereas our opponents, partly because they only thought in defensive terms and partly because they had drawn the false lessons from the war in Spain, did not.

In terms of the number of divisions, our Western enemies and we were fairly evenly matched. The problem was that we did not have enough tanks. The same applied to motor vehicles to carry our infantry, haul our artillery, bring up our supplies, and evacuate our wounded. Intense as our efforts since 1933 had been, in 1939 Germany still remained under-motorized. Thus the great majority of our forces continued to consist of old-fashioned infantry. In the *Heimat* (home country) they moved by rail. In enemy territory, they moved on foot.

To be sure, none of our divisions was entirely without motor vehicles. But we never came close to the ratio of one vehicle per six men as was the case in the English and, later, the American armies. Even if we had done so, we could not have provided them with the fuel they needed. Consequently, the bulk of our artillery and supplies had to be hauled by horses or else carried on horse-drawn vehicles. The more prolonged the war became, the greater the shortage. In 1914–18 we mobilized 13,000,000 men and 1,400,000 horses. In 1939–45 we mobilized 18,000,000 and 2,700,000, respectively. Figure out the rest for yourself.

Next, the Luftwaffe. The Treaty of Versailles had prohibited us from having any air force at all. As I said above, we were able to evade some of the restrictions by training glider pilots, disguising our bombers as passenger aircraft, and the like. But so puny were these efforts as to be hardly worth mentioning. In 1933 I put Göring in charge. *Draufgänger* (go-getter) that he was, he attacked the problem with great energy. Nevertheless, real progress towards rearmament only started in 1935 when we felt strong enough to let the world know what we were doing.

As with the army, the first problem was manpower. Almost to a man, those who had flown for us in 1914–18 were now too old to serve as anything but commanders and, to a limited extent, trainers. However, it lay in the nature of things that the Reichswehr should have few air commanders. Whom and what could they have commanded? Consequently, we had to fill the ranks with army personnel. One such was General Walter Wever whom Göring made the first Luftwaffe Chief of Staff and who was also the first to try and devise a doctrine for it. Unfortunately, he was killed in a crash. Another and more important one was Albert Kesselring. When Kesselring joined the Luftwaffe, he was already 48 years old; the first thing he had to do was to learn to fly. Later, he became one of my best commanders, and I promoted him to field-marshal.

During the Great War our aircraft had normally been as good as those of the enemy. Perhaps at times, and before we started running out of raw materials in 1918, they were a little better. But here, too, the years between 1919 and 1933 had taken their toll. Not having been able to experiment with the very latest technology, we were in danger of first building prototypes and then prematurely putting them into serial production. Unless we were very careful, the outcome would be an air force that was out of date before it was even properly launched. I shall not go into detail except to say that, at the time we went to war in 1939, our military aircraft and their ancillary equipment were better than those of Italy, France, and Russia (of course). They were not, however, superior to those of the Royal Air Force. In 1940–41, that fact was to cost us dearly.

Air power was a relatively new instrument. To be sure, it had been tested in Abyssinia and Spain. But those campaigns had been relatively small and low level. They could not bear comparison with what was facing us in Central and, even more so, Western Europe. As a result, no one had a very clear idea as how to use the Luftwaffe. Early on we decided that it would be independent of the other services. That was a decision that both our American enemies and our Japanese allies only reached after 1945.

With that, though, the consensus ended. At the time and later, the best-known work on the question was *Il dominio dell'areo*. It had been written by an Italian general, Giulio Douhet, as far back as in 1921. I know that some of my commanders, the invaluable Milch in particular, read it. But they did not agree with its conclusions. The air force they built was designed to assist the army in its operations, including both close support and interdiction. *Pace* Douhet, it was not made for the heavy strategic bombing of civilian targets later practiced by England and the United States. For that, thousands upon thousands of four-engine bombers would have been required. In the event, the few we built suffered from defects that the Luftwaffe technical office never succeeded in overcoming.

Except in 1897–1914, when Wilhelm II sank his heart, soul, and treasure into it, the navy had always formed by far the smallest part of our Prussian/German armed forces. It was so small, in fact, that Clausewitz did not even bother to mention its existence! My own inclination was to leave it so. However, the events of 1938–39 made it unequivocally clear that, my efforts at conciliation notwithstanding, England would not enter an alliance with us. It would, in fact, do whatever it could to obstruct us. Thus I was forced to change my mind.

I turned to Raeder and asked him for a scheme to expand the navy so that it might take on the English if necessary. He came up with "Plan Z," outlining an enormous buildup. It would only be completed, if it could ever be completed, in 1945. We were to have ten battleships, twelve battle cruisers, four aircraft carriers, three *Panzerschiffe,* five heavy cruisers, forty-four light cruisers, sixty-eight destroyers, and no fewer than two hundred forty-nine submarines.

As with the Luftwaffe, and in view of the fact that the army had to take first priority, the plan proved to be far beyond our industrial capacity. Considering how long other countries had taken to develop their naval aviation and how long China is taking to do so right now, how Raeder could have thought he could do it in just a few years was also something of a mystery. In the end, only a few of the vessels he had in mind were finished and underwent sea trials. Some of the heavier units which *were* finished, especially, but not exclusively the two battleships, turned out to be not assets but burdens. One, the *Bismarck,* was sunk on its very first operation in the Atlantic. The other, the *Tirpitz,* never participated in any operations at all.

Instead, anchored in some godforsaken Norwegian fjord, it had to
be protected against enemy aircraft and submarines. Not only at
enormous cost, but ultimately to no avail as well.

We ourselves entered the war with fewer than one quarter of the
submarines we were planning to build. To make things worse, some
of those were training vessels and weren't suitable for active operations. Of the rest, only one third could be on station at any one time.
Raeder could not, of course, build better submarines than those the
current technology permitted. But he *was* responsible for the fact
that we did not have more of them. Raeder, who took up office
in 1928, was an excellent organizer. He did as much as anyone to
rebuild our navy from 1933 on. However, he remained at his post
for too long. Strategically, his mind had gotten stuck in 1914. Like
his former master, Wilhelm II, and like *his* master, the nineteenth-
century American naval theorist Alfred Mahan, he was obsessed with
capital ships. He always thought we could not have enough of them.
I should have let him go much sooner than I did. Say, after the loss
of the *Bismarck* in May 1941 instead of in January 1943. By the
latter date he was 67 years old, high time for any commander to go.

In September 1939, many of these problems were still in the
future. Meanwhile, I had a war to run. On the evening of the
3rd of the month I left Berlin and boarded my special train, code-
named *Amerika*. It was a cumbersome contraption, but it had to
do. First came one or two armored wagons carrying anti-aircraft
guns. Then came my wagon, complete with a fair-sized drawing
room, a sleeping compartment, a bathroom, and compartments for
my adjutants and menservants. Other wagons carried a command
center with a conference room and an up-to-date communications
center, dining facilities, and quarters for my military escort, medical
staff, and press section. There were also some guest quarters. At the
rear came another anti-aircraft wagon. The whole thing was pulled
by two locomotives.

Traveling across country where there was no danger of air attack, we used to halt in the open, enabling me to take a short walk when I felt like it. When such a danger did exist, we stopped near railway tunnels so as to quickly take shelter in them in case of an alarm. The train also served as a forward base from which my entourage and I would take trips in our heavy six-wheeled Mercedes *Geländwagen*, cross-country cars. Doing so, we were regularly followed by a horde of motorized functionaries, all of whom kept jostling one another for what, today, is known as a photo op. There was also another train of the same kind. It was nicknamed Heinrich and carried Ribbentrop, Himmler, and Hans Lammers. The latter was Chief of the Reich Chancellery and thus my principal liaison to the bureaucrats at home. These trains were an innovation. Much later, the firm that built them, having passed under the control of the so-called German Democratic Republic, also provided a similar, but much more luxurious, one for Mao Zedong.

The war woke up the infantryman in me. Unlike Wilhelm II and other heads of state, I went into the most forward positions and watched the enemy through a periscope while the battle was still going on. During stops I shared the troops' food. Wherever I went, I was received with tremendous acclaim. And, of course, I made Goebbels and Hoffmann see to it that the appropriate photographs and films should be widely disseminated—not that they needed prompting! I held meetings with my generals—in fact it was at this time that I first met Jodl. But I did not feel obliged to interfere much. One reason was that they proved more competent than I, and perhaps they themselves, had thought. After all, they had not been in action for twenty years. And another reason was that the Polish defenses were antiquated and weak.

First, we destroyed much of their air force on the ground. Next, we shot down the rest in air-to-air combat. Doing so was easy, since almost all of their planes were obsolescent. Next, our mastery of the air enabled us to interdict their columns as they marched to the front. Above all, the Poles vastly exaggerated their own strength. Some of them even hoped to march on Berlin! They committed the classic error of concentrating their forces too far forward. This meant Posen instead of behind the Vistula as they should have. Determined not to give up any territory, they ended by being unable to defend themselves and losing all of it.

On the 6th I toured the battlefield of Tucheler Heide in northern Poland. A powerful Polish corps had been surrounded there and was desperately trying to break out. It was during this battle that they famously pitted their cavalry against our tanks. As the saying goes, the line between courage and lunacy is a narrow one, with none more so than with the Poles! The roads we traveled were strewn with the debris of war: wrecked vehicles and hideously mutilated corpses of horses and men. And not just soldiers either.

To be sure, Göring had explicitly ordered the Luftwaffe to stick to the laws of war. Given our military doctrine and the way our air force was constructed, doing so made good operational sense. But here and there mistakes were made. I am told that this happened because, observed from a fast-flying aircraft, columns of civilian refugees often look much like military ones. Both consist mainly of covered wagons, and both are smothered by dust or mud. I myself had been through enough slaughter to spare, so the sight did not affect me too much. But I presume that some of our younger troops had different feelings.

It was during my stay in this area that I was informed that Krakow, a key city hundreds of kilometers to the south where some Polish forces had fled, had fallen. At Krakow and elsewhere, our bombers had concentrated on railway yards and communication knots. Hence it had received little damage. Far less so, for example, than many Belgian and French cities did during the Great War and, again at the time of the Allied Normandy Landings. The case of Warsaw was very different. Already on 10 September, being surrounded on all sides, its situation was hopeless. But the Poles simply refused to surrender.

On the 25th I visited the commander on the spot, General Johannes von Blaskowitz. The record of the meeting is extant. He told me that, until then, our air force and artillery had only fired at military objectives such as enemy batteries as well as vital installations such as gas, water, and power stations. There was nothing particularly sinister about this. In fact our targets were not very different from those the U.S. and its allies attacked in Baghdad in 1991 and in Belgrade in 1999. We did not, of course, have the precision-guided munitions the Americans had built at such enormous expense. But our aircraft, especially the Stukas, flew much lower and were specifically designed to hit their targets accurately. Not only were there far more of them, but they were able to fly several times as many sorties each day as their late twentieth-century successors.

Blaskowitz was an officer of the old school. Not long afterward he started raising objections to the way the SS was treating the Polish intelligentsia and the Jews, condemning what he called "criminal atrocities, maltreatment, and plundering." To show him who was the boss, I transferred him to some minor post in the West while at the same time offering an amnesty to the SS personnel involved. At this point, though, he asked for, and received, my permission to try to persuade the Poles to surrender on reasonable terms. Officers would keep their daggers and be taken into honorable captivity. Ordinary soldiers and NCOs would be released as soon as we had finished processing them. That very evening we dropped millions of leaflets to that effect. Our efforts were to no avail.

This left us with no option but to subject the city to an all-out assault by our infantry and artillery. However, we had a problem. The Luftwaffe, it turned out, did not have a sufficient number of aircraft suitable for dropping incendiaries. So we were forced to use our Ju-52 transports for the purpose. We had a man stand at each

open door, wearing a harness so as not to fall down, to shovel the
bomblets into the empty space below! Accuracy, of course, was out
of the question. The city suffered horribly, and 26,000 people are
said to have died. But that was not my fault. In fact I had done my
best to prevent such a disaster from taking place. On 5 October I
visited Warsaw for the second time, using the opportunity to visit
Field-Marshal Pilsudski's former residence and to lay a wreath in his
death chamber. More important, I attended a grand victory parade
our army had organized. As the troops marched past smartly, looking
almost as if they had not just put a difficult campaign behind them,
I took the salute. Didn't Nietzsche write that victory is the best cure
for the soul? How right he was.

On 17 September Stalin sent his forces to invade eastern Poland
as the secret protocol in our agreement required him to. Our troops,
though, had not been informed. Consequently, Guderian's tanks
drove all the way east to Brest Litovsk. He was highly annoyed. Who
can blame him? Naturally he obeyed, but not before asking, and
receiving, permission to hold a common parade with the Red Army
on the 22nd. The campaign over, we reannexed the territories we
had lost in 1918–19 and then some. I entrusted the work of re-
Germanizing them to Himmler. He lost no time in throwing out
Poles and moving in people of sound German stock.

One advantage of the process was that it enabled him to look after
thousands of our *Volksgenossen* who, without having to be told, had
fled from the Red Army. And, of course, Himmler, making liberal
use of his special police units, had anyone who might resist us shot.
Taking account of our annexations and those of the Russians, we cut
Poland's territory by about three quarters. The rest I turned into
a *Generalgouvernement;* for some reason I do not recall, we used
the French term. The governor was my former lawyer and trusted
collaborator, Hans Frank. Over the next five years we exploited the
country to the hilt, partly because we were, after all, involved in a
world war and partly because the Poles deserved no better.

During all that time our opponents in the West did not lift a finger to help the Poles. Perhaps that was one reason why my generals, cautious as ever, were still pinning their hopes on peace with them. So much so, in fact, that, on 15 September 1939, Halder issued instructions not only for the withdrawal of most of our combat troops from Poland—that made sense—but for partial demobilization! I, however, knew more about international politics than the brass at Zossen did. I very much doubted whether we could achieve peace. Furthermore, I was of two minds. Prewar Poland was a large and rather underdeveloped country. Properly digesting it would have taken decades. But suppose the Allies had accepted our victory and agreed to make peace on the basis of the status quo. Was that really what we wanted? I was already fifty years old, and my time was running out. Besides, I had no doubt that we would have to settle accounts with the West. If not now, then later. But we no longer lived in the period of cabinet wars, when decisions were made by a few crowned heads and their mistresses. The illusions of politicians and generals notwithstanding, one cannot simply start and end a war whenever one feels like doing so.

Had the decision been mine alone, we would have struck as early as October 1939. But my generals, as so often, procrastinated. The war with Poland, they said, though victorious, had revealed not the forces' strengths but their various weaknesses. They did not have this, and they did not have that. They could not do this, and they could not do that. This and that had to be fixed, and, of course, they needed time to fix it. Could I, the great dictator, have forced them to act against their "professional" judgment? In theory, perhaps yes. In practice, no. The Wehrmacht, including the officer corps above all, was an exceptionally cohesive organization. That, in fact, was the real secret of its outstanding performance. Such an organization has to be handled with care, or else it will fall to pieces in one's hands.

The international environment was not getting any better either. The Spanish Civil War had finally ended, and ended well for us. But

Italy, instead of using the opportunity to join us, found one excuse after another why it should not do so. Whether it was Ciano who incited the Duce against us or the Duce who secretly gave Ciano his marching orders was, in the end, immaterial. The example of Rome was not without effect on other European countries. The Scandinavian countries, Benelux, and Switzerland all hedged their bets. Hungary, Romanian, Yugoslavia, Greece, Bulgaria, and Turkey, though more sympathetic to our cause, did the same. Even that great hypocrite, Roosevelt, was starting to give some trouble. In public he tried to present himself as a disinterested peacemaker, a stance he hoped would help him win the 1940 elections. However, documents rescued from the Polish Foreign Ministry in Warsaw showed that, behind the scenes, he had been goading England and France to hold firm against us. In the long run he would almost certainly join them in fighting us, just as his predecessor, the equally hypocritical Wilson, had done during the Great War.

More immediately, Stalin was using the international situation to strengthen his own position. First, in the summer, his armed forces dealt those of Japan a powerful blow at the Battle of Khalkhin-Gol in faraway Manchuria. Faraway it might have been, but it taught the Japanese what was what. It also put an end to any desire they may have felt to fight Russia in the future. Instead, they continued their hopeless attempt to take over China with all its huddled, teeming masses while also starting to prepare for war against England and the U.S.

Feeling that their rear was secure, the Russians attacked Finland so as to increase the distance between the Finns (and us) and Leningrad as well as to get a better hold on the Baltic. Finland was vital to us because it provided us with nickel from the mines at Petsamo. Without this raw material, which we needed to produce high-quality steel and for which there was no other source, we might as well have closed shop. We knew it, the Allies knew it, and the Russians also knew it.

The strange thing was that, with regard to this particular war, we and our Western enemies found ourselves on the same side. Both of us sympathized with the Finns as the underdogs. What is more, they were civilized underdogs resisting the Asiatic hordes coming at them. They fought as bravely as any people in history. Much later, one military expert rated them as Europe's best soldiers, saying they were even better than ours. Perhaps they were. However, given the enormous numerical and material superiority they were facing, there was only so much they could do. In the end they had to surrender to Stalin's demands.

Amidst all this, my generals kept coming up with objections to any potential offensive we might launch against the West. But step by step, I shepherded them toward D Day and H Hour.

Chapter 21

Victory in the West

On 6 October 1939 I addressed the Reichstag. This was in the midst of a period of several weeks during which the West and we put out peace feelers to each other. Once again, one of the intermediaries was the indefatigable Dahlerus. My speech, by convincing the German people that I wanted peace, served its purpose very well. But I cannot say that the talks were really meant in earnest. They were not, as far as I was able to determine, on the English side; adopting the pompous attitude so typical of them, they treated us as if they had just won a war and we had lost it! And not on mine. It was time to get serious. In other words, let the cannons have their say.

Preparations for "Operation Yellow," as we called the coming offensive against the West, proceeded slowly at first. To a large extent, it was Halder's fault. At the time Halder, a Bavarian by birth, was fifty-five years old. He had an unrivaled capacity for work and a schoolmasterly manner I found irritating. He tended to patronize whoever he met; that was why, at one point, I told him he would never know my innermost thoughts. As Chief of the Army General Staff, he carried a larger share of the responsibility than any other officer did. Yet, paradoxically, among all our top commanders he was the general with the least confidence in the offensive. He kept raising difficulties and asking that it be postponed.

His nominal superior, Brauchitsch, was even worse. His position between Halder and myself made him feel uncomfortable. So he made himself scarce by repeatedly leaving the headquarters and vis-

iting the troops. To sound them out, he said. At one point he even
wrote them an open letter concerning their sexual habits! Not exactly
an ideal team to work with, I would say. But this was 1939–40, not
1938. We were in the midst of a major war. I could not change
my most senior commanders while at the same time preparing the
offensive which would determine the fate of Germany for the next
thousand years. Or so I hoped.

Before we could tackle the West, though, there were two other
problems that worried us. One was the Allied intent to mine the
Danube and to disrupt our oil shipments from Romania. The other
was their attempts to do the same with respect to the Swedish iron ore
that was being shipped to us by way of the Norwegian Leads. Nothing
much came of the first plan. However, the second issue was vital to
our existence and could not be ignored. Our intelligence sources told
us, quite correctly as it turned out, that the English and the French
were preparing to mine the Leads. Next, they were going to land
troops at the ports of Narvik, Bergen, Trondheim, and Stavanger. We
decided to forestall them by occupying Norway ourselves.

As Raeder pointed out, doing so would provide us with another
advantage. During the World War our submarines and surface blockade runners had greatly suffered from a lack of proper bases. In large
part, it was a question of geography. Each in their time, Spain, the
Netherlands, and France had all suffered from the same problem.
Their way to the Atlantic, and hence the world's remaining seas and
oceans, was blocked by the British Isles standing in the way like
sentries in front of a palace. The fact that the Republic of Ireland
gained its independence soon after the First World War and remained
neutral during the Second helped, but not by very much. In 1939,
given how small and weak our navy was, we could not hope to avoid
being blockaded just as we had been in 1914–18. But we *could* do
something to give our submarines much greater freedom of action.
And we did.

Undertaking Operation *Weserübung* was one of the most risky military maneuvers in history. From Kiel to Narvik—look at the map! First, it had to be carried out in the teeth of the enemy's crushing superiority at sea. Second, northwestern Scotland and the Orkneys, including the main English naval base at Scapa Flow, were much closer to central and northern Norway than our own bases. They enabled the English to make better use of their fleet and air force than we could. Third, the English had carriers whereas we did not. In such a situation only boldness, careful planning, secrecy, perfect execution, a gift for improvisation, and, above all, a bulldog-like determination to hold on could offer a way out. Overall command was in the hands of Hugo Sperrle, the air force officer who had cut his teeth in Spain. So unprepared were we that, initially at any rate, he had to use Bädeker maps, like a tourist! Truth be told, though, neither he nor any other German general had ever commanded anything like this operation.

Our first troopships sailed on 7 April. On 9 April, the day on which hostilities proper began, we dealt with the tiny Danish air force, which was based around Copenhagen. Thereupon, the Danes, fearing we would bomb their capital as we had Warsaw, capitulated. Norway, a much larger and topographically very difficult, country, proved a tougher nut to crack. First, we sent naval forces into the Oslofjord in an attempt to reach the capital. However, the Norwegian coastal batteries were ready and opened fire. They sank the heavy cruiser *Blücher* and damaged the cruiser *Lützow,* forcing her to withdraw from the fight and to sail home for repairs. In the end we had to complete the job by flying in troops to occupy the local airfield. From there they marched into the city and took it over.

Proceeding from south to north, our landings at Kristiansand, Bergen, and Trondheim went well. We met the strongest resistance at Kristiansand, where the cruiser *Karlsruhe* was hit and almost went to the bottom. However, in all three places we ended by attaining our objectives. Having captured the ports, our forces set out to occupy southeastern and central Norway as well. The narrow mountain passes, melting snow, and occasionally fierce Norwegian resistance obstructed their advance and slowed it down. Time and again the troops had to call on the Luftwaffe to deal with the defenders. It took longer than we had expected, but by the second week of May they had more or less accomplished their missions.

The situation at Narvik, far to the north, was entirely different. Our commander on the spot was General Eduard Dietl, a Bavarian. I had known him since 1923, when he and his company had sided with us during the Putsch. Escorted by ten destroyers, he and his men took Narvik on 9–10 April. On their way out, though, the destroyers ran into a greatly superior English naval force that sank all ten of them.

Next, the English sent their troops ashore. The vast distance between our bases and Narvik prevented the Luftwaffe from softening up the Norwegian units in this area as it had done further south. Joining the English, they captured the town, forcing Dietl to retreat into the surrounding mountains. There, greatly outnumbered, he continued the fight. At one point, so desperate was the situation that I considered ordering him to withdraw across the border to Sweden, where he and his forces would be interned. In the end, our victories in Benelux and France and his own strong nerves prevailed. The English withdrew, but not before fighting a naval battle in which they lost an aircraft carrier and we had one of our pocket battleships, the *Scharnhorst,* badly damaged. In June I awarded Dietl the Knight's Cross of the Iron Cross. He was the first of my generals to receive that distinction; no one deserved it more.

Our troops had performed magnificently. We suffered 5,296 casualties. Of those 2,375 were sunk at sea, 1,317 were killed on land, and 1,604 were wounded. Six of our submarines went to the bottom. So did one out of two heavy cruisers, two out of six light cruisers, and ten out of twenty destroyers. Several other warships suffered heavy damage. So badly was the surface fleet hit that it never quite recovered. We also lost about ten percent of our merchant fleet. The

Luftwaffe's losses totaled 90 aircraft. But the objective of *Weserübung* was achieved. Denmark and Norway were now in our hands.

In Denmark we allowed the existing government to stay, under our control of course. In Norway things were different. The Norwegian government, with King Haakon VII at its head, had escaped to England. Hence we formed a new government under a former Minister of Defense, Vidkun Quisling, who agreed to take the job. Over his head I appointed my veteran Gauleiter, Josef Terboven, *Reichskommissar* for the occupied Norwegian Territories. During the rest of the war both occupied countries remained almost perfectly calm. Norway met our expectations by providing our submarines with first-class bases, whereas Denmark delivered a considerable amount of our food.

Compared to the tremendous drama now unfolding in the West, though, Scandinavia was a sideshow. Throughout the autumn and winter of 1939–40 the troops trained, and the problems that had plagued us in Poland were gradually solved. Meanwhile, my staff and I wrangled over the exact shape of the offensive to come. The French, remember, had built the Maginot Line to cover their frontier with us. That fact persuaded the Army High Command, with Halder at its head, to plan for a repetition of the Schlieffen Plan of 1914. The only essential difference was that, this time around, the Netherlands would not be spared.

Then along came General Erich von Manstein. Haughty in manner, addicted to bridge, he was widely regarded as the army's most outstanding strategic mind. At the time he was serving as Chief of Staff to Army Group A. The group was deployed opposite Northern France and Belgium between Army Group B on its right and Army Group C on its left. Working informally with Guderian, Manstein proposed moving the *Schwerpunkt,* or center of gravity, from our north to our center. The decisive point was to be Sedan, the little town where Moltke had encircled Emperor Louis Napoleon III and his army back in 1870. The problem was Halder. Halder was a conventional officer with a conventional officer's mind. Considering the Ardennes passes too narrow for motorized formations to drive through, he did not like the plan at all. To get rid of Manstein, he sent him to command a corps at Stettin! I, however, got wind of the scheme during a luncheon I held for some corps commanders.

In January one of our courier aircraft, violating my explicit orders, was forced to land in Belgium. The papers it was carrying fell into Allied hands. The incident strengthened my conviction that the original plan should be scrapped and a new one put into its place. Willy-nilly, Halder went along. Over the next few months we systematically took forces away from Army Groups B and C and moved them to Army Group A and its commander, General Gerd von Rundstedt. So vast was the concentration of troops and vehicles that its tail, stretching over 150 kilometers, reached back across the Rhine! Above all, we gave Rundstedt practically all the armored and motorized divisions we had.

The balance of forces between us and the Allies, Belgium and the Netherlands included, was as follows. We had 3,350,000 troops; they had 3,300,000. We had 5,638 aircraft; they had 2,935. We had 141 divisions; they had 144. We had 7,378 artillery barrels; they had 13,974. We had 2,445 tanks; they had 3,383. Here it is worth noting that many of their tanks, the French Char B in particular, were heavier and better armored than ours. They were so much better armored, in fact, that the light cannon most of our tanks carried were unable to penetrate them. As I said earlier, though, we had the better organization, the better ancillary equipment, and the better—much better—doctrine for using them. By this time we also had the more experienced commanders. But our most important advantage was the offensive spirit of our troops and their willingness to dare, risk, and fight. For that, I suppose, I can take much of the credit.

On the evening of 9 May I left Berlin in a Ju-52 flown by my faithful pilot, Captain Baur. First, to deceive any onlookers, we headed east. Next, we turned and flew to Bad Münstereifel, not far from Euskirchen, where the army engineers had prepared a field headquarters for me. I called it *Felsennest*, the Nest among the Rocks. There had been some last-minute worries. In particular, the weather which could have interfered with our air operations upon which so much depended. My chief meteorologist sweated blood, as they say. But things turned out as he had predicted: it was a cool, bright day of the kind people liked to call *Hitlerwetter*. Much later, I learned that some traitors high up in the *Abwehr*, the military intelligence and counter-intelligence organization, had contacted the enemy and betrayed the date of our attack. But we did not know it at the time, and in any case it did not matter.

Distances in the theater were much smaller than in Norway. But the risk we took was almost equally as great. For several years the Luftwaffe had been preparing equipment and troops for air-to-ground assaults. Now Göring sent gliders to capture the fortress of Eben Emäl in Belgium and paratroopers to take Dutch airfields at The Hague as well as the bridges over the Maas at Rotterdam. Both operations were the first ever of their kind. The one against Eben Emäl went perfectly and opened our way into northeastern Belgium. However, the paratroopers in the Netherlands got stuck and came under a fierce counterattack by the Dutch Army.

Meanwhile, to the east, our forces succeeded in penetrating the so-called Grebbe Line and entering "Fortress Holland." This was the 14th of the month, and negotiations aimed at making the Dutch surrender were already under way. Meanwhile, we sent bombers to relieve our hard-pressed paratroopers in Rotterdam. Just before they arrived, an agreement was reached. Our commanders on the ground launched red flares to warn the bombers away. But for some reason only a third of them received the order and acted accordingly. The remaining fifty-something struck at their targets. They were Dutch military positions and therefore perfectly legitimate according to the laws of war. Unfortunately, some of them missed and hit a margarine factory instead. The outcome was a huge conflagration that could be seen from dozens of kilometers away. The material damage was vast; yet the number of dead was only about 900.

In any case, the forces moving into the Netherlands and Belgium were intended mainly as decoys. Their real function was to draw the English and the French north into Belgium. Arriving on the river Dyle, they took up positions as if to defend against a second edition of the Schlieffen Plan. As they did so, Rundstedt's spearheads were making their way through the Ardennes, far to the south.

Luck was on their side. The French, their minds still caught in 1914–18, expected a long war. Believing that victory would go to the side with the last battalion in reserve, they deployed their aircraft well in the rear. So reluctant were they to use them that they ended the campaign with more operational ones than they had when it started! Our columns, moving bumper to bumper along the narrow roads and sometimes getting stuck in gigantic traffic jams, went almost unopposed. The fact that the French telephone network was hopelessly antiquated helped. By one account their Commander in Chief, General Maurice Gamelin, depended on a single line. And that one was inoperative for two hours every day because his secretary went for lunch.

On 15 May our advance guard reached the Meuse at Dinant. They called in the Stukas which silenced the French defenders, less so with their bombs, perhaps, than with the infernal scream they emitted as they dived, almost vertically, upon their targets. Driving west, our troops found themselves across the communications of the Allied forces on the Dyle. So fast was the pace of the advance that it worried me on occasion. That was particularly true on the 17th, when a French division, commanded by the aforementioned de Gaulle, counterattacked at Montcornet. Again, it was the Luftwaffe, acting in perfect cooperation with the army, which saved the day. Later, this General de Gaulle was to form a "Free French" government in London. Seeking recognition, for over four years he drove Roosevelt and Churchill so nuts that the former at one point wanted to arrest him! He also raised some troops, but their military contribution to the Allies' eventual victory was negligible.

The curious thing was that, at my headquarters, the roles had been reversed. Throughout the months before the operation, Halder had consistently suggested caution. Now, suddenly, it was he who declared we should press forward as fast as possible whereas I, to the contrary, wanted to rein in the Panzers until the infantry, necessarily marching at a considerably slower pace, could catch up and secure the corridor through which their supplies had to pass. We clashed over this question several times. After the war, working for the U.S. Army's historical service, he wrote a little book about me. In it he accused me—me, who had assumed all the risk both in Norway and in the West—of having bad nerves! Look who is talking.

In any case the French counterattack only held us up for one day, if that. On the 20th of May our spearheads, commanded by Guderian, had reached the sea at Abbeville. With that all communications between the French homeland and the Allied forces further to the north had been cut. Guderian, *Schnelle Heinz* (fast Heinz), as he was known, was understandably flush with victory. He asked for the right to be allowed to proceed north along the coast to Calais so as to close the circle on our enemies. And Halder, with Brauchitsch in tow, supported him.

I for my part was not so sure. The Panzers had covered some 300 kilometers from Sedan to Abbeville and were exhausted. Both men and machines badly needed rest and replenishment. And I was still worried about our rear. In this I had the support of all my senior commanders, including Generals Rundstedt, Hans Kluge (the excellent commander of 4th Army, which had been put under Rundstedt's command), and Ewald von Kleist, commander of the *Panzergruppe* named after him and Guderian's direct superior. Finally, I knew that the countryside around Dunkirk, though open, was waterlogged and unsuited for armored operations. So, having been stationed there during the Great War, did generals Keitel and Jodl. This was especially true of the latter, whose advice I came to value more and more.

Here, I want to put to rest two tales historians have come up with. First, it was not a question of allowing the Luftwaffe and Göring to get all the glory. In my view, if not in his own, he already had more than enough glory to spare. Second, I did not stop the tanks in order to enable the English to get away and thus to facilitate peace with London. What really happened was that our intelligence did not discover the Allied evacuation in time. It took us 72 hours to understand what the English were doing: running from the Continent and taking along as many French as they could. As we resumed operations, though, we found ourselves confronted with a perimeter they had erected in haste. Progress was slower than expected. Meanwhile, the Luftwaffe encountered the fresh English fighter squadrons which, up to this point, had been held back. Now, taking off from bases very close to the Pas de Calais, it inflicted quite a few losses on us. Still, the outcome of the struggle was never in doubt. On the morning of 27 May all of Dunkirk was in our hands.

It took us just two days to refit our forces, refuel them, and turn them around. Considering their size and the length of the front along which they were spread, doing so was a magnificent achievement. Our armored divisions, covered by the Luftwaffe from the air, rolled south and southeast. The bulk of the forces followed in forced marches. Here and there we encountered some stiff resistance. But the so-called Weygand Line, named after the new Chief of Staff who had replaced Gamelin, hardly existed. Again, the outcome was never in doubt. On 10 June the situation of France became even more difficult when Italy entered the war, sending 300,000 troops to attack, or rather to try to attack, across the Alpine Passes. On the same day Paris was declared an open city, and on the 15th our forces entered it. Meanwhile, farther to the southeast, Army Group C was slowly but methodically chewing its way through the Maginot Line.

In this desperate situation the French government had no choice but to ask for an armistice. Famously, I made sure it would be signed at the very spot, and in the very railway wagon, the French had used to receive our delegation at the end of World War I; later I had it moved to a Berlin Museum. Overlooking the scene was a statue of the then-Allied Commander in Chief, Field-Marshal Ferdinand Foch. A short film was made, showing how perfectly happy I was. With my adjutants looking on, I even performed a few dancing steps! And no wonder, after all the months and months of endless worries. On the next day, the 23rd, I realized an old dream of mine. I had Breker, who had studied in Paris under Aristide Maillol and knew the city well, show me around. In the company were Bormann, Speer, Hoffmann, and a few others. It was very early in the morning, and the streets were almost deserted. The few people who were about and who recognized me behaved as if they had seen a ghost. I also took the opportunity to visit some of the places where, a quarter-century earlier, my comrades and I had fought.

It was a victory of historic dimensions. Other Great Powers before us had gone down to defeat. So, in the end, did we ourselves. But not in six weeks! We set up arrangements for running the occupied territories. For the Netherlands I chose the faithful Seyss-Inquart. Though an Austrian by birth, he was a sincere admirer of Dutch culture. He did what he could for the country and remained at his post right to the end. Belgium's king had stayed in Brussels and later gave us so much trouble that I was prepared to let him leave for England to meet his mistresses! The country itself came under a military government, as did France. The unoccupied part of France retained a French government under Field-Marshal Philippe Pétain, the elderly but highly respected hero of Verdun, and a former prime minister, Pierre Laval. Pétain's role was symbolic, whereas Laval held whatever power there was to be had. The French were made to pay a huge indemnity and to bear the cost of our occupation as well. Considering what they had done to us at Versailles, they deserved no better.

There followed the usual victory celebrations. First, I made my official entry into Berlin to the most tumultuous welcome I could desire. Next came the distribution of decorations, promotions, and so on. Seldom had the world seen so much gold leaf concentrated in one building! To satisfy Göring's vanity, I invented the rank of *Reichsmarschall* for him. Big boy that he was, did he ever like the specially designed baton he got with it! I also created no fewer than twelve new field-marshals, a number unprecedented in our history. Surely the generals in question had deserved it. But I did not include Halder among them. It is true that he had worked out all the zillion details such a vast operation consists of. Nevertheless, I could not help feeling ambiguous about him. He was as disappointed as Göring was elated.

Forgetting their previous doubts, so many millions of good Germans flocked to see the newsreels that some movie theaters had to run them as many as ten times a day! Goebbels' film about the campaign, *Sieg im Westen (Victory in the West)* also proved to be a great international success and was translated into twenty languages. Personally, I felt like a gambler who had staked everything on a single card. Having made a huge but unexpected gain, he wants nothing better than to pocket his money and to leave the building. For a few weeks after the surrender of France we tried to negotiate with the English. That same evening, 19 July, I made them an official peace offer. It was a very generous one, I must say. My efforts were in vain, as it turned out. Instead of changing their attitude, they put their faith in "the New World." The ensuing life-and-death struggle ended by striking both our countries from the roster of Great Powers. Those who must bear the historical responsibility for this are Churchill, who had replaced Chamberlain in May, and his Jewish puppet masters.

Very much against my wishes, the war would go on.

Chapter 22

From West to East

Imagine a rivulet of water issuing from an overturned pail. As it advances, it loses momentum until it finally comes to a halt. At that point, it starts to recede. A military offensive behaves in a similar way. It must achieve its objective, i.e. victory. Failing that, it will exhaust itself and turn into its opposite, a defensive. This is what Clausewitz calls the culminating point.

In the summer of 1940 we stood in danger of reaching that point. Yes, our military, especially the Luftwaffe and the army, had more than proven itself. Yes, our victories had been past compare. But they did not succeed in breaking the enemy's will or enable us to dictate the peace. In fact they did not enable us to make any peace at all. At that moment time started working against us. Not, take note, because of the English. Commanding, as we did, not only our own resources but most of Europe's as well, we could handle them. But we faced the growing likelihood, indeed near certainty, that both Russia and the U.S. would end up turning against us.

In fact, Russia was already giving clear signs of preparing to do exactly that. In June Stalin occupied the Baltic States. Following up almost immediately, he did the same in Bessarabia and Northern Bukovina. Considering the agreement we had made with him in August 1939, he was formally within his rights. Still, his moves, following as they did upon his war against Finland, could not but make us think. We were even more concerned because the second one brought the Red Army within striking distance of our principal source of oil. We contacted Bucharest, asked for permission, and sent in 100,000 men. As they say, better safe than sorry.

Roosevelt, for his part, was siding up closer and closer to London. True, U.S. public opinion remained isolationist. The American people did not want to be fooled into pulling Whitehall's chestnuts out of the fire, as had happened in 1917–18. With presidential elections scheduled for November, there were limits to what the President could do. But he made no secret of where his sympathies lay and what, if given the opportunity, he would do.

It was with such considerations in mind that, on 31 July, I summoned my top commanders to the Berghof. The question, I told them, was why England did not give in. To that question I could see just one answer: Churchill was hoping that Russia would stab us in the back. Given Stalin's character, it was not an unreasonable belief! Therefore, I continued, it was essential to attack Russia so as to finish it off once and for all. Russia's defeat would also free Japan to resist the U.S. and make Roosevelt think twice before acting against us. With Russia's resources in our hands, we would no longer need the kind of overseas trade that had preoccupied the Kaiser and his advisers so much. This would enable us to resist the Anglo-Saxons forever if necessary.

Personally, I would have liked to have attacked Russia that very autumn. As so often, though, Halder objected. Preparations for such a vast undertaking would take too long. It was too late in the season—autumn and its rains were coming fast. And so on and so on. I was forced to concede that there was logic in what he said. As a soldier, I had served in the west. But I had had no personal experience with conditions in the east. Consequently, all I did was order some preliminary planning to go ahead. But my decision to postpone the campaign until the next spring left open the question as to how to handle the English. The natural thing would be to mount an invasion of the island. My generals and admirals had already started preparing some plans for it. I personally never really liked the idea. Though a hero on land, at sea I was a coward; perhaps it was my Austrian background. At any rate, the waves always made me feel slightly uncomfortable. Still, I allowed them to go ahead—pending final authorization, of course.

The problem was that our navy was much too small to stand up to the English one. It could not do so before the Norwegian campaign. And it became much less capable after the massive losses it had suffered during the fighting in that part of the world. Therefore, if our forces were to get across the Channel, the first thing to do was to obtain command of the air. I entrusted this mission to Göring and the Luftwaffe. Starting on the 10th of July, they launched a major offensive against the Royal Air Force. The objective, as Douhet had put it, was to ensure that we could fly and that they could not. Prime targets consisted of airfields, headquarters, communication centers, anti-aircraft defenses, and aircraft and ammunition factories. We also hoped to use our numerical superiority to force the English to take off and to engage in air-to-air combat. All this, let me repeat, meant proceeding well within the limits permitted by the laws of war.

While construction crews built review stands at Berlin's Pariser Platz in preparation for another victory, our generals and admirals were working on their plan, known as *Seelöwe* (Sea Lion), for invading England. In fact, working is too grandiose a term. Squabbling would be a more appropriate one. On one side were Halder and the army. They worried about possible counterattacks by the English Army—weaponless, as, following the evacuation at Dunkirk, it was—and demanded a landing on as broad a front as possible. On the other side were Raeder and the Kriegsmarine. Anxious about their (in)ability to protect the transports against the Royal Navy, they wanted to land on as narrow a front as possible. Another problem was that we did not have any specialized landing craft. Hence those transports would have to consist of requisitioned Rhine barges, not exactly ideal vessels for such a purpose. They could have served, if at all, only on the calmest days. In fact some barges were assembled at ports such as Rotterdam and Antwerp, and some exercises in embarking and disembarking troops were held. The two services went on arguing, but an agreement was never reached.

The first week of September having arrived, decisions had to be made. One reason for this was that the days were becoming shorter and the storm season closer. Either we acted quickly, or else winter would be on us. More serious still, what the enemy called "the Battle of Britain" was not going as well as we had hoped. Our intelligence had underestimated both the opponent and the magnitude of the task. The English, we discovered, had refused to let their best squadrons participate in the Battle of France but had kept them in reserve instead. Now, fresh, ready and—one must hand it to them—eager, they took off to fight us.

Our losses mounted. Worst hit were the Stukas. Thanks to their precision-bombing capabilities, they had played major roles in the previous campaigns. However, with their fixed undercarriages they proved too slow for modern air combat and had to be withdrawn. Our remaining bombers could not place their loads as accurately as the Stukas did. They also found that they could not cope with the English Hurricanes (*Huren-Kannen,* as our troops called them) and Spitfires but needed to be protected by friendly fighter squadrons. Our fighters, primarily the single-engine Me-109, were good enough for the task. But they did not have the range to reach all the targets we had in mind. Besides, each time one of our aircraft was brought down, both the machine and the pilot were irretrievably lost. By contrast the RAF, fighting over friendly territory, was able to salvage many aircraft and recover many pilots.

And then there was radar, a new contraption we encountered for the first time. The English, it turned out, had been busily working on a series of stations known as the Home Chain. It was finished just on time and immediately went into action against us. It acted as a "force multiplier"—an expression, of course, that only came into use decades later. Having backed it up with a sophisticated command and control system, our enemies were able to guide their fighter squadrons with unparalleled precision. It did not take our experts totally by surprise; in fact the navy had been working on something similar for a number of years. However, they were slow to realize its importance. Had they done so from the outset, then very likely victory would have been ours. Even so, it was a close-run thing. Though we did not know it at the time, in September the English defenses were tottering. Their production of fighters was still satisfactory; but they had started to run out of pilots.

To avoid defeat Churchill, using as his excuse some of our aircraft that had hit London by mistake, sent his bombers to attack Berlin. His "air pirates," as Goebbels called them, deprived people of their sleep. But their aim was bad, and the damage they inflicted minimal. Still, I saw myself obliged to respond in kind. To reduce our losses, we switched from day attacks to night ones. The latter were much less precise, forcing us to change our targets. Rather than focus on the Royal Air Force and its supporting facilities, as we had done up to that point, we attacked so-called "infrastructure targets." That included ports—in a country such as England, which depended on imports for its food, fuel, and raw materials, they were among the most important of all. Next came factories, power plants utilities, and railway stations. Briefly, they are the pillars upon which any industrial economy stands. Many of the targets were located inside cities. Mistakes were made, and many civilians also died. But I can assure you that, on the whole, we did not kill them deliberately. Even Coventry, the city on which we inflicted so much destruction as to turn it into a symbol, was targeted for no other reason than that it was a major industrial center; throughout the war, its plants produced no fewer than a quarter of all the RAF's aircraft.

The raids, which our enemies called the Blitz, went on throughout the winter and spring. Contrary to the visions of Douhet and so many others, there was no mass panic, no chaos, and no attempt to end the agony by overthrowing the government and suing for peace. People grumbled—how could they not do so?—but put on the stiff upper lip. Later, in the face of much heavier bombardment, our own people behaved in a similar way. Could it be that the reason why Douhet's visions failed to materialize was because he was an Italian thinking about Italians? Anyhow. The English suffered, but they held their own in the end. The aforementioned factors apart, the main reason that enabled them to do so was that, as I said before, both our doctrine and the limitations of our industry had made us focus on building relatively light two-engine bombers. They simply could not carry the loads we would have needed to bomb England to pieces.

Amidst all this, my decision to postpone Operation Sea Lion until at least the following spring came almost as an afterthought. But it left my fundamental problem—how to bring the war to a victorious end—exactly as it had been. In stepped *Grossadmiral* Raeder. His navy did not have what it took to invade England. But he did think that, acting in tandem with Italy, we could drive the English out of the Mediterranean and Egypt, much like Napoleon had tried to do in 1798. The outcome would have been to bring down the empire.

Personally, I never found the idea attractive. Not in late 1940, not in the summer and early autumn of 1942 when, with our forces standing a hundred kilometers from Alexandria, it was floated for the second time. I felt this way for good reason, as it turned out, for the most important lines of communication that kept England afloat were those in the North Atlantic, not the ones with India and the Far East. Besides, right from the beginning the military performance of our Italian allies left something to be desired. They tarried in Libya, and they lost the first naval battle at Punto Stilo near the Calabrian coast. Going from bad to worse, they allowed the English to use their torpedo bombers against their fleet at Taranto, sending half of it to the bottom. Still, for lack of a better alternative, I agreed to try it out.

First, we had to make our political preparations. In September we signed the Tripartite Pact with Italy and Japan, a logical extension of the Anti-Comintern Pact we had signed with the same countries four years earlier. It was a defensive alliance in the best tradition of such treaties; a step, albeit a fairly modest one, toward containing both Russia and the United States. Over the next few months Hungary, Romania, Slovakia, and Bulgaria also joined. Some did so voluntarily; some less so. In particular, keeping the Hungarians and the Romanians, the Romanians and the Bulgarians, off each other's throats was not easy. Still, the treaty helped consolidate our grip on Eastern Europe.

In the west, things proved more difficult. We needed the cooperation not only of Italy but also of the two other principal Mediterranean countries, France and Spain. France owned quite a few important bases, and, at Toulon, a strong fleet that had remained untouched by the previous events. Only with Spanish help could we hope to capture the key to the Mediterranean, i.e. Gibraltar. All three countries, needless to say, were at loggerheads with one another over Corsica, Nice, Savoy, and Tunisia, among other things. So important did I consider the matter that, on 22 October and with Ribbentrop in tow, I went on an extended railway journey. It took me all the way to Montoire, where I met Laval. His boss, Pétain, was an enormously impressive old man with steely blue eyes, but Laval himself always reminded me of a frog, as, indeed, he was often portrayed in the English press! Then I moved on to Hendaye on the Franco–Spanish border, where I met Franco. So much did his voice irritate me that, as I later told my staff, I would prefer having two or three teeth pulled than to repeat the experience! Franco's son-in-law and Foreign Minister, Serrano Suñer, a bigoted Catholic churchgoer, also got on my nerves. It was no wonder I did not succeed in papering over the aforementioned differences. In particular, Franco's refusal to join us in an attack on Gibraltar was galling. He owed us everything, and now he refused to join us.

Arriving in Florence on 28 October, I had a surprise waiting for me. Meeting me on the platform was a beaming Mussolini. Not since his visit to us three years earlier had I seen him so cheerful. He greeted me with the words, "Führer, we are marching!" From Albania into northwestern Greece, it turned out. We had, of course, known of the Italian preparations. With their typical lack of discipline, they were constitutionally unable to hide any large operation from anyone who wanted to know. Seen from a military-geographic point of view, Greece, and even more so Crete, reminded me of Norway. In any fight against the English in the Middle East, possessing them would have brought us important advantages.

Seen in such a light, Mussolini's move made good sense. But only, of course, if it had been carried out by the right army at the right season of the year and as part of a comprehensive plan. As it was, he had the wrong army, started his offensive at the wrong time, and did not have any plan at all. After a few days, his troops got stuck. Next, they were pushed back into Albania. At one point it even looked as if that piece of land might be lost. Meanwhile, the commander, the despicable General Ubaldo Soddu, filled his time by writing music for films.

As Raeder and Göring kept telling me, implementing the so-called "peripheral strategy" would have implied reducing the army in favor of the Luftwaffe and the navy. Doing so would have taken years. To gain the necessary breathing room, it was indispensable that we come to some kind of agreement with Stalin. In particular Ribbentrop, who following his agreement with Molotov considered himself a diplomatic genius, was in favor of the scheme. Thereupon, he invited Molotov to visit Berlin on 11–13 November. He even prepared a draft treaty! But the talks, which aimed to turn the Tripartite Pact into a pact of four, did not go well. Ribbentrop tried to seduce the Russians by presenting them with the prospect of gains in the Persian Gulf. Molotov, while refusing to commit himself, demanded, as his price, additional territory in Finland, Poland, Romania, and Bulgaria as well as the Straits of Denmark and the Dardanelles! Negotiations were still going on when English bombers paid Berlin a visit. They caused little damage, but a delighted Molotov was not slow to use the opportunity to have a little fun at Ribbentrop's expense.

Clearly, the peripheral strategy had failed. Truth be told, it had been stillborn. It went against my most cherished principles, and my heart had never been in it. By 5 December I had made up my mind. We would attack Stalin as soon as possible. Doing so would serve two ends. First, it would hack off the arm, a very strong arm as we later learned, that was standing ready to stab us in the back. Second, it would enable us to move toward the realization of our greatest objective: meaning, gaining living space for the German people in the east. Originally I had thought the two wars, the one against the West and the other against Russia, would be separate with a pause of perhaps several years in between. Now, with England defeated and unable to undertake anything serious against us in the near future, I came to the conclusion that I could and should fuse the two struggles into one.

Meanwhile, I had other worries. The most important one was Italy, whose troops were going from one defeat to the next. On 9 December the English 8. Army in Egypt attacked westward. By the end of January they were threatening Tripoli, the capital of Libya. This being decades before oil was discovered under the sand, Libya itself was of no importance to us. To misquote Bismarck, it was not worth the bones of a single Pomeranian grenadier. But I could not afford to see Mussolini fail. Apart from Japan, which was not yet in the war, he was the only important ally we had. Looking back, it probably would have been best for us if he and his feckless country had stayed neutral. That was an idea, incidentally, I had played with during the early 1920s. The Italians would have formed a buffer against the English in the Mediterranean and helped us import some of the things we needed. But one cannot always get what one wants. Least of all in retrospect.

I also had another problem. The English were helping the Greeks against the Italians. Next, they asked the Greek dictator, Ioannis Metaxas, to allow them to use his airfields to bomb the Romanian oilfields. Had they succeeded in their purpose, they would have brought our entire war machine to a halt. I had absolutely nothing against the Greeks. On the contrary, I rather admired their courage in fighting the Macaronis. I tried to solve the difficulty by having them join the Tripartite Pact. Pressed by the English, they refused. This left me with no choice but to order my staff to prepare to invade and occupy their country as well.

Thus it came about that we started preparing for operations both in North Africa and the Balkans. Our advance units reached Tripoli in January–February 1941. At their head I put General Erwin Rommel. I knew him from the time he had been in charge of my headquarters battalion. Having been awarded the *Pour le Mérite* in World War I, he was reputed to be a brilliant leader and excellent tactician. So rapid were his movements during the French campaign that the enemy called his troops the Ghost Division! He had not, however, previously given any sign that he was capable of higher strategic thought. Nor, given his somewhat jejune character, am I certain that he ever developed any such thing. In this he was typical of my generals. They were masters of their profession but of very little else.

Rommel's original assignment was to hold Tripoli. But on 30 March he disobeyed his orders and went on the offensive. He embarked on a spectacular drive eastward, bypassed Tobruk, and reached the Egyptian border. Over the next two years Rommel's "little hunting expedition," as Göring called it, probably cost us more than it was worth. His communications were always coming under attack. Repeatedly, we were compelled to divert the Luftwaffe to attack the English base at Malta. We also had to give the Italian Navy some of our precious oil. Losses at sea, especially of *materiel*, were quite heavy. Much later, it turned out that the English had been reading our codes and deploying their forces accordingly.

Originally, Rommel only had two German divisions under his command. At peak, he had four out of a total of perhaps two hundred. However, in proportion to its size the Africa Corps, as it became known, received more tanks and motor transport than did our formations in any other theater. Keeping them supplied in the desert created enormous difficulties. Hence, militarily, it might have been better if Rommel had halted at Benghazi, dug in, and waited for the English to do what they could. Even if Rommel had occupied Egypt, the British Empire, aided and abetted by Roosevelt, would have held. These, however, were the years of our victories. I, with public opinion in mind, could not order him to retreat.

Rommel's own qualities as a commander were one thing. But what enabled him to achieve his initial victories was the fact that the English had withdrawn many of their forces from Libya and sent them to Greece instead. In doing so they sealed the fate of that country. Throughout the winter we kept moving troops through Hungary, Romania, and Bulgaria in the direction of Thrace. Ere we could attack, though, there was the problem of Yugoslavia to be solved. The key railway on which our forces, engaging the Greeks, would have to depend passed dangerously close to the Yugoslav frontier. It was a risk I could not take. I put pressure on the Regent, Prince Paul, to join the Tripartite Pact. On 25 March he finally did so. A mere two days later, he and his government were overthrown by a military *coup*. It was one, needless to say, that had been prepared in London and was orchestrated from there.

Having grown up in pre-1914 Austria, no one detested the Serb *Bombenschmeisser* (bomb throwers) more than I did. But this went beyond my personal tastes. What was at stake was the honor, or credibility, as they say today, of the German Reich. I immediately ordered Halder to drive from Zossen to Berlin. Guessing my intent, he prepared some preliminary plans on the way; this was one of the few times I felt really happy to have him at my side. I gave him the go-ahead, and he set his staff to work. They only took ten days to do what had to be done: select the main axes along which our forces were to advance, bring them up and deploy them along the border, look after the logistics, set up a communications network, and the like. On 6 April, to show the Serbs who was boss, we opened the offensive by bombing the hell out of Belgrade. How the Serbs howled! Next, our ground forces went into action. Cutting through the 800,000 strong Yugoslav Army like a knife through butter, they moved on the city from several different directions and quickly captured it. By 17 April everything was over.

Meanwhile, our forces invading Greece from the north faced unexpectedly tough resistance. It was to no avail, however, since we circumvented the so-called Metaxas line by making a right hook through newly occupied Yugoslav territory. Driving south, our troops reached Thermopylae and forced their way through. We took some of the English prisoner. The remainder fled. The rest was easy. On 27 April our flag was hoisted on the Acropolis. Four days later, our spearheads reached the southernmost tip of the Peloponnese. The Greeks had no choice but to capitulate. At the last moment there was some difficulty because Mussolini insisted that they surrender to his forces, too. By now I had learned to despise those forces, especially their feckless generals, with all my heart. But again, circumstances forced me to agree.

It remained for us to occupy Crete as it was the most important strategic target of all. Back in 1940, both in Norway and France, the Luftwaffe had demonstrated its ability to move its bases forward at lightning speed. It did so on this occasion, too. On 20 May our offensive, combining paratroopers with gliders and transport aircraft, got under way. Opposing our troops were Commonwealth forces. Having just been evacuated from Greece, they were somewhat disorganized; nevertheless, they gave us a good, at times desperate, fight. In the end, assisted by some forces that arrived by sea, we prevailed. We also sent a good part of the English Navy in the waters around the island to the bottom of the sea; never again would any fleet that did not have strong support from the air dare confront one that did. But so heavy were our casualties that I developed serious doubts whether large-scale air assault had not had its day. After 1944, that did in fact prove the case.

I myself had left Berlin on 10 April. Again traveling in *Amerika,* I set up my headquarters at Fürstenberg in southeast Austria. As always, we made sure there was a tunnel close at hand to serve as an air-raid shelter if necessary. To be honest, with the campaign going like clockwork there was little for me to do there, and I soon turned back. On 31 May I addressed the Reichstag, praising the German soldier and congratulating ourselves on our victories.

I now found myself ruling an empire that stretched all the way from the North Cape to western Egypt. All of it had been acquired in fewer than two years and at the cost of very few casualties indeed. There had been no Verdun and no Battle of the Somme. I heard it said that, compared to me, even Napoleon and Hindenburg looked like miserable bunglers. So impressed was Keitel that he started speaking of me as *der grösste Feldherr aller Zeiten,* the greatest warlord of all time. That was typical of him. I wish he hadn't, though, because the phrase soon gave rise to a comic abbreviation, *der Gröfatz.*

No sooner had Crete fallen than some people, especially in the navy, suggested that, in view of our recent successes, we revive our peripheral strategy. I, however, turned down their request for a second time. Not only would the strategy in question take a long time to implement, but it would have left our problem with Russia intact. If anything, it would have made that problem even worse.

Chapter 23

"The World Will Hold Its Breath!"

To retrace my steps, the die was cast in early December 1940. But not in the sense that there would be a war of expansion against Russia. *That* had been an unalterable part of my plan for many years past. However, the war in question would be part and parcel of the one we were already waging. In other words, the two would be fused into one.

Russia, I knew, was like none of the opponents we had faced until this point. The country had assumed its more or less "modern" form under Ivan the Terrible in the sixteenth century. Ever since, it had often been invaded. But it was never really defeated. Charles XII tried and failed. Napoleon tried and failed. The Allies in 1854–56 had made some gains, but they were minor and were soon lost again. Japan had tried, only to have the verdict of history reversed, to a large extent, in 1939. The most successful were Hindenburg and Ludendorff in 1914–18. Even so, by the autumn of 1940 Stalin had regained almost all that Holy Russia had lost. Briefly, from the moment Russia started casting its shadow over Europe toward the end of the seventeenth century, it had, on the whole, gone from strength to strength. And it was no wonder; in 1940, its population equaled that of Germany, France, and England combined. These Slav subhumans truly breed like rabbits.

Other factors that made up Russia's strength included the extreme hardiness of its people and the vast spaces that made it immune to blockades and into which its army could retreat. Add a railway system that used a wider gauge than the international standard and a road network that was, in reality, no network at all, and the difficulty of invading the country will become clear. But that was not all. In 1917–18 the Judeo-Bolsheviks came to power. I say Judeo-Bolsheviks, not simply Bolsheviks, as not only were many of their leading personalities Jewish, but at one point no fewer than fifty percent of the NKVD generals were. They set up a ruthless totalitarian government compared to which the one I built was child's play. They started by killing millions of people during the civil war. Hardly had they stopped doing so than they turned on the peasantry, literally starving millions of people to death in order to obtain the necessary funds to industrialize the country. Then came the great purges of 1937–39, in which several hundreds of thousands more died.

Amidst all this, they somehow succeeded in building a gigantic military industry. That shows you what sheer terror can do! To be sure, both then and later the quality of that industry often left something to be desired. Not so much in terms of the most important weapon systems, such as their tanks, artillery, and aircraft, which tended to be crude but functional. Some, particularly the T-34 tank, which we began to encounter in late 1941, were better than ours. But with regard to refinement, operator comfort, and finish, it was as if the designers were saying, "We do not care about these things because the equipment will soon be lost in battle anyhow. So why spend more on them than we must?" The same applied to every kind of ancillary equipment, such as wireless, optics, and photography. No decent German would have used such junk! Even their watches stopped working after a short time.

Geographically, European Russia falls into two zones: a north and a south. They are separated by the Pripet Marshes, an elliptically shaped area some 480 kilometers long and 225 kilometers wide. It forms an almost impassable area of forests and swamps ideal, as it later turned out, for irregulars and bandits of every sort. Thus any invader will be faced with the question of where the center of gravity should be placed. The original plan, produced by some officers in the Army General Staff during the summer, was to go for the southern part of the front first. However, my Directive 21 of 18 December changed this. I did not want my divisions to get lost in the endless spaces of the Ukraine. Instead, the emphasis was on a rapid campaign aimed at destroying the opposing Red forces as close to the frontier as possible.

To achieve the goal of Operation Barbarossa, the name I chose for it, we formed three army groups. Proceeding from left to right, Army Group North, commanded by Field-Marshal Ritter von Leeb, was to advance from East Prussia toward Leningrad by way of the Baltic States. Army Group Center, commanded by Field-Marshal Fedor von Bock and the most powerful of the three, was to take the historic route leading from Poland to Moscow. Only Army Group South, under Field-Marshal Gerd von Rundstedt, was to march south of the marshes into the Ukraine. Further south still our forces in Romania were to proceed northeast along the Black Sea Coast. Each of the three Army Groups was to have the support of a *Luftflotte,* an air fleet.

A very serious problem we faced was that of intelligence. Compared with the West, Russia had always been secretive. That may have something to do with the Slavic soul, which tends to be inscrutable, devious, and undependable. Bad communications, which prevented news from spreading quickly and efficiently, did the rest. Stalin's terror, some of which was directed against alleged "spies" and "saboteurs," made things even worse. Compared to Russia, both his and that which he passed to his Communist successors, ours was a free and open country. His subjects, for that was what they were, were not even allowed to travel without a domestic passport! From Brest Litovsk to Vladivostok, every railway station had its cells to house those whom the NKVD caught on the way. From those cells to the concentration camps the road was often short.

All this may have had its uses in maintaining Stalin's regime. But it made obtaining the kind of information our commanders needed very difficult. The most elementary sources, of the kind that, in other countries, are freely available in any book or stationery shop, were absent. There were no reliable maps (some of the ones we had were deliberately misleading.) There were no guidebooks. There were hardly any technical magazines. There were not even any telephone books. Fortunately, we had, in the form of our Ju-86, reconnaissance aircraft capable of flying so high (50,000 feet), that no Russian anti-aircraft gun and no Russian fighter could shoot them down. During the last few months before the invasion they provided us with lots of vital information. But their range was limited, and they could not tell us what was happening deep inside enemy territory.

Thus we entered the campaign with less detailed information than we ought to have and wanted to have. To cite just one example, we ourselves committed about 3,500 tanks. We knew that the Russians had more. But how many more? Estimates varied enormously. One was as high as 24,000. I could not believe my eyes and prohibited that number from being disseminated. But it turned out to be correct, give or take a few thousand. It's no wonder that, later on, I compared myself to a wanderer who had lost his way in a snowstorm. Not knowing where he was, he crossed Lake Konstanz over the ice. Turning back and realizing what he had done, he himself turned into ice. I consoled myself by the plain fact that Providence had guided me during all these years. I trusted that it would continue to do so in the future.

There was another side to the picture. We were at the height of our military power. Our equipment had proved its worth during the recent campaigns. Our doctrines were sound, our commanders experienced, and our troops well trained and battle hardened. Military morale was as high as high could be. The homeland, though subjected to a few restrictions and beginning to feel the occasional impact of an English air attack, was solidly behind the forces. And me! Never in history had any ruler enjoyed the trust of his people more than I did. Not before, not after. So much so that, immediately after the invasion started, even the aforementioned Galen praised my war on "Judeo-Bolshevism" and told his flock to pray for my welfare! The exception, if any, were some of my senior generals. These were not the days of Blücher, "Field-Marshal Forward" as he was known, who took the bit between his teeth and marched toward the sound of the guns. Nor those of Moltke Sr. with his calm confidence that, with God on our side, things would turn out well.

The commanders in question had grown up under the Kaiserreich. Like so many other members of the old elite, they ended up looking down on us National Socialists. Not to put too fine a point on it, but they saw us as upstarts who had risen, God only knows how, from the gutter. Most were reactionaries, and few, if any, really shared our world view, let alone were committed to defending and spreading it with the kind of fanaticism which alone can make ideas have any influence at all. Servile as Keitel was, that even applied to him. He saw himself as an officer first; everything else was secondary. As the campaign approached, too many of them developed reservations of one kind or another. Not a few, I was told, read the depressing memoirs of Napoleon's aide, Armand de Caulaincourt. That is why, in January and again in February 1941, I gathered them and subjected them to what were, in essence, pep talks.

But that was not enough. On 30 March I called 200 of my generals for another speech. I wanted them to understand that Russia was not the West. This was a war between two *Weltanschauungen:* our National Socialist one and the criminal Judeo-Bolshevik one. It had to be waged accordingly. There was no room for outdated ideas of soldierly honor, no question of sparing the civilian population as much as possible. We were going to exterminate the Bolshevik Army Commissars. They formed the chassis, so to speak, that held the entire gigantic structure together. We were also going to destroy as

large a part of the Communist intelligentsia as we could reach. This
was no job for our army; that was why I was sending in Himmler
and his special security forces. They themselves were to close their
hearts to pity and do what had to be done. As to international law,
there was no need to worry about it. The Soviet Union had never
joined the Geneva Convention. They were going to ignore it, and
so would we.

Neither at the time nor later did any of them protest. Not necessarily, I well knew, because they agreed with me. But because they
thought, as we Germans say, *nicht so heiss gegessen wie gekocht* (the
broth is not eaten as hot as it is cooked). Almost to a man, they were
prepared to provide logistic support to Himmler's "special" units and
to look away while the latter did what had to be done. But in general
their motto was, don't get your hands dirty. Later, when some of
them were put on "trial" at Nuremberg, this attitude served most of
them well. It enabled them to present themselves as "pure" soldiers
while putting the blame on Himmler and me.

In the meantime, the buildup continued. Not only was it the
largest in history, but it is likely to remain so in the future, too. We
used 17,000 trains—imagine that—to deploy 138 divisions for the
operation. Of those 104 were infantry, 19 Panzer, and 15 motorized.
We also had 9 security divisions to hold down the occupied territories, 4 to help the Finns in Karelia, and 2 more which served as
a general reserve. We had 7,200 cannons and 2,770 aircraft, which
formed two-thirds of the Luftwaffe order of battle. The total number
of men was just under 3,500,000. The number of vehicles (not
motor vehicles, as one source erroneously says), was 600,000.

Not included on the list are 14 excellent Finnish divisions and
13 not-so-excellent Romanian ones. The latter distinguished themselves mainly by committing such excesses against the Jews that even
our own men were disgusted. Later, we had Italian, Hungarian, and
a few Slovak troops join us as well as a growing number of Waffen
SS units. Recruited by Himmler from all over Europe and issued

equipment on a priority basis, they fought like the devil. There were some problems, particularly with regard to the weather. But in the end everything was completed on schedule. To disguise our intentions, we spread the rumor that the buildup was meant as a cover for a coming invasion of England. A deception within a deception, one might say. To maintain that illusion, we kept on bombing London almost to the last moment.

At 0300 on 22 June we opened fire all along the 2,500-kilometer-long front. The Russians, it later turned out, had received plenty of warning. Nevertheless, they were somehow taken completely by surprise. After the war, the question how this could have happened became the subject of an entire literature. Was it the shortcomings of their communication system, which prevented them from alerting their formations in time? Was it our deceptive measures? Was it sheer blindness to what was going on? One thing is certain: had we not attacked, they would have attacked us. Not immediately, perhaps, as the Russian historian Viktor Suvorov in his bestselling volume, *Icebreaker,* claimed. But certainly later in case we showed the slightest sign of weakness. Ours was a preventive war, perhaps even a preemptive one. Certainly, my reasons for launching it were better than those of President Bush Jr. when he invaded Iraq sixty-two years later.

We started by destroying most of their air force on the ground. So unprepared were they that they had not even dispersed their aircraft and concealed them; hence the operation only took a few days. After that, our pilots were free to support the ground forces both behind the front and at it. Our armored and motorized divisions advanced at a speed rarely, if ever, achieved before or since. Behind them came the infantry, marching hell for leather, and behind them again were the supply trains and the railway companies, which worked day and night to convert the Russian system to the one everyone else used.

Passing from north to south, by early September we had surrounded Leningrad. I had decided to starve out the city, not take it by storm. Minsk fell on 3 July and Smolensk, just 400 kilometers from Moscow, three weeks later. The capture of each city, carried out by two successive pincer operations, brought the Red Army huge losses and us, huge numbers of prisoners.

At Smolensk, some 600 kilometers from our starting positions, we were obliged to stop and take stock. We worked day and night, yet we simply could not push the railheads forward fast enough. At this point an argument developed between Halder and myself. As had also happened in the campaign against France, Halder, who up to this moment had usually been on the cautious side, changed his spots. He argued that we should continue straight to Moscow as Napoleon had also done. His reasoning was that Moscow was the one objective the Russians could not retreat from. Therefore, an attack on it would enable us to deliver the Red Amy the *coup de grace.*

I myself saw things in a different light. Great as our victories up to this point had been, they had not broken the Red Army. Halder himself agreed with that conclusion. The reason was the primitive nature of the opponent. His troops, unlike the Western ones we had met in the previous year, can only be described as a horde of primitive animals. Sullen, totally at the mercy of their commissars, and driven ever forward by vodka and the lash, they just did not know when they were beaten. They went on fighting even when they were surrounded. When that became impossible, they melted away and joined the so-called Partisans.

We were trying to bite off more than we could chew. There was no point in moving forward while our rear was yet insecure. I wanted to reduce the size of our pincer operations. As fate would have it, a magnificent opportunity to do that had just presented itself. On our right, Army Group South had not advanced as fast as we had expected. With Army Group Center stretching farther east than it did, we were able to come at our opponent, Stalin's old drinking comrade Semyon Budyonny, both from the north (Bock) and west (Rundstedt). Doing so would not only destroy the Russian southwestern front but also give us the Ukraine, complete with its industry and grain. The Ukraine in turn would give us access to the Caucasus with its oil.

Halder, as usual, objected. To convince me he had Guderian fly back to East Prussia, where I had my headquarters, and talk to me. Guderian was a relatively junior officer. However, I respected him and let him have his say. When he was done, I answered in a single sentence: My generals, I said, do not know anything about the economic aspects of the war. He saluted, and that was that. Later, Halder berated him for having given way as easily as he did. But Guderian knew, and knew that I knew, that what I had told him was true.

The Battle of Kiev was a huge success. Never in history had a single operation inflicted so many losses on any army. Between dead and prisoners, the toll was around 700,000 men. The booty we took was astronomical. Even so, it turned out that we had underestimated the Russian colossus. Each time we destroyed one of their armies, even army groups, they put another in its place. To be sure, their divisions were not really divisions in our sense of the word. They did not have the commanders—Budyonny, whom Stalin had flown out of the pocket at the last moment, was notable mainly for his enormous mustache. Nor did they have the organization, the cohesion, the training, or the doctrine. But they were there, and the deeper into the country we advanced, the more stubbornly they fought.

This struggle over, our forces, assisted by the Romanians on our extreme right flank, continued their advance to the east. In November they crossed the Mius River and captured Rostov, the key to the Caucasus, after fierce fighting. But here we found a surprise waiting. On 27 November our armored spearheads came under fierce attack from the north. Rundstedt wanted to retreat whereas I prohibited him from doing so. When he disobeyed my orders, I fired him. In his place I put General Walter von Reichenau, one of the few senior army officers who was a National Socialist, heart and soul, and whose anti-Jewish orders were a model of their kind. He, however, claimed that Rundstedt had been right and enlisted Halder to support him. In any case it was too late for me to intervene. So Rostov was lost after some fierce fighting. It was a reverse, but one that we could easily correct in the spring.

For all the magnitude of our operations on this front, the really decisive battle was going on further to the north. It opened in early October, when our railway companies had finally completed converting the necessary tracks. At that point no fewer than three Panzer Groups, two forming part of Army Group Center plus one that had been brought over from the Leningrad front, started a concentric advance on Moscow. The weather was against us; the autumn rains were transforming the entire region into a single sea of mud. Our troops, dragging or pushing their vehicles forward, did not receive even the most elementary supplies. Some of my generals, notably Guderian, tried to describe their sufferings to me as if I did not know them at least as well as they did. Still, the men pushed on, slowly, painfully, making progress and taking prisoners by the hundreds of thousands. In November the ground froze, putting an end to the mud. However, the cold created new problems. Engines would not start as the oil that lubricated their parts froze. It was the engineers' fault. For years on end I had been telling them to focus on air-cooled engines, but they had refused to listen. Still, our advance continued step by painful step. Early in December some of our forward troops, looking into the distance, could see the spires of the Kremlin.

At that point we were suddenly hit by fresh forces: to wit, eighteen divisions, 1,700 tanks, and 1,500 aircraft Stalin brought up from Siberia in the nick of time. All of them were under the command of General Georgy Zhukov. Zhukov was the scion of simple peasants. As a child, he had been apprenticed to a shoemaker. He was a primitive but rock-hard commander the likes of which I was hard pressed to find among my own senior generals. It was said of him that, when one of his subordinates blundered, he would order the unfortunate man to put his deputy in his place and blow his brains out! In a way, it was all the fault of our dear Japanese allies. First, in April 1941, they had surprised us by signing a nonaggression pact with Russia, thus securing Stalin's rear in his coming fight with us. Next, they failed to catch a Communist spy, Richard Sorge, who told the Russians that they could indeed rest assured on that account. The attack on Pearl Harbor, by involving them in war against the U.S. and Britain, did the rest.

At the news of the Soviet counterattack many of my generals panicked. They demanded that we quickly build a new front further to the rear before retreating so as to shorten our communications, rebuild our forces, and wait for an opportunity to launch a counteroffensive. I firmly refused. I knew the mentality of the *Landser*, or simple soldier, better than they did. Once he was permitted to withdraw, there would be no stopping him. That, after all, was what had happened to Napoleon, whose retreat from Moscow, which initially had been quite orderly, turned into a rout. I therefore issued my order "not a step back." Whatever my commanders said after the war, to this day I have absolutely no doubt that, by doing so, I saved the army from disintegration. But at what a cost in anxiety and "nerves!"

Meanwhile, the Russians were having their own troubles. In early January their advance petered out. Major operations, hampered by the intense cold, came to a virtual halt. In front of Moscow as in the south, the reverse we had suffered was serious but very far from decisive. It was time to take stock. By that time I had rid myself of Brauchitsch. Throughout the campaign he had proved himself useless; come the crisis, his nerves gave way.

I myself took his place as Commander in Chief of the Army. It was an arrangement quite a few of my top people, both officers and civilians, did not like. They repeatedly urged me to appoint someone else or, failing that, to unite all the forces on the eastern front under one commander. They wanted to lighten the superhuman burden I was carrying, they said. But doing so would have put some three quarters of the entire ground forces under the authority of a single man. That was too much for comfort, I should say.

The winter of 1941–42 also brought us some trouble in the Mediterranean. First the English counterattacked and advanced westward, only to have Rommel turn the tables on them and recapture much of the ground he had lost. Tactically, the operations of the "Desert Fox," as our media called Rommel, were as magnificent as ever. But in view of the small forces involved their strategic significance was minor.

The question of resuming our Russian offensive in the spring apart, my greatest problem was the United States. Strictly speaking, those who claim that Roosevelt was not a Jew may have been right. But he liked Jews and surrounded himself with many members of the "chosen people." There were so many that his own behavior became typically Jewish. He had never been one of our greatest admirers. Now, having won a third term, he became bolder and bolder. In March 1941 he had Congress enact Lend-Lease, a program that enabled him to provide the English with weapons without the latter having to pay for them. Later, it was extended to Russia as well. In September his navy started escorting England-bound convoys from the U.S. east coast all the way to Iceland. An interesting form of neutrality, I would say.

Throughout the second half of 1941 my admirals, with Raeder and the submarine commander Karl Dönitz at their head, kept pestering me to allow them to attack American shipping. I, however, with the sinking of the *Lusitania* (1915) in mind, refused even though, by the end of the year, our relations with the U.S. had deteriorated to the point where they fired at our submarines at sight. Roosevelt, it seems, was goading us on, just as he did our Japanese allies. Then came Pearl Harbor—a mighty blow delivered without a declaration of war of which, of course, I fully approved. Japan, we thought, would keep the Americans busy in the Pacific for years to come. Four days later, I in turn declared war on the U.S. Partly because, in practice, we were at war already; and partly because doing so freed our hands and enabled us to fire back at the American warships that were firing at us.

Such was the situation at the end of 1941 and the beginning of 1942. The strain was tremendous; for months on end, each time I thought of snow, I shuddered. My physical health also suffered. I had severe headaches, and my eyes, which had long suffered from exposure to excessive sunlight, started deteriorating. How I longed to turn my back on military affairs and devote myself to fields more suitable to my nature! If I pulled through, then this was partly thanks to the drugs and injections Morrell administered. And it was partly thanks to my own strong constitution. But these are details. It is not true, as the German historian Andreas Hillgruber and the American one Timothy Snyder, among others, have claimed, that I already recognized that the war was lost. Some, including Fritz Todt, who was now my Minister of Armaments and came to tell me his views, thought so, but they were wrong. Japan was keeping the English and the Americans busy in the Indian and Pacific oceans, respectively, by destroying important naval forces and by capturing many strategic positions. In the Atlantic our submarines, finally unleashed, were having a ball, sinking more English and American vessels than ever. And we still had time until the U.S. could mobilize its full power against us and deploy its full force across the Atlantic. In fact that only happened in mid-1944. Admittedly, English air attacks on our cities were increasing. But they had not yet reached the point where they formed more than a nuisance.

Above all, time and again our forces in the east had proved their superiority over Stalin's hordes. The losses, in terms of both personnel and *materiel,* of the Red Army had been staggering. Ours were not light either but were still more or less tolerable. Most of

European Russia, which before the war had provided the enemy with practically all of his agricultural and industrial products, was in our hands. We had every right to expect that, once summer returned, we would be able to finish off that opponent once and for all.

Chapter 24

My New Order

For me, power has never been simply an end in itself. To be sure, having hundreds of thousands cheer me until they were blue in the face, as at the annual Party Day in Nuremberg, was not ungratifying. Even here in Hell, where all sounds are muted and nothing ever happens, the memory makes me shudder a little. But let me put it on record as clearly as I can: my objective, the only thing that really mattered, was to build a new order. In Germany, in Europe, perhaps—who knows?—in the world. In this respect the war had a double impact. It interrupted some of my attempts in this direction, but it also opened all sorts of new possibilities.

When one occupies a country, the first thing to do is to secure it and to make it secure. In the West, doing so was easy. Much easier than one would think by reading the vast literature about the "Resistance," its heroic deeds, and the terrible damage it supposedly inflicted on us Germans. We were, after all, dealing with more or less civilized people. "Civilized" in the sense that they were racially close to us. "Civilized" in the sense that they had been living under orderly forms of government for centuries on end. "Civilized" in the sense that most of them were town dwellers rather than semi-literate clodhoppers. As such, they neither had weapons at home nor would have known what to do with them if they did.

In all these countries without exception, we were able to rely on the existing civil services, police forces, and so on. Had that not been the case, things would have looked very different from the way they did. That was true in Denmark and in Norway. It was also true in the Benelux countries, the occupied part of France, and the Channel Islands. Essentially, all we had to do was make sure that the people at the top would follow our orders. In some of these countries we appointed military governors and in others, civilian ones. In Denmark, the country that did the best of all under our rule, we left the entire government, complete with the king and parliament, in place. One of the advantages of the various arrangements was that they were *not* uniform. In this way we were able to adapt to local conditions while at the same time making it harder for people in the various countries to cooperate with one another. Divide and rule was how the Romans ran their empire. In many ways I simply followed their example.

We did station some of our troops in the west, especially during the second half of the war. But we did that more in order to defeat a possible invasion than to hold down the local population. For *that,* all we needed were some HSSPFs (*Hohere SS und Polizei Führer*, Higher SS and Police Leaders), whom Himmler appointed and provided with the appropriate staffs. Plus one battalion of second-rate troops here and another there. Some were still undergoing their basic training, which meant that we got two soldiers for the price of one. Others were recuperating from their experiences on the eastern front, whereas others still consisted of overage personnel.

I received regular reports from Kaltenbrunner and others. They showed that, everything considered, the arrangements we made were a great success. To be sure, hardly a day passed without some act of sabotage taking place. But most were very minor: a few illegal leaflets and newspapers surreptitiously distributed in one place; a telegraph wire cut or a train derailed in a second; a couple of our men killed or injured when a shooting occurred, or a mine exploded, in a third. People in post-1945 "advanced" countries tend to take such incidents very seriously. They do that partly because they are being stimulated by sensationalist journalists who make their living by always magnifying them out of all proportion to the point where quite a few terrorist acts are staged specifically with the media in mind! And partly because the "long peace," as it is called, has made them weak in body and mind. But we, and I personally, had a world war to fight and win. Not a day passed that did not bring new problems demanding all my strength, mental, and, in a certain sense, physical as well. Hence it was only on exceptional occasions that such trivia was even brought to my attention.

When that happened, invariably, my role was to put some backbone into the Wehrmacht commanders and their ubiquitous legal advisers. This included those at my headquarters and those on the spot. Steeped in their old-fashioned "code of honor," quite a few of them were too soft to implement the barbaric retaliatory measures the situation required and I demanded and which, I should add, international law often permitted to be implemented against an occupied population that did not know its proper place. As, for example, when civilians who were not wearing uniforms or other identifying signs and not carrying weapons openly fired at our troops, when they were not under a proper chain of command, and so on.

We could not afford to treat terrorists with kid gloves. That is why I always insisted that nothing less than the death penalty, liberally used, would have any effect. A notable example of what could be done (though it took place in the east, not the west) followed the assassination of Heydrich, Neurath's successor in Prague. Heydrich was a strange character. Handsome and athletic—he was a champion fencer, ice skater, and horse rider—but with a face marked by a cruel streak, he was an insatiable womanizer. Specializing in discovering people's weaknesses and capitalizing on them by blackmail if necessary, he was an excellent bureaucrat. But he was also a *Draufgänger* (daredevil) and inclined to take greater personal risks than I thought were appropriate for someone of his rank. Perhaps this had something to do with persistent rumors about his Jewish ancestry. Though

repeatedly disproved, they may have made him feel insecure. In any
case he took flying lessons and flew a fighter plane both in Norway
and in France. Once, during the Russian campaign, he was forced
to make an emergency landing. Touching the ground, he had to be
rescued by some of our troops. When he told them he was the head
of the Reich Security Service and demanded to be treated accordingly,
they understandably thought he was out of his mind! Thereupon I
prohibited him from flying, but I could not prevent him from driving
his convertible sports car to work every day.

As one would expect from him, his rule was as harsh as harsh can
be. In the first two months alone several hundred Czechs were executed. But he also improved some people's lives, such as by making
sure Czech armaments workers got better rations than those of the
Reich and introducing some welfare provisions, such as paid holidays,
for the first time. His success in pacifying Bohemia and Moravia
made him a thorn in the eye of the Czech government in exile as
well as its English puppet masters. That was why, one fine morning
in May 1942, two Czechs working for the English secret service threw
a bomb at him, inflicting injuries from which he died eight days later.
In response, I ordered my people to do what had to be done. The
details do not matter. For me, what *did* matter was that, from that
point on, Bohemia and Moravia gave us very little trouble indeed.
The more time passed, the more we moved our war industries into
those districts. Not only were they among the few still beyond the
reach of enemy bombers, but they remained in our hands right down
to the end. As a result, alone in Europe the Czechs actually ended
the war with more capital stock and higher real wages than they had
when it started. Briefly, so weak was the "resistance" that it was not
even remotely capable of preventing us from exploiting the countries
in question to the hilt, let alone of putting our rule over them in
danger.

Meeting terror with terror, we put hundreds of thousands into
concentration camps. The next step was to open the way to economic

exploitation. There were no half measures and no false sentimentality here. The only thing that counted was our own interests and needs. The most important milch-cow in our shed was France. At peak we were able to divert as much as 30–40 percent of its output to our service. Jewish property apart, by and large that did not happen because we resorted to confiscation. In any case there were not enough Jews around for such measures to make a difference, macroeconomically speaking. At best it was only German individuals and companies who profited. Good for them, I say.

Instead, we did four things. First, in most of the countries we occupied we captured substantial stores of raw materials which helped sustain our industry. Second, we required that the authorities in Vichy pay the cost of our occupation at a level we ourselves determined. Third, we fixed the exchange rate in favor of the mark (marks, of course, were one of the few things we could produce in unlimited quantities and at practically no cost). Fourth, we made many leading industrialists cooperate with us. Seeing their opportunity, they did their best to produce what we needed. To provide employment and to ensure the existence of their factories until the end of the war, they said. The best example was in France, where the Renault Corporation worked hand in hand with us. For that it was nationalized after the war. But other companies, especially in the Netherlands and Belgium, were not far behind.

One reason why industrialists in all the occupied Western countries put their factories at our disposal was precisely because we told them that, if they did not do so, we would take their labor force away from them. Speer in particular was always in favor of having as many workers as possible work for us in their native countries. Partly because doing so saved us from having to hunt them and look after them; and partly because he wanted to reduce his dependence on Sauckel, a man from a much lower background with whom he was never able to get along. The figures speak for themselves. In 1940 the contribution of the occupied countries stood at a mere 3 percent of our German steel production. Four years later, it reached 27 percent, a nine-fold increase. Especially in 1942–44, a large part of our consumption of grain, fat, and meat was covered by the occupied territories, primarily Poland and France.

Still, our need for labor and more labor was insatiable. In the summer of 1944 the total number of foreign workers, including Polish, French, and Russian prisoners as well as civilians, stood at eight million. A handful, especially Westerners, were influenced by our propaganda and came of their own free will. Many others, especially during the last years of the war, were rounded up in *Razzias,* or raids. They were taken to specially constructed camps, packed into trains, and sent to Germany whether they wanted to go or not. Once they arrived, strict discipline and the shadow cast by our concentration camps did the rest. Foreigners of both sexes were employed in factories and on the land working in agriculture, where they helped families whose male members had been called up. The figures speak for themselves. At peak, the proportion of foreign workers in the Reich reached 19 percent. I am told that, in some of our more industrialized cities, German almost turned into a minority language. It was just the opposite of what I had intended, but as long as the war lasted, there was nothing I could do about it.

In July 1942 a major scandal unfolded in Berlin when a greengrocer, one August Nöthling, was fined for selling foodstuffs without asking for coupons. The list of his clients reads like a *Who's Who* of cabinet ministers, senior party officials, and high Wehrmacht officers. I ordered an investigation; in the end, though, for fear of hurting national morale I had to let the matter drop. In any case we succeeded in keeping our people, and incidentally those of the occupied countries in the West as well, tolerably healthy. There were no major outbreaks of plague and other infectious diseases. There was no repetition of World War I, when hundreds of thousands of our people died of diseases brought about by malnutrition and the

Spanish Flu. And there was nothing like the Thirty Years' War, when as much as one-third of the population of Central Europe perished. To the contrary, the population continued to grow. In the Netherlands it reached nine million for the first time. The same happened in Denmark, though on a smaller scale.

But it was not only foreign industrialists and workers who cooperated. Even before the war, every single one of the Western countries we later occupied had its own native Fascist/National Socialist parties or movements with programs more or less similar to our own. Call them *Action Française,* call them Rexists (in Belgium), call them NSB (the Dutch *Nationaal-Socialistische Beweging,* National-Socialist Movement), and the like. Many of their members came from the less developed districts of the countries in question. Their motives varied. Among them were antipathy for both communism and capitalism, a visceral hatred for the Jews, whom they blamed for all their problems, and even a certain Pan-European idealism, some of whose roots went back all the way to the years before 1914.

This last-mentioned sentiment was often directed not only against Russia but against the United States as well. With very good reason, as the post-war "Coca-colonization" of the western half of the continent was to prove. In many ways it was not too different from the kind that, starting in the 1950s, helped Europe push toward integration. At times the very same people were involved. An excellent example was Ludwig Erhard. Born in 1897, an economist by trade, in 1939–45 he worked for industry preparing plans for the reconstruction of Europe. Later, as West Germany's Minister of Finance and *Bundeskanzler,* he and his colleagues made a decisive contribution to European integration. And why not? If anyone knew how to turn a bankrupt economy around so as to provide work, prosperity, and social security for millions, it was our experts. And me, of course, pointing the direction in which they should go and giving them the backing they needed. Better than the French. Better than the English. Much better than the Americans who, at a time when we were positively crying out for labor in 1937–38, were still mired in a depression.

Other forms of cooperation were also widespread. For example, many artists in the occupied countries agreed to entertain our occupation troops or even to come to perform in Germany. For this, more than one of them subsequently paid a high price. And then there was the so-called "horizontal cooperation." One famous French actress even claimed that, while her heart was with her country, her ass was international! In every single country where our soldiers were stationed tens of thousands of local women were found who slept with them. A comparative handful did so because they were forced. But it turns out that the Americans raped far more Frenchwomen than our well-disciplined troops ever did. Some did it for food or money and others for love. Others still had a mixture of both motives. And why not? Nature itself has decreed that women should always seek the best-looking, strongest men to mate with. For a number of years, the best-looking, strongest men were ours. As occupation troops, they had more free time than the native men did, and, in comparison with those men, they were often generously provided for and paid. Even members of the SD and Gestapo sometimes found lovers among the local female population.

Starting in 1942, the Wehrmacht in Russia, combing the prisoner of war camps, recruited hundreds of thousands of so-called *Hilfswillige*, i.e. volunteers. Among them were some Muslim troops guided, I was told, by their faith in "Allah and Adolf Effendi." We even set up kosher butcher shops for them! It was a practice I strongly disliked. However, in the end I had no choice but to tolerate it. The most important indication of our success in enlisting the *willing* support of many Europeans in and outside the occupied territories were the tens of thousands who enlisted in Himmler's Waffen SS. They were very well trained, magnificently equipped, and led by superbly aggressive officers. Indeed, the Waffen SS may well have been the toughest, tightest organization that ever went into battle. Yet almost half of its divisions consisted entirely, or mainly, of foreigners. The largest contingents were supplied by the Netherlands, Hungary, and Romania. But we also had Belgians, Estonians, Italians, Russians, and White Russians. Whatever their origin, these men knew what they could expect in case we were defeated. If only for that reason, they fought like devils. In fact the very last defenders of the *Reichskanzlei* and me during the Battle of Berlin were the men of the Charlemagne Division. Pay attention, you hypocritical French.

I myself consistently turned my face against *Kleinstaaterei* (little-state mentality). Doing so, I did as much to assist in the birth first of the European Economic Community and then of the European Union as anyone else. But there were two differences. First, *I* would never have been so foolish as to give up our solid D-mark and to conspire with people such as the Greeks—the Greeks!—to create the Euro instead. Second, to think that such a union can be held together solely by consent without the use, or at least the threat, of force is pure illusion. As BREXIT showed all too clearly, come the first real crisis it will be torn apart. What was needed was a single government with a single army at its disposal. German ones, needless to say. Around this government and this army other Europeans, provided only they had the proper blood in their arteries, could and would coalesce.

In the east, things were different. Slavs with heavy infusions of Jewish and Tatar blood, the people there were subhumans, incapable of engaging in civilized behavior even if they had tried. Spaces were larger, the population sparser, towns smaller and fewer, and the forests and swamps more extensive and more primeval. To top it all off, the road network, which could have alleviated all these problems, was primitive and so practically nonexistent that, in some places, we had to use cavalry instead of motor vehicles! In Poland at any rate we had a civilian government in the form of the aforementioned *Generalgouvernement*. However, the quality of the personnel we were able to send there left something to be desired. Or perhaps they

were infected by the usual Polish flare for corruption; as one of my
subordinates put it, there is no such thing as a decent Pole. In any
case we, meaning the Reich, got considerably less out of the country,
considering its size and resources, than we should have.

The Baltic countries resembled those of the west in that we could
more or less rely on the local administrations. More so, in fact.
Having tasted the joys of Jewish-Bolshevik rule for a year or so, the
population hated and feared the Soviet Union more—*much* more—
than it did us. When we occupied the region in 1941, we found
the corpses of thousands of people whom the NKVD had murdered.
When we were forced to leave it in 1944–45, many of those who did
not flee were either summarily shot or deported to Siberia, never to
be heard of again.

Surprising as it sounds, the situation in Yugoslavia, Serbia included, was not too different either. First, we helped the Croats under Ante Pavelič to realize their dream of setting up an independent
republic. It was independent within the limits of our supervision,
needless to say. Their paramilitary forces, known as the Ustasha,
were a great help in fighting Tito's bandits and an even greater one
in cleansing the country of its Jews. Next, we set up a government in
Belgrade. Its head was General Milan Nedič, a former chief of staff.
His subordinates in the civil service proved no more, but also no less,
trustworthy than their colleagues in, say, Paris. After the war, those
of them who had not succeeded in getting away were executed.

The most difficult problem was Russia. Officially, Rosenberg and
his Ministry for the Occupied Territories in the East were in charge.
Rosenberg's greatest asset was his loyalty. But he still remained much
more of a dreamer than a doer. His written work was often incomprehensible; it was said that no one sold so many books that no one read.
Goebbels, Rosenberg's rival as the party's intellectual in chief, called
him Herr Almost. He almost managed to become a schoolmaster,
journalist, and politician, but only "almost." He proved utterly ineffective in dealing with the Wehrmacht, the SS, and various Reich

Commissars whom I had given the task of ruling this province or that so as to better exploit its resources. In fact, he was so ineffective that some subsequent historians suspected I had deliberately set out to create disorder! Let me say, once and for all, that such was not the case. It is true that, in the Third Reich, there was a great deal of infighting among various personages and organizations. Including, as I wrote earlier, the various branches of the armed forces. But there was no more than in other states, democratic ones included.

To resume, nor could there be any question of harnessing the Russian bureaucracy to our cart. One and all, they were Bolshevik subhumans. Following my orders, our men killed as many of them as they could catch. The outcome was that, throughout the vast territories we were holding, almost the only government left consisted of our security forces. I am told that the absence of a government or governments was one reason why we only got a small fraction of the products the territories in question did yield or could have yielded. There may be some truth in that. But what other choice did we have? One cannot treat such people as one would Westerners. The reason is that, to them, any attempt to do so simply looks like a sign of weakness. Give them a finger, as Ludendorff had tried to do when he encouraged some Ukrainian nationalist movements in 1917–18, and they will demand not just your hand but your entire arm, too. This was an error I was not going to repeat.

There were other reasons why our economic policy in the east was not, by and large, a success. First, the appropriate infrastructure was lacking. Second, the Russians evacuated what industrial plants they could and destroyed the rest. Trust me on this: when it comes to destruction, no one is a match for the Jewish-Russian-Bolsheviks. As late as German reunification in 1989, even many windows broken during the last days of the war had not yet been repaired. Basically, all we could do, especially in the countryside where our forces were spread very thin, was to take what we needed without bothering with formalities of any kind even if it meant, as if often did, burning entire villages *pour encourager les autres.* Such methods helped feed our troops on the spot. However, they also meant that few supplies were left to send home to the Reich. And even fewer we available for the millions of Russian prisoners we took.

In both Yugoslavia and Russia we faced guerrilla warfare and what, today, would be called terrorism. As in the case of the West, though, its true significance has been exaggerated by the post-war literature. It is not true, as Tito, his lackeys, and some other historians later claimed, that it was his "Partisans" who made us retreat from Yugoslavia. We departed because Hungary was being overrun by the Red Army, which threatened to cut our lines of communication and leave our forces stranded. And for every one of our soldiers who was killed by Russian bandits, many more died in battle with the Red Army. To be sure there were some, mainly old-fashioned generals, needless to say, on my staff who worried that the war in Russia would never really end. They claimed that we would have to engage at what, today, is known as counterinsurgency. I for my part answered that, far from fearing such a scenario, I would welcome it. It would provide our troops with the best training there is.

Those were short- and medium-term problems. Determined to leave my mark on history in the long run, I had very different plans. They were enough to keep our people, the Party, and all sorts of government organizations busy for generations on end! First, I was going to exploit the spaces in question to the hilt, economically speaking, even if doing so meant that as many as 30 million Slavs would have to starve or be expelled eastward across the Urals. After all, no less a luminary than Herbert Hoover, the former U.S. president and five-time Nobel Peace Prize candidate, at one point called ethnic cleansing a "heroic remedy;" so, referring to the "German problem" immediately after the war, did many other Allied leading figures. Next, I was going to bring in new settlers, including not just Germans but Danes, Norwegians, Dutchmen, Belgians, Swedes, and Finns as well. There would be no need for coercion; given to understand the vast

prospects we were opening, they would come over, banners flying
and drums beating.

My vision was rooted in the practice of the Greeks and the Romans
who set up colonies in every country they occupied. For all their
attempts to distance themselves from me, moreover, the Israelis in the
West Bank are doing exactly the same. The details I left for Himmler
and his staff to work out. I planned to establish large numbers of fortified farming homesteads *(Wehrdörfer)* grouped around newly built
towns. They would be populated by former soldiers who, in case of
need, would also be able to defend themselves and the large families
they would have. Our links to the east would consist of an excellent
new railway system. It was to use a royal gauge of four meters, not the
miserable 1.435 meters which nineteenth-century technicians copied
from the days of horse-drawn carriages and remains in use today. To
enable our people to really experience the meaning of space, thus
mentally preparing them for their imperial mission, we would build
thousands of kilometers of *Autobahnen,* the modern equivalent of
the famous Roman roads. So excellent would their construction be
as to enable our people to drive their Volkswagens all the way to
the Crimea at a steady 80 kilometers an hour. What is more, they
would not encounter a single pothole on the journey. The Crimea
itself would be renamed Gothenland. We'd set aside 100,000 acres of
its territory for rubber plantations. The rest would be turned into a
vast vacation resort, perhaps similar to the one we built on the Baltic.

As to the remaining natives, I intended to treat them as the American colonists treated the Indians. We would kill as many as necessary
and deport most of the rest, thereby rendering them harmless. In doing so, our Mississippi would be the Volga. Note that the Russians are
utterly without the sense of duty that motivates us Germans. Left to
themselves, they would live like animals, multiplying and wallowing
in their own filth. No German doctors, no German health system,
to look after them! Above all, we would never unleash the German
schoolmaster on them. All they would need would be a. reading (no

need for any writing) skills just sufficient to understand the signs on our *Autobahnen* to avoid being killed in road accidents, b. the ability to count to 500 or so, and c. the certainty that the Germans, like the Boer *baas* in South Africa, are masters and have a God-mandated right to be obeyed. To help instill the last-named quality we would take, year by year, a troupe of these *Untermenschen* and show them the glories of Berlin. Returning to their hovels, they could spread the news.

This brings me to my plans for Berlin. Like so many European towns, Berlin began its days as an obscure fishing village. In 1701 it became the capital of the Kingdom of Prussia. Located in the poor lands east of the Elbe far from the sea and therefore from world commerce, in terms of size, economic development, and cultural achievement it lagged far behind the great cities of the West. Some of the Hohenzollern, especially Friedrich Wilhelm II, did what they could to make it prosper and flourish. But real change only got under way during the years after 1871, when the billions paid by the French as war reparations came in. Here, I must hand it to Wilhelm II. His artistic taste was pompous, and he lacked any sense of proportion. But he really put his heart into the business. Even so, the city remained unworthy of the vast empire I was going to build.

Some of my projects, including the Olympiastadion, the new *Reichskanzlei,* and the East–West Axis, were completed before the war. To this day, the lanterns on both sides are the ones Speer designed and installed for me. Other projects only reached the planning stages or, at best, had some preliminary work done on them. One was the North–South Axis. 120 meters wide, no less, it would be even larger than the East–West one. To make it possible, 50,000 homes would have to be demolished and 150,000 people resettled. Compared to this, what Louis Napoleon had done in Paris and Mussolini in Rome was mere peanuts. The crowning glory was to consist of three enormous projects: a giant people's square, a huge victory arch several times as big as the Brandenburger Tor, and an even larger congress hall. It was going to be nine times as big as St. Peter's and capable of holding 180,000 people. To make sure it would last, everything would be built of granite.

Watching my vision being realized, if only in the form of models, could move me to tears. It's no wonder, as some of my earliest sketches for them went back as far as 1925. Who would have thought I, an aspiring politician just out of jail, would ever be in a position to realize them? As so often in my career, people came up with all sorts of objections. In particular, the engineers' experiments showed that the muddy, waterlogged terrain around the River Spree might not support the weight of the stones we were going to put on it. I did not share their worries. First, weighed down by cares as I was, I looked at our discussions of such matters as much-needed relaxation. They took my attention away from the war, if only for a moment. Second and more important, experience had taught me that the only thing "experts" are really good at is dreaming up reasons why things will not work. I had no doubt that some kind of solutions could be found. Had we won the war, they surely would have been.

I played with the idea of renaming Berlin, which some experts believe got its name from a Slavic word meaning "swamp," *Germania*. Both at the time and later—especially later, of course—my plans were subject to fierce criticism. Even Speer, the man in charge of the whole thing, who shared as much of my vision as anyone did, was not totally convinced. In his memoirs he says, half-apologetically but half-approvingly, that when his father, who was also an architect, saw some of our plans, he exclaimed that we had all gone stark raving mad! Others thought my ideas were megalomaniac, pompous, and even inhuman.

How typical of the small minds which most people possess, and by which, unfortunately, even I was so often surrounded! But such is the fate of great men. Presumably, when the Pharaohs built their pyramids, they had to cope with similar objections. Ludwig II, who, thanks to his erecting of several magnificent palaces, is the only King of Bavaria anyone remembers, certainly did. But let them spout their nonsense to their hearts' contents. To be sure, most of my projects were left incomplete. Others, such as the great parade ground Speer had built for me in Nuremberg, were destroyed by Allied bombing or demolished after the war. What a pity. Still, even today, whoever comes to Berlin can choose among several "Nazi Berlin" tours on offer. Quite a few visitors do exactly that, taking the tours or buying one of the many guidebooks on sale. The same applies to other cities in which I spent time. Better proof that my plans were indeed worthy of eternity would be hard to find, wouldn't it?

In conclusion, let me note that, in the wake of our victories of 1940, Churchill gave his "Minister for Economic Warfare," Hugh Dalton, the task of "setting Europe ablaze." In that he did not succeed. The parts of the Continent for which Dalton and his colleagues in the Special Operations Executive (SOE) were responsible, i.e. the west, remained as quiescent as one could expect under the circumstances. The parts with which they had nothing to do, i.e. the occupied Russian territories, gave us more trouble in a week than he did over five years. The only important exception was the Yugoslav coup of March 1941, which was conceived and coordinated partly in London. But even that did not affect the course of the war nearly as much as some historians have claimed.

Chapter 25

The Final Solution

The war, and even more so its outcome, prevented me from reshaping Europe as I had planned to do. At the same time, its outbreak allowed me to do certain things which, but for it, would not have been possible. By far the most important one was my attempt to rid the Continent of the Jews. I desired to do the same to the gypsies, of course, but compared to the Jews they were small potatoes.

Both during my life and later, many people have wondered why I devoted as much time and effort to the Jewish problem as I did. Eager to add his own little piece of wisdom, the French "philosopher" Jean Paul Sartre even claimed that, in reality, anti-Semites, me presumably included, were afflicted by self-hatred! But that is rubbish of the sort, indeed, that only a French degenerate can produce. Suffice it to say that the Bible itself provides the best explanation why, starting as early as Greek and Roman antiquity, the Jews have often been detested as much as they were. "A stiff-necked *Volk*, leading its own life and refusing to mix with others," As the Talmud says. And they were a professedly racist one as well, or how else could they have kept themselves pure during a period of some thirty centuries?

My original plan, as written down in our Twenty-Five Point Program, was to rid Germany of its 600,000 or so Jews. This was to be done by forcing them out of all the public positions they were occupying, denying them the rights and duties of citizenship, and making their lives in general difficult so as to make them leave. I intended to boot them in the behinds, in other words. The first organization to which we applied this policy was the Party. Applied, I say, because there were quite a number of Jews who would have been only too happy to become members. When we refused, they were actually offended! Having taken power in 1933, we did what we could to segregate the Jews and to make them depart for the few countries that were willing to take them in. Minus their property, of course.

Note that I say emigration, not extermination. To recall what I wrote in *Mein Kampf,* personally I would have liked nothing better than to put a few tens of thousands of Hebrews into the gas chambers. I didn't feel that way because I have a sadistic nature; far from it. I did not go hunting as so many of my predecessors, associates, and successors did. Rumor notwithstanding, never in my life did I attend an execution or a torture session. Nor did I delight in bloodshed as some of my men, notably SS General Erich von dem Bach-Zelewsky, did. As you can see from my so-called *Secret Conversations,* during the war I expressly told my associates that, had I been up to me, I would rather not have hurt a fly. However, when the vital interests of the nation were at stake, I immediately became *Eiskalt* (ice cold). I forced myself to put aside any feelings I may have had, allowing no one and nothing to divert me from my purpose. That, and nothing else, is the real clue to my personality. Mobilizing all my willpower, I did what had to be done by whatever methods were the most effective. This included poison gas, of course. Depending on the size of the chamber used, carbon monoxide and Zyklon B enabled us to dispose of hundreds of people within a matter of minutes. One cannot shoot rats or bacteria one by one, can one?

But there are certain things which just could not be implemented in peacetime. The reason why they could not be implemented was that the German people would not have stood for them. Not, at any rate, in their own well-tended, well-ordered land, where even revolutionaries don't step on the grass! The reason why they would not have stood for them is that, when you get down to it, they have always been, and still remain, a rather soft-hearted lot. How else could they have produced a Goethe, a Hölderin, a Beethoven, or a Schubert? That even applied to true henchmen, such as Heydrich and Eichmann. As I knew, the former was an excellent violinist. As I learned later on, the latter also liked to play the violin, albeit he did not do so nearly as well as his superior did. Their commander, Himmler, was an incurable romantic. He even tried his hand at designing porcelain. To execute his designs and those of others, he set up a company by the name of Allach and provided it with labor from the nearby Dachau concentration camp. Full of pride, he showed me the figurines it produced: shepherd dogs, kings, knights, soldiers, *Hitler Jugend,* and similar "authentically Germanic" stuff. It was to counter these romantic tendencies that, in my speeches and writings, I so often used terms such as *fanatisch, unwiderruflich, rücksichtloss* (fanatical, unalterable, ruthless), and brutal. I kept telling people that, in certain matters, there was no room for sentimentality. But I only partly succeeded.

I am not saying that there was no anti-Semitism in Germany. Thank God there was, and plenty of it, too. But there was not nearly enough. Most people, including even some Party members, were content to grumble about the "Jewish problem" and to leave it more or less at that. The great Wagner himself set the example. To be sure, he did pen a famous piece on "The Jews in Music." But this did not prevent him from working closely with Jewish directors, conductors, and singers. Thousands of others did the same. How else can we account for figures such as the "impressionist" painter Max Lieberman and the group of popular "musicians" who called themselves the Harmony Comedians making the heaps of money they did? That's to say nothing about Gerson Bleichröder, the pluto-crat who, for bankrolling Bismarck, had a "von" attached to his name. Or Walter Rathenau. Or Albert Ballin, the German equivalent of the

Thomas Cook family of travel agency fame. Or the circle of Jews who surrounded the German Crown Prince, Frederick Wilhelm, even as late as 1941. And many others like them.

To repeat, I am aware that a Jewish-American historian, Daniel Goldhagen, has written about the "exterminationist anti-Semitism" which, in his view, permeated our people from top to bottom. I wish! But it didn't. To see real "exterminationist" anti-Semitism in action, the learned professor should have looked at some of the sickening things people did to the Jews in places such as Croatia, the Baltic, the Ukraine, and the Romanian-occupied Russian districts along the Black Sea coast. They often did so as soon as our troops arrived on the scene—and often with very little encouragement on our part. *That* would have taught him what real savagery means. I'm assuming, of course, that he would have come back in one piece.

The measures we took worked well enough. Within five years of our coming to power almost a third of Germany's Jews had left the country, most of them after having been forced to leave their assets behind. A great many others, having their lives turned into ones of misery, were planning go do so at the earliest opportunity. Good riddance! At that point, however, we began our career of expansion by incorporating Austria into the Reich. That meant we were cursed with another 200,000 of these unsavory creatures. Taking the bit between their teeth, SA men forced Jews to clean the pavement of Vienna with toothbrushes. Photographs were taken and published around the world. They may have gratified the minds of some people as, up to a point, they did mine. But they damaged our image abroad and did little to solve the problem we were facing. That is why I ordered them to be brought to a halt as soon as possible.

Over the next few years this pattern was repeated over and over again. First in the Sudentenland, "home" to 120,000 Jews. Then in Bohemia and Moravia (120,000) then in Poland (3,000,000), then in the West (500,000), then in the Balkans (1,400,000), and finally in the Baltic and Russia (3,000,000). The more land we annexed or conquered, the more Jews, including some whom we ourselves had forced to flee from the Reich, came under our rule. Paradoxically, our very victories were working against us.

I became more and more frustrated. One early sign of this was my "prophecy," made in front of the Reichstag on 30 January 1939 not long after our occupation of the Sudetenland, to the effect that a new war would lead to the "extermination of the Jewish race in Europe." Probably no other sentence of mine has been analyzed and reanalyzed nearly as often as this one. Had the idea always been on my mind, or was it new? If it was new, when, how, and why was it born? And just what did the term "extermination" mean? What my nerdish critics overlooked, though, is the plain fact that, at that time, I had no idea that, in a little more than two years, our flag and that of our ally would be flying from the North Cape all the way down to the Pyrenees in the west, Crete in the east, and Sollum (in Egypt) in the south. Obviously, what I was saying was not that we, meaning I, would exterminate the Jews. Instead, I was saying that a new war would make people throughout Europe so furious at them that they would start doing what had to be done on their own. That, in fact, happened in many places.

It was against this background of frustration that, following the surrender of Poland, Heydrich had proposed, and I had approved, the confinement of its Jewish population in ghettoes pending deportation to some yet undetermined destination. Now, with our victory in the west a *fait accompli,* someone in the Jewish Department of our Foreign Ministry revived the so-called Madagascar Plan. The first to raise the idea was one of our forerunners, Paul de Lagarde, in 1878. It rested on the notion, whose roots go back to the seventeenth century, that the island's inhabitants were somehow linked to the Jewish race. That is why, at various times, it attracted the interest not just of French and Polish politicians but of Jewish ones, too. First, we would round up the five million or so Jews in the parts of Europe that now came under our jurisdiction or that of our allies. Next, we would pack them onto ships and send them to the island. There, supervised by the SS, they would form a penal colony. This, more or less, was what the English had done when they sent shiploads of convicts to Australia and what many other countries have done when they established penal colonies for undesirables of every kind. True, the island's French owners hated the Jews almost as much as we did. But they were in no position to object.

I personally backed the plan. Energetically carried out, it would have solved the Jewish problem in Europe within just four years. From Brest-Litovsk to Brest, so to speak. Unfortunately, it all depended on the English. They too did not like Jews any more than we did. That is proved by the fact that, for over three and a half centuries between 1290 and 1657, they were able to keep their country *Judenrein*. In this respect their record was much better than ours. However, this was 1940. Though we had thrown them out of the Continent, they still retained their command of the sea. And the English, we soon found out, would rather commit suicide than cooperate with us, even on a matter such as this one.

There things remained, more or less, until the summer of 1941. Proceeding from east to west, wherever we went, we identified the Jews, confiscated their property, and concentrated them in ghettoes. Some we killed, but not nearly enough to make a demographic difference. As we were making the final preparations for Barbarossa, though, we were faced with the prospect of increasing the total number of Jews under our control to between eight and a half and nine million. This time, there was no possibility of getting rid of them at all. What on earth were we to do with them? It was against this background that I concluded that they would have to be exterminated. Physically, I mean, not in any other sense. The first orders only referred to men, but very soon women and children were also included. This is nature's way; I simply could see no other. Leaving them alive would merely result in the rise of a new generation stronger, more vengeful, and more dangerous than the previous one.

Back in 1977 David Irving, a non-academic English historian who up until then had been seen by many as the Wunderkind of the profession, came up with the idea that I had not been informed about the extermination of the Jews. Supposedly, Himmler had carried it out behind my back, at times even against my explicit wishes. In his support Irving, forgetting how good I was at keeping my own council and manipulating others, quoted various conversations I had with various people. For this offense, as well as "denying the Holocaust" in general, the champions of free speech attacked him, ostracized him, and put him on trial. He even spent some time in an Austrian jail. Much as I commend him for combating postwar anti-German propaganda, I want to put it on the record: all of this is pure hogwash.

It is true, as Irving and others wrote, that my hold over Germany weakened after 1939. Many state prosecutors, police officers, and Gestapo personnel were called up. Their absence created a vacuum we couldn't fill. I myself was running a world war, which was enough to keep any man busy. As Commander in Chief, I had to spend too much time in my field headquarters and not enough at the *Reichskan-zlei* in Berlin. Disliking the latter city as I did, I avoided it whenever possible in favor of the Berghof. All this meant that some domestic problems which were brought to my attention had to be postponed until after the war. For example, my plan to prohibit civil servants from investing their money in anything but state bonds was delayed. And the question of what to do with tens of thousands of half and quarter Jews who served in the Wehrmacht, sometimes with their superiors' knowledge, sometimes without, was put on hold as well.

Perhaps the most important issue of all was the possibility, which both Himmler and Bormann explored at various times, of reintroduc-ing some form of polygamy. The First World War had cost the lives of two million German men. After Operation Barbarossa did not lead to the quick results we had expected, it began to look as if the second one would cost as many lives, if not more. Most of these would be in their prime, leaving open the question as to who would enable

millions of German women to have children so as to make good our
losses. Nor was it a question of numbers only. Throughout the ages,
war has often caused the sexual *mores* of stay-at-home women to go
downhill. Just look at ancient Sparta, where they associated with the
Helots! German women were no exception to the rule. The more
time passed, the more of them, both married and unmarried, took
up with whatever men they could find, foreigners included. Rolf
Hochhuth's 1978 novel, *A Love in Germany,* did not invent anything!
Draconian punishments, including public humiliation and spells in
a concentration camp, only had limited effect. The outcome was a
real threat to the purity of our race.

Presumably there were also some other issues that my staff considered too minor to merit my attention. But the extermination of
the Jews? No way. First, Himmler's mind was much too limited
to originate such a thing. Whatever his other virtues, he was totally
lacking in imagination. As I said before, when you get down to it, he
remained a pedantic, perfectly groomed, and splendidly uniformed
head clerk. Albeit one who sometimes came up with the most bizarre
ideas, such as his attempts to revive old Viking traditions and to
replace Christianity with some kind of sun worship. There was also
the time when he became involved with a scientific expedition to
Tibet in the hope of proving some crackpot theory about the origins
of Aryan man. The most he could have done was get a little ahead
of himself, as happened in the case of some German Jews whom he
liquidated before their proper time had come. But that was all.

Second, Himmler did not operate on his own. He needed others,
including many who were not under his authority, to work with.
Look at the list of those who attended the famous Wannsee Conference. They represented the Reich Party Chancellery, the Reich Ministry for the Eastern Occupied Territories, the *Generalgouvernement*
in Poland (where the extermination camps were just starting to operate), the Reich Ministry of Justice, the Reich Ministry of the Interior,
the Reich Chancellery, and the Reich Foreign Ministry. Other orga-

nizations, such as the military, which provided some of the transport, and the *Reichsbahn,* without which much of the operation could not have taken place, were also heavily involved. To claim that all these highly qualified officials could have worked together over a period of three years, taking millions of people from their homes, confiscating their property, concentrating them, transporting them from one end of Europe to another, and killing them without my knowledge is an insult to my intelligence. It's particularly insulting because, as became clear after the war, both Stalin and the Western Allies were aware of the operation almost from the beginning.

It is also an insult in another sense. Solving the Jewish question had always been one of my two most important objectives if not the most important one of all. Unformed as my thoughts were, very early on I realized that, one way or another, we would have to get rid of *that* pack. That is why any suggestion that the idea had been planted in my mind by others—for example the Mufti of Jerusalem, Haj al Husseini, whom I briefly met in November 1941—is ridiculous. Does anyone really think I needed an Arab *pithecanthropus* to teach me? It is also why, overriding those who wanted to keep at least some of them alive so as to exploit them for labor, I insisted that the operation be continued might and main as fast as possible and all the way to the last days of the war. The most I allowed was for some Jews to be killed slowly by hunger and overwork rather than quickly by shooting or gas. I do not apologize for what I did. To the contrary, I took and take full responsibility for it. Indeed, the fact that I always did so was one cardinal reason why people supported and obeyed me for as long as they did. Sitting here in Hell, my only regret is that I did not quite succeed. Had my post 1945 supporters had any sense, they would have taken a similar line. Far from trying to deny "The Holocaust," they would have confirmed it and glorified in it.

We, or rather Himmler, started by expanding our so-called *Einsatzgruppen.* We first used them in 1939–40 in Poland to avenge our *Volksgenossen,* whom the Poles had murdered, to exterminate tens of thousands of members of the local intelligentsia, and, yes, to kill some Jews. You should have seen the glee on the faces of our Polish prisoners of war when they watched their Jewish "comrades" being treated as they deserved to be! Next, we unleashed them in Russia. They and their cousins, the special police battalions, were a mixed lot. Most of the men were working class—sailors, dock, warehouse, and construction workers, truck drivers, waiters, and the like. They had never served and had only received a modicum of military training. After all, how much skill does shooting someone in the back require? Others, including many officers, were too old for front service. The fact that the killer units operated in the rear did not endear them to our fighting troops. But they systematically moved from one township to the next, rounded up the Jews, women and children included, took them to some more or less secluded spot, and shot them after making them dig their own graves.

Neither the Jews nor the local population mounted any resistance to speak of. The former were too stunned and handicapped by the need to look after their families to do so. Many members of the latter were only too happy to see the Jews go. Nor was there any shortage of Ukrainians, Byelorussians, and Balts who voluntarily offered their support to our men and carried out their assigned tasks with considerable enthusiasm. The Latvians in particular were a great help. Explaining why, before our coming, Stalin employed so many of them in the NKVD. That's to say nothing of the civilians who first pointed out the Jews and then used the opportunity to plunder whatever property they had left behind. Much as they tried to deny it later on, most of our senior commanders on the spot also did what I expected of them. No more, perhaps, but certainly not less.

A few months having passed, though, problems emerged. First, the number of Jews was too large, and the distances between their settlements were too great, for our operations to be as effective as they should have been. Rumor preceded the *Gruppen* wherever they went; this enabled many Jews to escape into the forests. Some had to be hunted down one by one, a wasteful use of our scarce manpower. Others formed bands or joined the "partisans" and became positively dangerous. Second, the grisly task got on our men's nerves. It caused many of them to turn to drink or worse. Even Bach-Zelewsky at one point suffered from psychosomatic symptoms sufficiently severe to require medical leave. Himmler, who always insisted on doing, or at least witnessing, everything he ordered his men to do and who in the summer of 1941 made a point of watching an "action," had first-hand experience with these problems. So shocked was he that he started looking for another solution—a final one, as the phrase went.

The idea of using special death camps as an alternative to these methods seems to have originated with Himmler and Heydrich. It first arose as a partial solution and then as a complete and "final" one. The day-to-day execution of the task was the responsibility of the camp commanders. The first appointment was that of Colonel Rudolf Höss of Auschwitz. Höss had spent his career serving on the staffs of various concentration camps, which made him well suited for the job. He also had a criminal record dating back to the French invasion of the Ruhr, when he had been convicted of murder. As a result, he was in no position to disobey any orders he was given. After having tried various means, including the exhaust of diesel engines, someone at the headquarters of Operation T-4 advised him to use cyanide gas. Construction of the camps started in the autumn of 1941. By early next year a number of them were ready to receive their first clients.

Like the personnel of the *Einsatzgruppen* and security battalions, those who staffed the camps were a mixed lot. Most were men, but about ten percent were women. Some of the men were young members of the SS, including the Waffen SS, who had been convicted of relatively trivial offenses. Next, they were offered a chance to redeem themselves, and that was that. Others were German civilians who answered ads the SD put in the papers without, of course, saying a

word about the nature of the work they were going to do "in the east."
When they found out, it was already too late. Others still were local
volunteers, who could be found in every nation in Eastern Europe.
They cost us little, and there were always more than enough of them.

Looking back, indeed one of the most surprising things about
the so-called "Holocaust" was not how much effort and how many
resources it required but how little. Far less than deportation and
resettlement would have. For example, the excellent Captain Stangl
at Treblinka did away with close to a million people over a period
of some fifteen months. Hardly any of those who entered the camp
survived, yet never at any one time did he employ more than 40 SS
men. That is what I call efficiency! The *Einsatzgruppen* and police
battalions combined never took up more than three quarters of one
percent of our forces in the east. On any average day, out of some
30,000 trains run by the *Reichsbahn,* no more than two carried Jews.

As late as December 1941, Frank in Poland "quite openly" told
his men, "We cannot shoot these 3.5 million Jews; we cannot poison
them." Now, however, what had previously been inconceivable was
turned into a horrible, but absolutely necessary, reality. It was against
this background that the aforementioned Wannsee Conference was
held in January 1942. It was not, as has so often been written,
held in order to extend the "Holocaust" from Eastern to Central
and Western Europe. That was something I had already decided
to do the previous October, just as our victories in the east were
approaching their peak and the Russians were preparing to evacuate
Moscow. Instead, the purpose of the meeting was to make detailed
arrangements for the way the Final Solution was going to be carried out from that point on. The importance—or, rather, the lack
of importance—of the conference was obvious just by seeing the
relatively low ranks of the participants. The most senior one was
Heydrich, who had received his orders from Göring. As I said before,
Heydrich was an excellent police officer who distinguished himself
by his ruthlessness and contempt for bureaucratic formalities. He

was also ambitious; rumor had it that he saw himself as my eventual successor. But to succeed me, he would have to kill Himmler first. That was something, I believe, of which the man with the iron heart, as I called him when I spoke at his funeral, was fully capable.

The details of the process by which the Jews were gathered, taken to the camps, made to surrender their clothes and valuables, marched into the gas chambers—disguised as shower rooms—and killed have been described countless times. I will not repeat them here except to say that, though I never went to watch the proceedings, I was kept fully informed by Himmler and others. The operation continued for about three years and went almost without a hitch. It was only here in Hell that I learned that, on occasion, it was necessary to delay some of the transports because the logistic requirements of our forces came first. At other times too many trains reached the camps at once, forcing the commanders on the spot to make the Jews wait in the open until their turn came. Here and there, a shootout occurred as a handful of prisoners stole weapons, rioted, and tried to escape. Most were caught almost immediately and executed. A few Jews managed to survive by making themselves useful and holding on until the end, especially at Auschwitz and especially toward the end of the war. But that was all.

In the summer of 1942 a certain SS Colonel Brack suggested to Himmler that, to provide our factories with the labor they so desperately needed, instead of killing the Jews, we should give some of them a temporary reprieve by sterilizing them en masse. Some experiments in this direction were made, but the technical difficulties proved too great. So the camps proceeded with their deadly work. They provided us with mountains of personal items, from shoes to suitcases and from coats to shaving brushes. Properly sorted, cleaned, and registered, they were distributed to the poor of the Reich. Much more importantly, thinking that they would be resettled, the Jews all brought some of their most precious belongings along. We laid our hands on mountains of foreign currency, diamonds, and gold. Some of the latter was pulled out of the mouths of the dead by *Sonder-kommandos*, special teams, made up of the Jews themselves. All this wealth went into the vaults of the Reichsbank. The latter used some of it to pay for imports of food, raw materials, and some industrial goods from countries such as Spain, Switzerland, and Sweden. Here, I should add that, although a great many people, both Germans and non-Germans, profited from the "Holocaust," that was not why I ordered it to be carried out. But I am repeating myself.

The most challenging part of the entire vast operation was not the logistics but the politics involved. The Russians' retreat left what we used to call "the occupied territories in the east" without any government. So our commanders on the spot, such as Erich Koch in the Ukraine, did as they were told and shot anyone who protested. The other extreme was represented by France and Belgium. Both were under military government. The generals, including some who later took part in the abortive coup of July 1944, dragged their heels, explaining why only about one-third of the Jews in those countries were killed. The French authorities also did their best to prevent the evacuation of their own, as opposed to foreign, Jews. The Dutch, with their typical respect for authority, any authority, were easier to deal with. When it comes to obeying orders, trust the Calvinists! That fact goes a long way to account for our success in sending some 70 percent of all Dutch Jews to the camps from where few of them returned. Thanks to the stupidity of some of our people on the spot, the Danes were able to ship all their 7,000 Jews to Sweden. Many Norwegian Jews, exploiting the long border between that country and their own, also escaped.

In Poland, Frank was always worried about possible outbreaks of starvation and disease. That is why, supported by Göring as the man responsible for the German economy, he did his best to prevent Himmler and Heydrich from using the *Generalgouvernement* as a Jewish dumping ground. Repeatedly, I had to order him to do as he was told, the Polish population be damned. Among our allies,

Croatia and Slovakia were very happy to oblige. The rest were less conciliatory. Not, heaven knows, because they liked their Jews any better than we did ours; but solely because they did not want their miserable "sovereignty" to be infringed.

Romania was governed by Field-Marshal Antonescu, a man whom I held in some respect. Among his entire people he was the only one, male or female, who could not be corrupted! During the first twelve months or so of Barbarossa his men did away with some 350,000 members of the chosen race, mainly in the provinces taken from Russia. Come the autumn of 1942, though, he obstinately refused to have more of "his" (i.e. Romanian) Jews taken away, allowing most of them to survive. Hungary's "Regent" Horthy did not like Jews either but nevertheless used all sorts of excuses to delay their deportation until the spring of 1944. It was only then that a change of government, brought about with our active assistance, took place. It finally created a situation where Himmler, again working by way of the ubiquitous Eichmann, was able to take care of the 600,000 Jews in the country. By contrast, Bulgaria never allowed us to deport any of its Jews at all. *Tant pis* for them.

Finally, there was Italy, our most important ally. In 1937–38 Mussolini introduced a series of anti-Semitic laws, not because we pressed him to but because he was developing an inferiority complex and wanted to prove that Italians, too, were a pure race. But the laws did not go nearly far enough. As a result, most of Italy's Jews remained, if not unmolested, alive and kicking. Italian officers and officials in southeastern France, Yugoslavia, and Greece also provided the Jews with some protection. Partly because they did not like what we were doing, and partly because the Duce told them to do so or at any rate did not object. It was only after the Fascist regime collapsed in July 1943 and we occupied most of the country that we were finally able to make real headway in the direction we wished. Even so, most Italian Jews, forming just one tenth of one percent of the population and being thoroughly assimilated, managed to survive.

Confronted with the facts, the attitudes of our enemies varied. Stalin, of course, could not have cared less. Shortly before his death, he himself started moving in the same direction, executing some Jews and removing others from positions of power. Brought into the secret, Roosevelt, knowing that his countrymen would never agree to go to war on behalf of the Jews, kept his cards close to his chest. Later, both he and Churchill worried that, had the full truth become known, public pressure would force them to change their strategy. Not only would their impotence to do anything have been exposed, but the outcome would have been conflict between them and their senior commanders, who did not want their troops to be diverted from their main mission. Caught between these millstones, they preferred to downplay the issue as much as they could until practically the end of the war.

Both Himmler and Heydrich were aware that, when it came to our treatment of the Jews, there were limits to what German public opinion would stand. That was why, throughout the 1930s, they did their best to steer the persecution of the Jews into bureaucratic channels. When we started evacuating German Jews in 1941–42, many of their Aryan neighbors expressed sympathy with them. Nevertheless, in the end the war facilitated our task. On the one hand, people had more important things to worry about than the fate of the Jews. On the other, it made secrecy easier to impose and maintain than before.

To be sure, completely concealing what was going on was impossible. In the whole of Europe there was hardly a single town that was entirely *Judenrein*. People were bound to see deportations and the like. Very often they were repelled by what they saw. One or two even had the gall to tell me that. The inevitable outcome of secrecy was that there were lots of rumors floating about. Everyone and his neighbor had seen or heard *something*. Everyone and his neighbor knew things were going badly for the Jews and that a great many of them were being taken away and killed. Had they wanted to, they could have known a great deal more. But they did not. As a result of all this, very few people had any idea of the full scope of the operation. That even applied to the leaders of the "opposition." Take that arch-traitor, Colonel Henning von Tresckow. No one had less sympathy for what we were trying to do and tried harder to get me killed. Yet in a letter to a friend and fellow conspirator he only mentioned "tens of thousands" of Jews being liquidated, not millions.

And how about the Jews themselves? Many, especially in the West, could not imagine what we had in store for them. When we told them that they were going to be "resettled" in the east, they believed us, more or less. They took it for granted that life would be hard but hoped they would survive. They often kept their illusions down to the very last moment. After they had been unloaded from the trains. After they had been separated from their families. After they had been ordered to strip naked. Right until the moment when, packed into the "shower rooms," the valves were opened and the gas began having its effect. As the ancient Greeks used to say, hope dies last. In this way the sheer "impossibility" of the task we had set ourselves made its execution much easier than it would otherwise have been.

But even that was not the end of the matter. Yes, I succeeded, more than anyone else in the history of the world, in doing away with lots of Jews. But I was not nearly successful enough, as the future was to show. One reason for this was that the remaining Jews profited enormously from their brethren's fate. The profited so much, in fact, that they have been able to establish and maintain an entire "industry" whose sole purpose is to extract reparations from every European country. Another outcome was the state of Israel. Not only did I force hundreds of thousands to emigrate, but I provided it with its *raison d'etre*. Seen from this point of view, I must have done more to help establish it than all Zionist leaders combined.

When the Jews were still scattered in the so-called Diaspora, they gave the world endless trouble. And now that about half of them are concentrated in a single country, Israel, they give it even more! Citing the very nonexistent moral principles they themselves had never respected, they demanded "reparations." So strong was their grip on Washington that they were able to block anyone who wanted to do business there without their consent! As a result, starting in 1953, all *Bundesrepublik* governments without exception have been bending backward to meet Israel's insatiable demands for money, weapons, and diplomatic support. Ask the people in Kiel. In 2016 they finished building the last of six super-sophisticated submarines for Israel, two of them at the German taxpayers' expense. And there are several more naval vessels on order.

One final point. Yes, I did unleash a world war, easily the largest and deadliest in history. Yes, I did kill masses of people both in the course of my military operations and when policing the occupied territories. Or simply because, as in the case of the Jews, I was convinced that they did not deserve to live and had to be exterminated like vermin. *Tempus vincet omnia,* they say. For everything else I did, people have, or would have, forgiven me. But not for this.

Good!

Chapter 26

The Hinge of Fate

History, they say, is written by the victors. Not so mine which, strange as it sounds, was written very largely by the losers: meaning, my generals. No sooner had the war ended than the U.S. Army started interrogating them about their experiences, particularly, but not exclusively, when facing the Russians. These were the early years of the so-called Cold War. And who had more experience fighting the Reds than we did? Several hundred former Wehrmacht officers joined the project, ultimately producing no fewer than 250 "studies" about various aspects of the war. And subsequent historians have not been shy about using them.

On the German side, the man who headed the effort was my old acquaintance Halder. Halder, it turns out, had long been involved with the opposition to the regime. In the summer of 1938 he and some others, including both officers and foreign office officials, were planning a *coup*. They even sent a representative to London to see whether they could gather support! My triumph at Munich convinced him and his fellow idiots that the German people would never follow them. As a result, from that point on he concentrated on his proper job, more or less. Always noted more for his meticulous attention to detail than for his strategic imagination and boldness, he became increasingly fussy until, in 1942, shortly before the Russians started their great offensive at Stalingrad, I decided to get rid of him. In his place I put Kurt Zeitzler, a less opinionated officer who was more prepared to do as I told him. It worked. His optimistic, at times almost clownish, spirit infected the General Staff, at least for the coming months. Later he abandoned me, but that that is a different story.

Once a traitor, always a traitor. The fact that Halder was now *ausser Dienst* (retired) did not prevent him from staying in touch with the group of conspirators who ultimately tried to blow me up and seize power for themselves on 20 July 1944. Thereupon, I had him imprisoned at the Dachau concentration camp, where he spent the last months of the war until the Americans "liberated" him. Looking back, my only regret is that I did not order him to be executed as his fellow traitor, Abwehr-boss Wilhelm Canaris, was. The war having ended, Halder agreed to work for the U.S. Army Historical Section. In this capacity he commissioned over a hundred former Wehrmacht officers to write "studies" about their experiences. The outcome was predictable. The officers in question were determined to "rehabilitate" themselves. They also wanted, if possible, to snuggle up to the victors upon whom their future careers depended. They did whatever they could to discredit me and to blame their own defeats on me. Halder himself set the example. In his aforementioned book he disputed my military abilities, claiming that I was basically an amateur. Albeit one, as he generously admitted, who was not without some natural aptitude for the business at hand.

Each of our victories, he wrote, was due to him and his super-competent, super-honorable, super-courageous fellow generals. Each of our setbacks was due to my obstinate, often ignorant, interference with their brilliant plans and my refusal to accept their suggestions. Others, Manstein above all, echoed his phrases. Particularly irksome was the latter's claim that I, being who I was and not knowing how to run a staff, based my relations with my subordinates on fear rather than on trust. I wish that, as the author of this particular piece of egregious nonsense, he would have spent one day working for Comrade Stalin in Moscow or, more recently Kim Il-sung in Pyongyang.

Just one day! Doing so would have cured him of his illusions soon enough, assuming, of course, that he lived to tell the tale.

One officer who worked for Halder was the aforementioned Kurt Hesse. He, however, differed from the rest by daring to criticize the behavior of U.S. soldiers during the war, saying that many of them were little better than hooligans. For this, the Americans fired him. Many other senior (and not so senior, but that is another matter) commanders also published their memoirs. Among them were Walter Warlimont, Rundstedt's chief of staff Günter Blumentritt, and Rommel's chief of staff, Hans Speidel. So successful was the last-named one at ingratiating himself—in other words, denouncing me and everything National Socialist Germany stood for—that he made quite a career for himself. He even served as Commander in Chief of the NATO ground forces in Central Europe. Yet he was a pure staff officer and never once commanded a major formation in war! Quite a few of the works in question were translated into English. Guderian's *Panzer Leader,* armed with a foreword by some English military scribbler whose name I had never heard, became a bestseller. And all were lapped up by a great many people eager to accuse me of every deed and misdeed under the sun. Studying my career, they based entire chapters on this junk.

Some of the problems we were facing were structural. The army's mental horizon still remained stuck in 1914 or, at best, 1918. Many of its officers seem to have thought that the air force, let alone the navy, did not exist. As a result, it did not have a single commander capable of coordinating joint operations. That is why I set up so many so-called OKW theaters for which the latter assumed responsibility. However, OKW, partly because it was younger than the other principal headquarters, never succeeded in establishing its authority either over the army or over the other two services. The fact that Jodl had been Halder's student at the disguised *Kriegsakademie* during the Weimar years did not help. Such was the tug of war between the various headquarters that a number of formations—not always the same ones, obviously—were permanently lost because they were being shuttled to and from one theater and another.

Göring, too, created problems. Göring was a Renaissance man who was transported into the twentieth century, exchanging his horse for a fighter aircraft on the way. His physical courage was unquestioned. Unlike me, he could and did kill without either compunction or remorse. No one was better than him at empire building. So long was the list of titles he carried that not even he could remember them all! He obstinately kept control over hundreds of thousands of men over and above those "his" Luftwaffe could effectively use, refusing to release them for more important duties. It was only my personal intervention which, in the end, forced him to arm them, form them into so-called Luftwaffe Field-Divisions, and send them to the front, which desperately needed them. Even so, they remained part of the Luftwaffe, not of the ground forces where they belonged. As a result, badly trained and badly commanded by unqualified officers, they suffered heavier casualties for fewer gains than they should have.

Another failure that must be laid at Göring's door was the fact that our navy had no air arm. The outcome was that our submarines, ably commanded by Admiral Dönitz and in some ways the most cost-effective force of the entire Wehrmacht, had to operate without its aid. Twice, in early 1942 and in early 1943, the submarines came within weeks of forcing England to surrender. Had they enjoyed proper support, they might very well have done exactly that.

Some historians have taken me to task for these problems and others like them. Lacking political experience, as most of them do, they erroneously assume that a "dictator" can simply order his commanders to do as he pleases. They overlook the fact that similar ones plagued the armed forces of every single belligerent during the war. David Irving, the historian who claimed I had not known about the extermination of the Jews, even wrote an entire book on the subject. Its title? *The War between the [Allied] Generals*. And don't forget about

the rivalry between the Japanese army and navy. Nor was the situation after 1945 any different. When the German Kriegsmarine was
reestablished in the 1950s, its commanders ordered English-built aircraft specifically in order to prevent the Luftwaffe, whose equipment
was American built, from taking them away! To this day, making the
services work together instead of at cross purposes represents a major
problem for every country that has them. Just spend a couple of days
at the Pentagon, and you will see what I mean.

Back to the military situation. Admittedly, in early 1942 it was not
as good as we had expected. But it was far from hopeless. In the short
term, indeed, my declaration of war on the U.S. helped our war effort.
It enabled Dönitz to sink not just English ships supplying England
but American ones as well. As had been the case since the middle
of 1941, our most dangerous enemy by far was Russia. I therefore
resolved to knock it out as soon as I possibly could. No longer able to
attack along the entire vast front, I selected two objectives. One was
Stalingrad, the city that bore Stalin's name and also commanded the
Volga through which Allied supplies were arriving from Persia. The
other was the Caucasus; it alone could provide us with the oil without
which we could not continue the war.

As in 1940, there was a last-minute hitch. Some idiot of an officer
flew a reconnaissance mission over the front. He was forced to make
an emergency landing in Russian territory, with the result that all
directives and maps fell into enemy hands. These people never learn!
Nevertheless, the operation, commanded by me personally from my
forward headquarters in the Ukraine, went like clockwork. Seldom
in history were such great advances made so quickly; 1. Panzer Army,
which was moving in the direction of the Caucasus, covered 500 kilometers in two weeks! On 4 July, just five days after the beginning of
the offensive, Manstein's 11. Army took Sebastopol, the main Russian
port on the Black Sea and an important symbolic objective which had
resisted our efforts to capture it in the previous year. On the next
day other forces occupied Rostov after fierce fighting. They crossed

the Don on 21 August, and reached the Volga north of Stalingrad two days later. Other forces captured Maikop. Unfortunately, the Russians had thoroughly destroyed the oilfields there. As a result, our advance petered out and came to a halt.

All eyes were now upon Stalingrad. Our direct assault on it opened on 10 September. Both the ground forces and the Luftwaffe participated, the latter using its Stukas in order to drop bombs almost literally at our own soldiers' feet. We made slow, but steady, progress. Gradually, though, we began to discover that the enemy, with typical Russian deviousness, had traded land for time. Contrary to our expectations, his resistance, instead of weakening, grew stronger and stronger. The struggle for the city went on for two months, during which it was almost entirely demolished.

Throughout October, I kept warning my generals against a possible Russian counteroffensive in the direction of Rostov. As so often, they refused to listen. This time the most important culprit was General Reinhard Gehlen, chief of *Fremde Heere Ost* (Foreign Armies East). Ere "Barbarossa" started, he had grossly underestimated the size of the Red Army. Now he insisted that Stalin would aim his blow at Army Group Center near Smolensk. On 20 November, just as our forces were approaching the Volga, the Reds did as I had predicted. A few days later, two vast Russian armies, one coming from the north and the other from the south, met west of Stalingrad. They cut off our 6. Army with as many as 250,000 troops. Gehlen apart, it was all the fault of our Italian, Hungarian, and Romanian allies whom, for lack of better troops and not because I had any illusions about them, I put in charge of our northern flank. The latter two in particular were always on the point of shooting at each other. When the Russians attacked, they ran.

I will not repeat the numerous accounts that have been written about the struggle that followed. There was a time when military history was written by serious authors in order to enable serious students to draw serious conclusions from it. Since about 1990, though, most of it has aimed at satisfying the curiosity of ordinary people—Western people, of course, who have never been within a thousand kilometers of a battlefield. That explains the heavy focus on individual soldiers, their deeds, their feelings, and their sufferings. I, however, had spent four years in the trenches. I knew what war is like and did not need this often maudlin stuff to remind me.

Still there is one point I want to emphasize. Had I agreed to evacuate Stalingrad, as many of my top commanders suggested, the Russians, driving west with nothing to stop them, would have cut off our forces in the Caucasus. It was the heroic resistance of 6. Army which saved those forces from destruction. Unfortunately, they had to leave much of their equipment behind. Furthermore, by continuing to hold the city, we bought time to bring up other formations. Had it been otherwise, the eastern front could never have been stabilized as eventually it was.

When I say 6. Army, I do not include its commander, Friedrich Paulus. Paulus had been Halder's deputy. Like him, he had never commanded a major formation in war. By appointing him to the post in December 1941, as part of the general reshuffle of that time, I hoped to give him an opportunity to show what he could do. As things became difficult inside the besieged city, he repeatedly begged me to allow him to break out. I, however, with wider considerations in mind, could not agree. Instead, I ordered him to stay put until he could be rescued.

Not long afterward, it became clear that he could *not* be rescued. Once again, it was Göring's fault. He had promised to supply the army by air but failed to keep his word. So many aircraft were lost in the effort that the Luftwaffe's transport command never recovered. For my part, I made Paulus a field-marshal in the hope that honor would prevent him from becoming the first officer of that rank in German history to surrender. He understood, of course, but betrayed my trust. Having been taken prisoner, he put himself at the disposal of his captors. Along with his chief of staff, General Arthur Schmidt, he formed the National Committee for a Free Germany. Over the next two years it did its mediocre best to make more of our men defect and join the Russians. How anyone could sink as low as he did is beyond me.

Meanwhile, in the Mediterranean, Rommel's tactical genius, assisted by an infusion of new tanks and other equipment, finally reasserted itself. In January 1942 he counterattacked the English 8. Army. In June, following a lightning campaign with few equals in history, he took the little town of Tobruk, which in the previous year had held out for 240 days. For that feat I gave him his field-marshal's baton. By this time even the enemy had fallen under his spell, extolling his supposed genius so as to excuse their own blunders. From Tobruk the Africa Corps continued its eastward drive. How the English ran! In July our spearheads reached Alamein, a desert dump just 100 kilometers from Alexandria. Understandably, our troops were enthusiastic about the prospect of exchanging the desert for the amenities a great city can offer. So was Mussolini, who was already planning a grand victory parade with himself, riding a white horse, holding "the Sword of Islam" in his hand, and accompanied by the march from *Aida*!

Not surprisingly, the Jews in Palestine panicked. Echoing our own accusations against their race, some hoped that the "fact" that, unlike their brethren in the diaspora, they were "working Jews" would save them. Others called on kabbalists—kabbalists!—to protect them against the Devil, i.e. me. They mumbled their prayers, cast their spells, and blew their *shofars* so hard as to render God deaf. Unfortunately, I was unable to deal with them as I would have liked to. The ongoing gigantic battle in Russia, as well as Rommel's own overextended communications, prevented us from supplying him. To ease his situation the Italians and we, assisted by some Japanese experts, seriously considered an operation against Malta. However, so heavy had the losses of our paratroopers in Crete in the previous year been that I decided to desist. Rommel's own attempt to break through the English lines at Alam Halfa did not go well either. Next came the English victory over the Africa Corps in October–November 1942, which caused Churchill to ring the church bells all over England. In one of his more bombastic speeches, delivered not long thereafter, he called the battle "the end of the beginning."

As so often in his long and mendacious career, he was exaggerating. To be sure it would have been better if Rommel had been able to remain where he was. However, given the relative unimportance of the theater and the fairly small German forces involved, his retreat from Alamein did not worry me much. The English commander on the spot, General Bernard Montgomery, was notable for his eccentric personality and behavior. The son of a bishop, speaking in the House of Lords after his retirement, he once suggested that the entire army be made up solely of bachelors such as himself! Militarily, he was mediocre at best. Proceeding cautiously and systematically, always afraid of falling into some trap that only existed in his imagination, sooner or later his advance would have petered out. That, in fact, had happened to his predecessors both in early 1941 and at the end of the same year.

The Allied landings in West Africa were something else. As happened all too often, our admirals, with Raeder at their head, were slow to realize what was afoot. When they finally did understand, they still believed that the Allied blow would fall on Corsica, Sardinia, and Tunisia rather than on Algeria and Morocco as it ultimately did. And, had the Allied commanders possessed any guts, it would have. As a result, when the battle started, our submarines were stationed too far east to take part in it. Once the enemy had gained a foothold, it was clear that North Africa would have to be defended at all costs. Not necessarily for military reasons but because I foresaw, which indeed was not difficult, that its loss would have important political repercussions in Italy. That is why I poured some 50,000 of our best

troops into Tunisia. Reinforcing those already there, they fought like
the devil and taught the Americans a sharp lesson at Kasserine. But,
ultimately, they could not hold out against the enemy's overwhelming
superiority on the ground, at sea, and in the air.

In January 1943 Churchill and Roosevelt, meeting at Casablanca,
declared that their policy toward us would be to insist on "unconditional surrender." The declaration was an extraordinary piece of
stupidity on their part, particularly because, as became clear almost
as soon as the war ended in 1945, they did not really mean it. As
they soon realized, they needed us to resist the Russian steamroller.
Meanwhile, the declaration enabled Goebbels to have a field day at
our enemies' expense by explaining to the German people that they
had no choice but to fight to the end. A few months later, in the
spring and early summer of 1943, I authorized Ribbentrop to send
out feelers to see whether it would be possible to reach some kind
of accommodation with Stalin. He, however, demanded terms that
would have left the whole of Europe, us included, at his tender mercies. Later attempts by Himmler and Göring, acting behind my back,
to contact the Western Powers in cities such as Stockholm, Geneva,
and Madrid fared no better. So the war had to go on.

The summer of 1943 witnessed three other important develop-
ments. First, the Western Allies, having cleared North Africa, invaded
Sicily. Thereupon, Mussolini fell from power. He was betrayed by the
King, the Fascist "Grand Council," and that vile toad, Field-Marshal
Pietro Badoglio, an aristocrat much given to wearing black gloves.
His motto was "I swoop like a falcon." In reality he was a weak,
vain, and devious man. In October 1922 he had refused to defend
Rome against the Fascist columns converging on it. In 1936 he
"proved" himself by using poison gas against barefooted Abyssinian
warriors. For that feat Mussolini made him Duke of Addis Ababa! As
Chief of Staff of the Italian armed forces early in the war, he was a
complete failure. Now, appointed Prime Minster by my old "friend"

Vittorio Emmanuelle, he immediately opened negotiations with the English and the Americans in order to bring about the surrender of his country while hoping I would not notice.

Needless to say, I did notice. And I knew better than to trust him. When the surrender came at the beginning of September, we were ready. Commanded by Rommel, our troops occupied most of the country, disarmed most of the Italian troops, and took them prisoner. Many ended up working in our factories; that way, at any rate, they did something useful. Our most dramatic move was to free Mussolini, whom Badoglio had imprisoned at some mountain resort and whose fate weighed on me like a nightmare. A daring commando raid succeeded in extricating him; I subsequently had him flown to my headquarters at Rastenburg, where I did my best to boost his flagging spirits. Next, I put him in charge of northern Italy, where he formed the so-called Salò Republic. I did that not because I did not realize that he was a spent force whose time had passed, but because there was no one else able or willing to take his place.

All too often, these brilliant moves had to be carried out against the advice of some of my generals. Meanwhile, the struggle in Italy continued. Having captured Sicily after 38 days of fierce fighting, the Allies crossed the Straits of Messina and landed at the toe of the boot. From there they hoped to advance north. When that did not work as well as they had expected, they used their navy to land forces at Salerno. When that did not work, they did the same at Anzio. In the whole of history, it is hard to find a less imaginative campaign! Each time they tried some maneuver my commander on the spot, Field-Marshal Kesselring, was able to save the bulk of his forces from being cut off. Making full use of the difficult topography, he and his men fought for every inch. Best of all, he was operating on internal lines. Partly because of the terrain, partly because of the heroic efforts of our railway companies, the Allies, in spite of their crushing superiority in the air, never succeeded in shutting off his logistic lifeline. For almost two years he held out against forces far superior to his own, diverting them from more important tasks. It was a real military masterpiece, I must say.

At the same time, the Allies mounted their largest bombing attack of the war thus far by bombing Hamburg. The city was an important center of communication, commerce, and industry. Above all, it was where many of our submarines were built. By this time our self-proclaimed "liberal" and "humane" enemies had perfected the technique of using incendiaries to set alight entire cities by causing a firestorm. The outcome was that tens of thousands—to this day, no one knows just how many—men, women, and children were incinerated. The smoke from the burning city could be seen from dozens of kilometers away.

On this occasion as on others, I refrained from visiting the bombed-out areas as Goebbels, taking Churchill as his example, suggested I do. Then, as now, I took full responsibility for the casualties that my efforts to secure the German nation a place under the sun necessarily incurred. However, I was worried that the sight of my people suffering such devastation might be more than I could stand. It might divert me from my historic task, and that was at a time when they needed me more than ever.

Starting with me and ending with the humblest fighter pilot, all of us were determined not to let anything of the kind to happen again. Göring, it is true, was too well known and too close to the very essence of the regime to sack. So I left him nominally in place, an enormously fat, pompous apparition with manicured nails and rings on his fingers. He continued to wave his field-marshal's baton, went on looting tours of the occupied territories in the west, and became more and more addicted to diamonds, silk underwear, and morphine.

Behind his back, I entrusted the real power over the Luftwaffe to two "new" men. They were General Adolf Galland, commander of the fighter arm, and General Joseph Kammhuber, chief of night fighters. In this capacity he set up the so-called Kammhuber Line, an integrated system of radars, headquarters, and communications. It detected enemy bombers as they approached and directed our pilots to them. We also greatly increased the production of fighter aircraft, including, above all, the new Focke Wulf-190 some of whose variants carried a powerful 30-millimeter cannon. It worked. In October 1943, such a colossal failure was the Americans' attack on the ball-bearing factories at Schweinfurt that they had to suspend their air campaign for several months. Not until the attacks on Berlin and Dresden in January–February 1945, by which time we had become practically defenseless in the air, did anything similar to Hamburg take place again.

Third, we mounted what was to prove our last major offensive in Russia. The fighting that followed our defeat at Stalingrad had left a Russian "bulge" around the city of Kursk. It jutted into our front from east to west. Now I decided to nip it off. One arm of the offensive, commanded by Model, was to advance from the north. The other, commanded by Manstein, came from the south. The stakes were enormous as were the forces on both sides. To this day, it remains the largest armored battle in history. Unfortunately Operation Citadel, as we called it, did not work out. Summer came late that year, forcing us to postpone the beginning of the offensive time and again. Another factor was the late delivery of our magnificent new Panther tanks. They developed teething troubles, which took time until they could be fixed. Even here in Hell, many years later, I can remember my feeling at that time. I knew that the offensive was critical to the outcome of the war; it made my stomach turn.

When the offensive finally got under way, it turned out that the Russians had discovered our intentions and were ready for us. They had built their defenses to a depth unmatched in history: dozens of kilometers of barbed wire, extensive minefields, anti-tank trenches, fortified bunkers, dug-in anti-tank guns, booby traps—well suited to the Russian mentality—what have you. Unknown to our field intelligence, they were also holding an entire armored corps in reserve, ready to be unleashed at any moment. Hard as our troops fought, they were unable to make progress. In the end I had to call off the offensive, thereby opening the way to a Russian counterattack.

Watching events from my headquarters, I could see the way all these developments were linked. The troops we sent to the Mediterranean were missing from our spearheads in the Ukraine. Focusing on fighters and home defense, the Luftwaffe had barely enough aircraft left to support our ground forces. That did not matter so much in Russia and Italy. As for the former, that was because air power had never been the Red Army's strongest suit. As for the latter, it was because the mountainous terrain prevented the Allied air forces from making their full impact felt. Try as they might, they never succeeded in cutting our lines of communication for any length of time. But in the open plains of the West the inability of our air force to keep the air over our troops clear of enemy fighter-bombers was to assume critical proportions. Its contribution to our eventual defeat was immense.

I want to put it on the record that it is not true, as so many of my generals wrote after the war, that I opposed any withdrawal on principle. Nor, by doing so, did I prevent them from "maneuvering" and staving off defeat. In fact, in a directive of September 1943, I authorized them to evacuate all of the Ukraine right back to the Dnieper. The objective was to gain breathing space as well as to transfer troops to the west where, as we knew, the English and Americans were preparing an invasion. However, whichever way we pulled the blanket, some limbs were left sticking out.

For me personally, the worst of it was the realization that we were unable to bomb the Allies' cities in retaliation for what they were doing to our own. Day by day the enemy, caring nothing for the laws of war, killed and injured thousands of German men, women, and children, rendering many more homeless and forcing the rest to live underground like rats. Hard as our civil defense organization worked, irreplaceable works of art were being destroyed. Photographs I received from my Gauleiters all over the Reich testified to these facts.

I must have seen thousands of them. Except, perhaps, during the last weeks of the war, the bombing did not make people question its basic legitimacy. But it certainly made them grumble at the government and Party, which they accused of not doing enough to help them. There were places where uniformed Party officials risked being assaulted.

In fact the responsibility rested squarely with Göring and the Luftwaffe. First, it was slow to develop radar. Though that shortcoming was later corrected, the Allies, using a device named Windows, managed to paralyze our apparatus, thus opening the way to the murderous attacks on Hamburg and other cities. Last, but not least, it failed to develop anything like the heavy bombers our enemies built by the thousand. In fact two of its most senior officers, the head of the Technical Office General Ernst Udet and Chief of Staff General Hans Jeschonek, committed suicide against precisely this background in 1941 and 1943 respectively.

And that was how *Vergeltung,* revenge, became the order of the day.

Chapter 27

Holding On

It cannot be denied that after Stalingrad, Tunisia, Sicily, Kursk, and Hamburg, things became hard for us Germans. As the saying goes, though, when the going gets tough, the tough get going. No one more so than me, I assure you! And I still had the German people squarely behind me. To be sure, our setbacks, which were accompanied by the loss of as many as 300,000 men who were killed or captured, had shaken them. But not in the sense that they were now prepared to give up. To the contrary, they only became more determined to fight on until final victory. Goebbels' declaration of "total war" in February 1943, though essentially symbolic by nature, helped.

Our political position in Europe, built with so much effort on my part in 1938–41, was also holding up well. True, Italy fell by the wayside, more or less. But many of its resources, including the concentration of heavy industry in the north, remained in our hands and continued to work for us. Finland remained our faithful ally. We retained our grip on Slovakia, Romania, Croatia, and Bulgaria with their vital raw materials, oil, and transportation systems. Sweden, Switzerland, and Spain, though coming under Allied political and economic pressure and growing increasingly wary, were still doing very much business with us. In the spring of 1944 the Hungarians made an attempt to break away. However, we had expected this and were ready. Assisted by some local movements, we were able to organize a Putsch, set up a new government in Budapest, and get the situation under control.

Another important beam of light in the darkness was our growing production of war material of every sort. In January 1942 Todt was killed in an air crash. He had always been open with me, and his death affected me so deeply that I did not want to speak about it. That is the way I am made: with my historical task always in mind, I suppress my personal feelings as necessity dictates. That, of course, does not mean that, deep down, they do not continue to manifest themselves. In Todt's place I put my former architect in chief, Albert Speer. Speer was a first class organizer; there was none better. But he did not have any experience in the field. His knowledge of weapons, the way they are produced, and the way they are used, was practically zero. My intuition did not desert me; before long, he proved to be an excellent choice. Until then, seeking to spare the German people the kind of hardship that they had suffered in 1914–18 and that had contributed to the Kaiser's fall, I had refrained from mobilizing all our resources for the war effort. Now Speer started doing so, with results that can only be called spectacular.

In his memoirs, published long after the war, Speer has some interesting things to say. First, he estimated that, had the reforms he pushed through been initiated earlier, we might have produced the wherewithal to arm a million more soldiers than we actually did. Second, he noted that Allied bombing cost us about fifteen percent of our total war production. That figure included both direct damage to every kind of property and the resources, primarily anti-aircraft defenses, shelters, and the like, which we had to divert so as to deal with the Allied bombers. All the more remarkable was the fact that, the bombing notwithstanding, throughout 1943 and the first half of 1944, our output of everything rose and rose. It was not just our production of fighter aircraft that increased but also of tanks, *Sturm-geschütze* (assault guns, essentially turretless tanks that were almost as useful as, but cheaper and easier to produce, than the real thing), armored personnel carriers, artillery barrels, submarines, you name it.

Periodically, Speer would report to me in writing, over the phone, or in person. Each time he did so he made me smile.

Several factors made the increase possible. First, as I have already said, we brought in masses of foreign labor to take the place of the men at the front. We even improved the conditions under which some of our Russian prisoners of war were held in order that, instead of expiring, they could work in our factories. Other workers were brought from the concentration camps. The SS used to rent them out to our industrialists at so and so many pfennig a man per day. Second, we stopped producing many inessential items and switched the factories that made them to war work. Third, Speer was able to rationalize production and standardize many products. An outstanding example were submarines. Previously, each one had taken forty-two weeks to build. After he took over, the figure went down to a mere sixteen.

Last, but not least, by 1942–43 our system for exploiting the occupied territories had overcome its teething problems and was functioning as smoothly as could be expected under the circumstances. In this field, too, Speer proved invaluable. He was a very hard worker, exceptionally handsome, highly cultured, a good listener, soft spoken, and incorruptible to boot. Briefly, he was the very opposite of some of the military blockheads with whom it was my fate to deal with for so long. Of course, he knew much more about our so-called "war crimes" than he was later prepared to admit. That included not just the use of slave labor, for which he was later imprisoned, but also the extermination of the Jews. Not only did he use their vacated apartments to house bombed-out refugees, but he also helped provide the rolling stock that transported them to the death camps. Here in Hell, watching him turn somersaults while trying to justify himself was quite amusing. On one occasion he denied being present when Himmler, on 6 October 1943, delivered a speech in which he described the fate of the Jews in some detail. Having been reminded that Himmler had addressed him by name as a member of the audience, he *still* persisted with his lies! But it *is* true that, typical technocrat that he was, he only took a very limited interest in ideology, our own National Socialist ideology included. If there was anyone foreign industrialists were willing to work with, it was him.

Some of the weapons we produced were old and trusty. A good example was the excellent M-1898 bolt action rile, which I myself had carried throughout my military service and which many of our troops went on using right down to the end of World War II. Many others were new, even revolutionary. Among the most important were jet aircraft. The reason behind our emphasis on jets was that we were unable to match the vast number of aircraft, both bombers and fighters, the Allies were producing and throwing at us. The jets used a propulsion system based on principles different from anything that had been tried before. The outcome was the Me-262, a fighter whose speed and climbing ability no Allied, let alone Russian, aircraft could match. Our pilots said that, the first time they flew it, it felt like magic.

With an eye toward *Vergeltung,* I initially wanted to have it configured as a bomber. In the end, though, I allowed Galland to persuade me over this question. By the time the war ended, it was in serial production. But it was just one of several new and revolutionary aircraft. Another was the Ju-287, a bomber with forward-swept wings which only reached the prototype stage. Yet another was a hypersonic, manned transcontinental bomber with a range of 5,000 kilometers. It was decades ahead of its time; had it been built, it would have been able to reach New York and repay the Americans for what they did to us.

We also had radio-guided flying bombs. In September 1943 we used them to sink the Italian battleship *Roma.* Just three small pilotless planes were needed for a 46,000-ton battleship; you can calculate the cost/benefit ratio for yourself. We developed several kinds of antiaircraft guided missiles and at least one guided anti-tank missile. Our submarines were the first to be equipped with radar-absorbing paint, snorkels that greatly extended the time they could spend underwater, and acoustic torpedoes capable of following ships as they steered a zigzag course. The so-called Walter submarines, the first of which were just about ready for action when the war ended, used a revolutionary propulsion system which gave them an underwater speed far greater than that of any similar vessel then in existence.

Nor did our land-based weapons lag behind. The 88-millimeter gun, dating to 1936, was originally meant for anti-aircraft work. Later, though, it was extensively used against tanks. In this role it was widely acknowledged to be the best in the world. Our tanks, the Mark VI Tiger and Mark V Panther, were the best armored and fielded the most powerful guns. Even more powerful was the *Königstiger* or Royal Tiger, which became operational during the summer of 1944. As a visit to any tank museum will confirm, these massive machines made the English and American ones in particular look like toys! Rejecting my experts' advice, I also played with the idea of building tanks weighing as much as 100, 200, and even 1,000 tons. Such mobile fortresses would have roamed over the battlefield, making mincemeat of any enemy tanks they encountered. Some work in this direction was done, but it never reached fruition.

It has often been said that dictatorships, by imposing secrecy and limiting the flow of information people can exchange, are inimical to scientific and technical innovation. If so, then perhaps my regime was not truly a dictatorship! To the contrary, our problem was a surfeit of talented tinkerers, inventors, and engineers. Each and every one of them wanted nothing better than to put his—there were hardly any hers yet—pet project at the disposal of the Reich so as to promote the war effort and to help us achieve the *Endsieg*. And avoid military service if he could, of course. The outcome was a lack of coordination and a waste of resources, of which I was well aware. Busy as I was with the conduct of military operations, though, I could not prevent it.

So advanced were many of our projects that, no sooner had the war ended, than the victors started squabbling among themselves in finding, arresting, and putting to work more of our leading scientists. Over the next few decades, many of their newly developed weapon systems testified to those scientists' involvement. Several of the scientists in question went to Egypt. Their intention was to help Nasser in his attempt to build weapons, especially fighter aircraft, ballistic missiles, and poison gas, with which to counter the Israelis. Whether because the Arabs were too incompetent or the Israelis too clever for them, though, nothing came of it. But that was not the end of the matter. As late as 1964, when America's first variable sweep aircraft took off, it showed the influence of a similar project of ours.

I myself always treated technicians and engineers with great respect. Nor did I have any difficulty doing so. Politically speaking, most of them were babes in the wood. If anyone was easily led, it was them. Normally, all they asked for was a pat on the head, as, for example, when I personally signed the decree making the rocket engineer, Wernher von Braun, a professor. How happy it made him! Needless to say, I did not claim to be an expert in their field. But I *had* spent years as a soldier at the front, and I *did* have a long-standing interest in technology in general and military technology in particular. The two combined gave me a good understanding of the so-called "interface" between weapons on one hand and the way they could and should be used on the other. That is why I regularly met with engineers and experienced front line officers. I examined new weapon systems in some detail and issued directives as to what should be produced and what should not. At times my proficiency enabled me to make a real contribution. For instance, in 1940–41 I insisted that our Mark IV tanks be equipped with a long, rather than a short, 75-millimeter gun. I also personally designed the fortified positions that made up the Atlantic Wall.

To avenge the destruction of our cities, we started building a giant cannon. Had it been completed, it would have been able to throw shells at London from its position near Calais. As Saddam Hussein's attempt to build something similar showed, in this field too we were far ahead of our time. The most spectacular new weapons of all were the V-1 and the V-2. The names we gave them notwithstanding, it was the V-2 which first appeared on the drawing boards. Originally, it was a private venture initiated by a couple of young enthusiasts who dreamed of one day flying to the moon. They did not have the necessary means to go forward, however, and were easily persuaded to start working for the army instead.

The main reason why the army took an interest in the rocket was that it hoped to outflank the Luftwaffe. But the latter, too, wanted to have some kind of unmanned weapon capable of reaching far behind the enemy front. That is why it started work on the V-1 with the aim of preempting the V-2. It was funny; it was sad; it was foolish. But this did not prevent the tug of war between the services from being replicated, in almost exactly the same form, in the United States during the 1950s. Clearly, then, it had nothing to do with any supposed inability of the National Socialist State, and me personally, to govern as has so often been claimed.

The V-1 was a comparatively simple, cheap system that could be and was produced in very large numbers. The same was not true of the V-2, a true technological marvel; watching (on film) the spectacle of a blazing, howling rocket taking off, I could see history in the making. However, it required many breakthroughs in the fields of metallurgy, guidance, and others. In the event both missiles proved disappointing. They had neither the accuracy nor the "throw weight"—to use an expression that only came into use during the late 1970s—needed to make a difference. The V-2, whose engine generated enormous heat, was also very expensive to produce in terms of precision-made parts, special steels, and the like. Our extensive use of slave labor notwithstanding, all in all neither program justified the vast efforts that I had been persuaded to put into them.

There was even a plan for putting a V-2 in a watertight container, to be towed by a submarine. Arriving off target, the rear compartment of the container would be flooded so as to point the missile upward and enable it to be launched at, say, New York. Unfortunately, the scheme did not reach fruition; it would have given the Americans exactly what they deserved. But not all our new weapons were high tech. A few were very simple indeed. One was the little Me-163 Comet, a revolutionary design with a rocket engine. It literally took off like a rocket and reached speeds unmatched by any contemporary machine. Once it had taken up a position above the approaching enemy bomber formation it would swoop down on them, shoot up as many of them as its short endurance permitted, and then glide down to earth. So simple, cheap, and capable of being mass-produced was the design that we could even afford to have the pilot abandon it and parachute to earth if necessary. Another was the *Panzerfaust*, a formidable anti-tank weapon capable of being handled by a single infantryman. Many, many Allied tanks fell victim to it.

Throughout all this, our main problem was quantity, not quality. Such was the enemy's material superiority that only our possession of nuclear weapons might have balanced it. After 1945, an entire literature developed as to why we never built the bomb. Let me make one point clear: contrary to what has so often been claimed, it had nothing to do with the expulsion of the Jews. We Germans had the best nuclear physicists in the world—including two Nobel-prize winners, Werner Heisenberg and Otto Hahn. Given the necessary resources, they and their younger colleagues could have built the bomb. As, indeed, our enemies always feared they might.

After the war, some of our scientists claimed that they had deliberately sabotaged the project to prevent me from having my finger on the trigger. Don't you believe that! These scientists will do anything to be the first in their field and to have their names engraved in history. The real reasons for our failure were quite different. First, one of the most prominent of the same scientists had erred in his calculations. He thought that far more enriched uranium would be needed to set off a so-called chain reaction than was actually the case. Second, the project was only brought to my attention late, in mid-1942 I think. The person who informed me about it was my dear old comrade in arms, Postmaster-General Wilhelm Ohnesorge. My Postmaster-General! Third and most important, at that point we could no longer afford any research project that would not yield results within a reasonably short time. In other words, the necessary resources were just not available.

Yet another reason for my continued optimism during this period was that we were finally getting the kind of generals I had always wanted. To a man, the older generation of senior commanders had served in the old Imperial Army and gained their spurs in the Reichswehr. They tended to be of noble origin. On the eve of our seizure of power there were proportionally more "vons" among them than there had been in 1914. Much like Halder and his predecessor, Beck, they did not believe in my genius. Almost without exception they tended to look down on me and my closest National-Socialist collaborators. Centuries of tradition, going all the way back to Friedrich Wilhelm I, had turned them into a closely knit clique. As a result, they frequently conspired against me and disobeyed my orders.

But now, at long last, things were changing. More and more officers of the older generation left. A few died in harness, as the aforementioned Reichenau did. Others retired either because they had grown too old or because I, acting through the Wehrmacht Personnel Office, made them do so. Moreover, during World War I most senior commanders invariably spent practically all their time in some comfortable country house kilometers behind the front. The situation in 1939–45 was entirely different. As the trenches were abandoned and mobile warfare took over, many generals set up their forward headquarters in some vehicle as both Rommel and Guderian did. The outcome was that quite a few of them were killed either when visiting their forward troops or by air attack. Among the generals who fell victim to just such an attack was Rommel, who was badly wounded.

Whatever the reason, new men started coming to the forefront. Very few of them had a "von" in front of their names. The most

important one was Dönitz, whom I later named as my successor.
Others were Waffen SS Generals Dietrich and Hauser and army generals Hube, Model, Rendulic, and Ramcke. Ramcke, a paratrooper
who proved his mettle defending Monte Casino, was exceptional in
that, while rising from the ranks, he had served in all three branches
of the Wehrmacht. The toughest of the lot was Schörner; no other
general meted out more death sentences for cowardice, defeatism, and
desertion. Had I only had a dozen like him, I might have won the
war! Right behind them came even younger men. Prominent among
them was SS Colonel Otto Skorzeny, the man who rescued Mussolini
and helped hold Berlin for me during the attempted July 1944 Putsch.
Another was Waffen-SS Colonel Joachim Peiper, our most successful
commander during the 1944 Ardennes offensive.

I cannot honestly say that these officers were less parochial than
their predecessors. If anything, they were the opposite. Paradoxically,
this quality of theirs had its advantages. It made it easy for me, with
my much broader background gained by reading and experience, to
overcome their doubts and to make them do as they were told. How
often did one of them come to my headquarters determined to tell
me "the truth" about the situation at the front, yet come out of
the conference with his spirits revived! Having fewer ties to the old
military traditions, in terms of *Weltanschauung* they were closer to
us National Socialists than their predecessors had been. Essentially,
though, they were apolitical. I sometimes got the impression that,
for them, even the prospect of victory mattered less for Germany's
sake than as a means by which they could advance their own careers.
Having fought their way up through one battle after another, they had
steel nerves and were as hard as nails. That was just what I needed at a
stage in the war when what counted was not brilliant maneuvers of the
kind Manstein was always proposing but a bulldog-like determination
to hold every position to the last soldier and the last bullet.

In brief, contrary to what so many historians, determined to prove
how deluded I was and totally misunderstanding the real situation,

have written, even as late as the spring of 1944 the war had not been lost. Our numerous setbacks notwithstanding, the Reich and its dominant position in Europe were still intact. Our soldiers were fighting bravely. They consistently inflicted more casualties than they took and earned the enemy's grudging respect. Churchill, who feared that invading the Continent might lead to a bloodbath similar to the one of World War I, in which 600,000 English subjects were killed, had a particularly strong respect for them. As we now know, had it depended on him, the Normandy landings might never have taken place. He would have gone for the Balkans, for Norway—briefly, anything but attacking us head on. And Stalin knew it; meeting him at Tehran in November 1943, he teased him about it.

As late as 1980, thirty-five years after the end of the war, the Pentagon was still busily paying the Wehrmacht the compliment of trying to learn from it. Our civilian population was also holding up well. To be sure, people were not exactly happy. Given our heavy losses, the growing shortages of food and consumer goods, and the rain of bombs that was demolishing their cities one by one, how could they be? But they did not go berserk as Douhet and even some of my own officers had predicted. Nor did they rise in rebellion and overthrow the government, as had happened in 1918. For those who were bombed out we were generally able to find solutions, albeit makeshift ones. The rest did their daily work, grumbled—more at the enemy than at the regime—and held on grimly. The frequent loss of relatives and property to air raids stoked their hatred of the enemy and radicalized many of them. Most also kept their faith in our final victory and eagerly waited for our new wonder-weapons to start making their effects felt. Above all, they continued to give me their trust and to follow where I led. So, almost to a man, did those whom I put in charge of them.

They, and, of course, I, were well aware that the long-promised, oft-postponed Allied invasion of Western Europe was coming closer day by day and that our chances of victory depended on our ability to repulse it. That is why I put Rommel in charge of the Atlantic Wall: to receive the invaders and to throw them back into the sea. Nor was the outcome of the coming battle by any means predetermined. As had been made abundantly clear to me in the context of our invasion of Norway, amphibious operations are the most difficult and most complicated of all military enterprises. Ask Churchill; not only did he lose the Gallipoli campaign, but he wrote an entire volume to justify himself. A sudden change in the weather can easily disrupt a seaborne invasion or even force it to be aborted. That, for example, was what happened to the Spanish Armada back in 1588. Notwithstanding his enormous superiority in men and *materiel*, General Eisenhower himself feared that he would fail. Given the fiasco at Dieppe in 1942, he well might. As late as 5 June, so atrocious was the weather in the Channel that we had to give up our air and sea reconnaissance. It is no wonder that, making his last preparations, he wrote down a note in which he took full responsibility for an eventual failure.

When the invasion finally came, I personally experienced it as a relief. So did many of my people. It is better to fight than to sit passively under the rain of bombs. Had the battle for Normandy gone in our favor, the situation would have been entirely transformed. Our enemies would have been demoralized. Conversely, our own people's morale would have been lifted sky high and their readiness to fight on redoubled. We would have been able to move as many as a million troops, including quite a few elite armored divisions, from the west to the eastern front. They would have been more than enough to destroy the Bolshevik hordes once and for all! Or else Stalin, who had long been unhappy with his Western Allies' procrastination, might have been more prepared to make an acceptable peace with us. In the event, though, the invasion succeeded. The main reason why it did so was that, when I told my generals to keep an eye on Normandy, they refused to believe me. Looking at the map, they kept insisting that the landings would take place at the Pas de Calais! The latter, they said, had always provided the shortest route and the best road network for an eventual invasion of Germany.

How this could happen I have never been able to find out even here in Hell. For many years the standard explanation was that our intelligence services had been misled by a brilliant disinformation campaign the Allies had planned and put into effect. This belief suited them fine. More likely, though, the real reason was different. Starting with Canaris, its head, and reaching way down its ranks, the Abwehr had long been riddled with traitors of the worst kind. Making full use of the veil of secrecy by which any intelligence organization is necessarily surrounded, many of them had betrayed us for years. The swine! As will be remembered, back in 1940 one of them had revealed the date of our attack on the West to the Allies. Later, Canaris himself not only refused to have anything to do with the persecution of the Jews but personally helped some of them escape to Spain and Switzerland.

Now, in the spring of 1944, they and their colleagues—the most important of whom was the aforementioned Speidel—deliberately sought to open the gates to our enemies. I myself received the news of the invasion at the Berghof during what was to prove my last stay at that much-beloved place. Misled by the Abwehr, I and my assistants at OKW, primarily Jodl, at first believed it was merely a diversion meant to disguise the real one, which would be directed against the Pas de Calais. That is why I refused to release the armored divisions which we had kept in reserve and which Rommel, as the commander on the spot, demanded. By the time the confusion was cleared up and the divisions were sent into action, it was too late.

Chapter 28

Götterdämmerung

Shortly after noon on 20 July 1944 my staff and I assembled for the usual discussion of the situation when a bomb exploded almost literally at my feet. There were 24 people in the conference room. Of those, four, including my long-time adjutant General Schmundt, were either killed outright or died of their wounds later on. Everyone else was injured to one extent or another. I myself escaped with perforated eardrums, hundreds of wooden splinters that had to be taken out of my legs, and singed trousers. Later, I sent the uniform I wore on that day to Fräulein Braun as a keepsake. But the show must go on. That very afternoon I shepherded Mussolini, who happened to arrive on the same day, through the devastation the bomb had wrought. As it had so often in the past, Providence held its protective arm over me.

Thanks to the abolition of "liberal rights," censorship, and, of course, the Gestapo, in my Reich any kind of overt opposition was almost impossible. In a proper *Führerstaat,* that was as it should be; the more so because, from late 1939 on, the state in question was engaged in a life-or-death struggle against practically the entire world. Clandestine opposition was something else. Early on we National Socialists assumed that, given the overwhelming popularity of our regime, we would not have to resort to drastic measures. In 1935 the number of those in concentration camps was down to just 4,000; so naïve was Himmler that he thought we might end up closing them altogether! As late as 1939, the number of inmates was still only 21,000. Relative to the size of the population, the number of prisoners in all our corrective institutions combined was no larger than in Switzerland, Finland, and the U.S. And relative to the size of the population, that was just four percent—*four percent,* I say—of the number Stalin's Gulag was holding at the same time.

It was only after war had broken out that the system, which now housed not just Germans but people from all over occupied Europe, started growing mightily. Many prisoners were "resistance fighters" who richly deserved their fate. At its peak in early 1945, the number was around 700,000. That was no more, and perhaps less, than the number of our *Volksgenossen* held in similar camps established by the Czechoslovak, Polish, Hungarian, Yugoslav, and Romanian authorities in the months that followed. But there was a difference. The inmates in our concentration camps had been arrested for a reason. In theirs, since the men had been called up, almost all were women, children, and old men whose sole crime consisted of being ethnically German. So atrocious were conditions that they died like flies. Finally, Himmler's strict controls made sure that, in our concentration camps, cases of rape were rare. In theirs, by contrast, it was so ubiquitous as to be almost self-evident. At times the victors simply took over our camps and used them for their own purposes. That was what happened, for example, at Auschwitz.

Inside Germany, the opposition could be divided into three kinds. First, there were a handful of rather peculiar individualists bent on killing me for any or no reason. As far as my person was concerned, this was the type I worried about the most. As the near-success of Georg Elser, who tried to blow me up in November 1939 showed, there simply was no way of stopping these people. But they were politically without any significance. Second, there were the Communists. Some of the principal figures had escaped to Moscow where, for reasons no one really understands, Stalin had many of them executed. The rest went on with their plotting. However, as long as the Reich lasted they never made any real headway. Part of the reason was that the Gestapo watched their every move, drove them underground, and prevented them from undertaking anything significant. And perhaps another reason was that, when all is said and done, Communism fits the German people as a saddle fits a cow.

The conservative, reactionary opposition was something else. Many of its leaders came from the highest classes of society. Some occupied posts that gave them real power. Prior to the 20th of July few if any of them were ever arrested or even suspected of plotting against me. Among them were some of Germany's most respected names, including, I am sorry to say, Yorck von Wartenburg, a descendant of the hero of the 1813 revolt against Napoleon, as well as Helmut James von Moltke, the great-grand-nephew of the great Moltke, and his brother Karl. An expert on "international law," Helmut James had long worked for the Abwehr. There, he had Canaris to protect him and assist him in his treasonous activities.

Others were officers whose families went back hundreds of years. At least one, Karl Gördler, had been the mayor of a major city (Leipzig). In 1933–36 he also served as Price Commissioner, where he flooded me with all kinds of confusing memoranda which I never bothered to read. Gördler himself was so pro-Jewish that the statue, in Leipzig, of the composer Mendelsohn-Bartholdi had to be dismantled behind his back! From Colonel von Stauffenberg down, most of the rest agreed that the Jews represented a problem which had to be tackled in one way or another. But they opposed our more extreme measures, and they certainly tried to keep their hands clean.

Others still worked for our Foreign Ministry. One and all, they never ceased plotting to remove me from power or, if necessary, to assassinate me. They also planned to set up an alternative government, to continue the war in the east, and to negotiate a separate peace with the West. That is just as I would have done, incidentally, had there been the slightest chance of success. The fact that none of the emissaries they sent first to London and then to neutral countries such as Switzerland and Turkey met with a favorable reception did not deter them. On several occasions their attempts to kill me failed, either for technical reasons—one bomb, planted in my aircraft, never exploded—or because of precautions I had taken such as by changing my plans. Stauffenberg, however, came as close to achieving his purpose as anyone had.

As things turned out, he and his bungling fellow conspirators, almost all of whom were medium-ranking officers, proved themselves no more able to plan and carry out a Putsch than a monkey can play chess. Stauffenberg himself succeeded in bluffing his way out of my East Prussian Headquarters, boarding a plane, and flying back to Berlin. Who would have believed it? However, at that point his luck ran out. Landing, he found that absolutely nothing had been done. Initially, he tried to convince his fellow conspirators that I had been killed. Thereupon they were going to activate a plan, known as Valkyrie, to gain control of the government quarter in the center of Berlin and to arrest Goebbels and other leading figures.

Fortunately, the commander of the Berlin garrison, Major Otto Remer, kept his head. First, he asked to speak to Goebbels by phone. Next, Goebbels put him in touch with me so I could assure him that I was, in fact, alive and well. Once that happened, any chance that the Putsch would succeed was gone. All that remained was to round up the conspirators. Or rather, round up those who had not committed suicide, as Henning von Tresckow did, and those who had not been executed by one of their own comrades, as Stauffenberg was.

Remer's reward was to be promoted to general, the youngest in the entire army. After the war, he became a right-wing, "Neo-Nazi" publicist and was put on trial for his efforts. Personally, the aspect of the Putsch that I found hardest to take was the fact that, among the conspirators, there were quite a number of officers whom I had known personally and whose careers I had promoted for years on end. The most important ones were field-marshals Rommel and von Kluge. In view of Rommel's great popularity I thought it best to allow him to commit suicide, and he obediently obliged. In return, his wife was given a pension, and he himself received a state funeral. Kluge, I am happy to say, did not wait to be arrested. He committed suicide of his own accord, thereby saving us the embarrassment of having to deal with him ourselves.

That very day in a radio address, I told the German people we would treat the conspirators precisely as they deserved to be treated. Himmler, who was always on the outlook for opportunities to expand the power of his Waffen SS at the expense of the Wehrmacht, did a thorough job. Over the next few weeks and months thousands were arrested. Given the elevated status of the accused, I knew we could not expect the courts to act as they should. They had, after all, been obstructing me for years, often looking for—and finding—reasons why people should not suffer the death penalty they deserved. In the case of officers the first step was to have them expelled from the army. That having been done, they, as well as the civilians, were put in front of a *Volksgerichtshof* (People's Court). I appointed Roland Freisler as the Court's President. He was a veteran National Socialist and, as even his enemies admitted, an excellent lawyer. At one point he forced the accused Colonel-General Höpner to admit he was an ass! Unfortunately, he was later killed in an Allied bombing raid.

How many people were executed in the wake of the Putsch is something I have never been able to find out either during my earthly life or here in Hell. One source speaks of 5,000. But that figure seems to include every kind of political prisoner who lost his life between 20 July and the end of the war, not just those connected with the events of that day; the real one was much smaller, perhaps as low as 200. It is true that we also arrested some family members of the condemned men. However, the Gestapo opposed such measures. Can you believe that? As a result, few were executed, and most survived the war. That even applies to Nina von Stauffenberg, who lived for another sixty-two years. Both Freya von Moltke and Erika von Tresckow, though subjected to interrogation, were let off the hangman's hook. The latter's two sons continued to serve in the

Wehrmacht as if nothing had happened. The war having ended and
National Socialism abolished, some of the survivors went on to make
a profit from their dead relatives. Had the man in charge of the
Gestapo been Stalin's dear friend Vyshinsky, with whom Freisler was
sometimes compared, then no doubt the outcome would have been
different.

In the whole of German history, there was no precedent to a
situation in which officers, violating their oath and throwing their
much-touted "honor" to the wind, tried to kill the Commander in
Chief. That was why, when Stauffenberg's name came up as the
perpetrator, I at first refused to believe the news. Had he used a gun,
or blown himself up as so many Islamic terrorists and even some
women have done, I could have respected him. But no, hoping
to live another day, he planted his bomb and slunk away. It was
no wonder that almost all his colleagues turned against him! Many
letters, both ones addressed to various government offices and private
ones intercepted by the *Sicherheitsdienst,* showed that civilians also
reacted with rage and horror. Some, convinced that only a miracle
had saved me, actually felt closer to me than they previously had. As
Stauffenberg himself had expressly foreseen, many of these attitudes
were carried over into the 1950s. It was only in the next decade that
(West) German government propaganda finally started making some
headway in convincing people that the criminals were really heroes
and deserved to be remembered as such.

The armed forces also continued to fight with undiminished vigor.
Even General von Blaskowitz, who back in 1939 had protested
against our "atrocities" in Poland, now expressed his abhorrence of
the "dastardly" crime and swore to stay with me to the end. Conversely, in November General Eisenhower called a crisis meeting to
ask why the Werhmacht's will to resist remained intact. To make sure
it did, we increased the number of NSFOs, *National-Sozialistische
Führungs Offiziere* (National Socialist Leadership Officers), whom
we had started appointing at the end of 1943. These were not the

cowardly Jewish types whom the Red Army appointed commissars. Far from it. We selected them from among decorated frontline officers, some of them invalids. Many were volunteers. Their tasks were to answer the troops' questions, to spur them to further efforts, and to deal with such things as *Zersetzung der Wehrkraft* (the kind of treasonable talk that undermines morale). Among them was a 29-year-old first lieutenant by the name of Franz-Josef Strauss. After 1945, he embarked on a spectacular political career; today Munich Airport is named after him.

Much later many historians, both German and foreign, had the gall to write that, by carrying on with the war, I deliberately sacrificed my troops' lives so as to prolong my own. In other words, they said that, by putting on a show of confidence, I betrayed them. Once again, I can only say, what hogwash. It's also an insult to their intelligence. First, they understood perfectly well the meaning of "unconditional surrender" on the one hand and Stalin's tender mercy on the other. For many of them, their fears turned out to be fully justified. Second, never in the entire war did I demand anything of my troops that I had not done many times over. That is something not many other heads of state can say. It is certainly not true of "democratic" American presidents who, from at least 1965 on, have been sending their uniformed men and, by now, their uniformed women, into one foolish war after another.

Field-Marshal Foch, whom I have mentioned before, once said that a battle won is a battle one refuses to acknowledge has been lost. That is why, starting in 1919, everything I ever said and did was designed to ensure that the kind of surrender that had lost us World War I would not be repeated. Again, the troops, *my* troops, understood all this very well. In 1944–45 the Americans, so typical of them, conducted a survey among German prisoners of war they were holding. It showed that most of the men cared about nothing but their personal affairs and that they had their doubts about everything else in the world. But there was one important exception:

they still retained their trust in me. After the Putsch, they trusted me even more. German civilians listening to my new-year address also drew confidence from my voice. And they were not prepared to throw in the towel. As so often in my life, I found myself standing like a lighthouse in a stormy sea. Should I, could I, have abandoned them to their fate?

Meanwhile, the war was not going well. In the spring of 1944 both Hungary and Slovakia tried to defect from their alliance with us. We were able to prevent that from happening, but we were not so fortunate with regard to Romania. The culprit was the young king, Michael I. He organized a Putsch, had Antonescu arrested, set up a new government, and promptly switched sides. For this Stalin—Stalin, who had murdered as many blue bloods as anyone in history—awarded him the Soviet Order of Victory. It was given, the citation explained, in recognition of "the courageous act of the radical change in Romania's politics toward a breakup from Hitler's Germany and an alliance with the United Nations, at the moment when there was no clear sign yet of Germany's defeat." But history has its own way of dealing with people such as him. The medal did not save him from having to flee the country when the Communists took over three years later. Only in 1997 was he allowed to return.

The defection was a heavy blow. Militarily it didn't hurt us much, because the Romanians were and are lousy soldiers more interested in graft than in fighting. Economically, though, it left us even more short of oil than we had been. That compelled us to continue the demotorization of our forces, which had begun as early as 1942. Next the fighting spread to Hungary itself, thereby threatening the neighboring *Ostmark*. In June 1944 the Allies finally succeeded in occupying Monte Casino, with the result that we had to give up Rome. As the coming months were to show, its loss did not mean much either in terms of geography or the resources at our disposal. The worst our troops suffered was that they no longer had access to the women of the city. At that time, it was serving as the largest brothel in the world.

At the end of July the Americans and the English broke out from their Normandy bridgehead. Our troops in the area fought like lions. However, in the end they were brought down by the enemy's enormous numerical and material superiority, especially in the air. By the end of August we had lost Paris which, contrary to my explicit orders, our commander on the spot did not burn down. The Allied invasion of southern France, which we simply did not have the forces to resist, did the rest. By mid-September we were well on the way toward losing not just all of France but Belgium, too. Fortunately, our troops succeeded in first blocking and then thoroughly demolishing the Port of Antwerp, delaying its use by the enemy. But the invasion had been coordinated with the Reds, who chose this moment to open their summer offensive. It hit our Army Group Center like a sledgehammer, costing us a million men between those who were killed, wounded, captured, and went missing. Fortunately, the offensive came to a halt in front of Warsaw. Whether that happened because they had run out of supplies, as they claimed, or because they wanted us to put down the Polish uprising that had broken out in the city first, as some historians have written, remains moot to the present day.

Once again, what should I have done? Resigned? Left the scene just as my country and people were going through the worst crisis in their entire history? Put a bullet through my head? That would have been easy. The more so because, following the failed Putsch, I no longer felt I could trust my collaborators as I used to. And the more so because, as a result, I was growing more and more lonely. Besides, my health was breaking down. Starting in 1914, for thirty years I had known nothing but combat and struggle. I continually bore a growing burden, often against what appeared to be overwhelming odds. Now crisis followed crisis. They were like the hurricanes which, I am told, keep hitting America's shores between June and November each year. Scarcely had I finished repairing the damage of one, more or less, than another even more dangerous one appeared on the horizon.

To be sure, I kept "functioning," as people say. Only in October 1944 did I have to spend a few days in bed. Once that episode passed, I resumed my duties, working day and night to defend the Reich. How I longed for the carefree days on the Berghof! Not only would Fräulein Braun have taken care of me, as she always did, but the mountain air would have done me a lot of good, particularly by helping me fall asleep at night. Instead, I was forced to spend most of the time at my Wolfschanze Headquarters in East Prussia. The army engineers had—so typically of them—selected the worst possible place they could find. It was swampy, with nothing but endless forests all around, stifling hot and infested with mosquitoes during the summer, and windy and ice cold in winter. And, for me to sleep in, there were a cell-like bunker and a narrow bed more suitable for a monk than for a Commander in Chief! Yet simply abandoning the damn place was not possible either. With the Russians about to attack, doing so would have been perceived as defeatism.

Briefly, there were enough problems to break anyone's will. But not mine. Only from time to time was a lighter note injected. For instance, once Speer's fellow architect and rival Hermann Giesler paid us a visit. He used to do excellent imitations of Ley, making me roar with laughter; together, we studied the reconstruction of our shattered cities after the war. How I loved drawing up plans for them! That is why, wherever I was, color pencils and similar supplies always had to be at hand.

The military situation, difficult though it was, also provided me with some reason to remain cautiously optimistic. With the exception of George Patton, a real go-getter whom my generals respected, normally, the American and English commanders were the epitome of caution itself. From Eisenhower and Montgomery down, they behaved as if they had never heard of operational maneuvers. Instead, relying on numbers, logistics, and the sheer firepower American industry kept providing them with, they preferred to advance on a "broad front." Almost to the end our men, provided only that they were reasonably supplied, were able to make mincemeat of them.

Proof of that fact came in September when, in sharp contrast to his usual method, Eisenhower launched a daring offensive. First 35,000 airborne troops of many nationalities were lifted and dropped deep into Dutch territory near Arnhem. Next, a ground offensive was launched with the intention of linking up with them. Had the offensive succeeded, many of our troops in the Netherlands would have been cut off and the country itself lost to us eight or so months earlier than it eventually was. Fortunately, Allied intelligence had failed to notice two Waffen SS armored divisions sent to the area to recuperate. Much to the disappointment of the Dutch population, which had already started celebrating, our brave Panzer grenadiers, ably commanded by Model, easily overcame the lightly armed paratroopers. Thousands were killed, and many others were rounded up and taken prisoner. The rest escaped. My own conclusion from the affair was that it confirmed the lesson of Crete in 1941: the days of large-scale airborne assault operations were drawing to an end.

This, however, was merely a local success. We Germans were holding the short end of the stick, especially because our production of war material, having peaked in July, started declining. The reasons for this were, first, the loss of France, and second, the unceasing Allied bombardment of our cities, which, at this point, was leaving many of our factories in ruins. At one point I had orders drafted for their prisoners of war, pilots in particular, to be executed in retaliation. But Keitel and Dönitz, fearing the enemy would respond in kind, talked me out of it.

To be sure, Speer had foreseen our difficulties. He and his deputy, Saur, took some measures to disperse our industry. But that only created another problem. Once the Allies had overrun France, they started using it to base their short-range fighter-bombers and light bombers. Unlike the heavy-four engine bombers, these aircraft had the precision needed to demolish not just railways stations but bridges, viaducts, and even moving trains. They particularly liked to attack locomotives. The boilers having been hit, they exploded in a most spectacular manner.

Throughout the autumn the *Reichsbahn* struggled on manfully, actually building or repairing more locomotives than were being destroyed or damaged. Still, in the end it was overwhelmed by the sheer number of interruptions. As a result, we could no longer provide our factories with fuel or move the components of weapon systems to the plants where they were being assembled. So short was fuel that the Luftwaffe was unable to train its pilots properly. The brave young men went into action nevertheless, sacrificing themselves. But again there was only so much they could do.

A strong power can afford to wage a battle of attrition while staying on the tactical defense. The weaker one, though, *must* attack. If not, it will be worn down. That is why, soon after the Battle of Arnhem, I started thinking about seizing the initiative. Like Schlieffen in 1893–1905, I was faced with the question on which front to attack: the east or the west. Like him, I let my choice fell on the west. Both militarily and politically the Western Allies seemed to be the easier nut to crack. Nor did they have the vast Russian spaces to retreat to. I also hoped that, once they had been defeated, Stalin would be easier to reason with. Should that not be the case, then hopefully we would still have the military means to deal with him and his hordes.

Preparations began in October. The man I put in charge was Rundstedt, the veteran commander who had proven himself in 1940 by attacking France and Belgium over the same terrain. He was, however, no longer the man he had been. At that time he had been eager to go. Now he did nothing but raise objections. Later he complained that I had not even given him the authority to move the guard in front of his headquarters from one position to another!

Yet I *did* give him thirty-five well-trained German divisions and fifteen hundred fighter-bombers. All we had and, since we had to denude our remaining fronts, more. The huge concentration of forces notwithstanding, secrecy was preserved. Perhaps the fact that we had thoroughly cleansed the Abwehr had something to do with this fact. In any case, when the offensive started on Christmas Day the Allies were taken totally by surprise.

As our objective, I selected Antwerp, the Belgian city that served the Allies as their main port through which their armies were supplied. Its loss would have resulted in the collapse of their front. The first days of our advance were a great success. In part, that happened because our troops, encouraged by their victory at Arnhem, were eager to go. And in part because the weather, which was cloudy, favored them by preventing the Allies from bringing their superiority in the air to bear. My poor opinion of the American troops was also confirmed. How they ran! Our men almost got to the Meuse. However, at that point the weather cleared, and their luck ran out. Another reason for that was that they were short of fuel. If *their* intelligence missed our preparations, *our* intelligence missed the existence in the area of a huge fuel dump. Had we known about it and captured it, things might have ended differently.

By the third week of January we were more or less back to our starting lines. I myself returned to Berlin, where people were joking that, if things went on as they were, one would soon be able to travel from the western to the eastern front by metro! I was still able to appreciate an occasional joke, but the remaining months were sheer torture. The German people also suffered horribly. During the winter the Russian hordes invaded East Prussia and Silesia. They could only be halted, temporarily as it turned out, on the Oder, about a hundred kilometers from Berlin. Countless civilians were killed and countless women raped. Some were even nailed to the doors of their houses! In response, whoever could packed his few belongings and fled. This was before global warming made its effects

felt. The temperatures were normally well below zero, and the roads
were covered by snow, with icy winds howling day and night. Many
perished on the way. Some tried to escape by sea, where our navy did
what it could. If anyone got away, then it was no thanks to Stalin.
One of his submarines sank a ship, the *Wilhelm Gutsloff*, which was
packed to the gunwales with refugees.

Meanwhile, the Allied bombing of our cities was reaching a murderous crescendo. As contemporary photographs show, in Berlin
every single house within kilometers of the government quarter was
left without a roof. In Dresden alone, anywhere between 30,000 and
70,000 people were killed. As the American author Kurt Vonnegut,
who survived the bombardment as a prisoner of war, later noted, it
was more beautiful than any his fellow soldiers had ever seen or could
imagine. It was also packed with refugees. However, there were no
important industries in the district. Its military value was exactly
zero.

Once our large and medium cities had been flattened, the Allies
turned their attention to the smaller ones. A good example was
Potsdam, another town with no military targets worth mentioning.
Perhaps what caused it to be selected was its symbolic value as "the
stronghold of Prussian/German militarism." On the night of 14–
15 April no fewer than 500 English heavy Lancaster bombers gave
it the usual treatment. As they did so often, the English aimed for
the railway station, or so they said. As they did so often, they ended
up destroying the entire city center instead. Among the wrecked
buildings was the Garnisonkirche, where Hindenburg and I had met
back in 1933. Thirteen years later, in 1968, Walter Ulbricht had
the remains blown up. Its place was taken by ugly office buildings
complete with some mosaics that showed the delights of life under
socialism. Not even smaller towns were spared. During the last weeks
of the war, so little was there left for the enemy fighter-bombers to
attack that they sometimes went after individual people in whatever
remained of our streets.

As our last remaining allies were overrun or deserted us, and as the remaining neutrals, coming under Allied pressure, refused to trade with us, our imports dried up. In particular, we were left without the nonferrous metals we needed in order to manufacture the special kinds of steel of which armor and weapons are made. Still, we fought on. We called up our last reserves: old *Volksturm* men and *Hitler Jugend* teenagers. We issued them what weapons we had, mainly anti-tank rockets, and told them to do what they could. But I never gave up my opposition to Japanese-style *kamikaze* attacks. They simply did not fit the Nordic spirit.

Mentally, I remained in complete command of my faculties; anyone who says the opposite is lying. But I looked and felt like a wreck. My hair was going gray. My back was stooped both forward and sideways. I was unable to control my left arm, which kept trembling. I suffered from flatulence and bad breath. Having moved to the *Führerbunker*, a dank, unpleasant labyrinth of corridors and rooms dug under the garden of the *Reichskanzlei*, I all but forgot what sunlight looked like. I used to drag myself along, holding on to the walls so as to keep my balance. And the bad news still kept coming day by day, and hour by hour.

In February, the first unmistakable signs of dissolution appeared. Civilians blamed soldiers for prolonging the war and refused to cooperate with them. Some even welcomed the enemy troops, the rich American ones in particular. Neither propaganda nor terror helped. On 19 March I issued my so-called Nero Order. Contrary to what some historians have written, it was not meant to "punish" the German nation by making it impossible for them to live. In fact it only referred to "military transport and communication facilities, industrial establishments, and supply depots, as well as anything else of value within Reich territory, which could in any way be used by the enemy immediately or within the foreseeable future for the prosecution of the war." Moreover, it was done at a moment of despair. I never really meant it or expected it to be carried out.

That's why I didn't have Speer executed when he told me, at our last meeting, that he had disobeyed my orders. As anyone can see from my political testament, I expected the nation to survive and, though it might take centuries, even to prosper. Why else would I analyze the past, record my experiences, and look forward to the day when a "truly united nation" would rise from the ruins?

On 12 April we received the news that Roosevelt had died—but this time there was no "Miracle of the House of Brandenburg." Eight days later, my 56th birthday was celebrated, providing some of my senior associates with an opportunity to swear their loyalty. But no sooner had they left than they started betraying me like rats deserting the sinking ship. Göring betrayed me, first by finding some excuse to leave Berlin and then by trying to take over leadership of the Reich. In response, I removed him from all his posts in the party and state and placed him under SS guard. Had the Americans not "liberated" him, he would not have survived. Himmler betrayed me. Going behind my back, for some two years he had been trying to negotiate with the Allies. As his intermediary he used Count Bernadotte, a member of the Royal Swedish family with whom, during the war, we had quite a few dealings. Now he became more insistent. He even tried to prove his "good will" by allowing several trainloads of Jews to reach Switzerland. Coming from *der Treue Heini,* "Faithful Hank," as he was widely known, such treason was particularly galling. However, there was nothing I could do about it.

I could do even less about two of his principal subordinates, SS Generals Felix Steiner and Karl Wolff. Steiner was charged with defending northern Berlin against the Russians but turned around and surrendered to the Western Allies instead. In return, he was spared an indictment as a "war criminal;" later, he wrote several books and led an organization that did its best to rehabilitate former members of the Waffen-SS. Wolff surrendered the German troops still holding out in northern Italy. He, too, escaped prosecution at

Nuremberg. Later, he was repeatedly tried and convicted; in the end, though, he died at his home at the age of 84.

Coming from men who had the words *"Unsere Ehre heisst Treue"* (Our Honor is Loyalty) inscribed on their belts, this was treason indeed. But at any rate I was able to catch up with another senior SS officer, Hermann Fegelein. Fegelein had started life as a stable boy before embarking on his career under Himmler, who ultimately made him his adjutant and sent him to the Berghof to act as a liaison officer between us. He was very attractive to women—as my driver, Erich Kempka, used to say, his brains were in his nuts. In June 1944 he married Eva's sister Gretl, with me acting as a witness. Now I had the satisfaction of having him shot for deserting his post. The squad I sent after him found him in bed with another woman and preparing to flee to Switzerland, for which purpose he had put aside gold ingots as well as loads of foreign currency. The swine.

Inside the bunker conditions were crowded. People were strewn about, so to speak, sleeping wherever they could; camp beds, armchairs, mattresses on the floor... Among those present were Bormann, the Goebbels family, and a some officers. There were also the usual servants, orderlies, telephone operators, and secretaries, all of whom continued to function calmly and efficiently. I only wish my generals had been as steadfast as they were! Best of all was Eva. Ribbentrop had begged her to make me change my decision and leave Berlin; she was, he said, the only person who might do so. But she refused. Young and eager for life though she was, she told him that it was for me alone to decide and that she would do as I did. So deeply did her loyalty touch me that, for the first time ever, I kissed her full on the mouth in the presence of others. During the next few days she went on fussing about me as she had always done.

At some time during the night of 28–9 April I married her. At the wedding I wore my field-gray tunic with the Golden Party Badge, my Class I Iron Cross, and my World War I Wounded Medal. She had put on a dark-blue dress. Hand in hand, me shuffling a little, we left my private apartment and entered the conference room, which had been rearranged for the purpose. The official in charge was one Walter Wagner, who had been summoned for the purpose; the witnesses, my old comrades in arms Goebbels and Bormann. Signing the form, Eva at first wrote "Eva Braun." Next, collecting herself, she struck out the "Braun" and put in "Hitler" instead. Though she was tired and pale looking after a sleepless night, our wedding made her as happy as, given the circumstances, happy could be. There was a wedding party of sorts during which, contrary to my usual custom, I drank a glass of wine.

Later, I dictated my personal testament to Frau Traudl Junge, my beautiful and highly intelligent secretary. It went through several versions. Once it had been completed to my satisfaction, I ordered three copies to be made. As the 29th went by, we helplessly listened to the Russian artillery rounds exploding outside. I also received some last-minute reports of the situation in and around Berlin. The city was surrounded. However, some fighting was still going on in Potsdam, where General Walter Wenck, proceeding along the Havel, was trying to mount a last-minute counteroffensive. His efforts were in vain, as it turned out.

To my inexpressible regret, I had one of my doctors poison Blondi. I myself refused to witness the scene, though I did look at the body after she had expired. I spent most of the night of 29–30 April having tea and talking with Eva as well as my three remaining secretaries. The next morning Eva and I got up late. Someone suggested that we form a party, break out, and try to reach the Luftwaffe base at Gatow a few kilometers to the west. From there an aircraft would take us to Bavaria. I curtly refused. Such was my physical condition that I could hardly even hold a pistol; hence I would be a burden on the rest. Besides, running away has never been my style. How could I leave my troops, who were still desperately fighting street by street, house by house? I said goodbye to Goebbels, who, along with

Magda, had resolved to take his life together with me. Next, I took my leave of my remaining staff. I shook their hands one by one and gave them poison capsules—the only thing I had left—to use in case they were about to fall into Russian captivity.

It must have been around 1530 when Eva and I went into my room and locked the door behind us. Wearing my favorite dress, a black one with roses at the neckline, and with her hair carefully done, she sat down on the right side of the narrow white and blue sofa with me on the left. She, eager to look beautiful even in death, took a poison capsule and died almost instantaneously. Whereas I, having bit a similar capsule, put a gun to my temple and pulled the trigger.

Chapter 29

Looking Backward

Once I had settled down here in Hell, my first concern was to learn what had happened to my closest associates. A few committed suicide. The most important one was Joseph Goebbels. Poor *Josephchen,* as his mother used to call him, was devoted to me like a dog to his master. Unlike people like Göring (in his early years) and Himmler, he did not have what it takes to build an independent power base of his own. Well aware of that fact, he stayed at my side to the end. What else could he have done? First, he had his wife, the incomparable Magda, kill their six children, a horrible but truly courageous act on her part. Next, he shot her and then himself. Bormann, who had also been in the *Führerbunker,* disappeared without a trace. Much later, it turned out that he had tried to escape and was killed in the process.

Himmler's attempts to negotiate with the Allies failed as they were bound to. His illusions shattered, he shaved off his mustache and put on the uniform of a private soldier in the hope of getting lost in the crowd. He was detected and ended his life by taking poison. Good! A score of my closest collaborators, both civilians and military men, were tried at Nuremberg. Twelve were sentenced to death, of whom eleven were executed by hanging. The twelfth, Göring, committed suicide before the hangman could get him. The rest got various prison sentences or were acquitted. Given the way they behaved during the last few months of my life in particular, I cannot say that I miss any of them. For years on end they had basked in my glory.

Had we won the war, each and every one of them would have come to me clamoring for his reward. But, physically at any rate, we did not; once I was gone, all they thought of doing was to put the blame on me in the faint hope of saving their own skins.

Among my senior commanders, Field-Marshal Model and General Burgdorf committed suicide. The first did so when his remaining forces were encircled in the Ruhr, and the second near my bunker a day or two later. So did Generals Hans Krebs and Robert von Greim, my last chiefs of staff of the Army and Luftwaffe, respectively. Another one who killed himself was Walter Hewel. Hewel was a veteran party member who had been with me since my time in Landsberg prison. Throughout the war he had formed part of my entourage, accompanying me in all my travels and often joining my circle around the fire at the Berghof. At one point he was involved in an aircraft accident which left him badly burned. Now, apparently suffering from psychological problems, he used the cyanide capsule and the pistol I had given him for the purpose.

The Chief of my Party Chancellery, Philip Bouhler, and his wife Helene also killed themselves—she by jumping out a window and he by cyanide. Other leaders scattered in all directions. Many were assisted by the Catholic Church. At the time, the reigning Pope was Pius XII. Earlier, serving as the Vatican's "foreign secretary," he had negotiated the Concordat with us. Contrary to his reputation, he was personally no anti-Semite. I am told that, when he was elected in 1939, the Hebrew-language press in Palestine gave him an enthusiastic welcome. However, he and the Church had always hated and feared the Communists much more than they did us National Socialists. He had very good reason for feeling that way. After all, I had never been an atheist. Repeatedly, I prevented Bormann from taking more extreme measures against the Church. Nor did I support Rosenberg's clumsy efforts to create a "National Reich Church," one that would have the swastika (or the sword; sources differ) as its symbol and a copy of *Mein Kampf* on the altar! When Gauleiter

Wagner of Munich foolishly ordered to have the crucifixes removed from the classrooms, I threatened him with a concentration camp. Finally, I always considered the belief in the Almighty a fundamental quality of man. Take it away, as the Communists tried to do, and see what happens.

Attempting to escape "justice" and to build new lives, some of my less important subordinates were assisted by various Western intelligence services, which valued their knowledge of Eastern Europe and experience in counterinsurgency and were quite happy to take them in. Once inside, the men could be kept in line by blackmail. Others went to South America, especially Argentina (where President Peron himself was involved), Bolivia, Chile, and Paraguay. As to money, that was something our dear Swiss friends took care of—for a fee, of course: *pecunia non olet*. Arriving in their new homelands, the men smoothed the way by paying bribes or else by assisting the local dictator in dealing with his opponents. Quite a few flourished. Klaus Barbie, the SS commander at Lyon, whom the French hunted for decades on end for alleged war crimes, could tell a pretty tale about that. Several of the men went to the Middle East in the hope of helping those good-for-nothing Arabs fight Israel. They met with no success, unfortunately. Others still decided to lay low. Some were tried and executed, especially in Eastern Europe. In the West, however, few of those who were sentenced to prison were made to complete their terms.

The most surprising—or, for those as familiar with human nature as I am, anything but surprising—thing was that, as the clock struck one minute after twelve, there were hardly any National Socialists left in Germany. Countless people who had benefited from my rule, cheered me half to death, served me for years, and flattered me until they were brown in the face suddenly wanted to have nothing to do with me. Almost to a man they had never seen anything, heard anything, or known anything, let alone done anything except that which they considered good, honorable, and just. From Halder and Speer down, many later "corrected" their diaries or used their memoirs in order to present me in a false light.

The few, most of them small fry, who admitted to something invariably claimed to have acted under duress. They sometimes had a legitimate reason, as was the case of von dem Bach-Zelewsky, whom we had in our hand because all of his three sisters had married Jews. And there was Franz Stangl, who had a police record just as Höss did. But there was often no reason. Here, I must hand it to women. Whether because they had less to lose—after all, not one of them had occupied a key position—or for other reasons, many of them remained faithful after my death. Winnifred Wagner apart, that included Leni Riefenstahl, Gertrud Scholz-Klink, Himmler's daughter Gudrun—who always insisted her father was "not a monster"—and Lina Heydrich, née von Osten, at the time Frau Heydrich met her future husband she was a much stronger anti-Semite than he. Later, she and her parents brought him to the Party, and the rest followed. At the time of her death, forty years after the end of the war, she was still swearing by me. The cleverest lot of all were my original countrymen. In 1938 they went out of their way to give me the most wonderful welcome I ever got. Later, though, they somehow succeeded in convincing everyone that Beethoven had been an Austrian and I, a German.

There were also a few exceptions. One was General Jodl, easily recognized in photographs because of his bald pate and prominent ears. Jodl had an excellent strategic mind and, even more importantly, the strongest nerves among all my top-level commanders. Speaking in a soft voice, neither impertinent nor by any means servile, starting at the time of the Norwegian campaign he was closer to me than any other senior officer. Whatever others might do, he later said, he could not bring himself to condemn me. Facing death at Nuremberg, he was also one of the few who kept his dignity from beginning to end, without hope or fear. On the morning of the day on which he was executed he made his own bed as, according to a centuries-old tradition, a Prussian officer is bound to do.

The other was Göring. I have already explained what he did, what he did not do, and how my opinion of him changed during the war, causing me to allow figures such as Milch and Speer to take away much of his power. Fighting for his life at Nuremberg, though, he surprised everyone by pulling himself together and becoming a man again. First, he lost weight and got rid of his morphine habit. Next, he proudly defended himself, the Reich, and me. So much so that Gustave Gilbert, the American-born prison psychiatrist (he was the son of Austrian-Jewish émigrés), had him isolated from the other accused lest he become a "bad influence" on them. How typical of those self-righteous Americans! It was as if the old Göring, the one I had known until 1940 or so, had made a comeback. As they say, better late than never.

As I wrote in my political testament, our troops had fought very well indeed. That was true both when they were on the offense and when they defended themselves, both when things were going well and, even more so, during crises. This has caused their performance to become legendary, so much so that some have attributed it to the use of drugs! They also turned the Wehrmacht into a model for others to follow. Throughout the Cold War our 1940 campaign against France, in the planning of which I played a decisive part, continues to be studied at all Western military academies, staff colleges, war colleges, or whatever. Even the Israeli Staff College used to organize regular tours to the battlefields in question! As I have shown throughout this book, though, our senior officers, especially those of the ground forces, were not as good. The later the date, the more numerous the doubters, the blunderers and, I am sorry to say, the outright traitors. That was why, from the last months of 1942 on, almost nothing we tried succeeded. The enemy's overwhelming numerical and material superiority did the rest.

Since then, I have often wondered whether, far from being too ruthless, I had been too soft and easygoing. Some people thought so. Perhaps I would have obtained better results if I had treated my collaborators as Stalin, the self-styled "Man of Steel," did his. Perhaps I should have played cat and mouse games with them as he was always doing. And perhaps I should have shot those who did not perform to keep the rest terrified. But my name was not Iosif Vissarionovich Dzhugashvili. I was a German, not some half-breed Caucasian chieftain magnified a thousand times over. I never used Stalinist methods to run my armed forces—except in the wake of the Putsch attempt of 20 July 1944, of course. Even then, I did not go nearly as far as Stalin had in 1937–39. If I pressed for more death sentences, which I did many, many times, I did not do so because I derived any pleasure from doing so but simply because, blessed with a judiciary that often proved weak in the knees, I felt doing so was my duty to the German nation. Wasn't it Stalin who, pronouncing his so-called "permanently operating principles" of war, wrote that the most important thing was to maintain the stability of the homeland? This, after all, was a time when countless excellent young men were dying every day. Against that background, what right did I have to let all sorts of psychopaths, criminals, and traitors live?

Much less was I a Zhukov who, at one point, told General Eisenhower that heavy losses did not matter to him because Russian women could be depended on to bear children. (With regard to that, incidentally, he was wrong. Currently, Russia's birthrate is among the lowest in the world, though still higher than our own.) Far from it. Whatever historians, especially feminist ones, may have written about the way we National Socialists "oppressed" women and "discriminated" against them, I always retained a soft spot for our beautiful and tender, but long-limbed, delicate, and vulnerable German women. Those with the "blue eyes, soft glance, and a heart that is noble and proud and good," as the poet Gottfried Friedrich Klopstock put it.

I also felt our German losses deeply. Too deeply, perhaps, as at least two of my top commanders, Manstein and Dönitz, thought. On one occasion, when someone told me of the sad songs my troops were singing at the front, I could hardly restrain my tears. How well I understood them! That, and not any lack of empathy, as Speer insinuates in his memoirs, was why, happening to find myself face to face with a trainload of our soldiers returning from the east, I ordered the curtains of my carriage drawn. That, too, was why I prohibited *Volksgenossen* whose houses had been destroyed by bombing from coming to Berchtesgaden and, later, refused to look at pictures of German refugees he presented me with. They might have caused me to weaken, and weakness is the last thing a man in my position can afford.

A well-known psychologist once said, "Evil consists in intentionally behaving in ways that harm, abuse, demean, dehumanize, or destroy *innocent* [my emphasis, AH] others—or using one's authority and systemic power to encourage or permit others to do so on your behalf." If so, I want to put it on record that I *never* knowingly committed a single evil deed. Not during my struggle for power. Not later. And not during my last days either. With the Reich collapsing around me, I *had* to complete my Providence-appointed task as far as was in my power to do so. I particularly needed to prevent the resurgence of Jewry by exterminating every last Jewish man, woman, and child I could. Do you say they were innocent? Bedbugs are innocent! They do what nature has destined them to, no more, no less. But is that any reason to spare them?

That is why, at this time, over and over again, I steeled myself to do what had to be done. The later the date and the more our overall situation deteriorated, the more difficult the dilemma and the more terrible the decisions that needed to be made. To quote Goethe, "Two souls, alas, are housed within my breast, and each will wrestle for the mastery there." It was this contradiction that gave many of my deeds the peculiarly horrible, twisted, character they had or appeared to have. Those which confused so many of my associates who, knowing my aversion to blood sports and even to horse racing, sometimes wondered at the things I ordered done. It is this seeming contradiction, too, which, starting in the 1930s, has baffled so many of my biographers and prevented them from getting to the bottom of me. Even though, proportionally and absolutely, my deeds were no worse than those of Stalin, Mao, Pol Pot, or even Saddam Hussein. All of them were members of the lesser races, and all of them were twentieth-century dictators who killed without losing a moment's sleep. To repeat, it was *die Endlösung* which turned me into the most hated man in history. That is a burden which, however undeserved it may be, I am happy to carry for my people's sake.

When the war ended, the victors took the opportunity to expel an estimated 10–12,000,000 of our *Volksgenossen* from Eastern Europe, where they and their ancestors had lived for centuries. It was by far the greatest forced migration in history, perhaps even exceeding the one that took place during the 1971 Indo–Pakistani War. It made my own efforts in this direction look positively puny. Germany itself was partitioned into four occupation zones. Later, the number was reduced to two: a western one and an eastern one. Later still, both the Western Allies and the Russians set up puppet governments in their respective zones. Staffed by Communist traitors who, unfortunately, had been able to escape my security services, the so-called German Democratic Republic remained a puppet right to the end, which came when it collapsed in 1989–90. The so-called German Federal Republic fared somewhat better, especially from an economic point of view. In fact it became filthy rich.

The price was having to kowtow to the victors. Culminating, in 1974, in the infamous scene when Chancellor Willy Brandt—a socialist and former deserter, incidentally, whom I would have shot if I had the chance—went on his knees in front of the Poles. The Poles! Need I say more? And the Jews, of course. There was never any question of combating them with every available means as I urged in my political testament. Instead, having blackmailed us into paying them huge sums in reparations, they grew even fatter and more impudent than before. Continuing their work after Roosevelt's death, so successful were they in corrupting Washington, D.C. that the U.S. paid Israel hundreds of billions of dollars in "aid." Meanwhile our own people were made to feel as guilty as hell. Afraid to look others in the eyes, in a certain sense they have been more traumatized by the "Holocaust" than the Jews themselves.

As I also wrote in my testament, from beginning to end what inspired me was my love for our people. In a Darwinian world where the strong prevail and the weak go under, I wanted to preserve our German identity and to strengthen it as much as possible. It was to that end, and that end alone, that I took every step and adopted every measure I ever did. For them I fought, for them I suffered, and for them I died. But without success. The old Germany, the convivial Germany of small towns, thinkers, poets, high-quality craftsmen, and heroes—briefly, the Germany I used to love—is no more. Instead, we have bankers and "public relations" persons. The former fleece whomever they can. The latter lie on behalf of anyone who pays.

Two processes are involved. First, starting as soon as it was established in 1949, the Federal Republic did whatever it could to "integrate" itself into Europe in the hope that the latter might forgive us our "sins." Doing so, our dear, fellow EU members took us to the cleaner's so often that we lost count; the reunification of 1989, far from reestablishing our independence, only reinforced the process. Second, starting in 1998 when the Social Democratic Chancellor Gerhard Schröder entered office, we admitted an ever-growing flow of non-Germanic people from Eastern Europe, Africa, and Asia. Currently, about a fifth of the population has an immigration background. As a result, the identity in question is on the point of becoming irretrievably lost. Much to my sorrow Germany, as it has been understood throughout the centuries, is abolishing itself. As a look at the center of Berlin and many other cities shows, in many ways it no longer exists. That makes me feel like vomiting.

In the whole of German history the twelve years of my rule, specifically including the glorious and heroic struggle for existence that was the war, are almost the only ones in which foreigners, and even many Germans, still take any interest at all. Everything else tends to be seen either as a prelude to the Third Reich or as a sequel to it. Just look at the bookshops, movies, and TV series. And not just in Germany either! Each time the leading news magazines are in need of money, which, in the day of the Internetz, they almost always are, they put a picture of me on the cover. Historians, journalists, and filmmakers have made fortunes by researching my life and times and are certain to do so in the future, too.

For all but a handful of grumblers, the years of the Third Reich—until, let us say, early 1942, when fortune started turning her face away from us—were the most joyous in German history. Neither before nor after have so many people, great and small, been ripped out of their humdrum, often poor and quite miserable, lives, transformed, elevated, welded together, and united in a single purpose. By 1939, some two-thirds of the entire population had become members of at least one Party organization. According to one story, so busy were various family members doing Party work that they only met once a year at the Nuremberg Rally! All this made sure that the Western Allies' subsequent efforts at "denazification" would remain a sick joke. This was true even in our show window, the Foreign Ministry, which was in charge of "restoring" our relations with the rest of the world. Until 1970 or so, half the personnel there consisted of former card-carrying Party members.

Back in the late 1980s my countrymen engaged in the so-called *Historikerstreit* over the question as to whether the "Holocaust" could or could not, ought or ought not, be compared with other historical events. Be that as it may, the more time passes, the more I feel I and my ideas have become part and parcel of Western civilization. This is not merely in the sense that practically all its members unite in holding me up as the ultimate evil but also in that, in many ways, they continued upon the path where I had led. Look at Europe. Look at North America. Look at Australia. All of them are talking about the need to combat growing socio-economic inequalities, though none have yet begun to tackle the problem as firmly as we National Socialists did. All have adopted programs meant to protect consumers' rights. All have developed vegetarian parties, some of them much more extreme and inclined toward violence than mine used to be. All have allowed, indeed required, doctors to take a much larger part in public life. All have mounted strong public health campaigns centering on the elimination of smoking, a filthy habit I have always opposed. And all have firmly embraced environmentalism and the protection of nature as part of their central ideologies.

All of these countries preen themselves on being democratic and liberal Yet all followed my example in putting in place impressive arrays of thought control, broadly known as political correctness, with the aim of muzzling people and making them toe the line. Going much further than we did, they expanded their supervision over about a vast variety of topics my people never dreamt of touching. This has now been carried to the point where one private company alone, Facebook, has appointed 7,500 censors to prevent people from saying what they think! Partly to force their citizens to pay their taxes, and partly to combat terrorism, all have also resorted to using the most modern technology to spy on people. Heydrich, Kaltenbrunner and Müller—Gestapo Müller, as he was known—would have loved to use hacking, data mining, and other modern inventions if only they could have imagined them.

Still not content, quite a few of the countries in question are employing their scientists in an attempt to find ways to look directly into people's brains. Neither the law—where it exists—nor respect for privacy, nor the potential for blackmail can stop them. Finally, all are busily working to improve the race by eliminating the unfit.

If not after they have been born, which for lack of an alternative was the way we tried to do it, then during the time when they are still in the womb. In these and many other fields I was the pioneer, and they are my followers. Even though most of them do not know it and would vehemently deny it if told.

In a growing number of Western countries, bleeding hearts and other milksops may talk of "integration," "diversity," and *multikulti.* They are welcome to continue spreading their vomit until that vomit turns around and hits them in the face as, judging by recent events, it has clearly begun to do. Racism, or ethnocentrism as those politically-correct morons call it, is again proving itself to be a basic human quality. One which, as self-sacrificing heroes such as Anders Breivik have shown, tsunamis of more or less official propaganda, dished out day and night by corrupt media, cannot eradicate. Least of all in Israel, which in some ways has proportionally more of my followers than Germany does! Yet another idea I often expressed is that Christianity, supposedly based on love, is a religion for weaklings and that we Germans would have been well advised if we had adopted Islam, truly a militant creed fit for men and warriors. Now that Al Qaeda, Daesh, and any number of other Muslim terrorist organizations are scaring the living daylights out of people the world over, the only ones who still do not know how right I was are those who will soon find out. Hopefully, they will learn before they have a knife stuck into their ribs or a bomb placed under their bums.

So numerous and so extensive are the fields in which people, knowingly or not, have taken their cue from my movement and me that I sometimes wonder whether we did in fact lose the war. Not the physical war, of course, as our much-shrunken borders attest to the present day. But the much more important one between different *Weltanschauungen.* Nor is that all. Notwithstanding that the Berghof had been thoroughly plundered and demolished several times over, very soon after our defeat it became almost as much of an object of pilgrimage as it was before I put an end to the practice in 1938. It is just like Mount Kyffhäuser, where Kaiser Friedrich Barbarossa is said to be asleep, waiting for the nation to call! On any given day one will find hordes of people, guidebooks and cellphones in hand, trying to trace the places where the most important buildings used to be. Others queue to enter the elevator that will take them, as it took me on the rare occasions I used it, to Kehlstein. Far over a million, by no means all German, came to see the local documentation center built by the Bavarian government. Had not the police intervened, my Munich home and other places where I used to stay would also have been turned into shrines for people to worship at. Surely there would have been souvenir shops selling Nazi dolls, Nazi music, and, who knows, working models of Nazi concentration camps complete with miniature Nazi gas chambers and ovens.

Take the attempt of the Austrian government to pull down the house in which my parents, having rented a flat, lived when I was born. The owner, a courageous lady in whose family the house had been for over a century, held out for five years, refusing to sell. As a result, she was finally expropriated, all in the name of democracy, freedom, and truth! But I am not worried. In the long run, the only outcome of such attempts to tinker with history will be to further increase the already large number of visitors who come to pay homage to me. Just as the destruction of the Jewish temple by the Romans 2,000 years ago only made the site on which it stood, or is supposed to have stood, holier still.

As I have already explained, our art was figurative. It was the kind which sought to elevate people's souls, not to fill their heads with the often obscene ravings of disturbed imaginations ripe for the lunatic asylum. That is why, starting in 1933 and continuing after 1945, it has been reviled as much as it was. That is also why, watching the world as I do, I am very happy to see that, in many places, abstract art is on the retreat, and figurative art, in some ways like that of the Renaissance, is well on its way back in. It is gaining popularity not because those snobs, the critics, like it but because the broad public, thanks to its sound instincts, demands it. Failing to find what it is looking for, it simply votes with its feet. As figurative art made a comeback, our own started doing the same. Some of our old pieces, long neglected and even given up for lost, have been rediscovered. Take the *Deutsches Historisches Museum* in Berlin, long a stronghold of political correctness. Just a few years back it mounted a show to "prove" how we wicked Germans had maltreated the poor Poles. Now it has, in the entrance hall, a copy—a poor one, alas—of Breker's huge statue of a nude, heroic man holding a sword. The one I personally commissioned and named *Die Wehrmacht*.

Worried about what "Nazi" memorabilia might stand for, some countries have tried to ban the trade in them. But to no avail. Most of the dealers and the collectors they serve are gentile. Some, however, are Jewish. Here and there, some of the latter justify their interest (and their profits) by claiming that their collections signify their "victory" over me. As if, in reality, things were not the other way around! Furniture and utensils are grist to their mill. So are every kind of *bric à brac,* uniforms, insignia, daggers, medals, stamps, bank notes, coins, photographs, posters, letters, diaries, magazines, books, banners, etc. Even as I was writing these words, a "treasure trove" of just such objects was discovered in Argentina; how it got there no one knows. Major items such as tanks, aircraft, and submarines are also eagerly collected and lovingly restored until they are as good as new.

Many, if not most, of the items in question were stolen from their German owners, both alive and dead. Other profit seekers have turned to robbing graves, especially in Eastern Europe, where most of our soldiers were killed and either had their bodies left in place or buried in makeshift cemeteries. So great is the demand as to form the basis of an entire industry. Those involved fake the items in question and sell them to the credulous. As for me, judging by the fact that everything I ever owned, touched, or laid eyes upon seems to increase in value a thousandfold, one might think I am some kind of a Catholic saint! I am told that, in 2009, three of my heavy six-wheeled cross-country Mercedes cars were sold for $3,300,000 each. A good investment, no doubt.

So popular am I personally that a Microsoft robot by the name of Tay, designed to mimic the thought of a 19-year-old American girl, surprised its creators by learning to say that I had been right! All this proves, if proof were needed, how unique, how incomparable, I was and am. More important, it puts the nobodies who have run Germany since 1945 on the horns of a dilemma. On the one hand, they want people to remember the Third Reich and me by way of what they call a *Mahnung* (warning) to future generations. On the other, they well know the true sentiments of many of our *Volk*. That is one reason why, in 2016, they were preparing to sue Facebook for failing to shut people up as, according to them, it should have done. They were also planning to fine it 500,000 euros for failing to remove every single piece of news they did not like within twenty-four hours. As these and countless other facts show, it would hardly be too much to say that everything the *Bundesrepublik* has ever said and done is explicitly meant to "face up to the past," as the saying goes, and condemn anything I ever stood for. In vain. The harder they try, the longer the shadow I cast. As one of our slogans used to put it: the German people is me; I am they.

Not only is *Mein Kampf,* which for decades was *verboten* in Germany and freely available there only to those soft-headed windbags, scholars, on sale again. It has, in fact, become something of a bestseller. This happened after some of the same windbags, employed by the aforementioned Institute for Contemporary History, had provided it with a "critical" apparatus meant to counter my "innumerable assertions, lies, and expressions of intent." Yet in reality that same apparatus brought to light how much I, a young man of no means who had not even taken the *Abitur,* had thought and read. The editors' hair-splitting comments, all 3,500 of them, surround the original text, making each page look as if it were pulled out of the Talmud. Perhaps that is why the Central Committee of Jews in Germany welcomed the edition as a "pedagogic tool!" To quote Nietzsche, "How are we to keep this colossus from doing what colossi do?" asked the chief dwarf. Short answer: no way.

People often accuse our system of being "totalitarian." If so, the Russian-Soviet one was much more so. Among other things, that is why the number of German POWs who died in Russian camps will never be known. According to some estimates, it was in excess of one million. The things the Russians did to some of our troops, especially Waffen SS men, who fell into their clutches defy the imagination. As to Russian POWs dying in *our* camps, I can only repeat that the Bolsheviks, by refusing to sign the Geneva Convention, brought the problem on themselves. Besides, trying to police *Untermenschen* whose only idea of justice is that which is meted out by the knout, what methods do you suggest other than those we used? Even the Western Allies, smug as they were, recognized that fact. Or else why did they allow my top anti-partisan general, the aforementioned Bach-Zelewsky, to avoid trial and to go on with his life?

Compared to those enacted by Stalin and some others, the measures I took to suppress the uprisings against me—the one of June 1934 and the one of July 1944—were positively benign. Take the case of Ernst Torgler. During the last years of the Republic he was my second most important Communist opponent in Germany. Acquitted of being involved in the burning of the Reichstag, I allowed him to go free on the condition that he leave politics alone. He kept the bargain and turned back to his profession as a journalist; in 1941, having been told by his son, who was serving on the eastern front, what life in the worker's paradise looked like, he wrote me, promising to renounce Communism forever! I also allowed both former Austrian Premier Schuschnigg and French Premier Daladier to survive. The same applies to Leon Blum, Jewish though he was. I intended the same with respect to the Italian Princess Mafalda, whom I had interned at Buchenwald. She was the daughter of my old "friend," Vittorio Emmanuelle, and I hoped to use her as a hostage. In the event, she died when the Allies bombed the camp. But not before the local medical staff did their best to save her.

As to violating the laws of war, look who is talking. Admiral Chester Nimitz, who commanded the U.S. Navy in the Pacific, said it at Nuremberg: If Dönitz was guilty of waging "unrestricted" submarine warfare, then he and his subordinates were equally so. Right from the first day of the war, he added! Bombing our cities, the English and the Americans killed incomparably more civilians than my Luftwaffe ever did. That's to say nothing about the firebombing of Tokyo and the dropping of two atomic bombs on Hiroshima and Nagasaki. And those incidents only refer to the years 1939–45, not to the seven decades that followed, which were by no means always filled with light and sweetness either.

In the decades since my death, innumerable scribblers, some Germans, others foreign, have presumed to condemn the path I took. The outcome has been endless rot. I should have become an artist and refrained from going into politics, they say. I should not have tried to avenge our defeat and reverse the verdict of Versailles, they say. I should not have gone after the Jews, they say. I should not have destroyed German democracy. I should not have torn up the Treaty of Versailles. I should not have rebuilt our armed forces. I should not have annexed Austria I should not have dismantled Czechoslovakia. I should not have gone to war with Poland. I should not have let the English off the hook when I had them at my mercy at Dunkirk. I should have launched my invasion of Russia earlier than I did (or, alternatively, not launched it at all). I should not have declared war on the U.S. I should not have ordered 6. Army to stay in Stalingrad. I should not have postponed the Kursk offensive. I should have gone for a kinder, gentler, new order. I should not have exterminated the Jews. I should not have prevented my generals from "maneuvering" (read, retreating), I should have thrown in the towel and "bowed to the inevitable" earlier than I did. As if anything is "inevitable" unless and until one bows to it! Many of these ideas came from ignoramuses who had never been in charge of anyone and anything. Others were impracticable. One and all, they meant that I should not have been who I was: Adolf Hitler.

True, I am dead. But in a growing number of places, my light is marching on.

Afterword

I am a Jew and Israeli. And I am proud of it. My grandparents, my parents, and most of my aunts and uncles went through the Holocaust in their native Netherlands. A few of my relatives died at Auschwitz. Some were deported to various camps but returned home, more or less sound in body and mind. All the survivors lost family and friends. All were legally discriminated against, persecuted by the police, had their property taken away, and were thrown out of their homes.

But that was only the beginning. Having escaped from the camp in which they were interned, during the last eighteen months of the war many of them were driven underground, forced to hide, and hunted down like rats. If most escaped the worst and survived, then it was no thanks to the German occupation authorities. Nor were the Dutch administration and police, who often assisted the Germans to the best of their ability worthy of gratitude. What saved my relatives was luck and their own resourcefulness as well as the incredible courage and kindness of some non-Jewish, people, including, in some cases, total strangers, who either did their best or turned a timely blind eye. Among them were a few Germans, including one close supporter of the Führer.

Much later, several of the rescued survivors, as well as their rescuers, wrote their memoirs. Others told me their stories. Some of the details are harrowing indeed. For example, what is one to say about the experience of my grandparents, who hid in a hole between a ceiling and an upstairs floor, from where they could hear their landlord, who had given them shelter, being arrested and beaten up

by the Germans? Or about my aunt and uncle who, when told that
they had been betrayed and that the police were looking for a young
couple with a baby girl, were forced to leave that girl under the bed in
a house about to be searched? Fortunately she was asleep, remained
quiet, and survived. But that was not the end of the story. To save her
life, the girl was handed over to a non-Jewish couple. They became
very attached to her and, after the war ended, initially refused to give
her back. In the end they did give her back. But what a tragedy for
both sides.

At my childhood home near Tel Aviv, the Holocaust was seldom
mentioned. Only many years later did I learn my parents' stories. My
mother escaped arrest and evacuation by joining a cousin of hers in
hiding under the floor of a wooden shower cabin; later, that cousin,
along with one of his brothers, tried to cross into Switzerland, was
turned back at the border, and ended up in Auschwitz. My father
lived under a false name with false papers. Twice, he was stopped by
Dutch SS men, and once he was summoned to the local German *Ort-
skommandant*. Each time he succeeded in bluffing his way through.
Five years after the war, in leaving the Netherlands and moving to
the fragile, dirt-poor Israel of those days, my parents' objective was
to make sure, as far as possible, that my siblings and I would not
have to experience what they had suffered. My mother in particular
tended to think in those terms. In early 1967, when they received
some reparations money, they used it to invite some of those who
had helped them to visit Israel. That was the kind of person she was,
and he, now 98 years old, still is.

I think I read my first book-length account of Hitler and National Socialism in 1962, when I was sixteen years old. The author
was Mr. Uri Avnery, the maverick owner, publisher, and editor of
a highly politically incorrect (as we would say now) weekly called
Haolam Hazeh (This World). The volume was called *Tzlav Hakeres
(The Swastika)*. So spellbinding was it that, over half a century later,
I can still recall entire sentences. Significantly, its purpose was not

simply to provide an account of what had happened. Rather, it was to warn against what the author saw as the rise of *Israeli* chauvinism and militarism. It was a warning which, as events following the 1967 War were to show, was not misplaced.

Since then, my interest in National Socialism and its leader has never flagged. I read and read and read. I also watched movies, visited some of the places mentioned in this book, and did research—including archival research—on parts of the historical periods that interested me. Like so many others, I wanted to understand what had happened and why it had happened as well as what had been swept away by history and what was still alive and kicking. Above all, I hoped to find the clue to the man. There just *had* to be some piece of information, perhaps hidden in some safe deep inside a lake or down in a salt mine, which would solve the riddle: how could anyone be born so utterly wicked? And how, being so wicked, could he make millions and millions of ordinary people follow him as if he was the Messiah? Like so many others, I failed.

Several times I tried to write my own biography of the Führer as so many others have done. Several times, convinced there was nothing of any importance others had not said many times before, I gave up. Then, one cloudy Friday morning in the spring of 2015 as I was cleaning my house, I was struck by an idea. To gain a real understanding of Hitler, I had to depart from the beaten path. Instead of writing about him from the outside, I had to focus on the way he understood himself; in other words, I had to give my work the form of a memoir or an autobiography. It would be, in some ways, similar to Richard Lourie's outstanding *The Autobiography of Joseph Stalin: A Novel* (1999). A book which, in my opinion and that of some others, provides as good a psychological portrait of the man as may be had.

Lourie, who was born in 1940, is an American Jew, journalist, and novelist. I, by contrast, am an Israeli historian trying to write what is perhaps best described as alternative history. Doing so, I felt obliged to stay considerably closer to the recorded facts than he did. I did not invent a plot; the plot was there for anyone to read. The description, in the prologue, of Hell and Hitler's life in it apart, I did not mention any people, moves, episodes, anecdotes, or conversations except those for which there is good evidence in the kinds of sources historians normally use. On the basis of my research and understanding of Hitler, though, I did allow him to express thoughts which, incarcerated in Hell (may he remain there forever) after his death, he very likely *would* have had. Most of those thoughts dwell on the way things were when he was still alive and active. But some, and by no means the least important ones, concern developments that have taken place after his death.

As a historian, indeed as a human being, I consider it my first duty to search for the truth and to record it as best I can. In this particular case the truth I seek is not about the "objective" world. Rather, I tried to uncover the *subjective* truth as it was seen or, in respect to the post-1945 world, probably would have been seen, through the eyes of one man—a man who, whatever else he may have been or done, single-handedly, in so far as anyone can do so, inflicted on humanity what may very well remain the greatest, deadliest catastrophe in its long, bloody history. And whose name, more than that of anyone else, is bound to remain synonymous with evil as long as there are humans left on this earth. Isn't that, or ought it not to be, the goal of any biographer worth his salt? There is only one difference. The method I chose was to try to get into his skin, as far as possible, so as to understand what made him tick. Even to the point of using the first person. Where there were gaps, I used what knowledge and understanding I thought I had in an attempt to close them.

My books are one thing. I am another. In writing this one, my goal was not to set forth my own ideas. Instead, I tried to understand Hitler's actions, views, and thoughts as I think he, observing the past and the present from Hell, would have explained them. So let the reader judge whether I have succeeded in this objective.

Acknowledgments

Writing this book was surprisingly easy. In fact, once I had made up my mind, it almost started writing itself. How come, I asked myself, such a simple idea had never occurred to anyone else? Still, I owe a debt of gratitude to a few people, one I am very happy to discharge.

Mr. Uri Avnery, for many years a famous Israeli journalist and happy troublemaker, encouraged me to forget about my fears and to go ahead with the project. Prof. Avihu Zakai, of the Hebrew University, Jerusalem, was the first to listen to my early rambling. Later, having read the ms., he drew on his wide learning to make several highly useful suggestions as to what Hell might be like. Prof. Emeritus Moshe Zimmermann, also of the Hebrew University, read the manuscript, and made some very important suggestions. So did my friends at Munich University, General (ret.) Dr. Erich Vad and Prof. Martin Wagener. Colonel (ret.) Dr. Moshe Ben David, as good a friend as they come, discussed the ms. with me many, many times. Last, but not least, thanks go to our family physician, Dr. Mark Zimmermann, who was there for me at a moment of black despair.

What can I say? Thank you all.

Martin van Creveld
October 2016

CASTALIA HOUSE